# Twentieth-Century Russian Literature

JOHANNES HOLTHUSEN

# Twentieth-Century Russian Literature

## A CRITICAL STUDY

SUPPLEMENT BY ELISABETH MARKSTEIN ON
*Censorship, Samizdat, and New Trends*

FREDERICK UNGAR PUBLISHING CO.
NEW YORK

Translated from the German
*Russische Gegenwartsliteratur*
by Theodore Huebener
Published by arrangement with Francke Verlag, Berne

---

For the Supplement by Elisabeth Markstein see page 277

# *Publisher's Preface*

Any comprehensive survey of contemporary Russian literature necessarily involves a description of the political as well as of the cultural background against which it has developed. In the turn-of-the-century artistic upheaval that culminated during the years of the Russian Revolution (1917–19), however, political issues were initially less important than the inner momentum of Russian literature itself. Not until the early 1920s did the gradual imposition of socio-political measures slow and arrest free creative development.

The years immediately preceding and following the October Revolution saw the avant-garde experimentation of writers born in the last two decades of the nineteenth century. Until 1922 the Revolution's so-called bourgeois authors generally retained their independence. The great exodus of publishers and writers that occurred in that year marked the beginning of the first more or less restricted phase of Soviet literature.

In the years that followed, Soviet writers were dominated by events connected with the consolidation of Stalinism, the trauma of World War II, and the changing political climate after Stalin's death in 1953.

In the study here presented to the reader, literary criteria are the principal means of classification, and the author has omitted from consideration a number of writers whose primary importance was political or ideological. Emphasis is placed on the most significant representatives of Russian literary development within the context of European literary history. Although biographical details have

83739

been kept to a minimum, the origin of new forms and styles has been treated in detail so that the reader may fully appreciate the literary range of given phenomena. Because of the difficulty in obtaining drama reviews and in securing authentic information on theater life, however, contemporary Soviet drama remains an almost unknown area.

Dates given in this study are generally those of a work's first edition. Certain dubious cases arise, however, because Russian editions tend to give the year in which a work was written rather than the year in which it was published. Wherever possible, long delays between writing and publication have been pointed out. For the convenience of the reader, all titles of literary works are provided in English. Such English title may be either a literal translation or the actual title of a published English version. The Russian title is given, in transliteration, in parentheses at the first mention of the work. It is followed by a date that indicates the first Russian publication.

# Contents

## PART I
## PRE-REVOLUTIONARY RUSSIA

### The Turn of the Century, 3

| | |
|---|---|
| Critical Foundations | 3 |
| The Decline of the Novel | 4 |
| Vsevolod Garshin and Sergei Andreyevski | 5 |
| Anton Chekhov | 6 |
| A Reconsideration of Values | 8 |
| Merezhkovski and His Followers | 8 |
| Journalism and the Realists | 10 |

### Symbolism, 12

| | |
|---|---|
| Early Symbolist Poetry | 12 |
| Konstantin Balmont and Zinaida Gippius | 12 |
| Valerii Bryusov | 14 |
| Fiodor Sologub | 17 |
| Other Early Symbolists | 18 |
| Symbolism's High Point | 19 |
| Aleksandr Blok | 19 |
| Symbolist Prose | 24 |
| Fiodor Sologub | 24 |

Valerii Bryusov                          26
Andrei Belyi                             29
Vasilii Rozanov                          33
Later Symbolist Poets                    36
Andrei Belyi                             36
Vyacheslav Ivanov                        38
Innokentii Annenski                      41

## *Realism, 44*

Two Masters                              44
Maksim Gorki                             44
Leonid Andreyev                          48
In the Realist Tradition                 49
Vikentii Veresayev                       50
Aleksandr Kuprin                         51
Mikhail Prishvin                         52
Ivan Smeliov                             54
Boris Zaitzev                            54
Ivan Bunin                               55
Realism Restructured                     59
Aleksei Remizov                          59

## *Beyond Symbolism, 62*

Mikhail Kuzmin, a Transitional Figure    63
The Acmeist Creed                        65
Nikolai Gumilev                          67
Anna Akhmatova                           68
Osip Mandelstamm                         71
Acmeism Reconsidered                     73
Sergei Gorodetzki                        73
Mikhail Lozinski                         73
Vladislav Khodasevich                    74
The Theory and Practice of Futurism      75

## Contents

| | |
|---|---|
| Aleksei Kruchenykh | 76 |
| David Burlyuk | 77 |
| Velemir Khlebnikov | 78 |
| Vladimir Mayakovski | 80 |
| Major Synthesizers | 83 |
| Boris Pasternak | 83 |
| Marina Tzvetayeva | 85 |
| Sergei Yesenin | 86 |
| Nikolai Klyuyev | 88 |

PART II

THE INTERWAR PERIOD

*Development of Prose, 91*

| | |
|---|---|
| The Serapion Brothers | 91 |
| Yevgenii Zamyatin | 93 |
| Lev Luntz | 98 |
| Veniamin Kaverin | 99 |
| Vsevolod Ivanov | 101 |
| Konstantin Fedin | 102 |
| Mikhail Zoshchenko | 103 |
| Gorki After the Revolution | 106 |
| Historical Novel | 108 |
| Aleksei N. Tolstoi | 108 |
| Olga Forsh | 109 |
| Yurii Tynyanov | 110 |
| Escapist Writing | 110 |
| Humor and Everyday Life | 112 |
| Pantaleimon Romanov | 112 |
| Valentin Katayev | 112 |
| Mikhail Bulgakov | 113 |
| Ilya Ilf and Yevgenii Petrov | 114 |
| Proletarian Writers | 115 |

Dmitri Furmanov 116
Aleksandr Fadeyev 117
Fiodor Gladkov and the "Construction" Novel 118
Six Major Figures 118
    Ilya Ehrenburg 118
    Isaac Babel 121
    Boris Pilnyak 125
    Leonid Leonov 128
    Yurii Olesha 131
    Mikhail Sholokhov 133

## *Developments in Poetry, 137*

Futurists 137
    Nikolai Aseyev 138
    Boris Pasternak 140
    Nikolai Zabolotzki 140
Serapion Brothers 141
    Nikolai Tikhonov 141
The Constructivists 142
    Ilya Selvinski 143
    Eduard Bagritzki 143
Some Aspects of Prewar Soviet Theater 145

### PART III
### CONTEMPORARY SOVIET TRENDS

## *World War II: New Orientations, 151*

The General Atmosphere 151
Socialist Realism in Fiction 156
    Six Exemplary Novelists 159

| | |
|---|---|
| The War Poets | 161 |
| Narratives of War | 162 |
| Vera Panova | 162 |
| Aleksandr Tvardovski | 166 |
| Viktor Nekrasov | 169 |
| Olga Berggoltz and Margarita Aliger | 173 |
| Emmanuil Kazakevich and Konstantin Simonov | 177 |
| Boris Slutzki | 181 |

## *The Older Literary Avant-Garde, 184*

| | |
|---|---|
| Coda | 184 |
| Some Poets, Novelists, and Memoirists | 185 |
| Anna Akhmatova | 189 |
| Boris Pasternak | 192 |
| Ilya Ehrenburg | 195 |
| Konstantin Fedin | 197 |
| Konstantin Paustovski | 201 |
| Leonid Leonov | 203 |
| Veniamin Kaverin | 206 |
| Nikolai Zabolotzki | 210 |
| Mikhail Svetlov and Semen Kirsanov | 213 |
| Leonid Martynov | 216 |
| Mikhail Sholokhov | 218 |

## *The Revolution's Critical Heirs, 220*

| | |
|---|---|
| The Redemption from Socialist Realism | 220 |
| Dudintzev and Others | 221 |
| The New Realists | 224 |
| Aleksandr Solzhenitzyn | 224 |
| Grigorii Baklanov | 228 |
| Yurii Bondarev | 230 |
| Nikolai Arzhak and Abram Tertz | 233 |
| Vasilii Aksenov and Anatolii Gladilin | 236 |

The Traditionalists                                          239
   Vladimir Tendryakov                                     239
   Vladimir Soloukhin                                      243
   Yurii Kazakov                                           246
   Viktor Konetzki                                         250

## *New Tendencies in Soviet Poetry, 253*

Lyric and "Chamber" Music in Poetry                          253
   Bulat Okudzhava                                         254
   Rimma Kazakova                                          255
   Yunna Moritz and Bella Akhmadulina                      256
Nonconformist Poets                                          257
   Gennadii Aygi                                           258
   Viktor Sosnora                                          259
   Iosif Brodski                                           260
The Poetry of Pathos and Sentiment                           261
   Robert Rozhdestvenski                                   261
   Yevgenii Vinokurov and Novella Matveyeva                263
Two Controversial Poets                                      266
   Yevgenii Yevtushenko                                    266
   Andrei Voznesenski                                      269

## SUPPLEMENT

## *Censorship, Samizdat, and New Trends, 277*

## *Bibliography, 291*

## *Index, 293*

# PART I

## Pre-Revolutionary Russia

# *The Turn of the Century*

During the 1890s literary life in Russia was pervaded by a profound skepticism but at the same time with new hope for the future. In the awakening of the artistic conscience of a whole generation, modern cultural criticism played a significant role. The awareness of the general decline of aesthetic standards cleared the way for the establishment of new criteria for artistic creation.

## CRITICAL FOUNDATIONS

Russian cultural criticism undoubtedly owed much to Nietzsche, whose influence at the turn of the century was very conspicuous. Outstanding contributions were also made by Nikolai Strakhov (1828–95), the friend of Lev Tolstoi and Dostoyevski, as well as by Konstantin Leontyev (1831–91).

In their criticism of positivism and the faith in progress of the nineteenth century, Strakhov and Leontyev combined a fervent apology for universal cultural attitudes and a vindication of poetry in its timeless character.

The Russian cultural critics cautioned against the alienation of native historic consciousness, as well as against depreciation of the poetic and against looking on humanitarian sympathy as something low and trivial. Dmitri Merezhkovski (1865–1941), one of the first bearers of this new cultural awareness, expressed his dislike of previous artistic expression in his collection of essays *Concerning*

*3*

*the Causes of the Decline, and the New Currents in Contemporary Russian Literature (O prichinakh upadka i o novikh techeniyakh sovremennoi russkoi literaturi,* 1893).

Thinking mainly of the "educated" public, Merezhkovski criticized its ready acceptance of the conventional "banal" tragedy supposedly based on contemporary themes; he likened the public's eagerness to that of fish snapping after the worm on the hook. He thus again elevated the moral problem of art to the level of the aesthetic problem:

> Exactly these honest ears of naive readers are the threatening sign of a general decline. The highest moral significance of art does not, in fact, consist of moving moralizing tendencies, but in the artist's unselfish and uncompromisable love of truth, his fearless sincerity.

By showing his appreciation of such poets of the transition period as Vsevolod Garshin (1855–88), Nikolai Minski (1855–1937), Konstantin Fofanov (1862–1911), and Anton Chekhov (1860–1904), as well as by reference to the thinker Vladimir Solovyev (1853–1900), Merezhkovski gave an example of unorthodox and entirely unprejudiced literary criticism, which rightfully placed him at the beginning of a new development.

Merezhkovski developed his own views only in his later critical writings, which, were dedicated to, among others, Tolstoi, Dostoyevski, and Gogol: *Tolstoi and Dostoyevski* (two volumes, 1901–02); *Gogol and the Devil* (*Gogol i chort,* 1906).

## THE DECLINE OF THE NOVEL

The crisis in the behavior of the Russian intelligentsia, which became apparent around 1890, also revealed itself in a deterioration in the art of fiction, which Merezhkovski had deplored.

The novel especially as the valid form of expression of social reality seemed to have outlived its time. The leadership in this genre had been assumed by second-rate writers. Not without reason did Chekhov avoid the novel and try to develop a new narrative style out of the short story and the anecdote.

The way out of the crisis was first forged by the smaller forms of literature, including the many "sketches," "portraits," and "studies" so abundant in the literature of the waning 1880s and 1890s. Vladimir Korolenko (1853–1921), a master of these forms, had considerable influence on the younger generation. Nikolai Garin (pseudonym of Mikhail Lovski, 1852–1906) showed a similar development in his stories, such as his travel sketches of Korea and Manchuria (1899).

## *Vsevolod Garshin and Sergei Andreyevski*

A writer of far greater endowment was Vsevolod Garshin (1855–88), who committed suicide. His somber but sentimental stories, which Merezhkovski called "lyrical prose," have continued to exert an influence on modern realism through their skillful portrayal of consciousness.

Sergei Andreyevski (1847–1919), a well-known Saint Petersburg lawyer and brilliant poet and critic of the older generation, is known for his *Book of Death* (*Kniga o smerti*), published at his request only after his death by an emigration publisher in 1922. The most significant parts of this two-volume work are the purely narrative sections of the first volume—presumably written in the 1890s—in which Andreyevski describes his first contacts with the phenomenon of death. The autobiographical narrative clearly shows the author's ardent admiration for Turgenev and Flaubert. In the opinion of the critic D. S. Mirski, it is "one of the finest achievements of Russian prose." The fragmentary essays of *The Book of Death* give a deep insight into the intellectual life and atmosphere shortly before the turn of the century.

Andreyevski also made a name for himself as a literary critic. His brilliant and sympathetic essays, collected in the volume *Literaturniye ocherki* (1902), contributed greatly to a revaluation and better understanding of Yevgenii Boratynski, Dostoyevski, Turgenev, Lev Tolstoi, Garshin, and Chekhov.

Literary criticism, which was so important in these years, was furthered in Russia in the 1890s by Merezhkovski and Andreyevski as well as by the vigorous editor and critic Akim Volynski (pseudonym of Akim Flekser, 1863–1926). Volynski played a leading role in the Saint Petersburg magazine *Severnyi Vestnik* (1885–98), in which the early symbolists were free to express themselves and which also offered religio-aesthetic ideas for a small but receptive group of readers.

Volynski undermined the practically unchallenged dominance of social literary criticism (in *Russkiye kritiki*, 1896); he was also the discoverer of Nikolai Leskov (*Leskov*, 1898) and the interpreter of Dostoyevski and Chekhov (*Chekhov*, 1898). His works include *The Battle for Idealism* (*Borba za idealizm*, 1900) and *The Realm of the Karamazovs* (*Tzarstvo Karamazovykh*, 1901).

## Anton Chekhov

An entirely new impulse, one that was fruitful for the future of narrative style, came from Anton Chekhov (1860–1904). Chekhov's stories and dramas show a sensitivity to language that was no longer to be found among the realists.

Chekhov's fascinating simplicity and his aristocratic laconism had already impressed young Merezhkovski, who described Chekhov's prose as being "compressed like verse," noting that Chekhov's precision in style and structure sharply distinguished his writing from that of the older forms of realism.

Chekhov had an extraordinarily intuitive grasp of the trifling incidents and misunderstandings of life. Even in his early humorous pieces a contemplative, skeptical view of life manifests itself. Chekhov, a physician who was afflicted by tuberculosis, possessed the profound insight of a diagnostician who has no illusions about the fortunes of life.

Chekhov's attitude toward reality is not emotional but ironic and melancholy. He does not propose to change man or to improve or to heal him, but only to console him. Chekhov's irony is a loving irony. Despite his hopelessness about making man better, he still thinks man, in his weakness and because of his weakness, is capable of loving his neighbor. There are no blessed spirits but also no damned in Chekhov. For him, there is life-long solace in humor, sentiment, further self-delusion, habituation, and forgetting.

These characteristics are especially obvious in Chekhovian dramas such as *The Seagull* (*Chayka*, 1896), *Uncle Vanya* (*Dyadya Vanya*, 1897), *The Three Sisters* (*Tri sestry*, 1901), and *The Cherry Orchard* (*Vishnevyi sad*, 1904). The "most undramatic dramas in the world" (according to Mirski), these plays nonetheless reflect the tragicomedy of interpersonal relationships through subtle dialogue.

Chekhov's dramas lack action, as has been pointed out often enough, but they are rich in atmosphere and in an ardent longing for something beyond the self. The dramatic effects are found only in the fact that the utterances of the characters are strikingly out of proportion to their inner emotions. Only through hints, gestures, and symbolic references does Chekhov express the actual psychological processes of his characters. Indeed, during his mature period Chekhov's poetic concepts emanate from the idea that direct speech always conceals the determining factors in a situation and that the truth lies in the undertones. Readers and playgoers must grasp the true meaning of Chekhov's nuances and not overlook any linguistic hints.

A very laconic artist who would rather understate than exaggerate, Chekhov likes to minimize his own role. Merezhkovski noted in 1906:

> Chekhov's simplicity is of such a nature that it sometimes makes one feel apprehensive. One gets the impression that with one step further along this path art comes to an end, that life itself is at an end; simplicity turns into vacuity, into mere nothingness. Everything is so simple that apparently nothing more is left and one has to look sharply in order to perceive everything in this "almost nothing."

A RECONSIDERATION OF VALUES

## Merezhkovski and His Followers

Merezhkovski initiated a reconsideration of values in Russian criticism that was of major significance for the twentieth century. Thus in historical perspective Merezhkovski's importance as a critic and an essayist is greater than as a writer of fiction. The pretentious trilogy *Christ and Anti-Christ* (*Khristos i antikhrist*) enjoyed a certain popular appeal for a time, but its importance is historical and cultural rather than literary. As historical novels all three parts are extremely tendentious and indigestible. They are entirely bound to modern ideological concepts.

The first part of the trilogy, *The Death of the Gods* (*Smert bogov*, 1895), is set in the time of Emperor Julian the Apostate. The second part, *The Romance of Leonardo da Vinci* (*Voskresshiye bogi*, 1901), is a novel about the Renaissance. The last part, *Antichrist, Peter and Alexei* (*Antikhrist, Piotr i Aleksei*, 1905), was to present an ideological synthesis in a portrayal of the era of Peter the Great.

In accordance with his special historical point of view Merezhkovski contrasts Christianity and ancient paganism during three periods in history and seeks to reconcile these two conflicting elements in European culture. In the main, however, he describes only the symptoms of degeneration in the cultures of antiquity (in Part I) and the signs of decay in Christian culture in Russia (in Part III). The influence of European "decadence" is clearly visible in this work.

At the beginning of the 1890s the names of modern non-Russian writers were beginning to be heard in Russia. In his critical writings Merezhkovski refers to Flaubert, Maupassant, Baudelaire, Verlaine, Poe, and Ibsen. In the Russia of the 1890s, however, mention was being made of Rimbaud, Mallarmé, Maeterlinck, and other representatives of so-called symbolism and decadence. Merezhkovski wrote of French symbolism as early as 1892, and the acceptance of new Western styles of writing in Russia can be dated with considerable accuracy.

In a few years intellectual and cultural forces elevated Russian critical awareness of the works of writers from Poe and Baudelaire, and of the latest writings of Mallarmé. The acceptance of symbolism began in 1892, and only five years later its epochal importance for Russia was clearly discernible.

From the point of view of cultural development the years in which symbolism took root in Russia were a period of creative initiative and intellectual liberation. New paths in all areas of art and thinking were pursued, and this new start at the turn of the century was later interpreted as the beginning of a new age. It was referred to as the "silver age" to distinguish it from the "golden age," which for Russians was the time of Pushkin.

The appearance of a number of new journals was an important factor in this cultural awakening. Among the most important was the art magazine *The World of Art* (*Mir iskusstva*, 1899–1904) of the cultural impresario Sergei Diaghilev (1872–1929). In its columns the symbolist writers and the representatives of the new religio-philosophical idealism were able to express themselves fully.

At the beginning of the century the symbolists published their own journals: *The Balance* (*Vesy*, 1904–09) and *The Golden Fleece* (*Zolotoye Runo*, 1906–09). The striving for the renewal of the ideological bases of Russian religious and secular thinking was so earnest, however, that Merezhkovski established *The New Way* (*Novyi Put*, 1903–04), a magazine devoted primarily to ideological questions.

At the same time the so-called religio-philosophical meetings in Saint Petersburg made a considerable impression. They, too, had developed out of the groups around Merezhkovski. These gatherings resulted not only in a discussion of the different directions and varieties of the new intellectual movement, but also in a fruitful meeting of minds of the intelligentsia and the clergy—two elements that, as a rule, had been strictly separated in Russia.

Prominent among the writers who devoted themselves chiefly to religious and ideological thought during these years were, in addition to Merezhkovski, Vasili Rozanov (1856–1919) and Lev Shestov (1866–1938). Shestov became especially well known in Russia as an authority on the philosophy of Nietzsche. He discussed it in connection with his treatment of Tolstoi and Dostoyevski in

*The Good in the Teaching of Tolstoi and Nietzsche* (*Dobro v uchenii Tolstovo i Nitzshe*, 1900) and in *The Philosophy of Tragedy, Dostoyevski and Nietzsche* (*Filosofiya tragedii, Dostoyevski i Nitzshe*, 1901). In 1905 Shestov's important philosophical work *The Apotheosis of Rootlessness* (*Apofeoz bespochvennosti*) appeared, with the significant subtitle, *An Experiment in Undogmatic Thinking*.

Several other outstanding writers of this era who had all been converted from Marxism to idealism were Sergei Bulgakov (1871–1944), Nikolai Berdyayev (1874–1948), and Semen Frank (1877–1950). Bulgakov, who had published a book entitled *From Marxism to Idealism* (*Ot marksizma k idealismu*), made efforts, together with Berdyayev, for the continuation of the journal *The New Way*. It appeared in 1905 under the new title of *Questions of Life* (*Voprosy zhizni*), but was soon discontinued.

## Journalism and the Realists

Through the development of the Russian press, and through the establishment of new journals and newspapers, some metropolitan and some regional, a number of younger hitherto unknown writers came before the public. The school of the modern realists thus established itself by way of journalism.

Young Gorki began his career as a correspondent for such provincial papers as *Samarskaya gazeta, Odesskiye novosti,* and *Nizhegorodsky listok.* Bunin appeared first as a staff writer on *Orlovski vestnik* and Kuprin as a reporter for *Kiyevlyanin and Kiyevskoye slovo.*

These new realists, who through circumstances were primarily bound to the provinces, developed their skills by writing sketches, studies, and documentaries about unusual ethnic types, about travel adventures off the beaten track, and about strange and unusual lives. Excursions, pilgrimages, and journeys became symbols of the time. Even Chekhov made an appearance as a travel writer in his report on the Island of Sakhalin.

Unusually non-bourgeois people and their destinies had already been portrayed by Vladimir Korolenko (1853–1921) in his stories. In fact, in de-emphasizing social pathos and stressing the irrational drives in human beings, Korolenko stands at the beginning of a new development. Merezhkovski even claimed that Korolenko was stimulated by religious inspiration. Gorki, on whom Korolenko had great influence, said in 1913 that the latter had helped him to understand the "Russian soul." Gorki's own early characters, the desperadoes of the harbors of the Volga and the Black Sea, his vagabond *bosyaki* (barefooters), are entirely in this mold, which remained rather constant for him.

Several years before the turn of the century, however, a return to a more compact writing in the novella and the novel could be observed among the younger realists. Sketches and light literature gave way to serious fiction. The settings, of course, were different from those of the great Russian classics. In many instances they became more exotic.

At the turn of the century Chekhov was the most widely admired writer. In the first years of the new century, however, the group known as "Knowledge" (*Znaniye*) began to publish its almanacs (1903–13). Chekhov, too, was asked to collaborate. In its second volume in 1904 it reprinted *The Cherry Orchard*. The third volume was a commemorative edition for Chekhov. It contained contributions by Gorki, Bunin, Kuprin, Leonid Andreyev, and other well-known figures.

The realists at that time had their periodic meetings, as the Sreda group, in the Moscow residence of writer Nikolai Teleshov (1867–1957), known for his stories of the Urals. He recaptured the mood of this group in his memoirs, *Notes of a Writer* (*Zapiski pisatelya*, 1952). In addition to Gorki, Kuprin, Bunin, L. Andreyev and Veresayev, many lesser writers whose fame has since faded attended the meetings, together with actors from the Moscow Art Theater, the singer Chaliapin, and finally Chekhov himself.

# *Symbolism*

Symbolism in Russia began in the 1890s, primarily as an aesthetic, partly decadent movement. It gradually divided into different currents, where ideological differences were initially stressed. Most of the points of contention now seem unimportant, because the various philosophies proposed by the symbolists were based entirely on the creation of myths. Indeed, the period from 1906 to the collapse of czarist Russia was, in one sense, the time of the creation of national myths, derived from remnants of Greek and Slavic mythology and from the beliefs of the early Christian sects.

Even early symbolism was dominated by a belief in mystic premonitions and apocalyptic visions, which only seemed to be confirmed by the Russo-Japanese War and the Revolution of 1905, as suggested in Andrei Belyi's essay *The Apocalypse in Russian Poetry* (*Apokalipsis v russkoi poezii*, 1905). Thus, Russian symbolist writing is perhaps still more full of tension than that of other countries. It is characterized both by aesthetic perception and by an acute awareness of the historical. This feeling for history turns into a mood of impending catastrophe as early as 1904.

## EARLY SYMBOLIST POETRY

### *Konstantin Balmont and Zinaida Gippius*

Among the writers typical of the turn of the century was Konstantin Balmont (1876–1943) and Zinaida Gippius (1869–1945), who as early as the 1890s belonged in the symbolist camp. Balmont skillfully handled the most difficult rhythmic and phonic forms of expression, producing striking effects rather than a well-constructed composition. For him, the charm of sound was the essence of the poetic. His metaphors, however, were often weakened by excessive alliteration and assonance, euphonic graduation of vowels, and frequently overloaded internal rhymes.

Balmont owed much of his inspiration to Poe, Baudelaire, Maeterlinck, and to some extent the German poets—particularly Heine, Novalis, and Lenau. Readily absorbing current literary developments during his extensive travels, Balmont became one of the most important disseminators of foreign poetry in Russia. His tireless activity as a translator contributed much to the cosmopolitan character of symbolist writing in Russia.

Balmont's most important works are *Under Northern Skies* (*Pod sevarnym nebom*, 1894) and *Let Us Be Like the Sun* (*Budem kak solntze*, 1903). In the latter, Balmont, influenced by the taste of the 1890s, portrays the demonic prose of the fallen angel who, in his search for the eternal Antigone, finds only the head of Medusa.

Balmont's cult of beauty, like that of all the decadents, was ambivalent. His poetry thrives among the "reeds, the swamp lilies, the red flower of crime, pestilence and death," as well as among the "ethereal abysses" and the "lush down of the snow." Posing as Nero, the poet is eager to see houses burn, as in *Burning Buildings* (*Goryashchiye zdaniya*, 1900). In the poem *Like a Spaniard* (*Kak ispaneta*), he portrays himself as a proud conquistador, seeking "copper, gold, balsam, diamonds, and rubies," but also "the blood that spurts from the breasts of the vanquished princes."

Characteristic of Balmont's poetic perception, however, is that despite the acts of violence conjured up by his imagination, he repeatedly feels himself crushed to the earth, forced into the "prison of the world," disillusioned and tortured, alone and unredeemed. The poet is left with only his "exquisite verse," but his metaphors run through his fingers like water.

Similar motifs occur in the more profoundly intellectual poetry of Zinaida Gippius. Influenced by the religio-philosophical ideas of her husband, Dmitri Merezhkovski, she also uses his dialectical abstractions in many of her images. Gippius is noted for her terse development of ideas as well as for her technique of lending variety to a thought by startling comparisons and parallelisms. The sentiments expressed in Gippius's verse are largely those of a masculine "I." The poems are compact and at the same time subtle in their composition. The syntactical structure, with its skillful placing of modifiers, is impressive. Her *Collected Poems* (*Sobraniye stikhov*) appeared in 1904. In subject matter, these poems, which have been influenced by decadent poets, express Russian literary motifs ranging from Dostoyevski to Merezhkovski. In Zinaida Gippius's later poems an element of the grotesque appears, as in *The Little Devil* (*Diavolionok*, 1908).

## Valerii Bryusov

The first important works of Valerii Bryusov (1873–1924), the son of a Moscow manufacturer, appeared as early as 1894 in the small pamphlets with the then startling title *Russian Symbolists* (*Russkiye Simvolisty*). One of the first poets to dedicate himself wholly to modernistic tendencies, Bryusov attempted to produce examples of Russian symbolist poetry instead of translations of French originals. His own poems were obviously based on French models, especially those of Verlaine, Maeterlinck, and Mallarmé. Among the contributors to *Russian Symbolists* was Bryusov's friend A. A. Lang, who wrote under the pseudonym Miropolski. Most of the contributors, however, were fictitious authors created by Bryusov to give the impression that there was an entire army of symbolist writers.

As a historian and philologist, Bryusov possessed extraordinary technical skill. In his poetry, moreover, he was as dedicated to experimentation as the most devoted scientist. In this respect, Bryusov clearly resembles the Parnassians. His precise cadences and the graphic nature of his expressions produce the effect of a potent, formal regulative principle of composition, even in symbolist poetry, which is characterized by vague allusions and phonic nuances.

Bryusov's poetic themes are definitely part of a literary tradition. Most frequently, they move in the ambiance of ancient or modern history, or in the area of poetic legends. Their symbols evoke the perpetual presence of the *mythos*.

In contrast with the later symbolists (Aleksandr Blok and Andrei Belyi), however, Bryusov is completely uninterested in the national mythos. His attitude toward history is purely eclectic and conditioned by aesthetic inclinations. Occasional utterances indicate that Bryusov considered ideologies merely as subject matter of purely aesthetic value.

Bryusov's extreme subjectivism, combined with an aesthetically based amoralism, produced a "decadent" attitude toward secular reality as well as an artistic protest against the ideological positions of the militant democratic intelligentsia. Consciously defying the *Zeitgeist*, Bryusov suppressed the national or social elements in his poetry. He therefore chose such unusual titles for his first volumes of poetry as *Chefs d'oeuvre* (1895), *Me eum esse* (1897), *Tertia vigilia* (1900), *Urbi et orbi* (1903), and *Stephanos* (1906).

The decisive development in Bryusov's art, as far as his poetry is concerned, occurred between 1896 and 1906, the years in which symbolism assumed its primacy in Russian literature. In later years, Bryusov merely repeated his earlier accomplishments. His poems in the volumes *All Motifs* (*Vse napevy*, 1909), *Shadow Mirror* (*Zerkalo tenei*, 1912), and *Seven Colors of the Rainbow* (*Sem tzvetov radugi*, 1914), are characterized by academic coolness and polished but noncommital rhetoric.

Bryusov's poetic language is selective in its vocabulary, but not too modish. The poet himself liked to compare his poems to a costly article of jewelry, as in *The Sonnet to Form* (*Sonet k forme*, 1895). Making a word his own was for him a careful polishing and faceting of rough gems that had hitherto been overlooked or disdained. Bryusov's poems are exceedingly rich in abstract concepts. He also gradually developed a strong taste for allegory, which reveals itself most clearly in *Urbi et orbi* and *Stephanos*.

Bryusov had a special predilection for arranging his poems in cycles. The titles of the separate cycles refer to a great variety of experiences, traditions, programs, and formal genres. The cycle *Favorites of the Centuries* (*Lyubimtzy vekov*) is characteristic of Bryusov's subject matter. Poems about a priest of Isis, Dante in

Venice, Don Juan, Mary Stuart, and Cleopatra are arranged next
to one another, without any suggestion of disharmony. Bryusov here
shows that he is a follower of modernist movements and at the same
time a traditionalist when he introduces Don Juan as a "mariner
of love":

> Yes, I am a mariner! An explorer of islands,
> I let myself be cast about daringly on the vast sea.
> I thirst for new lands, for other flowers,
> For peculiar dialects, for foreign ranges of mountains.

The cycle *The Eternal Truth of the Idols* (*Pravda vechnaya
kumirov*) was written from 1904 to 1906 as a sequel to *Favorites
of the Centuries*. Here mythological and historical themes recur, as
in *Theseus to Ariadne* and *Antony*. Bryusov also elaborates political
and social problems in "supra-historical" metaphors. The cycle
*The Present* (*Sovremennost*), also from the book *Stephanos*, treats
the Russo-Japanese War and the Russian Revolution of 1905, but
it also contains such titles as *Julius Caesar* or *The Huns of the
Future* (*Gryadushchiye gunni*). The latter is especially important
because of its "Mongolian" theme, which is linked with the Russo-
Japanese War and with reflections on the philosophy of history of
Vladimir Solovyev (*Ex oriente lux*). In Bryusov's poem, the new
assault of the Huns is welcomed, because it must draw the sickly
body of Russia through a wave of flaming blood toward regeneration.

Bryusov occupied himself intensively with Verhaeren's works as
early as 1899. He was attracted by Verhaeren's concern with the
modern city and its problems for the newcomer from a rural background, as dealt with in *Les Villes tentaculaires* and *Les Villages
illusoires*. The influence of Verhaeren is clearly shown in *Tertia
vigilia* and even more strongly in *Urbi et orbi* and *Stephanos*, as
well as in several narrative poems of the early 1900s, including
*Praise of the Crowd* (*Slava tolpe*, 1904) and *The Sallow Horse*
(*Kon bled*, 1904). All of these works present the theme of the
metropolis, anticipating the concerns of later Russian poetry.

In *The Sallow Horse*, Bryusov pays tribute to the apocalyptic
current in Russian literature. The sallow apocalyptic horseman
dashes through the chasm of a city street under neon lights and

electric billboards, which glow "from the terrifying heights of thirty stories." He hurries between omnibuses, automobiles, rushing pedestrians, and newsboys. Traffic stops only for a second, then continues as if nothing had happened. A lunatic escaped from the hospital is scarcely heard as he shrieks: "A quarter of you will perish through epidemics, hunger, and the sword!" [Bryusov as narrative writer, *see* p. 26.]

### Fiodor Sologub

The poetry of Fiodor Sologub (pseudonym of F. Teternikov, 1863–1927) is extremely formal, although his subject matter is very unusual. For Sologub, reality is ambushed by demons. The sun is the head demon—the symbol of a "bad" work of creation. Rejecting the hypocritical deception of daylight, Sologub favors the poetical transfiguration of the nocturnal elements of life. He seeks the ecstatic negation of the world and expresses his desire for union with the eternal repose of nothingness.

Sologub is the magician and sorcerer among Russian symbolists. His poems often sound like magical incantations. For Sologub, the basis of poetic expression is not melody, but the litany, with its "obstinate" repetitions and insistent conjuration.

Sologub was not one of the founders of Russian symbolism. Early in his career as a poet, however, he fell under the spell of the aesthetic currents of the departing century. First of all, his poems remind one of impressionistic painting. They take as their theme the feeling of individual isolation and metaphysical emptiness that preceded the renascence of idealism in Russia.

Sologub remained almost unknown until 1896. He soon developed a close spiritual affinity with the Saint Petersburg symbolists, however, because of his early translations of Verlaine. In four poetic works published between 1896 and 1904 he revealed his self-willed imagination and strange inclinations. During the 1905 Russian Revolution his poetry became somewhat satirical and grotesque. As an "anarchist" hostile to all orderly arrangements, Sologub welcomed the Revolution and sided with its victims.

In addition to some definitely revolutionary poems, in these years he wrote poems in popular rhythms (so-called lullabies and grotesque ballads) that are among the most successful of his creations. They were included in *The Circle of Flame* (*Plamennyi krug*, 1908), probably his most representative collection. Poems such as *The Dog of the Gray King* (*Sobaka sedego korolya*, 1905), *Quiet Lullaby* (*Tikhaya kolybelnya*, 1906), *The Devil's Swing* (*Chortovy kacheli*, 1907), and *The Hangman of Nuremburg* (*Niurenbergski palach*, 1907) belong to the permanent treasures of Russian poetry. In his pronounced pessimism, Sologub shows the influence of Schopenhauer. Beyond that, his ethical ideas indicate a relationship with Manichaean and Buddhist teachings.

In Sologub's works, the Christian relationship of God and Satan is abolished. The heaven of Lucifer, of the "flaming breath of freedom," exists with equal power beside the "heaven of Adonai," the heaven of the "dark and vengeful God." Man, from Sologub's point of view, is at the mercy of the "irony" of the powers of fate. He can reaffirm his freedom only in Luciferian daring, in the readiness for earthly death. [Sologub as narrative writer, *see* p. 24.]

## Other Early Symbolists

In addition to those poets previously discussed, a number of less well-known symbolist poets were, nevertheless, of importance to their time because of their originality. The most gifted were Ivan Konevskoi (pseudonym of Ivan Oreus, 1877–1901), the Lithuanian Jurgis Baltrušaitis (1873–1945), and Maksimilian Voloshin (1877–1932), also a painter.

Voloshin, a talented translator of French poetry, was also an important representative of the mythical-visionary style that was cultivated in the group around Vyacheslav Ivanov. After 1910, Voloshin's brightly colored poetry moved markedly away from symbolism and approached so-called acmeism in its formal characteristics.

Sergei Gorodetzki (born 1884) was also initially indebted to symbolism. By 1911, however, he had already entered the new acmeist movement. His revival of Slavic mythology and his partly religious, partly folkloristic symbolism inspired a number of younger poets.

## SYMBOLISM'S HIGH POINT

### Aleksandr Blok

The poetry of Aleksandr Blok (1880–1921) is generally regarded as the high point of symbolism in Russia. In his earlier years, Blok was primarily influenced by Russian romanticism and its aftermath (Zhukovski, Lermontov, Polonski, Fet, and Apukhtin). The decisive influence on his work, however, was the "sophiology" of Vladimir Solovyev as expressed in this philosopher's poetic works. From the beginning Blok's mystic, erotic concept of a feminine cosmic soul was linked with concrete phenomena. The earliest embodiment of his conception was the luminous figure of The Beautiful Lady. The most typical among them was The Unknown One, an ambiguous creature, demimondaine, clad in black silk and with black ostrich plumes on her hat.

The power of Blok's poetic monologue developed considerably between *The Verses of the Beautiful Lady* (*Stikhi o prekrasnoi dame*, 1901–02, printed in 1904) and the poem *The Unknown Woman* (*Neznakomka*) from the cycle *The City* (*Gorod*, 1904–06). He became capable of portraying virtually every human emotion, from joyful hope and expectation to self-torturing doubt.

Blok studied law and philology in Saint Petersburg until 1906. As early as 1902 he made contacts with the group around Merezhkovski; Zinaida Gippius became his sympathetic friend and attentive teacher. In 1903 Blok met the young Andrei Belyi, whose mystic inclinations resembled his own. Belyi had long been a close friend of Sergei Solovyev, a distant relative of Blok and a nephew of the philosopher Vladimir Solovyev, whom both Blok and Belyi admired.

With the cycle *The City*, Blok demonstrated his maturity as an artist. He did not develop his own inimitable style, however, until the poems of the cycle *The Snow Mask* (*Snezhnaya maska*, December 1906–January 1907).

In this work he combined the subtle musicality of his verses with an inspired imagery. Even in *The City*, which was strongly influenced by Bryusov, Blok had departed from the mists and the ethereal images of his youth. His somewhat folksy Germanic romanticism was replaced by the poetry of the big city. In *The Snow Mask*, Blok translated his former mystical experiences and his life in the big city into a visionary, metaphorical language, that is both symbolist and at the same time very Russian.

On the whole, Blok's poetry is more emotional than intellectual. His fleeting metaphors can be understood only in reference to entire cycles of poetry. Their function in the individual poem is often only musical. Certain complexes of metaphors can easily be singled out, particularly those that arise from elementary Russian phenomena. Thus from 1907 to 1914 the basic elements of his poems were the snowstorm, wine, gypsies; the flame, the dance, the droning of musical instruments; and the "fire of destructive life" ("zhizhni gibelnoi poshar"). Here Blok expressly uses such Russian literary motifs as Lermontov's *Demon*, Dostoyevski's *Double*, and Fet's poem *There a Man Has Been Burned* (*Tam chelovek sgorel*).

The frequent alternation between ecstasy and depression is very definitely recorded in Blok's poems of these years. Hopelessness and disgust with life frequently become religious self-torture and gnawing pangs of conscience, so that contrary currents enter Blok's poetry.

Blok's cycles of the years after 1907 bear such titles as *Horrible World* (*Strashni mir*, 1909–16), *Harps and Violins* (*Arfy i skripki*, 1908–16), *Carmen* (*Karmen*, 1914), and *Retaliation* (*Vozmezdiye*, 1908–13). Throughout these works Blok's attitude toward poetry is above all an attitude toward music. Such poems as *Dance of Death* (*Pliaska smerti*, 1912–19) or *Black Blood* (*Chernaya krov*, 1909–14) are musical, rhythmic variations rather than clearly perceptible treatments of a subject. Furthermore, through his free verse, that is, through the so-called "tonic" verse and decidedly unconventional rhyme technique that he used from 1910, he exerted a strong influence on the post-symbolist poetry of acmeism and futurism.

Blok's poetic work after the Revolution ended suddenly with the publication of the much-discussed poems *The Scythians* (*Skify*, 1919) and *The Twelve* (*Dvenadtzat*, 1918). This termination resulted in part from the linking of Blok's symbolism with definite ideological concepts. The cycle *Homeland* (*Rodina*, 1907–16) presents a new *mythos* in which the musical female soul of Russia waits for her redemption through the Revolution. In the poem *The Voices of the Violins* (*Golosa skripok*, 1910) the world soul appears as a "world orchestra," in which a special role is reserved for Russia.

Blok experienced the Revolution as a "musical wave" (Diary, August 7, 1917), and he fixed the historical moment as "a whirlwind of the atoms of a cosmic revolution" (Diary, August 15, 1917). After October, however, Blok realized that Russia could not play its part to the end without spiritual allies. As before, the mystic expectations became ironic destruction. In *The Scythians,* Blok followed the ideas of the social revolutionary R. Ivanov-Razumnik (1878–1945), who had issued his first almanac under that title in 1917. Here Blok assumed the stance of an "Asiatic": "Yes, we are Scythians! Yes, we are Asiatics! With slit and greedy eyes."

Blok then announced that Europe must solve the riddle of the Russian sphinx. Russia looks toward Europe "full of hate and full of love." Let the European neighbors in fraternal cooperation finish the work of liberation. If Europe fails, its fate is sealed. Russia will then no longer move a finger if the "Huns" should lust to "roast the flesh of the white brothers." The "barbaric lyre" for the last time calls the old world to a fraternal feast of work and freedom.

For Blok, the downfall of the old world was sealed in 1918. He still hoped, however, that the purely destructive forces would not gain the upper hand. He saw in this hour a last, somewhat dubious opportunity, to rescue his *mythos* of the cosmic soul. Blok's last attempt at a mystic integration is the expansive poem *The Twelve,* written in January 1918, a few days before *The Scythians.*

The somewhat strange song of the twelve "red" soldiers (the twelve is an allusion to the twelve apostles) consists of a series of twelve individual chants. Twelve soldiers of the Red Guard march through starving Petrograd in a snowstorm. Their political revolt is combined with rebellion against the old moral and judicial order. One of them, Petrucha, uses this historical crisis to take bloody revenge on a rival but accidentally kills his former sweetheart. Although he is badly shaken, his conscience is finally cleared. Encouraged by his comrades, he marches on.

In the twelfth part of the poem, no other than Jesus Christ appears at the head of the "red" troopers, "with the bloody flag, invisible in the snowstorm, protected by a charm against bullets . . . crowned with white roses." Such an artistic solution was obviously counter to all political and ideological logic.

The remarkable thing, however, as Blok himself writes in his diary (1918), is not "that the red troopers are unworthy of Jesus, but that Jesus leads them and that really someone else ought to have." With the mystical conclusion of *The Twelve*, Blok makes a final effort of faith, the last attempt to justify himself and his symbolic work. After January, 1918, Blok is no longer the same as poet and thinker. The poetry that appears after *The Twelve* and *The Scythians* is a swan song, and the poet becomes almost silent.

In addition to his work as a poet, Blok created a series of interesting symbolic dramas. He also wrote extensively about the theater. In 1918 he was even elected chairman of the repertory section of the state theater.

Blok thus became part of the great revival of the Russian theater that had begun in 1898 with the founding of the Moscow Art Theater by Konstantin Stanislavski (1863–1938) and Vladimir Nemirovich-Danchenko (1858–1944). Here the plays of Chekhov, Gorki, and Leonid Andreyev were produced in authentic and exemplary stagings, exercising a notable influence on the history of Russian theater. Stanislavski, however, subscribed almost exclusively to naturalism and realism, but Vsevolod Meyerhold (1874–1940), a former member of Stanislavski's group, became the principal director of the symbolist theater.

Meyerhold turned from Stanislavski's repertoire, which was dominated by Ibsen, Hamsun, Hauptmann, Lev Tolstoi, Chekhov, and Gorki. He discovered Blok and Sologub for the Russian stage, also favoring Przybyszewski, Maeterlinck, and Wedekind. In 1906, just as the first dramatic productions of the symbolists were appearing, Meyerhold was able to secure a forum for the new experimental style of the Saint Petersburg Dramatic Theater of the actress Vera Kommissarzhevskaya (1864–1910). During this period, moreover, a number of outstanding directors were active in Russia, notably the members of the *Mir Iskusstva* group: Sudeykin, Golovin, Somov, Rerich (Roehrich), Sapunov, Benua (Benois), and Bakst.

This new theatrical enterprise was marked by a high degree of cooperation among representatives of the various arts, as shown in the 1906 production of Blok's grotesquely ironic little drama *The Puppet Show* (*Balaganchik*). It was produced by Meyerhold with the collaboration of Mikhail Kuzmin, who composed the background music, and of the painter Sapunov, who designed the stage sets; the presentation, as Blok himself noted, opened entirely new perspectives for the drama. In planning the production, Meyerhold was particularly attracted by the style of the puppet play, in which the principal figures are Pierrot, Colombine, and Harlequin.

As literature, Blok's dramatic works were rather controversial, although of great importance for the theater of the time and for the stylized symbolist stage. The shorter dramas, including *The King on the Plaza* (*Korol na ploshchadi*, 1906) and *The Unknown Woman* (*Neznakomka*), mark a crisis in Blok's output in that they ironically destroy, even parody, his own "mystic" youthful period.

The pantomime style of the puppet theater corresponded both to Blok's own ideas and to Sologub's modern theories of the drama. Sologub championed the theater "with milieu," a theater of "abbreviations," in which the least possible play-acting would take place. In his view the content of the modern theater is determined by "the tragic play of fate with its marionettes, the spectacle of the dissolution (*istaiveniya*) of all earthly masks." Thus, although Sologub probably overemphasized the "statuary" principle in his own dramas, his ideas resemble those of the symbolist theater, as shown in the plays *The Triumph of Death* (*Pobeda smerti*, 1908) and *The Valet Vanka and the Page Jean* (*Vanka Klyuchnik i pazh Zhean*, 1909).

Blok's play *The Rose and the Cross* (*Roza i krest*, 1913) is developed within this framework of concepts. Set in 13th-century

France, it produces dramatic conflict through the interaction of historical reality and romantic imagination. The unfortunate knight Bertrand suffers death as a deputy for all those who love truly and purely. The drama as a whole has meaning only in the "sacred mystery of crucified love" (*Mochul skyi*).

SYMBOLIST PROSE

After the Revolution of 1905, the most important symbolist writing was achieved in prose—in the short story, the novel, and the essay. Thus the possibilities of the symbolist style were expanded in the development of the experimental narrative. Several prominent poets of the symbolist movement worked in this genre, among them Fiodor Sologub and Valerii Bryusov.

### Fiodor Sologub

Sologub's stories and novels, like his poems, reflect a divided world. Even more emphatically than in his poetry, the author stresses the dichotomy between freedom and lack of it, between Lucifer and Adonis, suggesting conflicts that are strongly marked by erotic elements in a fundamental cosmic dualism. In his works, Russian reality, which Sologub finds absurd, is presented in a double image that is at once satirically grotesque and poetically imaginative.

Sologub's best novellas combine both points of view harmoniously, as in *Shadows* (*Teni*, 1896), one of his earliest novellas, and most notably in *The Sting of Death* (*Zhalo smerti*, 1904), *Consolation* (*Utesheniye*, 1904), *In the Crowd* (*V tolpe*, 1907), *Death After the Announcement* (*Smert po ob-yavleniyu*, 1907), and *The Grieving Bride* (*Opechalennaya nevesta*, 1908).

In most of the works published after *The Way to Damascus* (*Put v Damask*, 1910), however, Sologub too often lapses into erotic mannerisms, as in the trilogy *The Created Legend* (*Tvorimaya legenda*, 1907–13). Here Sologub's erotic-anarchistic utopias, his "satanism," and his aesthetic ideas are reflected more clearly than in any of his other works, but the combination of poetry, the utopian, eroticism, and satire is occasionally quite artificial.

Sologub's narrative technique involves dissonance, as in the weird novella *In the Crowd*, in which a public festival degenerates into a gruesome and bloody catastrophe. (He had actually witnessed such an event on the Khodynka Field at the crowning of Nicholas II, in which thousands of the curious were trampled to death.) In this novella Sologub depicts the sudden change from exuberance and delighted curiosity to fear and terror; his cool exquisiteness recalls the work of Edgar Allan Poe, from whom he borrowed many artistic devices. Sologub attains a greater effectiveness by reflecting the experiences of the mob in the souls of children who are unsuspectingly and innocently drawn into the disaster.

Sologub frequently made children the central figures of his stories. Having worked as a teacher and later as a school inspector, he found schoolchildren and adolescents more interesting than adults. In his portrayals of the conflicts of children with one another (as in the novella *The Sting of Death*) and between the child's world and that of the adult, he delineated the conflicts of life in their most fundamental form.

Sologub's best known and most important prose work is *The Petty Demon* (*Melky bes*, first published in complete form in 1907). Set in a provincial town, it contrasts the gossip-filled life of people of rank with that of a lovable, gaily mischievous horde of schoolchildren, dominated by the suspicious, sadistic secondary-school teacher Peredonov.

Peredonov, who combines as a character all the malicious, suspicious, superstitious, and sadistic traits of the minority come to power, is one of the most convincing inventions of world literature. The characterization is derived from Sologub's understanding of Gogol's gloomy humor, Saltykov-Shchedrin's bitter sarcasm, and Poe's studies of cruelty and madness. Although Peredonov is only a petty devil, he is a tormentor to be feared.

In Sologub's view, everything evil is the work of man, a product of his alienation from himself. In his essay *Man Is Man's Devil* (*Chelovek cheloveku diavol*, 1907), Sologub remarks: "Who is really the tormentor? Man or the devil? Man is man's devil!"

In its stylistic and thematic concentration *The Petty Demon* is a remarkable work of art, notable for the skillful joining of its individual parts. It is also an excellent example of Sologub's unpretentious and temperate prose, which can produce an effect of calculated, ironic naïveté, as when he reports the grimmest and most absurd incidents in a simple and aphoristic tone. Sologub, however, always speaks from a distance, whether in poetic delicacy, in popular "stylization," or in careful and pedantic accuracy. This monochrome style, entirely unaffected by emotion, clearly reveals the dissonances in Sologub's psychological processes.


## *Valerii Bryusov*

Valerii Bryusov is one of the masters of the classically pure art of narration. His first volume of stories *Earth Axis* (*Zemnaya os*), appeared in 1907. In 1907–08, the journal *Vesy*, which he edited, printed his first novel *The Fiery Angel* (*Ognenny angel*). Bryusov was especially eager to preserve and renew certain established forms of the older tradition. He therefore used the literary device of the story with an established perspective. In this framework all action appears in a traditional form, usually as observed by an omniscient narrator, who interprets and evaluates the events.

Many of Bryusov's stories carry subtitles that indicate the general tone of his narratives, as in *In the Underground Dungeon* (*V podzemnoi tiurme*), subtitled "According to an Italian Manuscript of the Sixteenth Century"; *The Last Martyrs* (*Posledniye mucheniki*), "An Undelivered Letter Given to the Hangman for Burning"; and *Now, However, That I Am Awake* (*Teper kogda ya prosnulsya*), "Memories of a Psychopath."

Bryusov's action-filled stories attempt to provide a rational basis for the fantastic and mysterious and to support it psychologically through dispassionate analysis. An intensified, hallucinatory consciousness drives his characters to extremes, even though they remain calculating and evaluating observers of themselves and their environment. His narrative style is entirely sober and objective, in contrast to Dostoyevski's, whose language far more intensively shades into feverish fantasies.

In Bryusov's utopian story *The Republic of the Southern Cross* (*Republika Yuzhnovo Kresta*), published in *Vesy* in 1905, the viewpoint of the eyewitness is indicated by the subtitle "Article of the Special Number of the North European Evening Journal." The action, set in a future, highly technological age, is thoroughly preposterous and horrifying, but its rendering is so scientific and professionally dispassionate that the occurrence of similar catastrophes in mankind's future becomes a frightening possibility to the reader.

The Republic, in which everything is precisely planned and organized, is destroyed because of an inane, ridiculous error that goes undetected. Its inhabitants fall ill from *mania contradicens*, the addiction to contradiction, and must act in opposition to their own desires. In the ensuing confusion, all social and technical functions fail, all moral restraints break down, and absurd orgiastic destruction and base sensuality cast mankind into a ruinous frenzy.

The most horrifying and extraordinary of Bryusov's revelations is that even the most sensible and sober man is vulnerable to insanity, which he maintains is not confined to the mentally abnormal. Presenting a similar picture of man's insanity in his story *The Last Martyrs*, Bryusov presupposes—again in a distant, utopian future— that all men of sensitivity are to be exterminated once and for all. Poets, artists, and thinkers, members of a decadent orgiastic sect, seek refuge in their cathedral, where they celebrate their last, viciously wild divine service, until all are shot down by the artillery fire of the besiegers, except for one surviving witness.

Bryusov's most important prose works are his two historical novels, *The Fiery Angel* and *The Altar of Victory* (*Altar pobedy*, 1911–12). *The Fiery Angel* is set during the Renaissance in Germany, principally in Cologne. *The Altar of Victory* describes the decadence of Rome at the end of the 4th century A.D. Both novels deal primarily with unusual spiritual and erotic passions, as shown in a number of historical and legendary characters. Thus *The Fiery Angel* portrays the spiritual and secular dignitaries of the region between Cologne, Düsseldorf, and Trier; included are famous scholars such as Agrippa of Nettesheim, and finally even Doctor Faustus.

The action of the novel, however, is carried by fictional characters who fascinate the reader because they act simultaneously as entirely modern figures and as individuals whose era has long disappeared. Ironically observing the metaphysical and erotic problems of inwardly related epochs, Bryusov purposely chose periods marked by contradictory forces: the transition from pagan antiquity to Christianity, and from the Christian Middle Ages to Humanism and modern times. Merezhkovski had previously chosen these same epochs for his novels.

With scholarly self-irony Bryusov included extensive lists of sources and commentaries in both novels. He thereby once again established a dichotomy between the author and the "narrator," who does not look beyond the boundaries of his own world. The novels are told in the first person, in the manner of an eyewitness report, and the narrative style is skillfully attuned to the rhetorical devices of the epoch described. Thus, in the preface to *The Fiery Angel*, the narrator characteristically speaks of his "artless" story, "bare of every adornment."

The narrative language is closely related to the narrator's experience. In *The Fiery Angel*, it is that of a former soldier, who once studied medicine in Cologne and who in the Spanish service became acquainted with the West Indies. The narrator's background in natural science, medicine, technology, war, and seafaring provide an amazing number of descriptions and images, often forming interesting parallels to Bryusov's poetry and its numerous erotic allegories:

> My passion, which covered me with a flood of supreme happiness for two weeks, then retired from the shores of my soul, set the beach free and left on its sandy ground sea stars, shells, and algae.

The subordinate theme of *The Fiery Angel* is brought out in the detailed subtitle, which represents an entire table of contents:

> The fiery angel, or a true story, of the devil, who several times in the guise of a luminous spirit appeared to a virgin and incited her to commit many sinful offenses; of godless occupation with magic, astrology, wizardry, and necromancy; of the court trial of a virgin under the chairmanship of his eminence the archbishop of Trier; as well as of meetings and conversations with the knight,

Agrippa of Nettesheim, and with Doctor Faustus, a doctor three times over, written down by an eyewitness.

Contemporary readers considered the novel a roman à clef in which not only Bryusov himself but also the poet Andrei Belyi and the divorced wife of a noted publisher appear. There is evidence that Bryusov, following a widespread practice, occupied himself with magical and occult experiments. As far back as September 1900, he wrote in his diary, "I visit spiritualistic seances eagerly. I preach, teach, and have some influence."

Among his posthumous papers was found a continuation of *The Altar of Victory* entitled *The Dethroned Jupiter* (*Yupiter pover-zhenny*). In his stories, as well as in the historical novels, Bryusov's narrative style is characterized by an ironic objectivity of which he is truly a master. The accounts are presented as though the least plausible and abhorrent events were quite natural and could surprise only those wholly unworldly. On this subject, the preface by the narrator in *The Fiery Angel* is most illuminating: "I believe that everyone who has had the opportunity of being the witness of unusual and hardly intelligible incidents must record them in a truthful and unbiased manner."

### Andrei Belyi

Andrei Belyi (pseudonym of Boris Bugayev, 1880–1934), the son of a well-known mathematician and professor at Moscow University, is, in his versatility and far-reaching influence, perhaps the most interesting exponent of Russian symbolism; in any case, he is one of its central figures.

Belyi sought to give symbolism a theoretical basis—poetically, aesthetically, and logically. He wished to join *mythos* to *logos*. His great scientific talent, developed in his studies of natural science, philosophy, and philology at the University of Moscow, is evident in his essays, which examine symbolism in aspects other than the purely literary.

In 1909, the magazine *Vesy* published his novel *The Silver Dove*

(*Serebryanyi golub*). The novel belongs to that period in which Belyi was intensively occupied with problems of the occult. As early as 1908 he had become acquainted with the *doctrine secrète* of the Ukrainian Madame Blavatskaya and had begun to attend theosophic meetings. The record of such indoctrination is found in *The Silver Dove*, the theme of which is essentially the old ideological question of Russian intellectual orientation—West or East?

In this novel Belyi attempts to show how the student Daryalski, a man of Western civilization, is attracted and destroyed by the dark occult forces of the East. The mysterious Eastern soul of Russia is incarnated in the sect of the "Doves," whose emblem became the title of the novel. Belyi is convinced that fundamentally Western civilization easily succumbs to Eastern sectarian beliefs and occult temptations, once the physical power of opposition has been paralyzed.

The precipitate action at the end of the novel is tinged with virtually documentary features. Daryalski, the refugee from Western culture, becomes increasingly involved with the sect and is finally murdered by fanatical sectarians. His corpse is wrapped in bast mats and buried in the vegetable garden.

As Mirski has emphasized, Belyi's world is entirely immaterial and not to be measured by familiar criteria. Belyi's mental abstractions, with all their apparent seriousness, always retain something playful and noncommittal. Mirski recognized in Belyi "perhaps the greatest Russian humorist since Gogol." His novels, therefore, should be viewed not as tragedies, but as grotesques.

This is especially true of Belyi's next novel, *Saint Petersburg* (1913), which uses something of the stream of consciousness technique. The novel is exhaustive in its description of consciousness, which is grotesquely distorted and divided. Although the "narrator" is used as an intermediary, he is neither an interpreter nor a guide through the labyrinth. He is rather something like an ironic announcer of various scenes.

In *Saint Petersburg* the poetic conception gradually pushes aside the ideological conception and outmaneuvers it. Originally, Belyi had again intended to place West and East opposite one another within the framework of a larger trilogy, of which Saint Petersburg was to be the second part. He had planned to set the novel in the city that was the strongest bastion of the West—the capital of Russia. As work progressed, however, the original plan began to vanish. Belyi had in the meantime become a follower of Rudolph Steiner. Inspired by the new anthroposophic conception of reality, he gave free rein to his imagination and moved the center of gravity from the level of action entirely to one of consciousness. The metropolis of Saint Petersburg, which binds the structure of the badly confused plot, becomes completely unreal and exists only as a hallucinatory consciousness of the characters who act and suffer like sleepwalkers.

On the level of consciousness Belyi portrays the decisive filial conflict between the old Senator Ableukhov and his terrorist-affiliated son, who is to blow up his father with an infernal machine. Here also Belyi describes the penetration of the occult and astral forces. Only in the occult phenomena are traces of Belyi's original. ideological conception visible: the East in the apparition of the mysterious Persian Shishnarfne and in the Mongolian motifs ("thousands of horsemen of Tamerlane"), and the West in Peter the Great's equestrian statue brought to life.

Of particular importance, however, is the grotesque quality of the occult and astral phenomena, suggesting that Belyi intended to parody his own ideas and those of other symbolists. Similar features occur in the "ethereal appearance" of the "white Christ" in the rough draft of the novel, although this image is preserved in the finished novel only in the peculiar figure of the "white domino." This apparition is certainly an allusion to the appearance of Christ in the last part of Merezhkovski's trilogy *Christ and Antichrist*.

In Belyi's novel, Saint Petersburg appears essentially in geometric and architectonic motifs as a dead city through which only the dull-green waters of the Neva flow. Saint Petersburg has become a city of shadows and ghosts in which no one and nothing exist as in real life:

> Behind the Neva, there in the half-illuminated, green distance stand the silhouettes of islands and houses, to rouse the false hope that this region is reality, not a pitiable endlessness that blew the gray smoke of the clouds through the streets of Saint Petersburg.

Belyi created an entirely personal "phrased" prose style based wholly on rhythmic curves and phrases. He not only developed Gogol's ornamental style but also, as in the "symphonies," used such musical principles as repetition, variation, and leitmotif. In addition to his constant repetition of certain "phrases," his style is notable for its play on words, ironic allusions, and quotations with double meanings taken from his own works. All these subtleties are easily lost in translation, as are the synthetic structure of the works, the often significant pauses and caesuras, and the author's intonation.

The best example of this stylized prose is *Kotik Letayev* (1917), which elevates the description of consciousness in the Russian novel to the point to which James Joyce brought it in the English novel, that is, to the portrayal of the stream of consciousness as a simultaneously concrete and surreal (mythical) reality.

*Kotik Letayev* is partly an autobiographical work that begins with the first, still-unconscious perceptions of the child. It even describes prenatal experiences. The actual life story, which comprises the years of childhood, appears cryptic; it is pure *mythos.* Here, the boundaries of space and time dissolve. Reality, as Belyi says at one point, is in the eyes of the child—it is like a succession of soap bubbles that rise and burst.

The real living space of the child is the primeval world:

> I live through the cave period, I experience life in the catacombs, life in Egypt under the pyramids; we live in the body of the sphinx; the rooms, the corridors, are the hollow bones of the skeleton of the sphinx; if I could look through the wall, there would no longer be the Arbat, no longer Moscow; perhaps I would see the expanses of the Libyan desert before me, and in the middle, in front of it, stands a lion who is waiting for me. . . .

All objects that Belyi describes in the novel are intended only as metaphors, and only incidentally does Belyi call them by a proper name. The ill, feverish child is Theseus, the dwelling is the labyrinth, and the family doctor plays the role of the minotaur.

Belyi's other autobiographical writings, which were published after the Revolution and which include *Notes of an Eccentric* (*Zapiski chudaka,* 1919–22), do not reach the heights of *Saint*

*Petersburg* and *Kotik Letayev* despite their stylistic excellence. A similar evaluation applies to the two novels *The Eccentric of Moscow* (*Moskovski chudak*) and *Moscow Under the Push* (*Moskya pod udarom*), in which Belyi comes to terms with his past. More successful from an artistic point of view is *The First Meeting* (*Pervoye svidaniye*, 1921), an autobiographical verse narrative in Pushkin iambics. Here, Belyi's taste for the grotesque and for word play brings about a surprising effect of parody.

In 1923 Belyi returned from Berlin to Russia. Among the best of his later works are his memoirs (three volumes, 1931–34) and his discerning book on Gogol's style, *Gogol's Mastership* (*Masterstvo Gogolya*, 1934). [Belyi as poet, *see* p. 36.]

### Vasilii Rozanov

As a thinker of unusual substance and a writer of great stature, Vasilii Rozanov (1856–1919), although little known in the West, distinguished himself to such an extent that his journalistic works may justifiably be included in "literature" in the broader sense of the term. Particularly notable are his later books, *Solitaria* (*Uyedinennoye*, 1912), *Fallen Leaves* (*Opavsiye listya*, two parts, 1913–15), and *The Apocalypse of Our Time* (*Apokalipsis nashevo vremeni*, 1917–18).

Born in the Russian province of Vetluga, Rozanov went to Saint Petersburg in 1893. He joined the conservative groups and became prominent as a religio-philosophical writer. A follower of the Slavophiles, he found favor with Nikolai Strakhov and Konstantin Leontiyev. After 1899 he worked on the influential newspaper *Novoye Vremya*.

Like the decadents and the symbolists, Rozanov combined an unconventional attitude toward religious, social, and sexual questions—which constituted his search for a new foundation of human existence—with an open discussion of the historical and religious traditions of Russia. Although he did not seek to join the symbolists, he was accepted as one of the moderns, and the symbolists often requested his collaboration on their journals.

The extent of Rozanov's influence on the religio-philosophical ideas of the symbolists is difficult to evaluate. Merezhkovski and Gippius, as well as Berdyayev, certainly owed much to him. His later admirers included Aleksei Remizov, Ivanov, and many other writers who were close both to the symbolists and to quite different groups.

As an autobiographer and as a critic and journalist, Rozanov belongs among those exceptional writers who courageously examine difficult problems and act on them with almost naive impartiality. Untiringly zealous in his battle against religious, social, and sexual taboos, he fought against every kind of conformity and asked any embarrassing question that came into his mind.

Family and religion, family and sexuality, are the problems around which his provocative writings, from *The Family Question in Russia* (*Semeynyi vopros v Rossii*, 1903) to *The Dark Countenance* (*Temnyi lik*, 1911), continually revolved. According to Rozanov, Christianity had deviated too far from the Old Testament and was therefore no longer capable of absorbing all the truth of "the world" and "the earth." He deplored the fact that the New Testament lacked the Psalms. The metaphysics of Christianity had become a metaphysics of death. For him, the countenance of Jesus Christ was the dark countenance: "Christ never laughed. . . . The stamp of sadness, of ashen sadness, cannot be overlooked in the gospel."

Rozanov, who had welcomed the Revolution of 1905 approvingly as an almost "physical" movement, as a "poetic" upheaval borne by youth, was not deceived by the Revolution of 1917. The events of the period left him depressed intellectually and spiritually. His last publication, *The Apocalypse of Our Time* (*Apokalipsis nashevo vremeni*), is one of the bitterest books of recent Russian literature.

For Rozanov the curtain had fallen, as suggested in the fragment *La divina commedia* in *The Apocalypse of Our Time*:

Rattling, grating, and screeching, the curtain lowers itself over Russian history. The performance is over. The audience rises. It is time to put on the furs and to go home. One looked backward. But there were neither furs nor houses any longer.

Rozanov's later publications are essentially books of confession, comparable to those of Pascal, Rousseau, Nietzsche, Proust, and Joyce. His own soul is the hero of his books, but as one of the great modern Russian writers he also solves the difficult problem of portraying his interior life in literary form. In his meditations, based on the interior monologue, Rozanov initiates the reader into all of his idiosyncrasies, passions, memories, and dramas, even into his physiological reactions. Aphorism, anecdote, small talk, and quotations alternate, but Rozanov does not express himself in the ordinary "literary" sense. He holds back every word before it can find its proper syntactical place according to the rules of rhetoric. Often enough, he despises the rules of grammar and develops a peculiarly untidy and "unliterary" literary style out of the stream-of-consciousness monologue.

In technique, however, Rozanov's monologue is completely auctorial. It is carefully related to the literary situation and the reader. In the introduction to *Solitaria*, Rozanov carries on a dialogue with the reader over the question of why he writes:

> Why? Who gets anything out of it? Ah, dear reader, I have been writing a long time without readers—simply because it's fun. . . . With the reader, one gets bored more than when one is alone. He opens his mouth wide and waits, wondering what he is to have placed before him.

This curt, polemic tone is very characteristic of Rozanov. In the same book, he writes about himself:

> My soul is woven of dirt, tenderness, and sadness. Or, stating it differently, these are goldfish that gleam in the sun, but they are in an aquarium that is filled with swill. And they don't choke. In fact, rather, on the contrary. . . .

Rozanov's language and metaphors are peculiar to him, as is the case only with greater writers. He has therefore received a special place in literary history. Viktor Shklovski, who in 1921 in Soviet Russia still had the courage to write about Rozanov, evaluated his work as the exemplary case of the "creation of a formless form." Mirski did not hesitate to call Rozanov the greatest writer of his generation.

An excellent selection of the works of Rozanov, with an extensive introduction by George Ivask, was recently published in Russian (New York, 1956).

LATER SYMBOLIST POETS

## Andrei Belyi

Belyi was successively influenced by Solovyev, Nietzsche, and Schopenhauer, by Neo-Kantianism, and finally by Rudolph Steiner's theosophy. Belyi's theory of language and poetry initially concerned itself with the mystical "Theurgy" described in *About Theurgy* (*O teurgii*, 1903). Later he strove for a compromise between "magical verbalism" (*mochulski*) and philosophical criticism as set forth in *The Emblematics of Sense* (*Emblematika smysla*) and *The Magic of Words* (*Magiya slov*), collected in the omnibus volume *Symbolism* (*Simvolizm*, 1910).

Belyi's severe criticism of the scientific methods of perception led him to a mystical idealism that perceived the meaning of art in a "re-creation of life," as in the essay *The Meaning of Art* (*Smysl iskusstva*). Creation and perception meet in the symbol, which itself limits creating and perceiving. The way of creation thus leads to the way of perception. Belyi rejects the scientific method of perceiving: "The differentiation of what is known deepens what is not known"; its path is that of the "creative ecstasy" that transforms the artistic man into a "flame."

Belyi's art is deeply ecstatic and is determined by mystical experiences. "Without leaving the world we can reach that which is behind the world," he wrote in 1904 in his reflections on Chekhov. The passage to the world that is inaccessible to our scientific experience Belyi would find in the word itself: "The seed (the word) sunk in the depths of the subconscious, begins to sprout, breaks its dry shell (the concept), and begins again to germinate. This new life of the word points to a new organic period in culture" (*The Magic of Words*).

Like all symbolists, Belyi worked to overcome that "exhaustion" of language which Nietzsche had already deplored. He therefore struggled not only to free the word but also to renew the rhythmic structure of language and its syntactic arrangement. He first made this attempt, not in his early volume of poems *Gold in Azure* (*Zoloto v lazuri*, 1904), but in the early so-called "symphonies," experiments in rhythmic prose that strove for the unity of word and music as set forth in Nietzsche's essays on Wagner.

The quality of Belyi's descriptive writing and his use of color remained conventional, along the lines of the art of the turn of the century. Belyi, like Blok, borrowed not only from Solovyev but also from Maeterlinck, Oscar Wilde, and Nordic poetry. Wagner and Grieg represented for him the quintessence of music. The English Pre-Raphaelites as well as Stuck and Klinger determined his taste in painting. Quite consistently, Belyi named his first prose symphony *Nordic Symphony* (*Severnaya simfoniya*).

Similar influences appear in *Gold in Azure*. Belyi retains "blue-glittering velvet of the ether," "the golden fleece," "the golden wings," "pale, azure-colored satin," and "purple" sunsets. On the other hand, the work shows signs of the "apocalyptic" phase of Russian symbolism, which preceded the Revolution of 1905. This apocalyptic tendency was related to the poetry of the city. Thus, one of Belyi's poems, *On the Street* (*Na ulitze*), closes with the verse:

> Cold poisonous dust,
> Forms a ball blowing upward.
> Through dusty yellow clouds
> I hurry with open umbrella.
> And the factory chimneys spew
> Smoke against the fiery red horizon.

"Dust" was an important apocalyptic symbol in Russia. Together with volcanic darkening, with dragons, snakes and chimeras, clouds of dust were not only for Belyi but also for other symbolists, like Blok and Sologub, the signs of an epoch that no longer had a feeling of security. The time for bloody confrontations and social disturbances was approaching.

In the period 1904–05, the attitude of the younger symbolists

toward coloration and the poetic image gradually changed. The
feeling spread that one lived in a "characterless epoch" (Vyacheslav
Ivanov) and that the mystical hopes, which at the turn of the century
had animated men's minds, were moving farther and farther away.
Belyi soon bade farewell to "the golden fleece" and the "argo," to
the blue azure and the sun. His next two volumes of poetry bore
the meaningful titles *Ashes* (*Pepel*, 1909) and *The Urn* (*Urna*,
1909).

In these volumes, Belyi turned directly to Russian reality. The
titles of the poems, such as "On the Rails," "The Telegrapher,"
"The Arrested One," "The Funeral," and "From the Window of the
Railroad Coach" reveal a new realistic attitude, which does not,
however, imply a rejection of a magical concept of the word.
Mythical reality, which Belyi subsequently sought, is here closely
related to national and historical circumstances.


### Vyacheslav Ivanov


Vyacheslav Ivanov (1866–1949) studied classical philology and
history abroad before joining the Moscow symbolists in 1904 and
finally settling in Saint Petersburg in 1905. The most important
subjects of his research were the ancient mysteries and the cult of
Dionysus. Through his preoccupation with Plato, Nietzsche, and
Solovyev, Ivanov arrived at his own world view, in which mythical
and Christian traditions were successfully combined.

Among the Russian symbolists, Ivanov is the most demanding in
culture and education. His scholarship, in fact, is more remarkable
than his poetry. In his view the poet is the preserver of the old
mysteries and the foremost bearer of a renewed cult. He is therefore
in no sense merely a writer, but always a prophet, magician, and
seer. "Symbolism in the new poetry" says Ivanov in his speech *The
Heritage of Symbolism* (*Zavety simvolizma*, 1910)

> . . . appears to be the first and unclear memory of the sacred
> language of the magicians and sorcerers. . . . They knew other
> names for gods and demons, men and things, than those that the

people gave them, and with the knowledge of the true names, they laid the ground for their power over nature.

The *mythos* that Ivanov sought to save and renew is chiefly classical in character. From this antiquarian interest, however, he derived a genuine inspiration, producing symbols attuned to the spirit of the Russian language. The symbolists immediately welcomed Ivanov after the publication of his first volume of poems, *Guiding Stars* (*Kormchiye zvezdy*, 1902); in 1905 the poet became the spiritual leader of the Saint Petersburg symbolists. His group developed those forces that a few years later were to replace symbolism with the new movement known as acmeism.

Ivanov's language is hybrid in its combining of archaic and modern strains. It is, moreover, very ornamental and occasionally of an oracular obscurity. Like the baroque poets, Ivanov was fond of antithetical concepts. In his poems a prominent position is given to such pairs of opposites as empyrean and abyss, fire and water, macrocosm and microcosm, light ray and reflection, tone and echo.

Like Bryusov, though with different aims, Ivanov often displays his familiarity with Latin, Greek, and other learning. The volume of poems *Transparency* (*Prozrachnost*, 1904) was followed by the collections *Eros* (1907) and *Cor ardens* (two parts, 1909–11). Next to such poems as *Glossa, Eden,* and *Rosarium* are others such as *Sacra fames, Adamantina proles,* and *Mi fur le serpi amiche*—a quotation from Dante. Ivanov also liked to make use of less common poetic forms—the sonnet, the ghazel, and the dithyramb. In 1914, with Bryusov, he published the so-called *Carmina amoebaea.*

Ivanov's work is a rich source for lovers of studied, farfetched poetic images in which the most disparate things are combined (*Concetto*). Conventional and stale images never appear in Ivanov's poems. His sweeping imagination always travels its own path. In *Nomads of Beauty* (*Kochevniki krasoty*), for example, he combines the concept of freedom of the poet with the trampling of horses' hoofs and with Attila's horde.

In Nietzschean terms, Ivanov's poems are a synthesis of Apollonian and Dionysian elements. The apparently "barbaric" strains in his poetry are definitely intentional. Such conflicts also occur in his tragedy on Prometheus, *Prometei* (1916, printed 1919). This *Prometheus* is a serious attempt to combine the Prometheus conception of Nietzsche—Prometheus as a Dionysian figure—with the Christian concept of sacrifice. The tragedy is also a study of human freedom.

Ivanov's poetic output is larger than the few titles of the publications of collected works would indicate. Some of his poems were published in various journals. Others appeared only posthumously. New poems, especially those written from 1915 to 1920, and some from the later years of his emigration (Ivanov lived in Italy after 1924), were published in England in the 1950s.

Important cycles of the later years are the *Winter Sonnets* (*Zimniye sonety*, written in Moscow in 1919), *De profundis amavi* (Moscow, 1920), *Roman Sonnets* (*Rimskiye sonety*, 1924–25), and *Evening Glow* (*Svet vechernyi*, published in 1962), which indicate that Ivanov was committed to the symbolist style even during his emigration. In his later work, however, he avoided certain stylistic exaggerations. Mild wisdom and human feeling become increasingly important in his last cycles of poems, which are written in a simple and unassuming style.

Ivanov's critical essays occupy an important place in his work. They were collected in part in the volumes *Toward the Stars* (*Po zvezdam*, 1909) and *Furrows and Frontiers* (*Borozdy i mezhi*, 1916). Others are difficult to locate. Of the greatest value are the works about such individual writers as Dostoyevski, and about poetry in general. Ivanov's essay *Manner, Personality and Style* (*Monera, litzo i stil*, 1912) is, according to Adamovich, "probably the most important statement in Russian about the poetry of our time."

The philosophical essays, such as *The Boundaries of Art* (*Granitzy iskusstva*, 1914), are not quite convincing, despite their suggestive language. Ivanov's efforts to establish a universally valid cultural and philosophical definition of the theater, and especially of tragedy, are also rather ineffective. In this area, Ivanov is perhaps the most convincing follower of Nietzsche, but at times he completely misunderstood the objectives of the contemporary theater. Ivanov vigorously rejected the symbolism of the Western type. In his

*Thoughts about Symbolism* (*Mysli o simvolizme*, 1912), he expressly invokes only Plato, Goethe, Tyutchev, and Dostoyevski. His particular admiration for Goethe is most clearly expressed in the *Correspondence between Two Corners of the Room* (*Perepiska iz dvukh uglov*, 1921). In this remarkable work, written in collaboration with the critic Gershenzon (1869–1925), Ivanov serves as the apologist for Humanism and the classical tradition. In Germany, E. R. Curtius particularly stressed the importance of this essay.

## Innokentii Annenski

Only as he neared the age of fifty did Innokentii Annenski (1856–1909), a classical philologist and former secondary-school teacher, attain recognition as an outstanding poet and one of the great spirits in the literary turmoil of the period. In 1909, shortly before Annenski's sudden death, the young art historian and critic Sergei Makovski (1877–1962) was able to secure the poet as contributor to the newly founded magazine *Apollon* (1909–17), by means of which Annenski's work became widely known.

Because of his age and literary background Annenski really belonged to the precursors of symbolism in Russia. Although he appeared late on the literary scene, he became an inspiration to the younger poets who, as acmeists, repudiated symbolism.

Annenski's poetic sources were ancient Greece and France. His life work is the critical and poetic translation of all the dramas of Euripides, to which he occasionally added detailed, carefully thought-out treatises. The first volume of this monumental Russian edition, *The Theater of Euripides* (*Teatr Evripida*), appeared in 1906. Annenski was particularly influenced by French traditions. His models were the Parnassians (Sully-Prudhomme, Leconte de Lisle), the decadents (Tristan Corbière, Maurice Rollinat, Jules Laforgue), and the pioneers of European symbolism (Baudelaire, Rimbaud, and Verlaine). He also translated many of their poems.

His own first collection of poems, *Quiet Songs* (*Tikhiye pesni*), appeared in 1904, but under a mystifying pseudonym, so that the work did not receive the attention it merited. The second volume of poems, *The Little Box of Cypress Wood* (*Kiparisovyi laretz*), appeared posthumously, and in 1923 the poems that remained at his death were published.

In every respect, Annenski was a poet of extremely subtle perception, for whom poetic discipline was synonymous with an increased capacity for suffering. He saw his muse in the misery, the restlessness, and the anguish of the heart, which is expressed in the Russian word *toska*. This muse appears in one of Annenski's typical poems, *My Heartache* (*Moya toska*), written a few weeks before his death. Here the muse is more negative than positive. She is "without love" (*bezlyubaya*) and not even loved by her poet. She lives in doubt, hypocrisy, and vice. Wilting azaleas adorn her hair. She is exhausted like "a sweat-covered horse."

Annenski's pessimism is not declamatory and self-indulgent as is the case with some of his contemporaries. It is the expression of a profound skepticism even toward himself. An especially typical poem, *The Ideal* (from *Quiet Songs*), can be reproduced in prose as follows:

> Dull sounds with the flaring up of gas above the dead brilliance of the heads. And the black plague of boredom at the tables that are just being left. And there, among those with green faces secretly concealing the misery of habit, one tries to solve the loathsome puzzle of existence on faded pages.

Contemporaries assert that Annenski was here describing the reading room of a library.

Not only the atmosphere occasionally conjured up but also the vocabulary in Annenski's poems are deliberately prosaic. The decadent metaphors, the artistically varied nuances of color, and the suggestive articulation of sound—all contrast again and again with the completely everyday impressions that are evoked through corresponding turns of phrases, as in *Anxiety at the Railroad Station* (*Toska vokzala*—from *The Little Box of Cypress Wood*):

> O preliminary celebration of the eternal working days
> Sticky sting of discomfort . . . .
> In the dusty heat of the afternoons
> Noise and color of the railroad stations . . . .

Strangely enough, a railroad station was to be the very last station of Annenski's life, for, in November, 1909, he died of a brain clot in the station of Charskoye Selo.

The mental and spiritual condition of modern man is more clearly expressed in Annenski than in the pretentious myths of the symbolists. His apparently decadent style conceals a serious involvement with humanity, as in the volume *The Little Box of Cypress Wood*, and especially in the section *Trifolia* (*Trilistniki*). This volume also contains the remarkable poem *Nerves, a Phonograph Record* (*Nervy, plastinka deya grammofona*), in which the poet shows how an everyday occurrence on the street suddenly assumes threatening proportions.

Annenski's style also recalls Chekhov. Self-irony and understatement are, in fact, typical features of Annenski's verse. Sympathetic gentleness, too, is not lacking, not even in the tragedies based on ancient models (Melanippe, King Ixion, Laodameia).

Annenski's most important play is the "bacchic drama" *Thamyras citharoedus* (*Famira kifared*), written in 1906, but published posthumously in 1913. In this work, Annenski combines tragedy and satyr plays in a special dramatic form, in which antique and Russian traditions coexist.

The drama of the Thracian poet Thamyras, who dares to compete with the muses and is blinded, is developed by Annenski into a drama of human impotence in general. The mother—the nymph Argiope—becomes a silent witness to the suffering that must visit this family according to the will of the gods.

Humor also has a place in the play, as in the scenes with the nursemaid, but above all in the reflections of Papa-Silens and in the scenes of the satyrs. The play, which belongs among the most important creations of the Russian stage, was first produced in 1916, in the Little Playhouse, by Aleksandr Tairov, the creator of the "unleashed" theater.

Annenski's critical essays also deserve attention. The single items, with the exception of the Euripides studies, were widely dispersed and are only partly collected in the two volumes *Book of Reflections* (*Kniga otrazhenyi*, 1906–09).

# *Realism*

## *Maksim Gorki*

In the early 1900s, Maksim Gorki (pseudonym of Aleksei Peskov, 1868–1936) was one of the best-known Russian writers. His fame quickly spread beyond the boundaries of Russia. Gorki, whose life has already become a legend, was of *petit bourgeois* origin. He was born in Nizhni-Novgorod (today Gorki) on the Volga. Early in his life he was compelled to earn his own living. As a young man he worked at many jobs and moved about frequently.

His lack of formal schooling was compensated for by his unusual talent of observing human nature. He also possessed an instinct for crisis, which was then a strong feature of the Russian short story. His literary reputation rose rapidly from the middle of the 1890s and was quite sensational. At a time that longed for contact with unvarnished reality, Gorki, the spokesman for the lawless and the outlawed, the bosyaks and rogues at odds with society, the honorable thieves and harlots, definitely received much attention.

Unlike Chekhov, Gorki did not develop a new kind of narrative art. Exacting critics, Lev Tolstoi among them, soon reproached him for his arbitrary and contrived poetry. Indeed, Chekhov, who recognized the amazingly natural element in Gorki's talent and who exchanged many friendly letters with him, called many passages in his writings senseless. On the other hand, even Merezhkovski, usually among Gorki's sharpest critics, stressed the inherent truth of Gorki's compositions and noted that his types, like the devils in Goya's drawings, were frighteningly real. In the description of milieu, moreover, Gorki assumed a new tone that is especially marked in the "direct" and cynically hard crystallization of the dialogue, particularly the famous drama *The Lower Depths* (*Na dne,* 1902).

As a young man, Gorki had become acquainted particularly with the southern coast of Russia, from Akkerman and Odessa to the Caspian Sea. Out of such a background arose such types as the protagonist of *The Old Isergil* (*Starucha Iz,* 1895), the thief in *Tchelkache* (*Chelkash,* 1895), specializing in cargo piled on the docks, and, in *Malva* (1897), the still so young and cynical woman worker from the fish station.

The heroes of these stories, all written before 1900, are the bosyaks (those going barefoot, vagabonds, often uprooted bourgeois) in whom almost always an anarchic drive bursts forth. One of the prototypes of bosyakenism is significantly enough an intellectual in whom certain teachings of Nietzsche are reflected, in *The Rogue* (*Prokhodimetz,* 1898). "A good scoundrel is always better than a bad honest person" is the motto of this former bourgeois, who lives on vagabonding but who always speaks with a pose of moral superiority:

> Most of our neighbors are only pennies, small change, and the whole difference between them consists of the year of their coinage. One has been rubbed off more completely, one is still new, but the value is the same, their material the same, and in everything one resembles the other up to the point of disgust.

Paradoxically, Gorki seeks the "human" precisely in the asocial, in the one standing outside the law, in the enemies of society. Gorki really has no sympathy for the peasant, the Russian *muzhik,* the hero of the literature of the *narodniki* of the nineteenth century. His bosyaks reject and despise the peasant. Thus in *Tchelkache* the undignified antagonist Gavrila is a young peasant lad, and in *Malva* the bozyak Serezhka comments on the peasant son Yakov: "I don't like him. . . . He smells of the village . . . and this smell I can't stand."

Gorki's creative imagination is kindled in his defiance of the world and sometimes creates characters of great dynamism, such as the hero of the novel *Foma Gordeyev* (1899), whose revolt is directed against his own position as a merchant. *Foma Gordeyev* is generally considered Gorki's best novel. Here reality is not determined by society. It is an arena for wild impulses. In Gorki's skillful portrayal of the Volga region the representatives of the old merchant dynasties have the vitality and savagery of wolves. In the hero this energy leads to self-destruction when he can no longer find a purpose in life.

For Gorki, the despair over the inner emptiness of life is characteristic of his time. He therefore searched for a guiding idea to fill the vacuum. Before he found the answer in Marxism, which— as he believed—made all questions superfluous, he put in the empty place of God an optimistic and apparently very comforting human pathos, which reaches its peak in the famous passage from *The Lower Depths*: "Man—that is the truth . . . Man! That is splendid! That sounds . . . proud! M–man! One should respect man!"

*The Lower Depths* in Stanislavski's production was one of the epoch-making successes of the Moscow Art Theater, and Gorki, even if he remained indebted to Chekhov in drama, here created a play of great impact. The uncolored, even cynical dialogue, which is here adapted to the stage, is Gorki's real element, and one does not have to deplore the fact that Gorki's next plan, to write an allegorical drama in verse with the title *Chelovek* (*Man*), was not carried out.

Gorki's first "defiant" phase ended in the years after the turn of the century. In the second phase, Gorki projected himself as a revolutionary writer. Arrested in 1905 he soon left the country. In the United States, and soon thereafter on the island of Capri, Gorki became an "engaged" writer fighting for his cause. His novel *The Mother* (*Mat*, 1906), first published in English translation, pursues propagandist aims, as does the drama *The Enemies* (*Vragi*, 1906) and the journalistic reports *In America* (*V Amerika*, 1906), and *Interviews* (*Moi interv-yu*, 1906). In the same category is *Fairy Tales about Italy* (*Skazki ob Italii*), published in Russia between 1910 and 1913, in which Gorki primarily discusses the social situation.

Human optimism remains Gorki's greatest source of strength, as shown in his motto "Think of it, everything good comes from man!" (*Fairy Tales about Italy*). Gorki's belief in man sometimes resembles an almost religious faith that can hardly be explained merely as Marxism. In the peculiar story *The Confession* (*Ispoved*, 1908), dedicated to the great basso Chaliapin and set among monks, pilgrims, and sectarians, the belief in man turns into a miracle-working faith. In the story, a girl lame for four years rises and begins to walk again.

Gorki's greatest strength, however, is his ability to make a given milieu come to life from within. In the human "wilderness" of the backward provincial towns, Gorki is at home. Everything is caught visually so clearly that Gorki's characters are felt as oppressive reality. His portrayal of types and events is based largely on his own experience, which is vividly described in the predominantly autobiographical stories and novels that span the period from the early novella *Twenty-six and One* (*Dvadtzatshest i odna*, 1899) to the great trilogy *My Childhood* (*Detstvo*, 1913), *In the World* (*V lyudyach*, 1915–16), and *My Universities* (*Moi universitety*, 1923).

Particularly on Capri, Gorki found in reflective absorption a very simple style that outdistanced his earlier mannerisms. After the longer story *The City of Okurov* (*Gorod Okurov*, 1909) and in the less successful novel *The Life of Matvei Koshemyakin* (*Zhizn Matveya Kozhemyakina*, 1910–11) Gorki began a new series of short stories, which he later compiled in the cycle *Through Russia* (*Po Russi*). The twenty-nine stories united here (1912–17) fill only a thin volume. They are notable, however, for an especially pointed diction. They include *The Birth of a Man* (*Rozdeniye cheloveka*, 1912), *On the Steamer* (*Na parochode*, 1913), *The Woman* (*Zenshchina*, 1913), *Yerlas* (1916), *Strasti-Mordasti* (1917), and many other charming short stories.

The three autobiographical volumes (since *Childhood*) show that Gorki was at the peak of his descriptive art and that this middle phase was the richest in his production. Immediately after the Revolution, Gorki also published his literary memoirs. Those on Lev Tolstoi have rightfully become best known (*Lev Tolstoi*, 1919). To this period also belong the two books *Vospominaniya* (*Memories*, 1923) and *Zametki iz denvnika, Vospominaniya* (*Remarks from the Diary, Memories*, 1924).

## Leonid Andreyev

The fame of Leonid Andreyev (1871–1919), which was almost equivalent to that of Gorki, faded in the period after World War I. Andreyev's compromise between critical realism and melodramatic "nihilism" remained a special case from which no new impulses emerged. With undoubted ability, but without feeling for artistic proportions, Andreyev conjured up all possible moods of nervous repulsion and sensuous excitement, which logically led to a negation of life and which could not prove its meaning.

An epigone of Lev Tolstoi in his moral polemics, Andreyev tried —not infrequently resorting to allegorical garb—to put all of life on trial, to expose the reality of man as a senseless labyrinth or as a dismal torture chamber. The one-sided logical conclusions that Andreyev drew out of the thoughts of Schopenhauer, Tolstoi, Nietzsche, and other philosophers led him to alienation from real life and from art.

Andreyev's major dramas and stories appeared in the period from 1901–09. Even here a selection has to be made, because such allegorical stories as *The Wall* (*Stena*, 1961) evince entirely too much false pathos. The stories exclusively devoted to sexual problems, *In the Fog* (*V tumane*, 1902) and *The Abyss* (*Bezdna*, 1902), brought Andreyev at that time a certain scandalous fame, but they are hardly masterpieces.

The most successful stories are interestingly enough in the tradition of Tolstoi, as in *Christians* (*Khristiane*, 1905). Here Andreyev, like his great master, in skillfully pretended naïveté exposes a hallowed institution (the court).

Human loneliness and man's confrontation with death are described in the story *The Seven That Were Hanged* (*Rasskaz o semi povesennych*, 1908), which was dedicated to Tolstoi. Five terrorists and two murderers condemned to death are presented as each prepares to meet his death, each experiencing a slow self-alienation. Andreyev treated a similar theme in the story *The Governor* (*Gubernator*, 1906).

The governor, who is guilty of the death of forty-seven demonstrators, is condemned to death by his own conscience. He feels he can atone for his guilt only by deliberately exposing himself to an attempt on his life. Andreyev here makes the imminence of death a solemn ceremony to which everything else is subordinated. As death approaches, the physical existence of the governor becomes an empty form, a bare mechanism.

Less successful than these stories that were psychologically derived from Tolstoi is the famous description of the Russo-Japanese War, which Andreyev presented in *The Red Laughter* (*Krasnyi smekh*, 1904). The writer, who had no practical experience in war at all, raises the horror to such a fortissimo that the hyperboles neutralize one another. Tolstoi noted that, although Andreyev did in fact arouse horror, he failed to fill one with apprehension.

For a time, Andreyev was also rated as one of the great playwrights of Russia, especially after his play *The Life of Man* (*Zhizn cheloveka*, 1907) was produced by both Meyerhold and Stanislavski. In *The Life of Man* the stages of human life are presented in five tableaux, from birth to death, in purely symbolic, allegorical scenes. The thesis of the senselessness and the futility of life is less impressive, however, than the dramatically effective comments of the peripheral characters, the choruses of old women, relatives, neighbors, guests, and drunkards. In the irrelevance and meaningless nothingness, these accompanying voices foreshadow the dialogue in the modern theater of the absurd. The Moscow Art Theater also performed Andreyev's allegorical drama *Anathema* (*Anatema*, 1909), but it did not meet with the same success.

IN THE REALIST TRADITION

At the beginning of the twentieth century several new writers appeared in Russia. Born in the same generation as Gorki and Andreyev, they supported the tenets of critical realism. Some remained in Russia after the Civil War, whereas others chose exile, producing works that belong to the Russian literature of emigration. Each of these writers developed a new personal style, and their work is notable for its diversity as well as for its successful continuation of the realist technique.

*Vikentii Veresayev*

Among the realists, Vikentii Veresayev (pseudonym of V. Smido-vich, 1867–1945) had to work most intently to develop a personal style. A doctor and philologist who had studied for ten years at the University of Saint Petersburg and Dorpat, he became known in 1901 with his successful book *Notes of a Doctor* (*Zapiski vracha*). Until 1909 his principal literary theme was the destiny and final spiritual defeat of that "radical" intelligentsia that had been the center of the revolutionary movement in the second half of the nineteenth century.

After the suppression of the revolt of 1905, Veresayev no longer sought salvation in Marxism, but in "living life" in a pantheistic glorification of the vital principle in society, art, and nature. He became a follower of Nietzsche, Bergson, and Gorki, surrendering entirely to the allurements of biological thinking. He summarized his earlier attitudes in the fictitious "diary" of the renegade Cher-dyntzev, which appeared in 1909 as *Toward Life* (*K zhizni*).

In 1910 Veresayev produced the first volume of the great collec-tion of essays *Living Life* (*Zhivaya zhizn*), in which he undertook to present a rather arbitrary interpretation of Tolstoi and Dosto-yevski. Describing the conflict between instinct and intelligence, he favored Tolstoi, the writer of instinct, over Dostoyevski, whom the symbolists Merezhkovski, Belyi, and Vyacheslav Ivanov considered their great ancestor.

The second volume of *Living Life* contains a discussion of Nietz-sche in the essay *Apollo and Dionysos* (*Apollon i Dionis*, 1913–14). In contrast to the symbolists, Veresayev placed Apollonism, the affirmative joy of life, over the Dionysiac religion of the "suffering god." After a trip to Greece (1910), he returned to his philological studies, especially of classical Greek poetry, which formed a founda-tion for his theses. Evidence of this preoccupation with Greek poetry appears in the translations of the Homeric hymns, which were printed between 1912 and 1917.

At Veresayev's initiative, the Publishing House of the Writers (*Knigoizdatelstvo pisatelei*) was founded in Moscow in 1911. From

1913 to 1917 its almanac, *Slovo* (*The Word*), published the works of the "moderns" among the young realist writers, including Zaitzev, Bunin, and Aleksei Tolstoi.

After the Revolution Veresayev produced the notable studies *Pushkin in Life* (*Pushkin v zhizni*, 1926–27) and *Gogol in Life* (*Gogol v zhizni*, 1933), as well as memories of his youth and student years in Saint Petersburg and Dorpat, published as *Memories* (*Vospominaniya*, 1936).

## Aleksandr Kuprin

Next to Gorki and Bunin, Aleksandr Kuprin (1870–1938) was the most prolific realist writer before World War I. His collected works at the outbreak of the Revolution (1917) already comprised twelve volumes.

Like Gorki, Kuprin had to work his way out of the literary "provinces." After his first literary successes and personal contacts with Chekhov (1901) and Gorki (1902), he quickly joined the literary circles in the capital. From 1903 to 1908 he belonged to the collaborators of the *Znaniye* group. At that time, Kuprin already had many years of wandering behind him. His experience included contact with the most varied occupations, even with the circus and a touring theatrical group.

In Kuprin, a marked tendency toward social criticism is combined with the preference for the "strong" of this world, for robust health and vitality, for audaciously firm stands, for physical records of prowess. He likes circus acrobats and divers, air pilots and master spies, great adventurers and gamblers. His passionate admiration of the human body is especially evident in a later incidental comment on the circus: "There man is as he really is. Strong and daring, he raises weights, jumps, gallops on his horse, and in every one of his movements there are song and beauty of life."

This admiration is especially evident in *The Laestrigonies* (*Listrigony*, 1907–11), stories of the Greek fishermen from the little Crimean harbor Balaklava. Other typical narratives include *Staff Captain Rybnikov* (*Shtabs-Kapitan Rybnikov*, 1906), and the story

*Seasickness* (*Morskaya bolezn*, 1908). The latter, with its frivolous theme of the seduction of a woman married to a socialist, was harshly criticized by Gorki and other "left" intellectuals.

Kuprin's socio-critical novels are interesting milieu studies. Here, however, his penchant for sensational themes appears even more sharply than in the stories. A series of these novels begins with *The Moloch* (*Molokh*, 1896), a dramatic and somewhat decadent story of the Donetz industrial area. The major work of the series is *The Duel* (*Poyedinok*, 1905), a critical novel of military and garrison life, which Kuprin published as *The Pit* (*Yama*, 1909–14).

*The Duel* is a vehement and—after the Russian failure in the Russo-Japanese War—a very timely indictment of the inflexible military training and moral cynicism of the Russian officers corps. It is also an idealization of physical might and the right of the stronger power. The novel also shows the influence of Kuprin's early military career, as reflected in his story of cadet life, *At the Crossroads* (*Na perelome*, 1900).

One of the most remarkable of Kuprin's works is the novella *The Bracelet of Garnets* (*Granatovy braslet*, 1911). A minor employee, romantically inclined, unsuccessfully courts a rich princess. Put in his place by the relatives of the lady, he commits suicide. The story has several narrative high points and presents a fascinating picture of the Russian south around Odessa. The influence of Hamsun's *Victoria* is especially apparent, pointing to Kuprin's literary interest in Western writers, as shown by his portraits of Knut Hamsun (1908), Rudyard Kipling (1908), and Jack London (1911).

Kuprin emigrated after the Revolution, settling in 1920 in France. In 1937, homesick and suffering from ill health, he returned to the Soviet Union.

## Mikhail Prishvin

A sympathetic observer of nature, Mikhail Prishvin (1873–1954) studied agronomy in Riga and Leipzig. He was a passionate traveler and an expert in such studies as ethnography, botany, zoology, history, geography, meteorology, and ornithology.

Prishvin's *In the Land of the Frightened Birds* (*V krayu nepuganykh ptitz*, 1907) is the first of a series of collections based on his extensive travels, during which he visited the most distant parts of northern and eastern Russia. His brisk, vigorous style is colored by a colloquial speech taken from fairy tales, folk songs, and the dialectic peculiarities of the Russian provinces. Konstantin Paustovski has compared the unpretentious naturalness of Prishvin's language to the beauty of field flowers.

Prishvin's second journey, to northern Norway, is described in *On the Trail of the Magic Bread* (*Za volshebnym kolobkom*, 1908). His next work, *At the Walls of the Invisible City* (*U sten grada nevidimovo*, 1909), portrayed the pious inhabitants of distant northeastern Russia. His trip to the southeastern steppes of Russia forms the subject of *The Black Arab* (*Chernyi arab*, 1910).

Prishvin likes to combine folkloristic details and stories based on old fairy tales and legendary themes with his travel observations. Untouched nature and the untouched faith or superstitions of people fascinate him equally. Although social undertones are present in Prishvin's writings, they are never developed into the most important theme. His view of life tends to include mysticism or the occult—a factor that explains his deep interest in the hermit and the shaman.

Prishvin's realistic novels include the story of Nikon Starokolennyi (1912), a man in exile, living only with the Bible, thirsting for justice, building his house in Ilmensee, raising children, becoming rich and then poor again. His fate is magically intertwined with that of the biblical prophets and at the same time with the legendary traditions of the early history of Novgorod.

In the years immediately before World War I and the Revolution, Prishvin was obviously influenced by Remizov's style and subject matter. Finally, he even approached the group around Ivanov-Razumnik and the latter's "Scythian" ideology. Prishvin's story *The Last Judgment* (*Strahnnyi sud*) was included in the first issue of *Skify*. Later he became almost completely silent, producing no new works until the 1920s.

### Ivan Smeliov

In contrast to the majority of the realists, who adhered more closely to the tradition of Tolstoi or Turgenev, Ivan Smeliov (1873–1950) chose Dostoyevski as his model. After many years of obscurity Smeliov became widely known when his novel *The Waiter Out of the Restaurant* (*Chelovek iz restorana*) appeared in 1911 with a Gorki story in the thirty-sixth volume of the *Znaniye* series.

Smeliov felt a profound sympathy for the "humiliated and insulted." His novel about the first-class Moscow restaurant is a brilliant study of a social milieu. It recalls Dostoyevski, especially the early Dostoyevski, whenever incidents seen from the perspective of the waiter are reported hastily and almost breathlessly, and in its description of a dramatic, sometimes hysterical intensification of intrigue.

An intense romanticism marks Smeliov's later work, as in the story *The Never Emptied Chalice* (*Neupivayemaya chasha*, 1918), which describes the peculiar relationship between an icon-painter, formerly a serf, and a young woman landowner. Paradoxically, Smeliov, during the revolutionary years, abandoned social themes and turned to a poignant, wistful glorification of holy Russia. His patriotism is clearly expressed in the story *Of Foreign Blood* (*Chuzhoi krovi*, 1922), which describes the suffering and death of a Russian prisoner of war in Germany.

In 1922 Smeliov left Russia. He subsequently published another series of books describing the horrors of the Civil War. Here, pre-revolutionary Russia appears in a kind of new transfiguration.

### Boris Zaitzev

Boris Zaitzev (born 1881) began his career as a writer when still very young. Like Turgenev he came from the middle Russian city of Orel. His stories and novels are strongly influenced by Turgenev, and even more strongly by Chekhov.

Zaitzev's first works appeared in newspapers and anthologies. In 1906 the active publishing house Shipovnik issued his volume of stories *Silent Teams of Horses* (*Tikhiye Tzory*). These stories are marked by a suspended melancholy and a restrained lyricism, far removed from the more intense realism of Gorki or Kuprin. Zaitzev's narrative technique is predominantly impressionistic, and his style of description has often been compared with watercolors.

Zaitzev shares Prishvin's predilection for travel and travelogues. His long journeys to holy sites in Russia, Mt. Athos, and above all Italy, are described in writings published in 1922, the year of his emigration.

### Ivan Bunin

Among the most prominent writers outside the symbolist movement before the Revolution was Ivan Bunin (1870–1953). In 1933, while in emigration, he was awarded the Nobel Prize for Literature.

A member of Gorki's generation, Bunin, after the turn of the century, also joined the group around the publishing house Znaniye. Although Bunin came from an old, originally wealthy, noble family, external circumstances forced him to earn his own living at an early age. Like many other writers of the time, he led a rather unsettled life that brought him into contact with various social strata. Bunin, too, came to literature by way of journalism. His first stories reveal the typical sketchy and reportorial character of the time. In them he describes the life of the "little" people in their geographical and social limitations.

In the first years of the new century, Bunin frequently dealt with Russian "atavism," the survival of local and historical factors that still influence the present. In this connection, Bunin also soon discovered the symptoms of the decay of the old aristocratic culture, and the contradictions and grotesque discrepancies that arose out of unsuccessful attempts to adapt to a changing environment.

With his acrid and sometimes bitter irony he belonged to the "most cruel" and disillusioned chroniclers of mores of the period before World War I. His art of narration, however, still has one advantage by which his work distinguishes itself from mere socio-critical analysis, namely, the presentation of the world as a poetic whole. By means of a special narrative perspective, through the personal stylization of the dialogue, through the conjuring up of sensuous impressions, and through the symbolic setting off of single objective concretizations, as in the story *Antonov Apples* (*Antonovskiye yabloki*, 1900), Bunin creates a unity of form that recalls the classic stories of Tolstoi or Turgenev.

In quality as well as in quantity, Bunin's most creative period occurred between 1910 and 1916. Bunin, like Gorki, spent part of this time on Capri, where both writers often met. Gorki, who frequently recommended Bunin as a model to the younger generation, characterized the writer in 1912 as the "best stylist of the present," although Bunin had already turned his back on Russia.

The series of his best-known works is introduced through the epic narrative *The Village* (*Derevnya*, 1910). It is concerned with the story of the brothers Tikhon and Kuzma Krasov, who waste their lives in the dismal milieu of the provinces. As itinerant merchants from the "black suburb," they carry on their varied transactions, until Tikhon, the more successful, settles down as the owner of a tavern and a general store in the vicinity of the village Durnovka. Kuzma, filled with an insatiable thirst for learning, is an autodidact and "scholarly" sectarian. He wanders through the land, begging and seeking work. In contrast to his brother, he personifies the restless element of Russian life.

During the revolutionary unrest of 1905, the two brothers put aside their quarrels. This reconciliation, however, is only an admission that life has deprived them of their just rewards, that they have both been burned out and are condemned to mere vegetating. The sluggish and dark forces of the village have made them indifferent, dull, evil, and malicious. The milieu has sucked them up.

For Bunin, however, this milieu gains symbolic significance when he announces: "All of Russia is a village." The setting of the story is the store, the room, the railroad station, the cemetery, the market, the suburb, and the highway. Kuzma, in his wanderings, gets as far as Kiev, but as a characteristic impression Bunin singles out only the beggar boy in front of Lavra monastery:

The little one was bareheaded, had a linen bag hanging around his shoulders, dirty rags on the thin body. In one hand he held a wooden bowl, on the bottom of which a copper coin lay. With the other he pushed back and forth his crippled right leg, bare up to the knee, unnaturally thin, burned black by the sun and covered with a golden down.

Bunin preferred such motifs, which illustrate his thought that in Russia life and strength are senselessly wasted. *Zachar Vorobiov* (1912) is the thoroughly healthy, vigorous, but entirely naive and isolated "giant," who because of a bet drinks willfully and senselessly until he falls dead. Even more ghostly, however, is *A Man Old as the Hills* (*Drevnyi chelovek*, 1911), which describes an old man who has lived 108 years, only to be pushed around by heartless and miserly descendants. He has no memories of his life worth conveying because he never left the spiritual area of his village. His existence is absurd and superfluous; the long years are wasted and forgotten.

*A Beautiful Life* (*Khoroshaya zhizn*, 1912) is told entirely from the viewpoint of a narrow-minded, uneducated servant girl, who in crass egotism literally walks over corpses. With crafty calculation, she marries a second time and at the end "even becomes the owner of real estate." Bunin's naive tone allows him to express the character's viewpoint with notable skill.

"My life was a beautiful life," the story begins, "and everything that I wanted I got." The similarly naive ending modifies this statement somewhat: "To be sure our city is boring. Recently, I was in Tula: absolutely no comparison!"

In *Sukhodol* (1912) Bunin presents a fragmentary chronicle of the noble Khrushchev family. Their former ward, the old maiden lady Natalya, cherishes the manor Sukhodol even more than the family does. She relates incidents of its history from her prejudiced point of view and without chronological sequence. As in a carpet, the many details of the story are woven into a pattern, and finally lost in the legendary and fairy-tale elements. *Sukhodol* thus becomes a Russian myth of a decaying family manor. The boundary between "real" and symbolic reality is consciously kept in flux.

Bunin himself liked to recall the tradition that linked him, as a

descendant of the old established nobility, with Tolstoi and Turgenev, with Tyutchev and Leskov; but this does not completely
explain his independent creativity. Bunin never entirely shut out
modern developments from Chekhov through the symbolists, and
in the description of people and the material world, he is frequently
inspired by purely atmospheric stimulations. In addition to external
perceptions Bunin describes emotional attitudes and fleeting sensuous
impressions, especially the olfactory, as in *Sukhodol*:

> We who had grown up outside, ready for odors and not less
> eager for them than for songs and legends, we always remembered
> that special, pleasant, that somewhat hempseed-oil smell that we
> perceived when the people from Sukhodol kissed us. We also knew
> that the presents they brought along smelled of the old steppe
> village; the honey of blooming buckwheat and the musty oak wood
> of the beehive, the towels of the hayloft and the smoky rooms of
> grandfather's time . . . .

Bunin by no means ignored the religious life of the Russian
people; in his stories he describes pilgrims and prophets, religious
zealots and those "holy" fools who were particularly honored in
Russia, as in *Howling John* (*Joann Rydaletz*, 1913). Records of his
many trips to the Orient are found in the early cycle of poems *East*
(*Vostok*, 1905) and in such stories as *The Cry* (*Krik*, 1911), in
which he describes a passage through the Bosporus.

The stories written from 1914 to 1916 form a group by themselves in which Bunin is increasingly attracted by the literary description of death, whether in the psychological explanation of cruel
crimes of violence, as in *A Spring Night* (*Vesennyi vecher*, 1915),
in thoughts about suicide (*Kazimir Stanislavovich*, 1916), or in the
analysis of the unexpected, sudden, and really senseless death at the
wrong moment and in the wrong place, as in *The Gentleman from
San Francisco* (*Gospodin iz San-Frantzisko*, 1916).

In the latter, the "gentleman" spends a vacation in a deluxe hotel
on Capri. One day, shortly before the evening meal he suddenly
collapses. He does not have time to prepare himself for death:

> Even if he had felt a premonition of it in his soul that something
> would happen, he would have thought just the same, that it would
> not happen soon, in no case, that it would happen at once.

The death of the rich American is especially disturbing for the hotel, which, with scrupulous haste, tries to hide it. Death, however, has acquired the respect that it demands, as Bunin suggests in the motto from the Apocalypse: "Woe unto you, Babylon, strong city." Like many others, Bunin emigrated from Russia after the Revolution, and much of his work belongs to the Russian literature in exile.

## REALISM RESTRUCTURED

### Aleksei Remizov

Two basically different traditions mark the Russian narrative style of the twentieth century. One derives from Lermontov, Tolstoi, and Turgenev; the other from Gogol, Dostoyevski, and Leskov. Whereas the first tradition is represented particularly by the realistic school (Gorki, Andreyev, Zaitsev, Bunin), the other acquired followers among the symbolists (Belyi) and the realists (Remizov, Zamyatin). The concept "realists," however, begins to lose its precise meaning here, because the narrative styles introduced by Gogol (aperspectivism, hyperbolism, and the grotesque) continually transcend the sharply defined lines of realism.

Aleksei Remizov (1877–1957) was influenced by the "ornamental" narrative style of Gogol, as well as by the individualistically colored circumlocutions of Leskov. Remizov's characteristic narrative style is called *skaz*, which denotes a stylized narrative discourse based on oral traditions. In *skaz*, the stress is always placed on the personal style of the narrator, behind whom the author conceals himself.

Remizov uses this technique to emphasize the satirical aspects of his characters and situations. Barely revealing his own attitudes, he delights in uncertainties, and his narratives are often capricious and grotesque in their view of the world.

As in Gogol, the ordinary relationships of the significant and the insignificant are upset. Remizov's dreamlike perceptions are focused on apparently "senseless" details. He likes to describe how people act when they think they are unobserved as in the *The Fifth Pestilence* (*Pyataya yazva*, 1912). Here, the gossip of a small town and the timid narrow-mindedness of its inhabitants assume ghostly qualities.

Remizov, as the son of an impoverished merchant family, was well acquainted with lower-class life, including that of the proletariat. In his novels *The Pond* (*Prud*, 1908) and *The Sisters of the Cross* (*Krestovye siostry*, 1911), he mercilessly describes the world of the workers' quarters and the tenements of Moscow and Saint Petersburg.

Remizov loved children. Their fantasy world and peculiar logic continually attracted him, as in the stories *Princess Mymra* (*Tzarevna Mymra*, 1908) and *Petushok* (1911). His interest in fantasy extended to history, religious folklore, fairy tales, and Greco-Byzantine traditions. These elements dominate his literary activity from the *Leimonarium* (*Limonar*) of 1907 to the *Legends of King Solomon*, published in the year of his death. The fairy tales, based partly on Siberian, Caucasian, and even Tibetan themes, provided Remizov with excellent opportunities for the stylization and adornment of dialogue.

He was also strongly influenced by the Russian literary language of the seventeenth century. Through his marriage to the scholarly Serafima Dovgiello, to whom he dedicated all his works, Remizov was led to a systematic study of paleography and the older Russian literature. Even his handwriting assumed the style of the seventeenth century.

An autobiographical essay of 1923 shows that Remizov owed much to Dostoyevski and that he also admired Vasilii Rozanov. These authors may have influenced his rather free treatment of erotic subjects and his unusual style. Mirski has pointed out that only in Rozanov and Remizov does the "natural" syntax of the Russian language appear, without any imitation of the usually literary syntax that was historically formed by Greco-Latin and French syntax.

To be sure, the "spoken" language is only the apparent model for Remizov's art language. The intonation of this language deviates from the spoken colloquial language no less markedly than the neologisms of the futurists deviate from the vocabulary of ordinary Russian. As noted, the models of the older Russian literary language and the Russian folk language (fairy tale and legend) influenced Remizov's narrative style. In any case, his style is virtually untranslatable.

Remizov's most interesting literary activity occurred from 1909 until his emigration from Russia in 1921. Of the stories written during World War I, the most beautiful have been collected in *Mara* (Berlin, 1922). The Saint Petersburg stories of the revolutionary period have been gathered in *Noises of the City* (*Shumy goroda*, Reval, 1921).

The first little book, *Akhru-Saint Petersburg Report* (*Akhru, povest petersburgskaya*, Berlin, 1922), written in the emigration, consists of glosses and fragments in which Remizov portrays his literary friends in Russia. The title *Akhru*—a word from the "language of the apes"—with its facetious manifesto at the end of the brochure, was a pointer to Remizov's friends. It informed them of the continued existence of that silly order of which "Asyka I, king of the apes" was recognized as the master. Remizov's predilection for the grotesque is clearly demonstrated in the invention of this "Great and Free order of the apes," of which the author remained the "chancellor" until his death. Even later in Paris he amused his friends with his many scurrilous ideas.

Among the adapted or retold legends that occupy an important place in Remizov's literary activity, the *Nicholas Parables* (*Nikoliny pritchi*, 1917–24) are particularly notable, as are the Byzantine legends from the volume *Trava-Murava* (Berlin, 1922), which were written down between 1914 and 1917. In the longest of these stories, *Apollonius of Tyre* (*Apollon tirskii*, 1917), Remizov develops the narrative according to the pattern of the medieval novel. He does it, however, in such an arbitrary and humorous manner that the fifty pages belong stylistically among his masterpieces.

An eight-volume edition of Remizov's works appeared in Russia as early as 1912. Although his style influenced the Soviet literature of the 1920s, he is now considered a decadent and reactionary writer, and his works have not been printed for decades.

# Beyond Symbolism

The symbolists conceived of the poet's language as a zone of contact and mutual interaction between two spheres—the cosmic-mythical-primordial and the individual-typical-poetic. The impetus was thereby given to a series of new poetic concepts. These were not intended to explain transcendental realities but to make new possibilities visible. According to the symbolists, these new possibilities were created by the spirit of the language.

At the time of symbolism and, in many instances, its rebellious derivatives, the theory of literary composition was a theory of language. This theory of language had to continue to develop logically to the extreme examples of the violence of the futurists, who ultimately assumed that their "meta-logical" language (*zaumny yazyk*) was the true language of literary composition. Andrei Belyi's and Vyacheslav Ivanov's speaking of "the word become flesh" points forward, however, in a quasi-cultic terminology, to the linguistic efforts of the futurists. Belyi had already stressed in his treatise *The Magic of Words* that "the combining of words without reference to their logical meaning is the means by which man protects himself from the pressure of the uncertain."

Between 1910 and 1913 the reaction to the symbolists' magic-cult concept of language led to the writings and manifestos of the acmeists and futurists. The purely literary achievements of symbolism were thereby largely taken over, even though in various modifications. Only the ideological superstructure seemed no longer useful, and the symbolist *mythos* was mercilessly discarded.

Although symbolism continued to exist until 1920, and later in isolated groups, its inner weakening had already progressed considerably before World War I. The real symbolist epoch virtually ended with the years 1912–14. The following decade is clearly a period of transition, in which literary development remains continually in flux.

On the other hand, the Revolution of 1917 could hardly bring a new note into the situation during this stirring phase. A new caesura in the trend of literary development becomes visible only with the great wave of emigration between 1920 and 1922. As the activity of Russian publishers became increasingly restricted because of the Civil War, numerous publishers also settled abroad, especially in Berlin, where, between 1921 and 1923, more important new publications in the Russian language were issued than at home. The situation that had arisen in Russia after the end of the Civil War led to the separation of literature in exile from Soviet literature.

### Mikhail Kuzmin, a Transitional Figure

The poet Kuzmin (1875–1936) occupies an important position at the periphery of the representative trends in the years of transition that followed the heyday of symbolism.

As early as 1906, Kuzmin issued a cycle of poetry with the title *Alexandrian Songs* (*Aleksandriskiye pesni*), in which the *Chansons de Bilitis* of Pierre Louÿs were recognized as the model. The poems, in free verse, not only show Kuzmin as an artist extremely conscious of form, but are also a form of literary confession. The refined but at the same time markedly literary cultivation of the feeling of late Alexandrian antiquity became a determining factor for Kuzmin's poetry as well as for his dandified appearance in the literary world of Saint Petersburg.

Although Kuzmin's poetry cannot be imagined without symbolism, it is related more closely to the tradition of Latin and romance writers. In its "clarity," it is closer to the taste of the Parnassians than to that of the romantically oriented Russian symbolists. Kuzmin's favorite epoch long remained the Rococo; as a musician, he esteemed Mozart highly. Kuzmin himself was an expert in music; he had studied the theory of composition with Rimski-Korsakov and liked to set his own poems to music.

In its rhythmic technique Kuzmin's poetry is particularly varied and interesting. It cultivates the freedom introduced by the symbolists and fascinates by its completely unconventional moods. His most important volumes of poetry before the Revolution are *Nets* (*Seti*, 1908), *Lakes in the Fall* (*Osenniye ozera*, 1912), and *Clay Doves* (*Glinyaniye golubki*, 1914). Many poems seem predominantly illustrative; Kuzmin, in fact, occasionally wrote poems according to themes of plastic art, as in *Landscape by Gauguin* (*Peyzazh Gogena*). An entire cycle from the years 1914–17 bears the title *Fujiyama in the Tea Cups* (*Fuzi v bliudechke*). It consists of little miniatures that show Kuzmin's delight in visual presentation.

The connection with Rococo was also established in Russia through the painting of the time. Such painters as Benois, Sudeikin, and Dobuzhinski brought historical scenes of the eighteenth century into fashion.

Even if some of the lyrical creations of Kuzmin belong to "cabaret art," he never deviated from a strict taste; nowhere does a false mannerism appear. Kuzmin is anything but a naive poet; behind his ease, there is much self-irony, and one divines the melancholy of an overripe culture in his coy pose.

Later, during the years of the Revolution, Kuzmin suddenly emerges in an entirely different aspect—as a poet of deeply religious inspiration, as shown by his cantata *Saint George* (*Svyatoi Georgi*, 1917), which was included in the volume *Evenings Not of This World* (*Nezdeshniye vechera*, 1921). In 1922 Kuzmin published, in one of the last pre-revolutionary almanacs (*Peterburgski Almanakh*), "gnostic" poems with such titles as *Sophia*, *The Teacher*, and *Hermes*. During these years Kuzmin did not avoid the influences of futurism. *Saint George*, for example, stands much closer to Mayakovski than to symbolism, in its verse technique as well as in its expressive language.

In his prose, Kuzmin was most successful where he subordinated his narrative technique, with its studied style, to an external law. In the historical novel as well as in the rogue novel and the biography of adventure, Kuzmin's efforts were much more successful than in the area of the social novel and the "modern" novella.

Novels such as *Tender Joseph* (*Nezhnyi Iosif*, 1909) and *Those*

*Traveling by Sea* (*Plavayushchiye puteshestvuyushchiye*, 1915) offer, to be sure, interesting insights into the life of the already somewhat morbid middle-class intelligentsia before the Revolution. From the artistic point of view, such works as the novella *Wings* (*Krilya*, 1906), which became famous because of its homosexual theme, are constructed far less convincingly, than perhaps *Aimé Leboeuf's Adventure* (*Pochozhdeniya Eme Lebefa*, 1907) or *The Journey of Sir John Fairfax Through Turkey and Other Remarkable Countries* (*Puteshestviye sera Dzhona Firfaksa po Turtzii i drugim z mechatelnym stranam*, 1910).

In these works, Kuzmin borrows from the Latin storytelling art (Petronius and Apuleius) and from the European narrative art of the eighteenth century. Henri de Regnier must also be named as one of Kuzmin's models. In 1910 Kuzmin published in the magazine *Apollon* his manifesto of "Clarismus"—*About Splendid Clarity* (*O prekrasnoi yasnosti*)—in which he attacked symbolism and made a plea for logic and clarity in expression and for absolute correspondence of the form of portrayal and the object described.

Kuzmin's production of novels is rather extensive. His shorter stories are striking because of their graceful stylization, *e.g.*, the volume *The Green Nightingale* (*Zeleni solovei*, 1915). As early as 1910 Kuzmin had written the *Deeds of Alexander the Great* (*Podvigi Velikovo Aleksandra*). Shortly before the Revolution, he thought of beginning a monumental narrative work, for which he chose the name *The New Plutarch* (*Novyi Plutarkh*). Because of contemporary circumstances this plan was frustrated, although a first story did appear in 1916, *The Wonderful Life of Joseph Balsamo, Count Cagliostro* (*Chudesnaya zhizn Iosifa Balsamo, grafa Kaliostro*, book form, 1919). After 1923, there was silence in the Soviet Union about Kuzmin, although he was still active as a translator. His translation of *The Golden Ass* by Apuleius appeared in 1929.

## THE ACMEIST CREED

The doctrine of "acmeism" (derived from Greek *akme*: peak, flowering, maturity) was confined entirely to poetry and was a reaction to the overemphasis of the magical character of the language held by the symbolists, and to the romantic undercurrents of symbolism in general. Acmeism sought again to stress simple things, pure colors and forms, clarity of expression, and consistency in the use of words. The proximity to the physical and material was emphasized and an unequivocal affirmation of life was demanded, an acceptance of the world as a unity of the beautiful and the ugly, as a synthesis of "God, vice, death, and immortality" (Gumilev).

The world view of the symbolists, their sensitiveness, and their prophetic attitude no longer found favor with the acmeists. In 1913 Nikoloai Gumilev (1886–1921), the authoritative theoretician of acmeism and one of its founders, declared in his manifesto *The Heritage of Symbolism and Acmeism* (*Naslediye simvolizma i akmeizm*): "As Adamists we are a little like the wild animals of the forest, and in no case would we like to exchange whatever of the animal is in us for neurasthenia."

Gumilev no longer valued Edgar Allan Poe and Baudelaire, Maeterlinck and Mallarmé, but considered such poets as François Villon, Rabelais, Shakespeare, and Theophile Gautier valid models for acmeist literary composition. Innokentii Annenski was named the Russian precursor of acmeism because of his "romanesque" irony and his incorruptible feeling for language, although in his essential premises he had remained a symbolist.

Acmeism as an actual school developed in 1912 out of the Guild of Poets (*tzech poetov*) founded the year before by Sergei Gorodetzki and Gumilev. This group received moral support from the magazine *Apollon*, and included Anna Akhmatova, who in 1910 had become Gumilev's wife, and soon thereafter Osip Mandelstamm, Mikhail Lozinski, and several younger poets, who emigrated at the beginning of the 1920s. One of these was Georgii Ivanov, who went to France to live and was revered as the most distinguished of the émigré poets.

Immediately after the Revolution (1920), the Guild of Poets was renewed, and the three almanacs of this second guild could still be printed in Saint Petersburg in 1921–22. A slightly changed reprint appeared in 1922–23 in Berlin after a part of the guild had settled abroad. In the emigration the organization soon disintegrated.

## Nikolai Gumilev

Gumilev, whom the Guild of Poets generally considered their master, became a victim of the Civil War in 1921. In connection with the exposing of a monarchist plot, the poet was arrested and condemned to death by shooting by the secret police, the Cheka. For Gumilev, the "engaged" life at the edge of danger formed not only the key to his personal existence but also the substance of his poetry.

Decorated in World War I with the cross of St. George, Gumilev, in his war poetry *The Quiver* (*Kolchan*, 1916), affirmed war as a religious and aesthetic experience; his earlier volumes also show an admiration for the heroic.

In 1910 Gumilev became known through the volume *Pearls* (*Zhemchuga*), the subject matter of which extends from tropical, remote regions and exotic motifs (*e.g.*, the old conquistador, the parrot, the captains), and from classical mythology (the return of Odysseus, Agamemnon's warriors), to the great themes of European poetry (*The Descendants of Cain, Adam, Christ, Don Juan, Beatrice*). Following the acmeist canon, descriptive poetry, often restricted because of its subject matter, predominates in *Strange Sky* (*Chuzhoye nebo*, 1912). A tendency toward the dramatic and the ballad, however, kept Gumilev from overemphasizing minute visual details.

The poems of the last volume, *The Pillar of Fire* (*Ognenny stolp*, 1921), are replete with magic concepts and the philosophy of the Orient. Here Gumilev seriously discusses the problem of art (*The Word, The Sixth Sense, Prayer of the Masters*). One of the best-known poems of this volume is *The Streetcar That Strayed* (*Zabludivshisya travai*), in which the trip through Saint Petersburg in a streetcar that cannot be stopped allows views of the stations that lie between life and death—stations on a road of suffering, but also of understanding.

Georgii Ivanov (1894–1958) made his literary debut in 1912 with his first collection, *Embarkation for the Isle of Cytherea* (*Otplytiye na ostrov Tziteru*), after the title of a picture by Watteau. These poems clearly show Kuzmin's influence. Ivanov's second collection, *Heather* (*Veresk*, 1916), contains typical, though stylized, features of acmeism, strongly recalling the *poésie légère* of the eighteenth century. The stylistic and playful, graceful attitude is typical of Ivanov's early poetry. *Gardens* (*Sady*, 1921) was the last of his work to be published in Russia. His later work belongs to the literature of exile.

### Anna Akhmatova

Anna Akhmatova (born 1888 or 1889) is without question the most outstanding Russian woman poet. Her maiden name was Anna Gorenko, and as the name indicates, she came from the south of Russia. The last years of her girlhood were spent in Saint Petersburg, where in 1910 she married Nikolai Gumilev; they were divorced in 1918. Although she joined the acmeists, her poetic talent developed more or less untouched by Gumilev and his poetic inclinations. Her temperament remained essentially feminine and fundamentally different from that of her husband.

Compared with Gumilev's dynamic verses, Akhmatova's poems are like delicate pen sketches, though betraying a stronger intensity of feeling. As far as the poetry of Akhmatova remains realistic, actually experienced and related to the visual, she submits to the postulates of acmeism. In her unobtrusive musicality and graceful mobility, she stands closer to Kuzmin's creations than to Gumilev's style.

In her first poetic sequences, Akhmatova preferred the form of the occasional and mood poem, sometimes in epigrammatic brevity. Her poetic utterance is spare, terse, and precise; single poems have the effect of having been painted on small tiles. Even in her early phase, the poet is an accomplished master of the art of confining dramatic scenes in a short form, as in *The Gray-eyed King* (*Seroglazy Korol*) from the first volume *Evening* (*Vecher*, 1912). Here the constantly intensifying dramatic situation is expressed in almost epigrammatic form.

The influence of acmeism appears most markedly in the precise and clear imagery of Akhmatova's descriptions, as in the first verse of *Venice* from *The Wreath of Roses* (*Chiotki*):

Golden pigeon-coop at the water
That dies green and friendly;
A light salty wind blots out
The narrow traces of black boats.

Akhmatova's early phase is almost wholly confined to the two volumes *Evening* and *Wreath of Roses*. In the latter, the elegiac tone increases, corresponding to a deepening and intensification of feeling. The imagery gradually becomes richer and more daring, and the love experience that is central to the subject matter becomes more intense and richer in problems. The poet attains her full maturity with *The White Flock* (*Belaya staya*, 1918), in which are combined the poems written between 1913 and 1917—years that were personally serious and difficult for her.

Here, as in *Wreath of Roses*, a woman's love remains the determining and great theme of her poetry, which without restraint exposes all the stirrings of the soul. Akhmatova produced several of the most beautiful Russian love poems, in which tenderness and consciousness, passion and objectivity, attain the best possible union. "I have learned to live simply and wisely"—thus begins a poem in *Wreath of Roses*, and through the wisdom of clarity and simplicity the poet deals with the problem of her role as a loving woman.

In *The White Flock* the predominantly autobiographical and intimate, diarylike style of her mood poetry finds support in the religious element and at the same time establishes a form that is poetically constant and final: "For a long time now my lips no longer kiss, but they proclaim," as the poet wrote in 1915. The world—originally completely filled with the femininity of the poet, with her tender memories of the odor of lindens, parks in the summer, the hammock, the open terrace, a white shoe given as a pledge, a pair of gloves beside a riding whip, blue pipe smoke, and the sea smell of oysters on cracked ice—loses its limitations and expands beyond its confines to include a greater destiny: war, the fate of Russia.

Because of the unusual intensity of the descriptions in Akhmatova's poems, the critic Poggioli recently placed her beside Proust. Akhmatova, however, is very Russian; her Saint Petersburg is the Saint Petersburg of Pushkin and the Russian classics:

> But for nothing will we exchange the splendor
> Of the granite city of fame and disaster,
> The gleaming ice of the broad streams,
> The dusky gardens without sun,
> And the hardly audible voice of the muse.
>
> (from *The White Flock*)

The elegiac muse, her companion during the years of the war, reveals a relationship to Annenski's muse:

> And the muse in her ragged dress
> Sings dragging and sadly
> In her cruel and young heartache
> Lies her miraculous power.
>
> (from *The White Flock*)

This elegiac mood is also continued in the volume *Road Grass* (*Podorozhnik*, 1921), in which the poet surrenders "singing and remembering" to her harsh lot and the trials of the time. In the midst of the darkness, however, there is present now and then a warm light, a calm and clear joy, which the poet confers upon the passing objects. In *Road Grass*, as well as in *Anno Domini MCMXXI* (1922), her voice gains still more strength and resilience. Her love poetry is attuned to memory and farewell; the landscapes of the soul become increasingly symbolic:

> A transparent reflection on things and faces
> As if all over petals were strewn
> Of those little yellow pink roses
> Whose name I do not know any more.

In Anna Akhmatova love of homeland was so overpowering that she disdained to leave her country for political reasons. From 1922 on, she was condemned to silence; after *Anno Domini MCMXXI* the poet no longer published. Only in 1940 could another volume of her poetry appear—*The Willowtree* (*Iva*), which demonstrated that Akhmatova had remained true to herself. In 1946 she incurred Zhdanov's official disfavor, and only in 1958 was a selection of her poems again published in the Soviet Union. The selection *Poem without a Hero* (*Poema bez geroya*), written at the beginning of the forties, has so far appeared only abroad (New York, 1960–61).

*Osip Mandelstamm*

Before 1923 Osip Mandelstamm (1891–1937?), sometimes considered the most important poet after Aleksandr Blok, published only two not very extensive collections: *The Stone* (*Kamen*, 1913) and *Tristia* (Berlin, 1922). The latter, in revised form, was subsequently published as *The Second Book* (*Vtoraya kniga*, Moscow, 1923). Son of a Jewish merchant family in Warsaw, Mandelstamm studied at the Sorbonne and in Heidelberg.

To reduce Mandelstamm's poetic work to a common denominator would be a futile undertaking, for the poet, in accordance with his cultural background, was primarily a Russian, but one distinguished by an unmistakably Jewish mentality.

In respect to verse and genre, his poems are rather conservative, based on the attainments of Russian classics (Batyushkov and Pushkin). In view of the language of the poetic images (the poetical "semantics"), however, Mandelstamm is a decided avant-gardist among the acmeists. From the visual aspect, Poggioli has compared the poet to the early Picasso and Giorgio de Chirico; for Ivask, his poetic suggestiveness recalls Mallarmé. These comparisons suggest the magic of Mandelstamm's subject matter, as well as the hermetic unity of his world, which sometimes makes the approach to his poems difficult.

In Mandelstamm's poems the attempt to project heaviness (*taizhest*) is combined with tenderness (*nezhnost*), which he seeks to balance, as in a poem of 1920:

Ah, heavy honeycombs and delicate nets,
More easily I pick up a stone than that I repeat your name. . . .

Like heavy water I drink the polluted air,
Time has been broken up by the plow and the rose has become
        earth.
In a slow whirlpool drift heavy delicate roses,
The heaviness and the tenderness of the rose you have woven into
        double wreaths.

Mandelstamm's poetry is, in fact, directed toward two poles, which were revealed to him most clearly in sacred architecture. Again and again, he returns to the metaphor of the cathedral, as in *Hagia Sophia* (1912) and *Notre Dame* (1912). This metaphor becomes especially impressive in a poem in *Tristia* where the "eternal cathedrals" of St. Sophia and of St. Peter are named "storehouses of air and of holiness," in which "the grain of the profound, full faith" is preserved. For Mandelstamm, the sacred structure is an important symbol not only of faith but also of art freeing itself from the burden that opposes the objectification of beauty. In contemplating the "bizarre ribs" of Notre Dame in Paris, Mandelstamm says, "Out of a burden of misgivings I, too, will some day form a work of beauty."

Mandelstamm included a selection of his poetry of the years 1921–25 in the volume *Poems* (*Stikhotvoreniya*, Moscow, 1928), which once more summarizes his total poetic production in its essential parts. Above all, there are poems from the years 1922–23 in which Mandelstamm, despite agony, privation, and uncertainty, gives life a new chance, even if the last refuge is only a sheep stall:

> Gently stroking the wool and shaking up the straw
> Like an apple tree starving in winter
> Under the blanket of bast,
> Full of tenderness and senseless pressing
> Against what is strange,
> And groping around in emptiness and patiently waiting.

Fifty-seven of the posthumous poems, written mainly in the 1930s, were published in 1961 in a New York almanac of the Russian exiles. Here, too, Mandelstamm shows himself at the former height of his art. Little is known of Mandelstamm's later fate in the Soviet Union. In the 1930s, he was exposed to harassment and persecution, and he may have died in 1939 or 1940 in a Far East camp.

## ACMEISM RECONSIDERED

### Sergei Gorodetzki

The earliest writer to turn away from acmeism was Sergei Gorodetzki (born 1884). After the Revolution, he placed his talent in
the service of a graceful poetry of propaganda. In 1912 he had
written, with Gumilev, a programmatic essay on the relationship of
symbolism and acmeism, which, under the title *Some Currents in
the Russian Poetry of the Present* (*Nekotoriye techeniya v sovremennoi russkoi poezii*), had been printed in the magazine *Apollon*
(January 1913). Gorodetzki's earliest volumes of poetry, still standing close to symbolism, were *Yar* (1907) and *Perun* (1907). From
the acmeistic period stem the collections *The Pasture* (*Iva*, 1913)
and *The Blooming Staff* (*Tzvetushchyi posokh*, 1914).

Gorodetzki's best poems are without doubt imaginative in their
verse structure and often baffling in their rustic and "barbaric" ex-
pressiveness. To Gorodetzki's credit, he inspired and encouraged a
number of younger poets, especially Khlebnikov and Yesenin, not
only through his championing of them but also through providing
them with themes from Slavic mythology and religious folklore.
These exist in his poetry in unprecedented abundance. Even Igor
Stravinski was once deeply impressed by Gorodetzki's poetry and
set several of his poems to music.

### Mikhail Lozinski

The highly gifted and deeply religious Mikhail Lozinski (1886–
1955) also remained in Russia after the Civil War. His only book
of verse, *The Mountain Spring* (*Gorny kliuch*), appeared in 1916,
but several years later he became silent and devoted himself only
to translations. From Lozinski stems among other things the exemplary Russian version of Dante's *Divine Comedy* (completed
1946).

## Vladislav Khodasevich

Vladislav Khodasevich (1886–1939) was descended paternally from a noble Polish family. Although he was close to the acmeists in many respects, he did not belong to them, at least as far as his relationship to symbolism was concerned. The poet, who made the highest demands on himself, did not include in his "collected verse" either of his early volumes of poems, *Youth* (*Molodost*, 1908) and *The Happy Little House* (*Shchastlivyi domik*, 1914). Thus the two cycles *The Way of the Grain* (*Putem zerna*, 1920) and *The Heavy Lyre* (*Tyazhelaya lita*, 1922) form the nucleus of his work prior to his emigration in 1922–23.

Although Khodasevich's poetry, like that of the acmeists, is particularly concerned with the concrete world of things, his tendency toward a mystic interpretation of reality is not to be overlooked. The title poem of *The Way of the Grain*, for example, refers to a passage in the gospel of St. John. Thus, in 1917 Khodasevich expressed the hope that Russia would die and be born again like the grain of wheat: "Everything that lives must go the way of the grain of wheat."

The poem *About Myself II* (*Pro sebya II*, 1919) may be considered self-revealing. For Khodasevich, poetic contemplation is linked with the myth of Narcissus as an act in which the poet bends probing over a surface of water, and at the mystic moment of becoming one with it, is drawn into the deep: "While falling, the unclean glance of my earthly eyes extinguishes silently, but a flaming wreath of stars arises from there over my head."

In the form of his poetry, Khodasevich is a late descendant of Pushkin. A critical study of Pushkin, *Pushkin's Poetic Economy* (*Poeticheskoye chozyaistvo Pushkina*, 1924), was the last book that he was able to publish in Russia. As with Pushkin, in Khodasevich the prose of life is raised to an absolute level, occasionally caught up in a condition of transcendence. In the interesting poem *Ballad* (*Ballada*, 1921) the bare objects in a poorly furnished cold room suddenly start to move, the entire room is submerged, and the poet remains alone on a black mountain, as the eternal Orpheus in whose hand lies the "heavy lyre."

The harsh reality of the years of privation and hunger is featured particularly in the little verse narratives in *The Way of the Grain*, namely, *The House* (*Dom*) and *The Second of November* (*Vtoroye Noyabrya*) and also in many individual poems, such as the allegorical *Automobile* (1921), in which the poet extends his "blind hands" and tries in vain to grasp reality:

> Here stood a world, simple and whole, but since the time that this thing (that is to say, the automobile with the black wings) drives around, there are in my soul and in the world white spots as from acids poured out.

## THE THEORY AND PRACTICE OF FUTURISM

In Russia after 1910 a special group of young poets emerged. In imitation of the Italian avant-garde, they finally called themselves futurists. In Italy, however, the artistic center of gravity lay more in the plastic arts (Carra, Boccioni, and Severini), while in Russia futurism developed as a remarkable poetic art, which gradually broke through the narrow confines of sectarianism. The question of dependence on non-Russian currents is of secondary importance, because in the revolution of art of 1909–12, a total European breakdown occurred, out of which new forms of the plastic arts developed as well as new forms of poetry, such as expressionism and futurism. Personal contacts at that time furthered new ideas and new experiments of interested groups that were quickly made known. Marinetti, the spokesman for Italian futurism, visited Russia as early as 1910. On the other hand, the brothers Burliyuk, who belonged to the earliest branch of Russian futurism, exhibited their pictures in Munich.

The problem of form as interpreted by Kandinski came to be the driving force of the new movement; in this respect, there were no closed boundaries. In Germany, for example, documentary evidence of preoccupation with form is supplied by the journal *Der Sturm* from 1910 to the outbreak of World War I; and it is evident that the Russians, too, were recognized to a great extent for the part they played in the development of new forms in these years. Their contribution is most conspicuous in the plastic arts represented by Kandinski, Yavlenski, Malevich, Tatlin, and Anton Pevsner. The connection that the Russians saw between poetry and modern visual presentation is emphasized by the fact that the group of futurists took the name cubo-futurists to distinguish themselves from the so-called ego-futurists, who had really usurped the name unjustly. Following a suggestion by Khlebnikov, the Russian futurists had also called themselves the *budetliane* (from *budet*, meaning "will be").

The ego-futurists in the years 1912–14 formed a short-lived community under the spiritual patronage of the poet Igor Severyanin (pseudonym of Igor Lotarev, 1887–1941). Later, several representatives of the so-called imagists (R. Ivnev and V. Shershenevich) emerged from the ego-futurists. This group had little to do with futurism. In their work, attempts to shock the reader, in Severyanin's manner, were considerably softened by a certain mundane playfulness. The titles of his collections already indicate this tendency: *The Thunder-Foaming Cup* (*Gromokipiashchyi kubok*, 1913), *Pineapple in Champagne* (*Ananasy v shampanskom*, 1915), and *Crème de violettes*, 1919.

Only the cubo-futurist group deserves serious literary attention. Its most important representatives, Velemir Khlebnikov and Vladimir Mayakovski, occupy an outstanding place in Russian literature between 1910 and 1920.

### Aleksei Kruchenykh

The theoretical formulation of the leading ideas of futurism go back in great measure to Aleksei Kruchenykh (born 1886). Kruchenykh operated with a new theory of language, which, despite all its extreme exclusivity, helped to establish poetic insights of general importance. Kruchenykh was the theoretician of the word "in itself," as is indicated by the title of a manifesto *The Word as Such* (*Slovo kak takovoye*, 1913), which he drew up with Khlebnikov. The principal idea was that the word as an element of form is more important and more interesting than the word in its lexical meaning. According to Kruchenykh, the poetic word is the "metalogical" word (*zaumnoye slovo*), which is to be actualized in its form and sound.

In its one-sidedness, this theory of meta-logical language did not bear any convincing fruits in Kruchenykh's poetic experiments. As a requirement for method, however, the new concept of the word as a formal element of structure was in many respects justified.

Only art was important for the futurists. As the manifesto expressed it:

> A work of art means art of the word. From this results quite of itself the expulsion from the work of art of any tendency toward "literature" of any kind (*literaturshchina*). . . . Every message that does not emerge of itself from art is wood that is painted like iron.

### David Burlyuk

Among the theoreticians, the painter and poet David Burlyuk (born 1882), who is now living in the United States, deserves consideration. It was not until his emigration that he set down his thoughts in final form with reference to his theory of entelechism (*entelekhizm*). He was definitely an inspiration to his time, however, and he was the real organizer of the futurist movement. Mayakovski, who, as a student of art, came under the influence of Burlyuk in 1911, confesses in his autobiography: "In lasting love, I think of David. A wonderful friend. My real teacher. Burlyuk made a poet of me" (1928).

Burlyuk's own poems are technically interesting because of their abbreviated syntax (the omission of prepositions); they display a remarkable artistic imagination. New poems, written during his emigration, appeared in 1930 in New York: *Entelechism, Theory, Criticism, Verse, Pictures* (*Entelekhizm, Teoriya, Kritika, Stikhi, Kartiny*, 1907–30).

Among the less-known futurists are the poetess Yelena Guro (1877–1913), Vasilii Kamenski (1884–1961), and Benedikt Livshitz (born 1886). Kamenski became prominent after the Revolution with a historical drama *Stenka Razin* (1919), which is a mixture of futurist literature and political catchwords. His memoirs appeared in 1931 in Moscow under the title of *The Way of an Enthusiast* (*Put' entuziasta*). The memoirs of B. Livshitz, *The Marksman with One and a Half Eyes* (*Polutoraglazyi streletz*, Leningrad, 1933), are also important for the history of futurism.

### Velemir Khlebnikov

Velemir Khlebnikov, born in the vicinity of Astrakhan in Southern Russia (1885–1922; first given name, Viktor) can be considered the most original writer of the futurists. Relying on a totally utopian philosophy of history, the visionary Khlebnikov was successful in turning to a modern epic style in which the poetic landscape spread far into the past and into the future.

The elementary, heroic pathos of the Revolution, toward which Khlebnikov assumed an affirmative attitude, is pictured in his works as a breaking in of the primeval world, as a new bubbling forth of the prehistoric springs of life. Khlebnikov's most important groups of motifs are, therefore, natural history (geology and paleontology), Slavic antiquity, the treasure of folk legends and the mythology of the Slavic, Oriental, and Asiatic peoples. Some of these paths had already been taken by Ivanov and Gorodetzki, but the linking of old-Slavic, old-Oriental, and the Central Asian mythical past was developed quite independently by Khlebnikov.

His most important collections of poetry are (disregarding the numerous individual publications) *The Model Book of Verse* (*Izbornik stikhov*, 1914), *Works I* (*Tvoreniya I*, 1914), and the volume *Verses* (*Stikhi*, 1923). In the years 1928–33, a group of Khlebnikov's friends published posthumously a volume entitled *The Unedited Khlebnikov* (*Neizdannyi Khlebnikov*), containing the greater part of the remaining poems. At the same time, the collected works appeared in Leningrad in five volumes (1928–33).

Khlebnikov's predilection for the primitive and archaic, for a prehistoric "exotic," is hardly to be compared with the aspirations of the symbolists. Khlebnikov's poems have an entirely different appearance, even in their linguistic substance. By a return to the pure elements of word formation Khlebnikov creates his own language. Just as in the case of Kruchenykh the meta-logical relationships between word stems and expansion through suffixes, between the sound of the word and its meaning, are moved into the foreground.

With reference to language, Khlebnikov is as much a futurist as a historian, and where the stock of words of the dictionary is inadequate, he invents particularly expressive neologisms in the original spirit of the language, relying intuitively on the actual available stock of words.

In this manner Khlebnikov became an arbitrary interpreter of the language and of its historical origin. Mayakovski called him the creator of a new "periodic system" of words. In his last years, Khlebnikov occupied himself especially with the theory of a poetic, primeval language, which he designated "star language" (*zvezdnyi jazyk*) and which he applied in the fragments *Scar on the Sky* (*Tzarapina po nebu*, 1925).

Khlebnikov's early poems, however, already point beyond pure experiment. The grotesque narrative in verse, *Zhuravl*, published in 1910 in the first almanac of the futurists, develops through an ingenious play on the word "crane" and the conflict between man and the monster of machine technology. Here already Khlebnikov's inclination toward surrealism appears, becoming even clearer in the historic-utopian prose story *Ka* (1916).

Khlebnikov worked out the futurist manifesto *A Slap in the Face of Public Taste* (*Poshchechina obshchestvennomu vkusu*, 1913) with Kruchenykh, Burlyuk, and Mayakovski. It appeared in the almanac of the same name. Here Khlebnikov also published his verse narrative *I and E* (*I i E*), with the subtitle *Story of the Stone Age* (written in 1911).

In the years following the most important stories in verse, predominantly of an idyllic character, are *Chadzhi-Tarkhan* (1912), *The Shaman and Venus* (*Shaman i Venera*, 1912), and *The Nymph and the Spirit of the Woods* (*Vila i leshi*, 1913). The works of the later years include the longer poems, *The Night in the Trenches*

(*Noch v okope*, 1919), *The Poet* (*Poet*, 1919), *Ladomir* (1920), and *Search by Night* (*Nochnoi obysk*, 1921).

A special genre of cyclical stories, predominantly in verse, which Khlebnikov himself called "retold tales" (*sverkh-povest* or *zapovest*), is represented by the dramatic series *Zangesi* (1922), performed twice in 1923 in Saint Petersburg by students under the direction of Vladimir Tatlin, the founder of constructivism.

Velemir Khlebnikov died in 1922 in extreme poverty as the result of complete physical exhaustion.


## Vladimir Mayakovski

From youth, Vladimir Mayakovski (1893–1930) was closely connected with the later Revolution. He was also well known in the West. Born in Transcaucasia, the son of a forestry official, Mayakovski came to Moscow in 1906 as a high school student, and then attended various art schools from 1908 to 1914. At this time, he was already politically active and was arrested several times. In 1911, he joined the avant-garde painters' group Jack of Diamonds (*Bubnovyi valet*), and in 1912 he was introduced to the futurist group by David Burlyuk.

Mayakovski's early poems are still completely under the influence of Khlebnikov and Burlyuk. Mayakovski, however, aimed at the "de-bourgeoisizing" of the language, not so much through a change in normal speech as by means of a deliberately vulgar diction and polemical images. In his first longer composition in verse, the "tragedy" *Vladimir Mayakovski* (1913), the author calls his words "simple like the howling of animals." Even here, however, one is already touched by the "threatening, accusing earnestness" (Pasternak) of this unusual language, continually breaking forth in hyperboles. In self-criticism, Mayakovski says in the prologue to his tragedy: "Through a thunderstorm of mockery, I bear my soul on a plate to the repast of the coming years."

In the poems of the years 1914–15, especially in the verse narrative *A Cloud in Trousers* (*Oblako v shtanakh*) and *Flute Made of a Spinal Column* (*Flejta-pozvonochnik*), Mayakovski's screaming and not infrequently blasphemous images developed in a more orderly manner and were composed into given complexes (big city, biblical metaphors, the human body in cosmic measure). His language creates a significant tension between sarcasm and naïveté, between pathetic cynicism and injured sensitiveness.

Although Mayakovski early declared himself for Communism and collectivism, his poetry is first of all ultra-individualist. The lyrical theme of his poetry is always Mayakovski himself, who puts into the limelight not only his iconoclastic social views, but also his own personality. He has a predilection for turning himself into a tragic figure, even where his verses speak in grotesque hyperbole, as in a short poem of the cycle *I* (*Ya*, 1913): "Where the cities are hanged and in the noose of a cloud the crooked necks of the towers grow cold, I walk alone and cry bitterly."

Mayakovski's early poems and verse narratives are the tortured monologues of an unhappy and jealous lover. Even in the poem *Man* (*Chelovek*, 1916–17), a personal destiny fills in almost entirely the fantastic picture of the time and its morals.

Political satire at this time still occupies a modest place. It is only in the agitatory piece *Mysterium buffo* (*Misteriya-buff*, 1918, new version, 1921) and in the verse narrative *150,000,000* (1919–20), which refers to the population of Russia, that contemporary satire becomes a strong counterweight to the usual romantic-heroic pathos.

With the gradual surmounting of the original futurist poetry, Mayakovski developed his own poetic style in the years 1915–23. It established him as one of the great masters of the twentieth century. Critics and especially Mayakovski's vehement adversary Khodasevich have pointed out that Mayakovski's innovations—such as *vers libre*, extreme variability, freedom of rhyme, and the graphic featuring of lesser syntactical units—had already been used before him. The fact remains, however, that Mayakovski was the first to set the new rhythmic forms and the new rhyme in Russian poetry as a valid standard, so that these innovations have since been considered style media of great value.

Mayakovski also created a really new poetic language, a new poetic expression, leading Roman Jakobson to say, in a memorial to Mayakovski in 1930, that through him the word seemed qualitatively different from everything that had appeared previously in Russian verse.

The moving apart of syntactical units and the transformation of the line of verse into a "step-ladder," which had also been tried out by Andrei Belyi, are by no means the most crucial of Mayakovski's innovations, although they strike one first. Mayakovski's poetry might be termed "poetry de-poetized" inasmuch as its expression is so contradictory to poetry up to this time. Mayakovski belongs to the very few really purposeful poets who carry their agitation and polemics on a great wave of an elementary poetic imagination and an instinctive mastery of language. This is clearly shown in the verse drama *Mysterium buffo*, successfully staged by Meyerhold in 1918. In this work, Mayakovski parodied the form of the spiritual drama. He attempted to bring the language in verse close to the "slogans on banners at mass demonstrations" and the "war cries of the street."

To be sure, the verse narratives are more valuable from the poetic point of view, especially those of the later years, such as *About That* (*Pro eto*, 1922–23), in which Mayakovski once more returns to the theme of unrequited love.

On the other hand, Mayakovski was not too modest to let his emotions occasionally take a turn toward publicity, as in *150,000,000*:

> 150,000,000 speak with my lips.
> Through the rotary press of the steps
> On the water-marked paper of the paved squares
> This edition has been printed.

Throughout his life Mayakovski remained "intoxicated with himself" according to the critic Okup, and images such as "I hold my heart high like a flag" can hardly be measured with the criteria of the intimate verse of Anna Akhmatova. Mayakovski remained until his self-willed end, and perhaps even in this end, the tragic, rebellious character whose aim it was to destroy through his words hypocrisy and bourgeois contentment, even in the Soviet state.

That Mayakovski let elements of bad taste slip in cannot be denied, especially in the case of the later poems, after 1920, which are of a feuilletonist character. Mayakovski's verse is marked for good and for bad by the reciprocal penetration of agitation, satire, and genial imagery.

The extent of Mayakovski's publications is considerable and cannot be detailed here. The collected works are available in two good editions: 1935–38 (12 volumes) and 1955–61 (13 volumes).

MAJOR SYNTHESIZERS

*Boris Pasternak*

Boris Pasternak (1890–1960), who only became known outside of Russia in 1958 through his novel *Doctor Zhivago* and through the award of the Nobel Prize, still belongs by virtue of his early poetry to the generation of the futurists. After studying in Germany, Pasternak, the son of a highly regarded impressionistic painter and a member of the educated upper class of the bourgeoisie, joined the group *Tzentrifuga*, which from 1913 had made quite a stir and was not far removed from futurism.

In addition to Pasternak, this group included Sergei Bobrov (born 1889) and Nikolai Aseyev (born 1889), who, during the 1920s, together with Mayakovski, participated actively in the movement of the *Lef* (left front of the arts). Aseyev and Bobrov together published Pasternak's first work, a volume of poems *The Twin in the Clouds* (*Bliznetz v tuchakh*, 1914). To this was added during the year of the Revolution the collection *Away over the Barriers* (*Poverkh baryerov*, 1917).

Pasternak's poetry strongly stresses the musical principle of composition, but attempts simultaneously to illustrate the varied stimulations of the senses through daring metaphors. In the poem *Venice* (1913), for example, Pasternak describes a cry, which "like a black fork bores into the fog up to the haft." The objective consolidation of impressions thus sometimes places Pasternak's poetry close to surrealism.

In *My Sister, Life* (*Sestra moya zhizn*, 1922), the collection of poems composed in 1917 but published only several years later, love and nature increasingly become the center of gravity of Pasternak's poetic universe. Thematically, however, both areas overlap continually with the innermost problem, from which Pasternak's poetry springs—the problem of art. Thereby, Pasternak's images in their elliptical reduction become more difficult to peer through and more relevant. In the years between 1917 and 1922, Pasternak developed into a "poet for poets" who expressed all problems only indirectly.

At the periphery of the currents of the time, Pasternak during these years tried to acquire not only the heritage of the symbolists and the futurists but also that of romanticism. In the introductory poem of *My Sister, Life,* he expressly places himself in relationship to Lermontov and the latter's poetic story *Memory of a Demon (Pamyati demona).*

The high point of Pasternak's first great productive period is the volume *Themes and Variations (Temy i variatzii,* 1923). It shows an enrichment of vocabulary through elements of prosaic colloquial speech, the language of technology, and "scholarly" concepts. In the use of poetic means of style, Pasternak becomes surer and more universal; he can risk falling in with Pushkin, as he tries to do in the series of poems *Themes with Variations.* In subject matter, these poems can be traced to Pushkin's famous poem *To the Sea;* they simply vary the romantic theme in modern diction. The Shakespeare theme, too, which preoccupied Pasternak later on, is already broached in the poem, *Shakespeare.*

Pasternak's far-reaching imagination becomes especially impressive in poems like *Mephistopheles, The Shirt of the Patient,* or *The Kremlin in the Snowstorm at the End of 1918,* in which the fantastic and surrealistic elements are held together only by a common point of reference. Above all, Pasternak develops the technique of graphic abbreviations in the volume *Themes and Variations* to a kind of metaphorical algebra whose deciphering demands some effort.

Pasternak's experiments in the field of prose are still sporadic in these years. Besides *The Adolescence of Zhanya Luvers (Detstvo Luvers,* 1922), *Letters from Tula (Pisma iz Tuly,* 1922) demonstrates a noteworthy skill in developing vivid perceptions and allowing them to flower in human consciousness. Pasternak seeks to portray not events but consciousness. The autobiographical story

*Letter of Safe-Conduct* (*Okhrannaya gramota*) appeared in 1931; in it Pasternak's relationship to art, nature, and life is vividly revealed.

## Marina Tzvetayeva

Marina Tzvetayeva (1892–1941) was the daughter of a Moscow university professor, who was director of the Rumyantzev Museum. Next to Anna Akhmatova, she is the greatest woman lyric poet in modern Russian literature. Because of her commitment to folk poetry and to themes of Russian history, she is the representative of both a romantic and a national Russian current.

By transforming the traditional, she made her contribution to the development of modern poetry. Consciously standing apart from the major literary currents and schools, she developed her predominantly baroque and heroic style, which occasionally is of "darker" roughness.

Tzvetayeva's language is characterized by lofty rhetoric, but it is at the same time directed wholly to the rhythmic life of the word and the verse. The poet is no less influenced by symbolism than by futurism, to which the expressionist note in her poetry seems related. Of importance is above all the poetic syntax, the accumulation of expressive one- and two-syllable words, the striking personal intonation. The strict paratactical linkings (omission of connectives) give the rhythmic movements an individuality that is underscored by the numerous syntactical parallelisms.

Even before World War I there appeared two collections of poetry, *Evening Album* (*Vecherni albom*, 1910) and *Magic Lantern* (*Volshebnyi fonar*, 1912). Only during the war, however, did Tzvetayeva's poetry acquire its typical and unvarying expression. Her later volumes are *Measured Stakes* (*Versty*, Moscow 1921–22), *The King's Girl* (*Tzar devitza*, Moscow, 1922), *Manual Work* (*Remeslo*, Berlin 1923), and *Psyche* (*Psikheya*, Berlin 1923). The cycle *The Camp of the Swans* (*Lebedinyistan*), in which numerous poems of the Civil War were collected, was published in 1957 for the first time in Munich.

The themes and motifs of these volumes are versatile and original. The horizon of poetic experiences and confrontations extends from Greek mythology to Russian folklore, from biblical narratives to contemporary history. With all her womanliness, the author did not feel that her poetic "I" was in any way subordinated to that of the male. This is particularly clear in situations in which the great poets are introduced as partners in conversation. In all historical or legendary roles that the poet seeks, she steps beside the man as a rival, a rebel, as a sister, or as a lover.

Her works have not yet been completely published. Although Tzvetayeva, who left Russia in 1922, returned later (1939) to Moscow, she suffered complete oblivion. In 1941, after the evacuation of Moscow, the poet took her own life for reasons that have never been clearly defined. Only twenty years later (1961), a selection of her poems was issued again in Russia through the government publishing house.

The vivaciously written literary essays and memories of the poet were collected and published in New York under the title *Prosa* (*Proza*, 1953).

## Sergei Yesenin

At the beginning of the 1920s, the writer Sergei Yesenin (1895–1925) attained great fame in Russia. Even today his works enjoy considerable popularity. Yesenin's home was Riazan, and he came from a peasant family. After attending a teacher-training institute, he settled in Saint Petersburg in 1913. There he fell under the influence of symbolism (Blok, Belyi, Gorodetzki), but in his later years he accepted by degrees the innovations of the futurists.

As a young and sensational talent "of the people," the still-adolescent Yesenin quickly gained respect in literary circles of the city. His first volume of poetry, *Funeral Service* (*Radunitza*, 1916), was favorably received. Very soon, Yesenin was drawn into the group around Ivanov-Razumnik, in whose almanac *Scythians* of 1917–18 his mystic, folkloristic verse narrative *Marfa, the Wife of Posadnik* (*Marfa posadnitza*), *Otchar*, and *The Singing Call* (*Pevushchi zov*) appeared. Yesenin's sympathy with the Revolution is shown also in the narrative poem *Comrade* (*Tovarishch*, 1918), in which Christ, as with Blok, is on the side of the workers. Until 1919 Yesenin remained loyal to the ideas of the "Scythians," as shown by the poems he wrote at this time, *Inoniya* and *The Return* (*Prishestviye*, 1918; dedicated to Andrei Belyi) and *The Transfiguration* (*Preobrazheniye*).

These poems, even in their blasphemies, are still mystical, messianic, and overflow with symbols and emblems of Christian origin. The vocabulary and diction are partly based on religious folk poetry, but the pathetic imagery is also strongly influenced by futurism. In Yesenin, the proletarian revolution is thought of as a cosmic movement; its frame of reference is the patriarchal peasant world. Rye and buckwheat, peas and raspberries, bees and birds, sheaves of oats and fields, studs, calves, sheep, and dogs are linked metaphorically with cosmic events. The milk pail becomes the "pail filled with azure," the mystic East is an East that brings forth young calves, and the Mother of God herself "calls the calves into Paradise."

During the years 1920–22, Yesenin intermittently kept close to the imagists, who had partly been recruited from former advocates of futurism. The imagists (among others, Vadim Shershenevich, Ryurik Ivaniov, Anatolii Mariengof, and Aleksandr Kusikov), who had founded a publishing house, issued numerous volumes of poetry in addition to almanacs, whose titles were intended to cause a sensation, as for instance, *The Cookshop of the Dawn* (*Kharchevnya zor*). In their poetry, however, compared with futurism and symbolism, these poets displayed little innovation. Their poetic images were noisy and actually dilettantic, even though Shershenevich tried to claim the poet of the *Song of Songs*, King Solomon, for the genealogy of imagism.

Yesenin himself, even as an imagist, maintained the peculiar style of his poetic language, which resembled the folk song and was filled with genuine feeling. The poems of these years, *The Mares' Boars* (*Kobylyi korabli*, 1920), *The Song of Bread* (*Pesn o khlebe*, 1921), *The Prayer of the Forty Days* (*Sorokoust*, 1921), and *The Confession of a Hooligan* (*Ispoved khuligana*, 1921), stand without exception far above the level of the rest of the imagist poetry.

Yesenin's last poems of the years 1922–25 are again quite simple, not stilted; more and more a tragic undertone appears. In this phase of his work Yesenin sings of the big city and its disreputable bars, but also of the "lost" Russian village. The lyrical moods of these poems are of a poignant and sometimes dreamy delicacy. Remarkable, too, is the later cycle *Persian Motifs* (*Persidskye motivy*, 1924–25), inspired by a trip to Persia.

On December 28, 1925, Yesenin, whose restless and scandalous life had become a legend, committed suicide in a Leningrad hotel room. His works were published in numerous editions in Russia and by the Russian emigré press. The publication of a new edition in five volumes was begun in 1961.

### Nikolai Klyuyev

Nikolai Klyuyev (1887–1937), a very prolific writer, was also a poet of peasant origin. His reputation was founded by his early cycles of poems, which were collected in 1919 and published under the title of *Song of Praise* (*Pesnoslov*). In the final cycle of this book, *Red Howling* (*Krasnyi ryk*), Klyuyev expressed what seemed to be great hopes for Soviet poetry. Later, however, somewhat like Yesenin, he turned in bitter disappointment from the consequences of the Revolution and lived in secret opposition to the regime. In 1933 he was arrested and deported to Siberia, where he died in 1937.

Klyuyev was particularly well acquainted with the life, moods, and views of the religious sectarians living in the underground. In part, he incorporated elements of their beliefs into his poetic mythos, which manifests Christian and pagan features. Klyuyev especially esteemed Russia before Peter the Great, and in one of his poems he calls the seventeenth century Protopope Avvakum his ancestor. But in 1917 Klyuyev, too, fell under the influence of the romantic utopian dreams of Ivanov-Razumnik. Thus, in *The Valley of the Unicorn* (*Dolina Yedinorova*), published in Pesnoslov, he gave expression to his ideal of the union of a sectarian cult of "brotherliness" with a romantic glorification of the "East."

Klyuyev's mystic hopes for a new peasant paradise acquired a strongly exotic hue through his dreaming of a "White India" (*Belaya Indiya*) as the center of the reconciliation of Europe and Asia.

# PART II

## The Interwar Period

# *Development of Prose*

The society of the Serapion Brothers was founded during the winter of 1920–21 in Saint Petersburg. Largely as a result of the vigorous intervention of Maksim Gorki,˙they were provided with the basic necessities of life so that they could combat the total stagnation of intellectual life after the Revolution.

During the years of the Civil War, Saint Petersburg, despite hunger and distress, presented the image of a metropolis that had recovered spiritually and artistically—in which life seemed to be touched only externally by the Revolution. As centers of intellectual life in Saint Petersburg, the newly organized institutes above all exerted a refreshing influence. There were, for example, the House of the Scholars (*Dom uchenykh*), the House of the Writers (*Dom literatorov*), and the House of Art (*Dom iskusstva*), in which absolute artistic freedom and freedom of thought could still be enjoyed, something that was propitious for the launching of new programs and new experiments.

In this free and creative atmosphere, there arose that circle of young writers who called themselves the Serapion Brothers, a name coined by E. T. A. Hoffmann. The nucleus of this organization was the Studio for Literature at the House of Art, in which Yevgenii Zamyatin (for prose) and Nikolai Gumilev (for poetry), until his arrest, served as instructors.

The most widely known members of this new literary brotherhood were Mikhail Zoshchenko, Lev Luntz, Veniamin Kaverin, Konstantin Fedin, Nikolai Tikhonov, Vsevolod Ivanov, Nikolai Nikitin, and Mikhail Slonimski.

Without doubt, Zamyatin was an important model for the writers, most of whom were at the beginning of their careers. Actually, the "neo-realism" sought by Zamyatin, with its cult of semantically "displaced" narrative language and its marked stress on the narrative form, had been in the air for quite a while. The young critics and language theoreticians who had founded the Society for the Study of Poetic Language (*Opoyaz*) took up questions of prose style in their writings. They made use of the insights they had obtained through their analyses of poetic language—symbolisn and futurism—for a new kind of "formal" criticism of prose. Above all, Boris Eichenbaum (1886–1959), Viktor Shklovski (born 1893), and Yurii Tynyanov (1894–1943) must be mentioned in this connection.

The investigations of these so-called "formalists" were concerned with the secrets of style, especially of the "ornamental" tradition, but also with general problems of composition and narrative technique and with figures like Cervantes and Laurence Sterne (Viktor Shklovski). A new, formal concept of the *sujet* as the structural unity of the narrative material and narrative procedure was developed, particularly by Shklovski. Thus the problems of the architectonics of narration, which had been neglected almost entirely since the classical period, moved into the center of the studies.

Shklovski, who was one of the most brilliant essayists and literary theoreticians of the 1920s and who was active in the House of Art, became closely attached to the society of the Serapion Brothers. Many of his books are even closer to fiction than to the essay. With works like *The Zoo, or Letters Not About Love* (*Zoo ili pisma ne o lyubvi*, 1923) and *A Sentimental Pilgrimage* (*Sentimentalnoi puteshestviye*, 1924), he established his own genre.

In his books, Shklovski liked to experiment with the technique of Laurence Sterne, by interlarding his stories with reportage-like sketches and essay-like deviations. In this way, in the two instances mentioned, Shklovski deliberately loosened up and expanded the genre of the epistolary novel in one case, and the genre of autobiography in the other.

The organization of the Serapion Brothers had first of all set for its goal the creation of a narrative prose style independent of the realistic tradition of fiction hitherto observed. Despite all the good will shown to the new literary avant-garde by the influential Maksim Gorki, it must not be overlooked that the point of view represented by the Serapion Brothers was a definite rejection of the older realism, which included Gorki as a writer of fiction.

The views of that time are most clearly reflected in a treatise that Zamyatin wrote in honor of the painter Yurii Annenkov. In this work, *About Synthesism* (*O sintetizme,* 1922), which almost has the character of a manifesto, Zamyatin stressed that the older realism viewed the world with the naked eye. This approach had to be replaced by a "complicated" optical system, following the experience of the fine arts in cubism and suprematism. Without humor, fantasy, and the grotesque, the desired synthesis, neo-realism, was not to be attained. It is illuminating in this connection that Zamyatin reminded the reader of the early pioneers of this type of art, namely, Hieronymus Bosch, the "Hell" Breughel, and Gogol.

In view of this attitude, the return to E. T. A. Hoffmann is understandable, although only Luntz and Kaverin—the writers most consistently oriented toward the West—were influenced directly by the spirit of Hoffmann's fantastic stories.

The Serapion Brothers defended themselves repeatedly against the reproach that they were enemies of the proletarian revolution. Zamyatin, too, felt attacked and expressed himself on this point in his critical essay *The New Russian Prose* (*Novaya russkaya proza,* 1923):

> Writers who are enemies of the Revolution do not exist in Russia at the present time. They have been invented so that it would not be too boring. The motive for this has been that these writers do not look upon the Revolution as a consumptive young lady, who must be sheltered against the slightest breath of air. [For poetry of Serapion Brothers, *see* p. 141.]

### Yevgenii Zamyatin

Yevgenii Zamyatin (1884–1937) was originally trained as a marine engineer. He is one of the foremost Russian writers, who belongs to that early avant-garde whose attitude toward questions of art was affected by the period of transition that culminated in the formation of the Serapion Brothers.

From the point of view of stylistic development, Zamyatin is no more distant from the "symbolist" Andrei Belyi than from the "realist" Aleksei Remizov. The "neorealistic" style, thus named by Zamyatin himself, perhaps owes more to the later development of symbolist prose than to the realistic prose of the same period.

In the story *At the World's End* (*Na kulichkakh*, 1914), one of Zamyatin's early works, there appears a stronger dependence on the conventions of realism, although Zamyatin has already acquired the "ornamental" tradition of style and makes full use of the familiar style of narration, of *skaz*, in the manner of Remizov. This transmission of the tradition originating with Gogol and Leskov was to become the style, over the years, of so many Soviet Russian writers.

In *At the World's End*, Zamyatin's special gift for satire is as striking as his art in isolating details, in which he was an apt pupil of Gogol. The story, in which Zamyatin describes the degeneration of the normal forms of community life in a small garrison at the edge of the Pacific Ocean, is the model for all his later satires, in which the basic motif of being cut off from real life continually reappears. In *At the World's End*, the geographical isolation and the narrowness of the milieu arouse in the officers various forms of brutalization and loss of feeling, and in this atmosphere spleen becomes the last refuge from general dissolution.

When Zamyatin was ordered to England during World War I, he wrote a clever satire on English puritanism that appeared in 1918 in the second almanac of the "Scythians" under the title of *The Islanders* (*Ostrovityane*). Under the obvious influence of Belyi, Zamyatin's narrative style had meanwhile developed further from *skaz* toward the rhythmic-symphonic ornamental style; through the numerous plays on words and grotesque metaphors, Zamyatin's realism was now transformed into surrealism, as in "The moon strolled the whole night over the park with a monocle in his eye and looked down with the benevolent irony of a porcelain pug dog" (*The Islanders*).

The geometric (and cubist) motifs, moreover, indicate the impression that Belyi's novel *Saint Petersburg* had made on Zamyatin. This new style influenced the stories that Zamyatin wrote directly after the Revolution. The grotesque story *The Man Hunter* (*Lovetz chelovekov*), written about the same time (1917–18) as *The Islanders*, is related to the latter in subject matter. It is set in London during World War I and the attacks by zeppelins lend the atmosphere a weird fascination.

Zamyatin's principle of composition is, as already indicated, the isolation of his characters from the "real" world, the limiting of the scene of action to a formalized space. In the mathematical correctness and the sterilized condition of the small English town in *The Islanders*; at the edge of the polar sea in *The North* (*Na severe*, 1918); in the loneliness of the monastery at the seashore in *The Miracle* (*Znameniye*, 1918); in the ice-cold Saint Petersburg tenements of the years of hunger in *The Cave* (*Peshchera*, 1920); or on the platform of the streetcar going by in *The Dragon* (*Drakon*, 1918)—everywhere the connections with reality have been demolished, one is in a "closed" society, outside of space and time. Everything that is outside remains veiled or dissolves in mist.

The isolation of the scene of action, moreover, offered the writer increased possibilities for metaphorizing, shunting his views into mythical realms. This approach characterizes *The Cave*, a story with a metaphorical title, and *The Dragon*, in reality a red guard, an unreal being, which in the wintry mist on a moving streetcar acquires very hazy outlines. Interesting, too, is the metaphorical transposition in the story *Mamai*, whose title conjures up the time of the reign of tha Tatars in Russia:

> In the evening and at night, one no longer finds houses in Saint Petersburg, only six-story stone hulls of vessels. As a lonely six-story world, the vessel floats on stone waves between other lonely six-story expanses; with the lights of countless cabins, the ship glimmers in the restless stone ocean of the streets.

Written in 1920, the stories *The Man Hunter, The North, The Cave*, and *Mamai* appeared in print in 1921–22.

Zamyatin himself, in a later explanation of his works, pointed out that the subject of his stories as a rule developed from certain graphic symbols that give the actual support to the entire composition and its "musical texture"; he called these symbols "integral" pictures, as in *Behind the Scenes* (*Zakulisy*, 1930).

One of Zamyatin's later works, the masterful story *The Flood* (*Navodneniye*, 1929), is carried along by such an "integral" picture. In this strictly classical novella, the outward happening (a flood in Saint Petersburg) is linked with the psychologically portrayed tragedy of jealousy, which results in a murder, by means of the metaphorical realization of the "flood" in the psychological area.

The satirical strain in Zamyatin's writing continues in the utopian novel *We* (*My*), which was begun in 1920. It was printed only abroad (in 1924, in English translation); Zamyatin was therefore sharply criticized. The complete Russian text appeared for the first time in 1952 in New York; in the Soviet Union, it could never be published.

In its social fantasy, this novel stands close to the technical-social utopias of H. G. Wells, so highly esteemed by Zamyatin, although the structure, as in *The Islanders*, is borne here by mathematical symbols and formulas. *We* is a so-called anti-utopia, which describes the bending of man under the "beneficent yoke of reason." The measures of a totalitarian state of the future aim to correct "the contortions of life" and to lead men out of the "uncivilized condition of freedom."

Through the medium of the diary notes of a subject of the "United State," which in the *nth* century has already existed for a thousand years, the point of view is so arranged that all observations and comments appear to the reader in an ironic refraction. As the story begins, the engineer of the *nth* century is a devoted servant of the state. He is working on the construction of a giant spaceship, the *Integral*, which symbolizes technical and social reality. The tyrannical state seeks not only to integrate the "equation of the universe" but also to turn mankind into a real collective mass: "Yes, to straighten the barbaric curve, to bring it into line with the tangent, with the asymptote, the straight one . . . the great, divine, exact, wise straight one—the wisest of all lines. . . ."

The real action of the novel begins at the point where doubts first arise in the narrator's mind. These are nourished by an unforeseen erotic relationship. Real life, relegated behind the big "glass wall," breaks through many secret channels, with its irrational symbols, into artificially normalized life, and the "wilderness" presses forward, apparently unchecked. A general infection develops, together with a revolutionary situation dangerous for the state. The rulers can correct the situation only by carrying out a brain operation on the narrator.

The conclusion, with its despairing irony, gives one a jolt. The engineer is finally healed of all "deviations" and writes like a docile child:

> Daytime, clear, barometer 760 . . . no more fantasies, no stupid metaphors, no feelings; only facts. For I am healthy, I am completely, absolutely healthy. I smile, and I cannot do otherwise but smile; out of my head some kind of splinter has been withdrawn, in my head it is light and empty.

Zamyatin, who politically entirely favored the Revolution, just a few years after that event became a great and courageous heretic who was not afraid to say in his novel:

> And why then do you think there is a *last* revolution . . . their number is infinite. . . . The "last one" is a child's story. Children are afraid of the infinite, and it is necessary that children should not be frightened so that they may sleep through the night.

Zamyatin developed similar thoughts in his various journalistic essays of criticism, especially in *About Literature, Revolution, Entropy and Other Things* (*O literature, revolyutzii, entropii i o prochem*, 1924). Here, Zamyatin turned again and again against the "sleeping sickness" of dogmatism and against the sterility of the official policy in literature: "If there were no heretics, one would have to invent them."

Zamyatin absolutely rejected the concept of "socialist realism" and put it on a level with "bourgeois" realism:

> Projection on movable, warped surfaces is infinitely closer to reality. . . . Realism, which is not to be primitive—not real but a heightened reality—lies in dislocation, in deformation, in crookedness, in nonobjectivity.

The theme of heresy, which Zamyatin developed journalistically, recurs in his literary work. In 1922 his drama *The Fires of St. Dominic* (*Ogni sv. Dominika*), which had as its subject the Inquisition in Spain, implicitly established a parallel to the Soviet state. Other stories by Zamyatin appeared sporadically about the middle of the 1920s, such as *The Story of What Is of Supreme Importance* (*Rasskaz o samom glavnom*, 1924) and *Infamous Stories* (*Nechestivyye rasskazy*, 1927), but it grew more and more difficult for the writer to oppose the growing pressure of political circumstances. In 1931 he asked for permission to leave the Soviet Union, which was not denied him. Zamyatin settled in France, where he lived in complete retirement until his death.

## Lev Luntz

Lev Luntz (1901–24) worked under the special aegis of Gorki. With Luntz's untimely death one of the great hopes of Russian literature passed away. He published only a few stories and four dramas. The last of these, *The City of Justice* (*Gorod pravdy*, 1924) appeared posthumously. As in the case of Zamyatin, dreams, satire, and fantasy are the media in which Luntz prefers to work when he is dealing with Soviet reality. This method is greatly intensified in the short story, *Circular Letter No. 37* (*Izchodyashchaya No. 37*), in which the director of a Soviet chancellery transforms himself by self-hypnosis into an official document, the symbol of bureaucratic functioning.

Luntz also distinguished himself as as a theoretician among the Serapion Brothers, especially with the manifesto *Why We Are Serapion Brothers* (*Pochemu my Serapionovy Bratya*, 1922). Here, Luntz definitely espouses artistic freedom at the time of the consolidation of Soviet power, when he rightly emphasizes: "A work can reflect the epoch but does not have to, and it is not inferior for this reason." Shortly thereafter, another polemic of Luntz appeared under the title *Toward the West* (*Na zapad*). It was published by Gorki in the Berlin magazine *Beseda* (1923). Luntz here formulated the thesis that Western literature of adventure was unjustly undervalued in Russia and that the disdain with which one looked on a thrilling plot only showed the provincial backwardness of Russia.

In ill health, the poet left Russia in 1923 and died near Hamburg.

## Veniamin Kaverin

An eccentric world, only loosely bound to reality, is presented in the first stories through which Veniamin Kaverin (pseudonym of V. Zilber, born 1902), became famous. While still a student of Oriental languages at the University of Saint Petersburg, Kaverin was inspired by Yurii Tynyanov and Yevgenii Zamyatin to engage in literary activity. At first, he cultivated the ultraformalistic style. His prize-winning first story *The Eleventh Axiom* (*Odinnadtzataya aksioma*, 1920) bases its composition on a purely mathematical problem: two parallels meet in the infinite, and the story therefore operates on two parallel planes.

The volume that he published in 1923, *Master and Journeymen* (*Mastera i podmasterya*), brought together romantic stories that are chiefly set at a geographical and historical distance—some, for instance in Germany. In them, the fantastic motifs of E. T. A. Hoffmann and Edgar Allan Poe have left perceptible traces. At that time, Kaverin, according to his own admission, made an effort to expunge, as far as possible, the national characteristics and the milieu (*byt*) from literature, or to alienate them so that the reader would face only that "poignant" side which bordered on the fantastic.

Kaverin's early stories are strictly attuned to a single adventurous motif, so that the subject matter becomes a kind of algebraic formula (Zamyatin). One of Kaverin's favorite motifs is the game of chance with high stakes, as in *The Big Gamble* (*Bolshaya igra*, 1925), the gamble with one's own fate. In fact, Kaverin's stories are unthinkable without the concept of gamble. His imagery borrows heavily from this sphere; sometimes, in fact, the title indicates a game of chance, for example, *A Card of Diamonds* (*Bubnoyaya mast*, 1927).

Kaverin bases his stories extensively on the tradition of the picaresque and adventure novella, which serves as the form for his grotesque and fantastic inspirations. Gamblers, impostors, frauds, charlatans and swindlers are the heroes of his stories.

The story *The End of the Den of Thieves* (*Konetz chazy*, 1925), which is dedicated to the memory of Lev Luntz, features a band of criminals who draw an apparently harmless Soviet citizen into their sinister operation. Kaverin here presents a description—in which the diction is also true to life—of the underworld of Saint Petersburg in the postwar years.

Reality is presented in a predominantly cinematographic style in the novel *Nine-Tenths of Fate* (*Devyat desyatych sudby*, 1925). An adventurous intrigue of the time of the Civil War is developed, showing how, even in an apparently pure life, a little cog may jump out of the mechanism and destroy the entire balance. Again Kaverin's penchant for employing a mathematical scheme appears; he formalizes the principal motif as nine-tenths against one-tenth.

The novella *The Auditor* (*Revizor*, 1926) is based partly on Gogol (*The Nose, The Auditor*) in the development of its subject. It describes the grave consequences of an exchange of persons that is caused by mixing up garments in a steam bath. The effects are here decidedly surrealistic; with the appearance of a grotesque Priapus, the symbolism definitely approaches the obscene.

In the *roman à clef The Troublemaker or Evenings on the Island of Vasilyev* (*Skandalist ili vechera na Vasilyevskom ostrove*, 1929), Kaverin presents a burlesque and partly autobiographical description of the academic and literary life of Leningrad. Here, too, Kaverin frequently uses the technique of the film—startling cuts and sudden closeups. The last in the series of Kaverin's formalistic novels is *The Anonymous Artist* (*Khudozhnik neizvesten*, 1931), a story in the first person in eight episodes and an epilogue. These describe various meetings with an unappreciated and ostracized painter, who can prove himself in Soviet Leningrad only in the role of Don Quixote.

Technically the novel is especially interesting because it is itself the genesis of the novel. It takes the form of a literary diary, consisting only of preliminary studies of a novel that is not yet born. The meetings with the characters of the novel are accompanied by various commentaries and suppositions by the author. The "omniscient" overview, however, is missing. The descriptions are governed by a complicated manner of observation that points to the world of the painter as well as to the film:

> For a moment, the room in back was reflected like a blurred closeup in Arkhimedov's eyeglasses: talking and drinking mouths,

hands stretched out toward glasses, a silhouette that telephoned, gesticulating excitedly, a waiter with a swinging tray stopped at full speed—a scene that had all the earmarks of an abruptly interrupted dream.

Kaverin's next work, the novel *The Fulfillment of Wishes* (*Izpolneniye zhelany*, 1934), is set in the academic milieu with which the author was familiar in his youth. Here again an adventure plot is developed, but for the first time Kaverin puts the emphasis on the social and psychological level. From the political point of view, the increasing demands of the era, *i.e.*, the approach to socialist realism, made themselves felt here; Kaverin later looked on this novel as the turning point in his artistic destiny.

## Vsevolod Ivanov

An entirely different trend among the Serapion Brothers was represented by Vsevolod Ivanov (born 1895). He was not concerned so much with the dynamics of plot or the whole structure as with the stylization of detail and the personal touch of narrative language.

Ivanov's range of themes was determined largely by his experiences during the war of the partisans in the eastern regions of the Russian Empire. They form the background for the famous story *Armored Train* (*Bronepoezd*, 1922), which was successfully dramatized. The scene of action is the Siberian railroad line at Vladivostok, where the Communist partisans fought against the troops of the "white" Admiral Kolchak in 1919.

Instead of developing a picture of political or historical perspectives, Ivanov seeks all the motives in an individual and in his local milieu. As in Zamyatin's works, man acts within the smallest elbow room, in a narrow, almost animal-like atmosphere.

Ivanov's so-called "primitivism" is based on the peasant coloration of his vocabulary as well as on the sensuous charms of the local color of the images. Zamyatin declared facetiously that Ivanov wrote chiefly with his nostrils.

Ivanov is considered the discoverer of the romantic "exotics" of the Civil War, as the poet of the vital and colorful undercurrents of the Revolution. From the historical point of view, his prose is indebted to the "ornamental" style, as shown by his two other stories, lengthened to novels: *Colored Winds* (*Tzvetniye vetra*, 1922) and *Blue Sand* (*Golubiye peski*, 1923).

In the 1930s, Ivanov adapted himself to the style of socialist realism imposed by official criticism of that time. The novel *The Adventures of a Fakir* (*Pokhozhdeniya fakira*), published in 1934–35, is based on the experiences that the writer gathered in his youth as a member of an itinerant circus. The historical-biographical novel *Parkhomenko* (1938–39) presents the portrait of a well-known front-line officer of the Civil War. Both novels were completely revised for the edition of his collected works (eight volumes, 1959).

## Konstantin Fedin

One of the most prominent writers today of the erstwhile Serapion Brothers is Konstantin Fedin (born 1892). His contemporary novel *Cities and Years* (*Goroda i gody*, 1924) caused quite a sensation. Fedin, who was forced to live in Germany during World War I as a civilian internee, became acquainted with expressionism there and was inspired by it in his own writing.

The plot of the novel, which extends to Germany, is developed psychologically. It is more indebted to modern European narrative style than to the predominantly antipsychological Russian trends of the time. Fedin experiments here above all with the chronological overlapping of the various parts of the novel and the foreshadowing of its end and thus of a solution to the problem that it poses. He is clearly less concerned with the dynamic of the adventure plot than with the psychological motivation and the illumination of the specific, at times somewhat obscure happenings.

The Civil War novel *The Brothers* (*Bratya*, 1928), which depicts the collision of the Revolution with the destiny of an artist, has a similar narrative structure. Fedin views the problem psychologically and depicts the struggle of an apolitical composer immersed in pure music to maintain himself and his work in the face of the conflicts of the Civil War, which divided families. The novel borrows heavily from Dostoyevski.

In his stories and novellas of the 1920s, Fedin treats the various motifs with remarkable sureness. The theme is usually the dawn of the new era, the Revolution, which upsets the living conditions of social classes hitherto secure. Fedin handles the psychological conflict that arises from the difficult adaptation to the changed circumstances.

Longer sojourns abroad in 1928 and in 1931 to 1934, resulting in part from illness, gave Fedin the opportunity to observe, of course from the Soviet viewpoint, the European crises of the pre-World War II years. The two novels *The Rape of Europa* (*Prokhishcheniye Yevropy*, 1933–35) and *Sanatorium Arktur* (*Sanatorii Arktur*, 1940) are drawn from this background.

Fedin started his literary career as dramatist with a series of historical scenes entitled *Bakunin in Dresden* (*Bakunin in Drezdene*, 1922). This play, dedicated to Maksim Gorki, owes its origin to Gorki's ambitious plan of a dramatic cycle, in which all important phases of world history were to be represented. Gorki had hoped to obtain the collaboration of a large number of authors for this enterprise.

## Mikhail Zoshchenko

One of the great stylists, Mikhail Zoshchenko (1895–1958) occupies a specific and outstanding position among the Serapion Brothers and a general one in the Soviet literature of the 1920s and 1930s.

By coincidence, Zoshchenko was a fellow-countryman of Gogol. He was born the son of a painter in Poltava (Ukraine). After a brief period of study in Saint Petersburg, he took part in World War I and in the Civil War, finally settling in Saint Petersburg in 1921, where he joined the Serapion Brothers.

Zoshchenko is known to the non-Russian reader chiefly as the author of humorous, satirical short stories, but actually his importance as a narrative writer is greater over a far broader area. Novellas and longer stories that combine a romantic-sentimental and a romantic-burlesque treatment of the topic are the works that most clearly show his humor and consummate mastery of the style called *skaz* (continuous narration with ironic persiflage).

The satirical, humorous sketches, the novellas, and the novel-like works have one thing in common: the author is deliberately obscured by the narrator. The narrator leads an independent existence and secretly moves up to become the chief figure in the story. By the application and the further logical development of *skaz*, Zoshchenko succeds in having all events controlled by the role of the narrator. The narrative situation is fixed in relationship to a tangible subject ("auctorial" situation).

Zoshchenko's malicious short stories, written during the period 1922–36, are in part pure works of art that are attuned to a basic melody up to the final figure of speech. As early as 1923 Zamyatin praised Zoshchenko's "consummate mastery, hitting the mark from the start," of which, unfortunately, as must be added, translations can give only an approximate idea.

The chief reason for the untranslatability of Zoshchenko is that countless words and entire expressions (slang and popular clichés used in political appeals and instructions) always simultaneously allude to a second level of consciousness that is never clearly expressed. The apparently casual conversational tone has a mediating function: it conjures up the picture of the half-educated, half-informed average citizen, naive or crafty, according to the demands of the situation.

Even in the short stories, with their frequently intricate and absurd situations, comedy is not the sole determining factor. The function of punch lines is not only to provoke laughter; they also point out the jeopardizing of what is human in a society that threatens to get lost in a labyrinth of half-truths.

Zoshchenko's ironic pessimism appears even more sharply in the novellas in which the comical and tragic sides of the commonplace touch one another directly. After *The Goat* (*Koza*, 1923) and *Wisdom* (*Mudrost*, 1925), there appeared in 1927 the volume *What the Nightingale Sang* (*O chom pel solovei*), to which Zoshchenko gave the subtitle *Senitimental Novellas* (*Sentimentalnyje povesti*). This anachronistic subtitle was added deliberately; it gives expression to the romantic irony of the story, but at the same time provides the cue for a concealed literary polemic.

In lengthy ironic prefaces to the individual stories, Zoshchenko discusses the literary situation of the time and takes a detached attitude. In this effort, however, the mocking tone often appears as only a mask for saying unpopular things. Thus in the title story, *What the Nightingale Sang*, the author insists on his right to create an ordinary, modest love story, even if one should therefore consider him a "ridiculous person of the previous century" and suggest that he should throw himself in front of a streetcar. This motif is taken up again, after the story reaches an unforeseen, sad ending. The author begs the reader for indulgence and expresses the hope that this story will look good a few hundred years later:

> The author always thinks just of that: of the future, of wonderful life in, let's say, three hundred years, perhaps even less. Yes, dear reader, may these three hundred years pass as quickly as possible, as in a dream, and then we will really want to live! Yes, if even then, however, it isn't better, then the author is ready, with an empty and cold heart, to consider himself a superfluous figure against the future as it unfolds. Then, too, he can throw himself in front of the streetcar.

Quite similar is the long preface to *A Terrible Night* (*Strasnaya noch*, 1925). Here Zoshchenko asks the ironic question: Where is the author to get the "wild flight of fancy," when Russian reality isn't like that at all?

> And as for the Revolution, that's one of those things again. It is impetuous. And lofty imagination it has, too. But let someone try to describe that. Untrue, it would be said. It doesn't agree, it would be said. The question was not approached scientifically. And the ideology, is nothing wonderful, either, it would be said.

This witty preface contrasts in a peculiar manner with the actual story, which is somewhat similar to Gogol's *The Overcoat*. The triangle player of the city orchestra, full of fear that he might suddenly lose his job, is seized by an acute terror, behaving like a madman and causing a great disturbance. Out of his mind, the poor musician flees from his pursuers up a church steeple, where he sets the heavy bell in motion, "as if he made a deliberate effort thereby to rouse the entire city and all mankind."

The comic side is, on the whole, stressed more than the sentimental, and, here, as elsewhere, Zoshchenko's moral stands closer to the mimic artist Charles Chaplin than to Gogol and his social metaphysics.

Other stories of this genre in the following years are *A Jolly Experience* (*Veseloye priklyuceniye*, 1927), *The Lilac Is Blooming* (*Siren tzvetet*, 1930), and *Michael Sinyagin* (*Mishel Sinyagin*, 1930).

Zoshchenko's most important books of the 1930s are the novel *Recovered Youth* (*Vozvrashchennaya molodost*, 1933) and the collection of illustrations and anecdotes *Blue Book* (*Golubaya kniga*, 1934–35). *Recovered Youth* is apparently an attempt to produce a sort of "cultural film," as the author called it, out of the numerous single episodes pieced together to form the action of the novel, by introducing popular-scientific comments. In the same way, the *Blue Book* was to be transformed through thematically linked historical and pseudo-historical anecdotes into a humorous cultural history, or a "history of human relationships." Both books are looked upon by critics outside Soviet Russia (Gleb Struve and V. Zavalishin) as skillful mystifications in which a sharp criticism of Soviet cultural philosophy expresses itself.

Finally, Zoshchenko devoted himself entirely to biographical writing and popular-science, historical books: *The Black Prince* (*Chernyi printz*, 1937), *Kerenski* (1937), and *Taras Shevchenko* (1939). In 1946 Zoshchenko's work was ideologically condemned by Zhdanov, although in 1957, shortly before his death, the author was, to a certain extent, reinstated.

## GORKI AFTER THE REVOLUTION

The initial primacy of prose over poetry under Soviet rule is primarily related to the final fading away of the voices of symbolism, which had found their sounding board precisely in poetry. The course of the 1840s was repeated, when poetry had also disappeared from the center of literary development. To this were added the historical challenges of the Revolution and the Civil War: the forceful and fateful reaching into the world of the individual's experience.

It is not, however, to be assumed that the immediate description of experiences in World War I and in the Civil War was given a position of preference over themes that had no closer relationship with the present. The activities of the Serapion Brothers show that the new wave of prose definitely encouraged a variety of tendencies on which a new phase of literary life could thrive for a long time. Beside this, however, there existed many an older tradition, such as that of the novel of social criticism and the historical novel, that had only to be revived.

The older generation evaluated what had been created earlier. Under new conditions it could critically verify its own historical point of view and its own view of life. This was the situation in which, for example, Maksim Gorki and Mikhail Prishvin found themselves at the beginning of the 1920s.

After the Revolution, Gorki was not very active as a writer. Until his departure for Germany at the end of 1921, he placed his efforts and his authority entirely at the service of assisting the suffering and distressed intellectuals as well as planning a great cultural program. Gorki, in the words of Zamyatin, had become something like an "unofficial minister of culture," an organizer of publicly approved works for the starvring, derailed intelligentsia.

After the completion of his autobiographical trilogy with the book *My Universities (Moi universitety*, 1923), Gorki did not turn to some great theme of the present, but returned to the plans and ideas of his youth. With *The Artamonov Business (Delo Artamonovykh*, 1925), he created a bourgeois family novel, which is very close in spirit to *Foma Gordeyev*. In Sorrento, Gorki began the uncompleted novelistic chronicle *Klim Samgin's Life (Zhizn Klima Samgina*, 1925–36), whose first part appeared in 1927. Here, too, Gorki sought to depict a typical prewar destiny in the life story of a representative of the Russian intelligentsia over a period of forty years, up to the Revolution.

After a longer silence the first part of Mikhail Prishvin's autobiographical chronicle, *Kurymushka*, appeared in 1924. Later, in the edition of 1930, the chronicle was given the title *Kashchei's*

*Chain* (*Kashcheyeva tzep*), after a legendary figure of Russian folk tradition.

The subtle nature studies of the phrenologist Prishvin were set down in the documentary collection of sketches *Nature's Calendar* (*Kalendar prirody*, 1925–26) and in the poetic miniatures of the book *Thaw in the Woods* (*Lesnaya kapel*, 1940–43), which developed out of his collected diary entries.

## HISTORICAL NOVEL

### Aleksei N. Tolstoi

Count Aleksei N. Tolstoi (1883–1945) belongs to the generation rooted in prewar society. After his return from the emigration (1919–23), he occupied an important position in Soviet literature. Aligning himself with the tradition of classical Russian literature, Tolstoi, after experiments in lyrical poetry (1907–11), turned to fiction. From 1917 he gave ample proof of his ability to handle historical subjects with his novels *The Day of Peter the Great* (*Den Petra*, 1917) and *Story of Troubled Times* (*Povest smutnovo vremeni*, 1922).

During the emigration Tolstoi wrote *Nikita's Childhood* (*Detstvo Nikiti*, 1921), a story based on his childhood memories. This tale provided the prelude for his great contemporary historical novel that was later expanded into three volumes under the title of *The Road to Calvary* (*Kozhdeniye po mukam*, 1922–41). The first part, *The Sisters* (*Siostry*), was begun in exile and covers the period in history up to the Revolution.

Even in the 1920s A. N. Tolstoi's prose was not "modern" in the sense of a particularly characteristic language or an experimental style. His conservative attitude toward styles did not, however, counteract his tendency toward occasional eccentric themes. During his emigration Tolstoi had turned to science fiction and thereby to a fantastic style in the manner of H. G. Wells. The best known of these works, *Aelita*, was written shortly before his return to Russia (1922) and describes the confusion caused by a Communist expedition on Mars.

Stronger socio-political and anti-Western tendencies appear in the equally fantastic story *Seven Days in Which the World Was Robbed* (*Sem dnei, v kotoryye byl ograblen mir,* 1925). The title, paraphrasing that of John Reed's book *Ten Days That Shook the World,* was later changed to *The Alliance of the Five* (*Soyuz pyati*).

The historical-philosophical novel *Blue Cities* (*Golobyye goroda,* 1925), set in the present, was less favorably received by the critics, and Tolstoi soon returned to the theme of Peter the Great. The first volume of *Peter the Great* (*Petr Pervyi*) appeared in 1930, and was also successfully filmed, but the novel was never completed. A somewhat "archaic mechanizing" (Mirski) and a markedly subjective treatment of the historical figure of the novel, are counterbalanced by the fascinating panorama that Tolstoi here presents of a society in dissolution, a panorama in which many a historical experience of the author is reflected. The second volume of the novel appeared in 1934, and the third was begun in 1944, but remained a fragment because of the author's death (1945).

Tolstoi's works for the stage met with varied success. By 1912 he was known as an author of several comedies, but the Moscow Art Theater had to reject some of his plays. Altogether during his life Tolstoi wrote forty-two plays, but success came to him very gradually. Several times he was inspired by other authors. In *Danton's Death* (*Smert Dantona,* 1919), he imitated Georg Büchner, and in *The Revolt of the Machines* (*Bunt mashin,* 1924) he was influenced by Karel Čapek's visionary drama *R.U.R.*

Tolstoi's historical dramas became particularly well known. They include *The Plot of the Czarina* (*Zagovor imperatritzy,* 1924) and *Azef* (a play about the czarist provocateur of the same name, 1926), as well as a drama about Peter the Great, *On the Rack* (*Na dybe,* 1928–29).

## Olga Forsh

The frequent displacement of the immediate present by a contemplative return to the past led in the 1920s and 1930s to a large number of good historical novels. Examples include *Enclosed in Stone* (*Odety kamnem,* 1925) and *Contemporaries* (*Soveremenniki,*

1926) by Olga Forsh (born 1873). *Enclosed in Stone* describes in the revived memories of an old man the bitter lot of the revolutionaries in the 1860s. *Contemporaries*, on the other hand, is a novel that belongs to the very popular genre of the biographical literary-historical novels. In it, Olga Forsh comes to a confrontation with Gogol and his painter friend Aleksandr Ivanov.

Olga Forsh's self-ironic burlesque contemporary novel *The Insane Ship* (*Sumasshedshyi korabl*, 1931) is a description of the literary bohème of the postwar years in the Saint Petersburg House of Art. Later, basing her work on the postulates of socialist realism, the author turned to a literary figure of the eighteenth century in her trilogy *Radishchev* (1934–39).

### Yurii Tynyanov

A peculiar kind of structure, like that of a film, is revealed in the literary-historical novels of the researcher and literary theoretician Yurii Tynyanov (1894–1943). In his books, he presents the biography of the poet V. Kyukhelbeker (W. Küchelbecker) and the last years of the poet and diplomat Aleksandr Griboyedov. These two books are entitled *Kyukhlya* (a playful abbreviation of the name Kyukhelbeker, 1925) and *The Death of Wazir-Muchtar* (*Smert Vazir-Muchtar*, 1927–28); Wazir-Muchtar was the name given Griboyedov in Persia.)

The various narrative episodes alternate without any transition at all, and the pretense of a documentary is stressed by the selectivity and timeliness of the tone. A sympathetic understanding, supported by excellent factual knowledge of the era of the Dekabrista revolt and of the Russo-Turkish War of 1828–29, gives this work an unusual intellectual interest.

## ESCAPIST WRITING

An entirely different method of evading contemporary themes is revealed during the 1920s in the increase in adventure and detective stories of the greatest variety. The interest in English and American literature of this genre was so great that a Russian woman writer, Marietta Shaginyan (born 1888), published her novel of adventure *Mess-mend or a Yankee in Petrograd* (*Mess-mend, ili yanki v Petrograde*, 1924) under the ironic pseudonym of Jim Dollar. In 1927 the magazine *Ogonek* published an adventure novel of pure entertainment, its twenty-five chapters written by twenty-five different Soviet writers, among them Kaverin, Aleksei Tolstoi, Aleksandr Grin, and L. Leonov. It was entitled *Great Conflagrations* (*Bolshiye pozhary*).

This hunger of the Soviet reader for adventurous romance and exotic adventures was appeased in the 1920s especially by the experienced Aleksandr Grin (pseudonym of A. Grinevski, 1880–1923). For his fantastic stories, Grin even invented a place of action that he dubbed Grinland (Grinlandiya).

Grin's stories and novels are filled with the romance of seafaring, fairy tale-like encounters, and adventurous destinies. In several of the stories, critics thought they had discovered polemic discussions of the Bolshevist revolution (V. Zavalishin). There is no doubt that Grin's creative energies were not exhausted by the creation of purely entertaining literature.

A similar attitude appears in the works of Konstantin Paustovski (born 1892). In his stories, too, seafaring, and adventure play a dominant role, as shown in his early work *Sketches of the Sea* (*Morskiye nabroski*, 1925). Paustovski, who knew the port of Odessa, was greatly attracted by the romantic atmosphere of the Black Sea. Indeed, he called one of his best-known geographical-historical novels *The Black Sea* (*Chernoye more*, 1935).

Paustovski's role as a writer was not, of course, limited to these genres, but it is typical of him that his themes (adventure, exotic experiences, scientific discoveries, man's creative intervention in nature) led him far from the commonplace and from current political issues. In the 1930s Paustovski's predilection for documentary descriptions drew him to the genre of the historical and historical-biographical story, as in *The Fate of Charles Lonceville* (*Sud'ba Sharlya Lonsevilya*, 1932) and *Orest Kiprenskii* (1937).

## HUMOR AND EVERYDAY LIFE

The most lasting successes in describing the everyday life of Russia were attained primarily by those authors who, like Zoshchenko, treated their material humorously. Several writers made use of the apparently innocent narrative style of the humorous short story in the effort, on the one hand, to give reality its due and on the other not to expose themselves ideologically.

### Panteleimon Romanov

The humorous short story, such as Chekhov had cultivated, was revived by Panteleimon Romanov (1884–1938), who enjoyed great popularity in the 1920s; his most successful short stories appeared in 1927 in the volume *Beautiful Land (Khroshiye mesta)*. Here Romanov examines peasants and the bourgeois, and their comic helplessness in confronting the new demands of life.

In the years 1926–30 Romanov produced a number of stories and novels in which the relation of the sexes to one another, as well as modern family life, were described in polemic and satirical form. In such novels as *The New Table of the Law (Novaya skrizhal, 1928)* and *Comrade Kislyakov (Tovarishch Kislyakov, 1930)*, he presents a lively, unvarnished picture of Soviet everyday life. Romanov was less successful with his longer, never completed, contemporary panorama *Russia (Rus, 1923–26)*. Planned as a trilogy, this work never proceeded beyond the first part, which ended with the outbreak of World War I in 1914.

### Valentin Katayev

Valentin Katayev (born 1897) made a name for himself as the author of satirical, humorous stories and several successfully produced comedies of everyday life. His greatest success was the story *The Defrauders (Rastratchiki, 1927)*, in which the satirical description of the milieu is set against a background of adventure. Two employees of a Moscow trust company embezzle 12,000 rubles and begin a gay trip on which there is little more to do than spend the entire sum in as many ways as possible until they are seized by the law. Katayev fascinates the reader with the novel's thrilling action, the colorful pictures of manners and morals, and the lively narrative style.

After a novel on the assigned theme of the Five Year Plan— *Time Ahead* (*Vremya vpered*, 1932)—Katayev once more had success with an unproblematical work, the widely read novel *The White Sail Gleams* (*Beleyet parus odinoky*, 1936), the title of which is a quotation from a poem by Lermontov. In the center of the historical action, which is set in the Odessa of 1905, is a little boy whose childish point of view determines the plot to a large extent.

Katayev, who possessed a remarkable dramatic talent, not only adapted *The Defrauders* and *Time Ahead* for the stage but also produced very entertaining comedies like *Squaring of the Circle* (*Kvadratura Kruga*, 1928) and *The Flower Path* (*Doroga Tzvelov*, 1934), which deal with the lighter side of everyday problems: love, marriage, and the lack of housing.

## Mikhail Bulgakov

Mikhail Bulgakov (1891–1939) is the author of the controversial *The White Guard* (*Belaya gvadiya*, 1924), in which he dared to present the "white" troops fighting against the Revolution in a far more humane manner than usual. This caused Bulgakov to be relegated to a twilight position, although the dramatized version of the novel under the title of *The Days of Brother and Sister Turbinych*, (*Dni Turbinykh*, 1926) enjoyed a great success on the stage.

Gogol's grotesque humor is reflected in the satirical stories that Bulgakov published under the title of *Devil Haunting* (*Dyavoliada*, 1925). The stories have a fantastic or dreamlike background; real life appears usually in distorted form. The two longer stories in the collection are *Devil Haunting* and *The Fatal Eggs* (*Rokoviye yaitza*). On the surface, they are mysterious adventure stories. A shorter story, *The Adventures of Chichikov* (*Pochozhdeniya Chichikova*), is a kind of sequel to Gogol's *The Dead Souls* in which Chichikov, Gogol's protagonist, resumes his unsavory activities in the Soviet Union, thereby carrying out an improbable career for himself. He continues until he is apprehended by Bulgakov, who exposes the whole story as a dream. The moral that might be read into this amusing fantasy is that in Russia everything has remained as it was since the time of Gogol.

### Ilya Ilf and Yevgenii Petrov

Perhaps the most popular of the humorous, satirical novels of the 1920s, but which also possess literary merit, are the work of two co-authors. The novel *Twelve Chairs* (*Dvenadtzat stulyev*, 1928) was jointly written by Ilya Ilf (pseudonym of I. Fainzilberg, 1897–1937) and Yevgenii Petrov (pseudonym of Yevgenii Katayev, the brother of the author Valentin Katayev, 1903–42). This satirical, picaresque novel is based on an extraordinarily simple and conventional plot.

Primarily it is nothing more than a treasure hunt in which two rival groups chase after a diamond that an old lady has hidden in the upholstery of a chair during the disorders of the Revolution. Because the twelve chairs originally belonging to the set have been scattered to the four winds, the present location of all the chairs must be found and each one searched. The episodes of this adventure novel are simply strung along as on a thread, the search leading back and forth through Russia.

The merry treasure hunt, however, is only the external motivation for a picture of the manners and morals of the time. Soviet life during the NEP period (New Economic Policy, 1921–27) appears in all its confusing contradictions. The structure of the novel and the witty diction are borrowed from Gogol, to whom Russian prose of the first three decades of the twentieth century is immeasurably indebted. The relationship to Gogol is already apparent in the first sentences of the novel:

In the district town N., there were so many barber shops and funeral parlors that it seemed as if the inhabitants of the city were born only to be shaved and shorn, to let their heads be refreshed with Vegetal and then to die forthwith. But actually in the district town N., people were rarely born, shaved, or carried to their grave.

Typical of Gogol's marked influence are also the numerous witty digressions about the different expressions for the process of death, about the "alienation" of the traveler in railroad stations and on trains, about different kinds of stops and closing mechanisms on swinging doors, and many other things. The novel achieves a modern touch by the frequent acceleration in the description of the incidents, somewhat as in the silent motion picture, and through scenes described chiefly in a pantomimic style.

The hero of the story, the swindler and adventurer Ostap Bender, is fundamentally a "positive" scoundrel, an irrepressible rogue and quick-change artist. The authors were well advised when, despite his ignominious end in the *Twelve Chairs*, they later revived him in their new novel *The Golden Calf* (*Zolotoi telenok*, 1931). This second novel poses the following questions: "How is one to exist secretly as a millionaire under Soviet conditions?" and "What are the tragicomic consequences of the acquisition of a foreign million?" Here, too, the plot is spun out rather fantastically and leads, as in the *Twelve Chairs*, through many levels of Soviet society.

The last book jointly written by Ilf and Petrov was the gay report on their trip to America, which they published under the title of *One-Story America* (*Odnoetazhnaya Amerika*, 1936).

## PROLETARIAN WRITERS

The so-called "proletarian" or class-conscious writers did not appear in the foreground of literary life until 1923. Yevgenii Zamyatin, in his reflections on the *New Russian Prose* (*Novaya russkaya proza*), could still write in that year that not a single proletarian fiction writer had become part of literary history, not even through the back door: "Despite the creation of special incubators, one has not been able to hatch proletarian literature." Zamyatin also contended that one could not expect more from the *proletkult* associations than they were able to give: "Dogma, statistics, and agreement prevent anyone's being seized by that illness that is called art, least of all by its complex forms."

These ironic marginal comments point to one of the most delicate problems of Soviet literature: To what degree is it sound for literature, as art, to be put consciously in the service of politically controlled public instruction and information? Because, under the circumstances, this question can no longer be directly asked in the Soviet Union and even less answered in the unequivocal manner of Zamyatin, the discussion of many fundamental literary questions has not moved forward one step in Russia since the early 1920s.

It was not to take very long, however, until the concept of the "proletarian" novel did become a literary factor. The literature that had hitherto set the standard was accepted as a creation of the "fellow-travelers," that is, those writers (*popuchiki*) who were sympathetic to Communism.

### Dmitri Furmanov

A definitely class-conscious contribution to the literary depiction of the Civil War was supplied by Dmitrii Furmanov (1891–1926) and Aleksandr Fadeyev (1901–56). Furman, born in the Volga area, was not even of purely proletarian origin, but came from a peasant, bourgeois milieu. After finishing secondary school, he studied at the University of Saint Petersburg for several years. After a short interval as anarchist and pacifist, he joined the Communist Party in 1918 and took part in the Civil War as a political commissar. In 1923 he published his famous novel *Chapayev*, in which he showed his appreciation of the personality of the partisan leader Chapayev, in whose division he had served for a time.

In this novel Furmanov does not confine himself to the bare reality of the Civil War, but also gives his attention to the ideological education of his hero. Furmanov, to be sure, treats the political problems in a rather unorthodox manner, but the emphasis of the narrative is on the interpretation of characters and of events, no longer just on the happening per se.

Artistically, Furmanov was dissatisfied with his novel, as he admitted in a letter to Gorki (1925). However, *Chapayev*, because of its ideological thesis, is highly regarded in the Soviet Union as a classical work of an incipient proletarian realism.

## Aleksandr Fadeyev

Another successful book, written a few years later, was the novel of the Civil War with which Aleksandr Fadeyev made his name as a proletarian writer. With *The Defeat* (*Razgrom*, 1926–27), Fadeyev entered the first ranks of the pioneers of socialist realism; he later became its best-known exponent.

Fadeyev himself had taken part in the partisan war in the Far East, which forms the background for the action of his novel. Since his earliest youth, he had been acquainted with the life of the people in the area of Vladivostok; his father had settled there as a surgeon.

In his novel, Fadeyev proceeds from a psychological analysis of the characters; his descriptions, which are indebted to psychological realism, have been occasionally compared with those of Lev Tolstoi, as far as external form is concerned. The combination of psychological realism and political-party loyalty was later to be raised to the dogmatic concept of socialist realism. Fadeyev's enthusiasm for instruction is as clear in *The Defeat* as is his unshakable faith in the future and the goodness of man. He looks on the human problem chiefly as one of social backwardness. In one passage of the novel, he says:

> Levinson, if he had not been himself, would have been another if there had not been in him that powerful craving, not to be compared with any other wish, for the new, beautiful, strong, and good man. But how could one speak of a new, beautiful man, as long as countless millions were forced to eke out an antediluvian, wretched, unspeakably mean life?

## Fiodor Gladkov and the "Construction" Novel

Epoch-making for the genre of the "construction" novels, later so popular, is the novel *Cement* (*Tzement*) by Fiodor Gladkov (1883–1958), which appeared as early as 1925. The plot is concerned with the resumption of production in a cement factory on the Black Sea that had been closed during the Civil War.

In his novel, Gladkov tries to describe people who have made the transition into a new social order, experiencing the development of a new set of morals, and wrestling with severe conflicts. Gladkov makes no effort to beautify reality, but his effort to force the individual characters into a dialectical scheme often leads to peculiarly incongruous situations. The narrative effects, which remind one of the older school of Kuprin (*Molokh*) and L. Andreyev, are also greatly exaggerated and seem novel only at first glance. The luxuriating imagery of the language is in Gladkov's case actually an artificial adornment, as is his forced treatment of erotic themes reminiscent of prewar literature. From the literary point of view, Gladkov is in this regard still an imitator of decadence and of early modernism.

The real significance of the novel lies in the treatment of the social theme and in the pronounced party loyalty with which Gladkov places his characters in relation to the Revolution. The novel was intended to give answers to very definite questions that were of economic and political importance.

## SIX MAJOR FIGURES

### Ilya Ehrenburg

The work of the much admired and much denounced Ilya Ehrenburg (born 1891) occupies a special place in Soviet literature. Ehrenburg came from a well-to-do bourgeois family, grew up in Moscow, and turned his back on Russia at the age of eighteen.

From 1909 to 1917 he lived in Paris, where he led the life of a homeless bohemian and wrote poetry. He turned to prose only after he had gone through the years of the Revolution and the Civil War in Russia. In 1921 Ehrenburg again went on one of his many extended trips.

Ehrenburg achieved literary renown with the novel *Julio Jurenito* (*Neobychainiye pochozhdeniya Khulio Khurenito i yevo uchenikov*), which appeared in Berlin in 1922. Ehrenburg himself declared even after decades that he had never ceased to love this book, which he considered a kind of autobiography. The structure is that of the picaresque novel, but the style is satirical and mocking. In part it is also feuilletonistic, as suggested in the second half of the subtitle: ". . . also many different opinions of the master on pipes, on life and death, on freedom, on chess, on the Jewish people, and several other things."

The novel about the emotional cynic, anarchist, and agent provocateur Julio Jurenito, whose disciples belong to the most varied nations and races, is, according to its contents, a satirical encyclopedia of European civilization and a grotesque history of World War I and its consequences. Even today *Julio Jurenito* remains Ilya Ehrenburg's most revealing work, and one cannot appreciate the role that the writer plays in the Soviet Union without recalling that rogue and master of parodoxes, Julio Jurenito.

In this work, every national psychology is led *ad absurdum*, and parodistic passages soften the seriousness of the supporting action and of the historical reflections. The tragedy of Europe becomes a farce, and the apparent championing of high ideas turns into flippant conversation as soon as "master" Jurenito begins to speak. The interesting facet of the book is that Jurenito also feels himself repelled by Soviet reality. An agitator and an intelligent anarchist, he dislikes the double standard of morals of the authorities in the Soviet Union, and he misses the existence of a radical and honest profession of an examination of values. For Jurenito, the new power apparatus is a whip that has been "adorned with violets." Instead of idealistic terrorists, he finds only "hypocrites who drape the crater of Vesuvius."

Julio Jurenito is, however, a true existentialist. He decides, under the circumstances, to leave life, because his ideas are not acceptable in the land of the Revolution. His time has not yet come.

Ehrenburg, who proudly called himself a "Soviet citizen of Jewish nationality," deliberately chose the role of agitator and troublemaker. His literary work is devoted to the destruction of national egoism and nationalistic obsessions. Zamyatin was probably right when, in 1923, he called Ehrenburg a quasi "esperantist" writer.

Ehrenburg is the author of about a hundred books, which, however, for the most part are light literature. Neither is it likely that his documentary novels, clever and witty as they are, will obtain a lasting place in literature. Noteworthy, however, are his historical and contemporary miniatures, which are collected in a volume of stories entitled *Thirteen Pipes* (*Trinadtzat trubok*, 1923). Binding the anecdotes to the various pipes produces a pithy style of narration. The dance of the thirteen pipes spreads over continents and destinies; the pipe becomes the symbol of Ehrenburg's cosmopolitanism.

*The Visa of the Time* (*Viza vremeni*, Berlin, 1929) deserves special mention as a brilliant travel book, one that reveals Ehrenburg's keen powers of observation. It offers a vivid cross-section of the Europe of the 1920s from Paris to Istanbul, especially France, Germany, Poland, and Czechoslovakia. Here, too, Ehrenburg liberally supplies malicious comments and humorous comparisons, *e.g.*, "By its odor, Athens reminds one extraordinarily of our Russian city of Gomel."

It is characteristic that Ehrenburg's best books were published for the greater part by Russian publishers abroad. This is true, too, of the picaresque novel *The Stormy Life of Lazik Roytshvanetz* (*Burnaya Zhizn Lazika Roitshvanetza*, Berlin, 1929), little known in Russia. The hero, the poor little Jewish tailor from Gomel, dreams of "great justice," but is given the role of the agent provocateur, which he plays consistently but unwillingly. Roytshvanetz is the "pure fool," something like a Jewish Candide, who happens to turn up in Bolshevik Russia.

When Lazik succeeds in fleeing from Russia, he continues playing his role in the emigration. In Berlin, Paris, London, and other places, he gets into humiliating, shameful situations, sometimes even landing in jail. His long journey ends in Palestine, where, flayed and abused by life, he collapses at the grave of Rachel in Jerusalem. With their nonchalant cynicism, Ehrenburg's books repel many a reader. His flippancy can lead to unpleasant exaggerations, which are not uncommon in his works. One has to take into consideration, however, that Ehrenburg's manner is a kind of fool's cap and that behind his irreverence lies a concealed genuine emotion that gives life and poetic color to his style.

### Isaac Babel

In his *Comments on Present-Day Russian Literature* (*Randbemerkungen zur heutigen russischen Literature*, 1930), a critical study written in German, Ilya Ehrenburg links Isaac Babel to Pasternak and Zamyatin as examples of Russian writers who could claim a permanent place in European literature. This association is neither accidental nor unfounded. In addition, contrary to the official view adopted in the Soviet Union, it is not because of the sensational aspects attached to their work that the West looks on these writers as representative of the epoch.

Isaac Babel (1894–1941), the son of a Jewish merchant, was born in Odessa, the city that was once called the "Russian Marseilles." His upbringing was in accordance with strict Jewish orthodoxy, but when he was still quite young he learned to read French, as well as Hebrew. In later years, Babel was to remember his parental home as "filled with the smell of onions and Jewish destiny." As a child, Babel's curiosity and lively imagination compelled him to ferret out hidden aspects of life in the port of Odessa. Because of his intelligence he was also able to penetrate effortlessly into the world of books. The works of Guy de Maupassant were a revelation to him.

Babel's first stories were published in 1916 in Gorki's monthly *Letopis* (1915–17), and he took to heart Gorki's advice to work harder and not to rely on his initial success. In the following years, Babel was caught up in the turmoil of the Revolution and the Civil War, and it was not until 1923 and 1924 that his name began appearing in the new journals *Krasnaya Nov* and *Lef*.

Service in General Budennyi's red cavalry and participation in the 1920 campaign against the Poles were decisive experiences for Babel. From the diary notes collected during this period evolved the stories that were to appear in their final form under the collective title *Red Cavalry* (*Konarmiya*, 1926). Several of the cavalry tales had first appeared in magazines along with stories of the cycle that makes up *Tales of Odessa* (*Odesskiye rasskazy*), which also appeared in book form in 1926.

The cavalry and Odessa cycles share characteristics in form and language. They consist of short stories and vignettes that illuminate a specific geographical and historical background. Each cycle is woven around a fixed set of characters.

Babel's stories focus on selected archetypal symbols, psychological motives frequently appearing only on the periphery. Striking images and loud colors that recall expressionist painting are used to make points of emphasis. Man's animal nature is stressed, and the mechanisms that control it are shown to be involved even in acts of heroism. Although Babel does not treat the mounted Cossacks or their Polish enemy as heroes, they are not seen as conventional criminals, because they act in accordance with the laws that obtain in war.

Babel never pushes his animalistic theme to the point of reducing human factors to pure instinctual forces. As a matter of fact, primitive actions appear in his stories as important and complicated rituals. It is, of course, no accident that Babel chose as the setting for his stories human communities narrowly dependent on one another and functioning under intensified group demands, *i.e.*, the soldiers in *Red Cavalry* and the underworld figures of Odessa in *Tales of Odessa*.

In this respect the narrator's point of view is significant in some of the cavalry tales. For the narrator, the world he depicts is really a foreign world to which he feels drawn but to which he cannot belong either intellectually or physically. This dichotomy gives the stories their inner tension and contrasting coloration. The solidarity of the Cossack army is highlighted by the fact that the narrator, known as "four-eyes" to the frontline soldiers (Babel wore glasses), has to sweat and strain to break into the charmed circle of their natural society. The fantastic events of the war remain in the narrator's consciousness as an enigma that converts him into a passive, brooding being:

I had lost all courage and walked further and further, bent under the crown dark as the grave [*i.e.*, the night]. I pleaded with destiny to give me the simplest of all abilities, the ability to kill a man.

The Russians, like the Poles, swear, murder, and rape, their outward behavior ignoring conventional morality. But inwardly they live according to their own strict law and adhere to a code of honor. It is this fantastic aspect of wartime reality, a reality inaccessible to conventional modes of understanding, that Babel wanted to depict. By focusing on the "distortions" of ordinary life, he was able to solve a difficult artistic problem. The picture of man painted in his tales corresponds to the deliberate distortions found in the "blasphemous" pictures of Pan Apolek's paintings of saints, which Babel describes so lovingly in *In St. Valentine's Church* (*U svyatavo Valentina*).

Babel's Cossack heroes have their analogue in the underworld heroes and bandits whose "king" in the *Tales of Odessa* is the young and cunning Benya Krik. Preoccupied with the figure of the Jewish gang leader from Odessa's Moldavanka ghetto, Babel created Krik's counterpart in the cavalry cycle with Ilya, the rabbi's son, whom the narrator calls the "last prince" and whose few possessions he rummages through after the boy's death: "They fell upon me in a mean and depressing rain—pages of the *Song of Songs* and revolver cartridges."

Babel spent his youth in the Moldavanka Jewish quarter, and it was as familiar to him as the Ukrainian and Galician villages that form the impressive backdrop of the Cossack army's campaign. He draws on his younger years in his autobiographical stories *In the Basement* (*V podvale*, 1931) and *Awakening* (*Probuzhdeniye*, 1932). Some of the figures in these autobiographical sketches also appear in the bandit stories *The King* (*Korol*, 1923), *A Father* (*Otetz*, 1924), *How It Was Done in Odessa* (*Kak eto delalos v Odesse*, 1923), and *Liubka the Cossack* (*Lyubka Kazak*, 1924).

With great artistic skill, Babel depicts the vanished colorful life of a port that opens on the world. Emphasizing the exotic elements, he employs a variety of telling metaphors: "A red watermelon with black seeds, seeds as slanting as the eyes of crafty Chinese girls." In the Odessa cycle as in the cavalry cycle he shows a special predilection for the dazzling colors of the sun and of flesh in all their nuances—pink, raspberry red, carmine, reddish brown, orange, and yellow. His preferred color spectrum recalls the early stories of Gogol, with whom he shared an ability to create lush, oriental images. Animal references are common in Babel; the sun is described as hanging from the sky like "the rosy tongue of a thirsty dog"; pregnant women sitting together on a bench in the evening "fill themselves with all kinds of mixed news, as the udder of a cow in the meadow is filled with the rosy milk of spring." Undertones of imagist poetry can sometimes be found in Babel's work.

Like most Soviet writers of the 1920s and 1930s Babel was confronted by the deep chasm that separated the Revolution from traditional Russian ways. Because of this gulf Jewish traditions had also become anachronistic. In such stories as *The End of the Old Folks' Home* (*Konetz bogadelni*, 1932) and *Karl-Yankel* (1932), Babel has vividly described the tragicomic consequences of the clash between old habits and the new social order.

Babel's family had settled in France, and in 1932–33 he joined them for some time. From this period dates the story *Dante Street* (*Ulitza Dante*, 1932), Babel's homage to Paris. Many of his manuscripts of the 1930s remained unpublished. Among them was a novel, the first part of which only appeared in a magazine in 1931 as *Gapa Guzhva*.

In his plays *Sunset* (*Zakat*, 1928) and *Maria* (*Mariya*, 1935) Babel provides in dramatic form brilliant milieu studies of the dissolution of traditional social standards. *Sunset* centers on the family of Mendel Krik, the drayman whose son Benya was previously introduced as the underworld king in *Tales of Odessa*. *Maria* contains interesting discussions of the role in Russia of the Jews, the "wonderful people" that produced "Heine, Spinoza, and Christ." Jewish themes are woven into all of Isaac Babel's work.

In the 1930s Babel grew increasingly antagonistic to the dominant, official concepts of art and had to resign himself to silence. He was arrested in 1939 and nothing is known of his fate. It was not until the mid-1950s that official sources acknowledged that he had been a victim of the Stalinist purges and Babel was to some extent "rehabilitated."

## Boris Pilnyak

An extensive and stylistically versatile body of prose was left posthumously by Boris Pilnyak (pseudonym of B. Vogau, 1894–1938?), who, like Babel, became a victim of political persecution. Pilnyak was the son of a veterinarian of Volga-German descent and spent his youth in several provincial towns near Moscow, which he later described affectionately. Pilnyak's first works were published before the Revolution, although he really became known with his novel *The Bare Year* (*Golyi god*, 1922).

From the beginning, Pilnyak was enthusiastic about literary experimentation, finding his stylistic models, among others, in Belyi and Remizov. His theme is the cultural-philosophical interpretation of the Revolution, which he, like the followers of the "Scythians" movement, understood as the expression of a truth on two levels— a truth the two sides of which are Europe and Asia. As a romantic anarchist, he tried to recognize in the great process of fermentation that had seized Russia the features of a primitive and "national" revolt in which the historically developed, unique character would assert itself against the rationalism of the "Western" currents.

In this way Pilnyak became, in his Slavophile-romantic interpretation of history, the poet of dying Russia and the archeologist of a vanishing culture, despite his purely sentimental affirmation of the Revolution.

The novel *The Bare Year* contains all the elements typical of Pilnyak. The rhapsodic chronicle of the year 1919 depicts Russia shaken by hunger, fever, and terror, and shows how the scales of history incline now to one side, now to the other. The finale consists of the memories of a country wedding, and here Pilnyak presents the face of Russia that seemed to tell him a purer truth than the face formed by the Communists in leather jackets:

> The wedding will be celebrated at the "black streams" according to the canon of the centuries like a liturgy, in the thatch-roofed peasant huts, under sheds, in the street, in the fields, in the woods, in the snowstorms, during the day and at night. It resounds in song and the beating of drums, it slinks around like an intoxicating

drink, it is gaily painted and brightly colored like a new ridge pole, in evenings as blue as the paper of sweets.

*The Bare Year* can be characterized as a literary experiment because in it a loose series of episodes replaces a consistent novel-like plot. The combining element is above all linguistic and stylistic; it consists of leitmotifs, stereotyped narrative segments, and certain symbolic-metaphorical passages referring to one another. Several chapters are provided by Pilnyak with the subtitle "triptychon," and the reciprocal relationships of the various scenes is thereby placed in a metaphorical correlation of symbols.

Pilnyak's poetic-ornamental language is given such a marked personal coloring that all the characters that appear are infected by it. Only in a later phase is Pilnyak successful in creating individual and typical characters with their own life and environment. In the early period, Pilnyak deliberately waives the attempt to create live characters; his style of presentation is strictly monological.

Characteristic of Pilnyak's frequently difficult scheme of composition is the novel *Machines and Wolves* (*Mashiny i volki*, 1925), which is thematically and stylistically derivative of *The Bare Year* and even contains numerous quotations from the earlier novel. In fact, Pilnyak liked to transpose entire segments from one work into another, sometimes with variations, sometimes unchanged. Pilnyak provided for such ease of transposition through the stereotyped character of his metaphors and through his epic syntax, which occasionally turned into interior monologue.

In *Machines and Wolves* the tendency toward the interior monologue is even stronger than in *The Bare Year*, and the narrative language manifests all the peculiarities of the uninterrupted stream of consciousness, as it appears in Belyi, James Joyce, or Alfred Döblin. The preference for the Russian of the seventeenth and eighteenth centuries is revealed (as in Remizov) by the historical digressions and the documentary notes that Pilnyak slips into his monologues, such as news clippings, posters, folkloristic texts, or statistical information.

The transition to a form of composition involving more action is made in tales like *The Tale of the Unextinguished Moon* (*Povest nepogashennoi luny*, 1926) and *Ivan-Moskva* (1927). The former tells of a well-known general of the Red Army who is forced to undergo an operation that causes his death, through the assistance of the doctors. The writer's clear reference to General Frunze's fate was not forgiven, and Pilnyak's public image further declined when he published the story *Mahogony* (*Krasnoye derevo*) with the Berlin Petropolis Publishing House in 1929.

In *Mahogony*, Pilnyak again returns to his old cultural-philosophical theme and shows how disappointed hopes are reflected in the consciousness of the inhabitants of a small city at the upper Volga that Pilnyak calls "the Russian Bruges." The symbol for the end of the prevailing historical period is represented in the story by the "dying" of the bells, which are needed for the building up of industry and which tumble down from the church tower with a dull rumble.

The real heroes of the story *Mahogony* are foolish eccentrics, disappointed revolutionaries, and political sectarians. In them, Pilnyak sees the continuity of Russian history:

> Mendicant friars, collectors of alms, clairvoyants, street singers, beggars, pilgrims, the poor in spirit, cripples, prophets, fools "in Christ"—all these are the trimmings of the mentality of Holy Russia, which is sunk in eternity, beggars in Holy Russia, fools of Holy Russia for the sake of Christ.

Pilnyak tried unsuccessfully to reestablish his public prestige with the novel *The Volga Flows into the Caspian Sea* (*Volga vpadayet v Kaspiiskoye more*, 1930). Even the theme of the industrialization of Russia could not save Pilnyak from further isolation. Furthermore, considerable portions of *Mahogony* had been worked into the new novel, and the sympathy of Pilnyak for those standing in lost positions was not sufficiently concealed. In the 1930s Pilnyak remained a barely tolerated writer, and after 1936, during the years of the purges, he disappeared. Nothing definite is known about the circumstances of his arrest and his death.

Pilnyak's numerous novellas and shorter stories fill several volumes of his collected works, which were printed in 1929–30 (eight volumes). Most impressive of all are perhaps the stories collected in the volume *Simple Stories* (*Prostyye rasskazy*), especially those of the years 1925–28, *e.g. The City of the Winds* (*Gorod vetrov*, 1928).

## Leonid Leonov

One of the most gifted novelists and one who is already classified as a classical writer of the 1920s, when there was so much literary activity, is certainly Leonid Leonov (born 1899 in Moscow). Coming from an intelligent peasant family, Leonov grew up largely in Moscow, but also spent some time in the country. He completed the course at the Moscow Gymnasium and served in the Red Army, where, among other things, he was active on the soldiers' newspaper.

Leonov's first works appeared entirely in bourgeois publishing houses and in non-Communist almanacs (1922–23). Not until 1924 did Leonov became a co-worker on the journal *Krasnaya Nov*. His first literary work, the promising, fairy-tale-like story *Buryga* (1922) was printed in the almanac *Shipovnik*, edited by Fiodor Stepun, shortly before his emigration. The early stories give clear evidence of the stylistic versatility of the author, because they realize the efforts of the young writers of this generation to escape the prewar realism (Gorki, Kuprin, and L. Andreyev) by drawing on other styles of narration. Leonov not only attempted the typical *skaz* of the older Russian tradition, as in *Kovyakin's Notes* (*Zapiski Kovyakina*, 1924) but also experimented with the fairy tale in the style of Hans Christian Andersen. Examples of this are *Valya's Doll* (*Valina kukla*, 1923), the oriental story *Tuatamur* (1924), and the romantic, fantastic stories *The Wooden Queen* (*Derevyannaya koroleva*, 1923) and *Yegorushka's Downfall* (*Gibel Yegorushki*, 1924).

Evidence of the deep spiritual debt to Dostoyevski can be found in the story *The End of the Little Man* (*Konetz melkovo cheloveka*, 1923). The tormenting experiences and dream fantasies of the shy Fiodor Andreich Licharov, "professor of erstwhile sciences," recall the most depressing scenes in Dostoyevski's *The Double*. The background is formed by the decaying, one-time Saint Petersburg, which threatened to change into a "desert" through the privations of the postwar period. In the rather long narrative, Leonov for the first time shows his gift for psychological portrayal; *The End of the Little Man* is the first step toward the novel.

*The Badgers* (*Barsuki*, 1924), a novel that Leonov wrote soon thereafter, is devoted to the psychology of a peasant rebel who has not lost his love for the land even after his contacts with life in the city. After the Revolution, he organizes a peasant revolt against the Soviet power. The novel in three parts shows a complicated structure, which in general is typical of Leonov. His narrative style is adjusted to a many-sided plot; the various short scenes change rapidly between the different loci of action. At intervals, Leonov presents longer epic transitions—descriptions of landscapes. Even a number of novellas are introduced into the plot.

Leonov's style is realistic, but he skillfully evades all traditional clichés. He makes no exaggerated use of metaphors although he does not avoid images. Describing life in the oldest quiet business streets of Moscow, where the action of the first part is set, Leonov writes:

> Dull and stately, as under the currents of a big stream. Only the sociable cooing of the doves, only the whimpering whining of a street organ, only the tolling of the evening bells, peaceful and snow-covered. Life here resembles a slow wheel, but every spoke is for itself.

In his novels, Leonov gives a rather objective picture of the environment. The social conflicts, which in many instances cut across familiar and general human conflicts, are not simplified for the sake of a doctrine. They maintain their sense even beyond the historical circumstances. The victory of order over the anarchic greed of the peasants lies in the logic of the narrative and signifies no devaluation of the feelings of these human beings harassed by the state.

A far-reaching description of social and human problems during the period of the NEP is presented by Leonov in his novel *The Thief* (*Vor*, 1927). He defends the belief in a better future under socialism, but does not gloss over the dreary conditions of the present. This is probably the best description in the entire Soviet literature of the mid-1920s in which *The Thief* is set.

*The Thief* is the novel of the city of Moscow, the metropolis on whose middle and lower social strata (petit bourgeois, mechanics, artists, and thieves) Leonov focuses. Leonov's model again is Dostoyevski, in this case, however, less with reference to the manner of description than to the different characters and their relation to one another. The thief Mitya Vekshin, who became a criminal because of hurt pride and disappointments, is the central figure in a whole whirl of happenings. He combines the traits of Raskolnikov and of Mitya Karamazov. Leonov sees social significance in the fact that Mitya, a former commissar in the Red Army, unable to realize his romantic dreams in the everyday reality of the NEP period, becomes part of the underworld because of this disillusionment.

In Leonov's view, the lovelessness engendered by the Revolution is to blame for Mitya's fall:

> In those years, one fought for the great achievements of mankind and thought little of the human beings themselves. A great love, spread equally over all, does not offer the individual more warmth than a wax taper.

Leonov extends the psychological problem in *The Thief* to a problem of literature in general. The key figure is the writer Firsov, who writes a "novel within a novel," a novel about Mitya, whose former and present life he examines in detail. Leonov occasionally alludes to the conditions with which literature had to contend in the Soviet Union:

> One should look at monumental structures only from the distance. For the time being, therefore, one should today only note the facts, but not comment on them. . . . (Firsov) only sketched a little house with grilled windows. It is clear that his thoughts went in two directions.

Mitya, however, is not yet lost for a better future, according to Leonov. "Mitka's forehead is bright and mutinous," Firsov writes in one of his notes. The ideological chastening of the thief is indicated at the close of the novel.

In the following novels, which came closer to the tendency of socialist realism, Leonov sought to differentiate his characters and to give them lifelike human contours. In *The Thief*, he had placed these words in the mouth of the writer Firsov:

> Man does not exist in pure culture, but, so to speak—in the ornament! (That is, from my point of view, something like a curtain, or perhaps false gold, a necktie pattern, the manner of holding a cigarette, the style of one's thoughts, family tradition, the level of culture. . . .) Man without ornament is naked.

With the novel *Sot* (1930), Leonov kept the promise that he had given at the close of *The Thief*. *Sot* is a novel of industrial construction, and here Leonov, for the first time by his own admission, attempted to present a picture of the "collective soul." The building of a paper factory in a distant wooded region of Russia is, however, not the sole theme of this book. Technical and social progress find their opposition not only in the lassitude of Russian character, but also in the antagonistic attitude of the monks of an old monastery, who have been startled out of their peaceful existence. The variegated resistance of "dark" Russia to the construction of a new life is given expression here.

As least successful we must consider Leonov's second industrial novel, *Skutarevshi*, which was published in 1932. Here he solves from a purely ideological viewpoint the then much discussed and immediate problem of the spiritual reeducation of the prerevolutionary intelligentsia.

A long and literarily pretentious novel is *The Way to the Ocean* (*Doroga na okean*, 1935), in which Leonov tries to maintain the narrative on different time levels. A historical and a utopian plot accompany and reflect on the contemporary story, which is determined by the political and human problems of the railroad commissioner Kurilov.

Although Leonov's narrative art degenerated more and more in the 1930s to that of an applied art, his psychological style stands out impressively from the contemporary works of pure commentary or propaganda that were the result of the official literary fiat.

### Yurii Olesha

The work of Yurii Olesha (1899–1960), who wrote almost as prolifically as Leonov or Pilnyak, is distinguished by a subtle artistic observation. Born in the Ukraine, Olesha grew up in Odessa, the city that was to give modern Russian literature so many of its outstanding talents—Babel, Valentin Katayev, Ilf, Petrov, and Eduard Bagritzki, among others. In 1927 the publication of his novel *Envy*

*The Interwar Period*

(*Zavist*) immediately established his reputation as one of the fore-most Soviet writers.

*Envy* focuses on the antagonism between a vigorous but wholly Philistine government functionary, Food Commissar Andrei Babi-chev, and his nonconformist brother, Ivan, who lives in a fantasy world, dreaming of a "conspiracy of feelings" against the soulless rhythm of the materialistic, workaday world. Between these two figures stands the novel's hero, Nikolai Kavalerov, Andrei's protégé. A bright intellectual, Kavalerov hates Andrei because of the latter's superior physical strength. Reacting similarly to the provocations of Andrei, Kavalerov and Ivan join in a conspiracy against the com-missar's complacent self-assurance.

The action of the novel develops from this situation, and the story ends with the ignominious defeat of the two "softer" protagonists. The first part of the novel presents Andrei and Ivan as they exist in Kavalerov's imagination. In Kavalerov's interior monologue An-drei is observed with "jealous" eyes and assumes superhuman pro-portions.

In his incisive descriptions of states of consciousness, Olesha uses an art in which a peculiar optical slant draws everything under its spell. Isolated objects have a tendency to free themselves from their moorings, as if gliding about in a dream, and swell the corners of consciousness. In this aspect of his art, Olesha is close to French surrealism and its related movements. The French influence on his writing is also revealed by a significant reference in one of his novellas to the psychology of Henri Bergson.

In Olesha's descriptions of consciousness, an effort is made to shift close attention from objective perception of the thing being observed and to merge with the object itself, so that the object becomes an experience. The physical appearance of the different figures and the details relating to them are of decisive importance. For example, of Andrei Babichev it is said ironically: "On the metallic disks of his suspenders the sun concentrated in two glowing bundles; things are fond of him."

Olesha devoted an entirely programmatic story, *The Cherry Stone* (*Vishnevaya kostochka*, 1930), to the problem of inner artistic perception. In it the origin of poetic vision is described in detail

from different points of view. The cherry pit, buried in a large building lot, is not only a souvenir of an unrequited love but a symbol
of the secret powers of imagination, which even in the midst of
technical construction can grow and bloom, just as a cherry tree
will spring up from a tiny pit.

Similar concerns are reflected in Olesha's various autobiographical
fragments and short stories of the years 1928–31. The novel *The
Three Fat Men* (*Tri tolstyaka*), set in the realm of the imagination,
was written in 1924 but not published until 1928. In it Olesha especially addresses himself to young readers and offers a colorful and
adventurous plot rich in fantasy.

Olesha also proved his skill as a dramatist, his best-known work
being *The List of Good Deeds* (*Spisok blagodeyanii*, 1931). The
critic Gleb Struve has characterized the play as an "inner dialogue,"
and in fact the outward action is subordinate to the development
of artistic consciousness in the play's principal character, the actress
Goncharova.

The drama contains many literary allusions that point up Olesha's
themes. Goncharova, converted to the cause of Communism only
after some implausible events during her stay in Paris, achieves her
greatest triumph by playing Hamlet. She particularly admires the
movie actor Charlie Chaplin, and the play anticipates Olesha's comparison of Chaplin with Denmark's Hans Christian Andersen—
*Thoughts About Chaplin* (*Mysli o Chapline*, 1936)—by using
themes from Andersen's fairy tale *The Ugly Duckling*.

For many years, Olesha's name was not mentioned in the Soviet
press, but he was "rehabilitated" some time after Stalin's death, and
a selection of his work—*The List of Good Deeds* was omitted—was
reprinted in 1956.


### Mikhail Sholokhov


As an outstanding representative of the so-called "proletarian"
current in literature, Mikhail Sholokhov (born 1905) moved into
the front ranks of Soviet writers in the second half of the 1920s.

Sholokhov was born in a province at the lower end of the Don River. His mother was a simple peasant, his father the son of a merchant whose family had originally come from Russia. Sholokhov belonged to that generation that had not experienced the war and the Civil War. His family sent him in 1915 to the gymnasium, first to Moscow, then to the vicinity of Voronezh, from which he returned in 1918 to his parental home after having half completed his studies. Young Sholokhov lived on the Don for two years under the rule of the Whites, then under the rule of the Reds, before he went to Moscow in 1922. There he became a simple workman. In 1923 he published his first literary contributions in Communist juvenile journals.

Two years later, Sholokhov returned to the Don, where he began to work seriously at his literary style and where he wrote *The Tales of the Don* (*Donskiye rasskazy*), published in Moscow in 1926. In these stories Sholokhov describes the life of the Cossacks and the adventurous circumstances that the Civil War produced in his homeland.

Sholokhov's further literary activity remained linked to the Don. In 1926 he conceived the idea of a great epic work of Cossack life, and in 1928 he produced the first volume of his famous novel *The Silent Don* (*Tikhii Don*), which is today ranked among the classic works of Soviet literature.

In the treatment of historical material, Sholokhov is a representative of the conservative trend, and in comparison with Pilnyak and Babel he does not seem exactly an avant-gardist. The greatest influence on his work came undoubtedly from Lev Tolstoi and Maksim Gorki, two writers who, for their part, stood on entirely different levels. From Tolstoi, Sholokhov borrowed the form of the historical epic; reminiscent of Gorki are the crassness of the descriptions and the easily responsive psychology despite much volubility.

The first retrospective volume of the novel was followed in the same year (1928) with a second book, in which the events up to the year 1918 are described. The third book appeared in magazine form in the years 1929–32. Its completion was delayed by Sholokhov's work on a novel about the collectivization of agriculture—*Seeds of Tomorrow* (*Posnyataya tzelina*, 1931). In 1938–40 both parts of the last book were issued, in which the fate of the Cossack Grigori Melekhov is slightly changed.

*The Silent Don* is, internally, a rather disjunct novel. One gets the impression that Sholokhov's political attitude is hardly able to adjust itself to the compelling and elementary motifs that penetrate the story as a "super-historical" power. Ideologically, Sholokhov is on the side of the new "red" might, but with his heart on the side of the "epic" Cossack character, which is not ready to submit to the strange new order without a struggle. Grigori Melekhov represents the primitive, strong Cossack element that has been crowded out of its normal course by historical events. He resists the patriarchal way of life of his ancestors as well as Sovietization, which is inwardly foreign to him. His personal idea of life and freedom cannot be brought into harmony with historical reality; he becomes a rebel against history.

The historical outlines and the subconscious elements that break through are in sharp contrast to one another (Mirski). The way out, which only Sholokhov could select, in order to save the victory of history, was the disgrace of his hero. In his premature collapse, Grigori Melekhov is very similar to Gorki's Foma Gordeyev. Both were born at the wrong historical moment, and both must accept the failure of life in view of the social order.

Grigori, in logical accord with his point of view, finally fights on the side of the Whites and, at the end, even in the ranks of a band that slowly continues guerrilla warfare into which the struggle has turned. Only when Grigori's physical resistance has been broken does he return, (at the close of the novel) to his native village. At the end, he is by no means chastened, only beaten.

With the local color of the lusty life of the Don Cossacks, Sholokhov without question created an effective literary frame, which largely explains the attraction that this novel exerted and still exerts on its readers. Artistically, however, the novel can at no point be compared with *War and Peace*, because the panorama is developed far more on the surface than in depth.

Sholokhov's second novel, *Seeds of Tomorrow*, is convincing as a documentary. It discusses the unmerciful collective measures that in the course of the Five Year Plan made incisive changes in the structure of agriculture in the Don region.

Sholokhov, who undoubtedly identified himself with the will of the party in this instance, too, maintained the distance and objectivity of the epic writer. Sholokhov's avoidance of timid opportunism later secured for him the uncontested reputation of a moral authority.

# Developments in Poetry

During the period from the end of the Civil War until the outbreak of World War II, the course of poetic expression in Rússia was far less tempestuous than in the two decades preceding. The spiritual, ideological latitude was considerably narrowed, and the formal devices in general show only a more or less skillful variation of what had been hitherto attempted.

The still-surviving representatives of symbolism, of acmeism, or of similar currents were either silenced rather soon (Sologub, Kuzmin, Akhmatova, and Mandelstamm) or chose exile (Ivanov, Tzvetayeva, Khodasevich, and others). On his return to the Soviet Union Andrei Belyi produced only prose works. Only Bryusov experimented with a new mingling of symbolist and futurist style devices in his last volumes of poetry, which manifested a stress on socialist themes, *Distances* (*Dali*, 1922) and *Mea* (1924).

Yesenin has been discussed in a previous section; he died in 1925. Velemir Khlebnikov, the spiritus rector of the futurists, died in 1922. Of the poets who had drawn much attention to themselves before the Revolution, only Mayakovski, Pasternak, and Aseyev were destined to play a role for a longer time.

## FUTURISTS

The followers of futurism, among them also theoreticians and critics like Osip Brik and Nikolai Chuzhak, united after the Civil War in an independent front, which they called *Lef* (*Levy front iskusstv*—Left Front of the Arts). Under the title *Lef*, there even appeared during the years 1923–25 a special journal edited by Mayakovski. The group to which especially the poets Mayakovski, Aseyev, and Sergei Tretyakov (born 1892) belonged, and to which Pasternak, too, was close for a while, soon fell into conflict with the official political dictates on art through its rejection of realism. They just barely eked out an existence on the officially tolerated periphery. Even the renewed getting together (*Novyi Lef*) in 1927 could not obviate the fact that the Front had finally played out its role.

With that, the era of the politically engaged and pro-Soviet futurism was practically over. Interestingly, this period coincides with the drives against "formalism" in prose and in literary criticism. There was an analogous development in the fine arts and on the stage, which clearly indicates the conscious directing of the entire campaign.

In the case of Mayakovski, political themes are definitely dominant between 1923 and 1930, the year of his death. A difference of genre, however, continues to be maintained between the satirical, light, occasional verses, and the heroic "poems." To the last group belongs especially the narrative in verse *Vladimir Ilyich Lenin* (1924) and the rhapsodic chronicle *Beautiful!* (*Khorosho!*, 1927) with the original title of *Oktober* (*Oktyabr*), which was intended for the tenth-year celebration of the October Revolution, as well as the fragment *Roaring with Laughter* (*Vo ves golos*, 1930).

To the formal achievements of his earlier poems Mayakovski adds hardly anything new. His extremely free rhyme technique, his special poetic syntax, and the rhythmic sequence in stages are now put entirely into the service of agitation and revolutionary aims.

### Nikolai Aseyev

Like Mayakovski, Nikolai Aseyev (born 1889) seeks a visualization of a bridge between the "formal" revolution of futurism and the revolutionary reality of the 1920s. Of all the Russian poets,

Aseyev came closest to the style of Mayakovski, whom he had studied in detail. Aseyev was even superior to Mayakovski as a theoretician, for example, in *Diary of a Poet* (*Dnevnik poeta*, 1929). His discussion of rhyme, melody, and intonation shows an alert critical sense and a genuine theoretical talent.

Before the Revolution, Aseyev, along with Pasternak, had belonged to the group "Tzentrifuga"; his early poems were essentially outside of futurism, at least thematically. Aseyev made contact with revolutionary futurism through his volume of verse *The Bomb* (*Bomba*, 1921), which appeared in Vladivostok. There in the Far East, together with David Burlyuk and Sergei Tretyakov, during the first years after the Revolution, Aseyev belonged to a very lively branch of futurism, exerting its influence for a time from the periphery.

After Aseyev had settled in Moscow, he appeared before the public with the little volume *The Steel Nightingale* (*Stalnoi solovei*, 1922), with a narrative in verse about Budennyi (*Budennyi*, 1922), and with a selection of his poems of the years 1912–22, *Selections* (*Izbran*, 1923).

The heroic themes of the years of the Revolution and the Civil War were followed in part by poems critical of the times, some of them glorifying the technology of the period of the NEP. Significant for this epoch are especially the stories in verse of the mid-1920s, for example, *Lyrical Digression* (*Liricheskoye otstupleniye*), *The Fire* (*Ogon*), and *Elektriada*. A special position is occupied by Aseyev's verse ballad *The Black Prince* (*Cherny printz*, before 1925), in which a piece of very artistically woven musical elements is analyzed in its smallest units of verse, corresponding to the arbitrary syntactic structure. The subject of this narrative is the fate of the English vessel, allegedly loaded with gold, that was sunk (1854) during the Crimean War in the bay of Balaklava. The same theme, incidentally, is also used in Zoshchenko's later story *The Black Prince*. The later volumes of Aseyev's verse, from *Thunder Against Marble* (*Gromy o mramor*, 1926) to *Renewal* (*Obnova*, 1934), use the unheroic themes of everyday. They do, however, contain poems of purely feuilletonistic character or that paraphrase political shibboleths.

## Boris Pasternak

Boris Pasternak devoted himself to the genre of the verse narrative (*poema*), which, during the 1920s, had been given greater prestige by the futurists. His epic poems dealing with the history of the Revolution, *The Year 1905* (*Devyatsot pyaty god*) and *Lieutenant Schmidt* (*Leytenant Shmidt*), appeared in 1927. A more intimate tone is manifested in the story *Spektorski* (1931; fragments as far back as 1925), originally intended as a novel in verse, in which Pasternak obviously attempted to place a modern counterpart at the side of Pushkin's lyrically ironic novel *Yevgenii Onegin*. The individual scenes, however, remained fragmentary. The charm of the "poem" lies above all in the personal reflections and memories of the narrator. Pasternak has here brought together poetic description and ironic commentary on the basis of a double scheme.

With the publication of his volume of verse *The Second Birth* (*Vtoroye rozhdeniye*, 1932), Pasternak shows at the beginning of the 1930s that he is a mature and self-assured poet who had no intention of joining any movement. The new poems as a whole possess a simplicity and naturalness that Pasternak himself characterized as "heresy." This is expressed, possibly, in verses such as the following:

> The surge roars and without a change
> One wave goes down after the other,
> And the foam washes their traces away
> From the hills of sand, like graphic symbols.

## Nikolai Zabolotzki

A final offshoot of Russian futurism can be seen in the works of the gifted Nikolai Zabolotzki (1903–58). His first collected poems appeared in 1929 under the title of *Columns* (*Stolbtzi*) and caused quite a sensation among the critics, who condemned Zabolotzki severely.

Zabolotzki's poems, which tend to assume a mocking, ironic tone, teem with nonsensical comparisons and farcical metaphors that are reminiscent of the painting of the primitives (Struve). The powerful language, tending toward word play and surprising harmonies of sound, suggests a relationship with Velemir Khlebnikov, to whom Zabolotzki felt a strong attraction. The poems are entirely directed toward colorful and teeming life; they take one to the markets and the streets of Leningrad, to the circus, to the football field, and into the beer halls.

A kind of burlesque utopia is presented in Zabolotzki's "poem" *The Triumph of Agriculture* (*Torzhestvo zemledeliya,* 1933), which likewise frightened the critics. Disregarding futurism, this work can more easily be related to the heroic-comic epics of the eighteenth century (G. Petrov), and there is no doubt that Zabolotzki's poem was no song of praise for collectivized farming.

After this poem, which was considered a scandal, Zabolotzki, before the war, published only a collection of poems entitled *Second Book* (*Vtoraya kniga,* 1937). Subsequently, he is said to have been arrested and interned various times. After the end of the war, new poems of Zabolotzki appeared in print, which, to be sure, were less provocative and "objectionable."

### SERAPION BROTHERS

#### Nikolai Tikhonov

Soviet poetry was enriched especially in the 1920s by the rediscovery of the ballad. One of its masters was Nikolai Tikhonov (born 1896), who, in 1922, joined the Serapion Brothers. Tikhonov also wrote stories in prose, but his reputation is based more lastingly on his poems, in which the romantic pathos of the Serapion Brothers seeks expression through the ballad form.

The two volumes that appeared in 1922, *The Horde* (*Orda*) and *The Brew* (*Braga*), already manifest a new tangible romanticism of the generation of World War I and the Civil War, which, as Tikhonov says in one of his poems, had made "fire, noose, bullet and hatchet" its serviceable spirits. Stylistically, Tikhonov owed more to the school of acmeism than to futurism, and his dynamic verse is closely related to that of Gumilev, who also devoted much attention to the ballad.

Aside from treating varied aspects of the war, Tikhonov's early poetry also presented exotic themes, as in *Afghanistanian Ballad* (*Afganskaya ballada*), as well as historical themes according to the taste of the Serapion Brothers, as in the poem about Swift. Best known of the early collections are the *Ballad of the Blue Package* (*Ballada o sinem pakete*) and *Ballad of the Nails* (*Ballada o gvozdyakh*), in which the dramatic passages are very effective.

There followed in 1927 the volume of verse *The Search for a Hero* (*Poiski geroya*), in which Tikhonov dealt with numerous themes, among others that of Swift (*Gulliver Plays Cards*). In 1936, with the volume *The Shadow of the Friend* (*Ten druga*; the title alludes to a poem of K. Batyushkov), Tikhonov places his art at the service of the political theses. The poems that he produced after his trip to the International Congress of Writers in Paris (1935) are devoted to the conflict of proletarians and antifascists in different countries of Europe.

## THE CONSTRUCTIVISTS

In the second half of the 1920s, a special group was formed by the so-called constructivists, who had appeared in 1924 with a "Declaration of the Literary Center of Constructivism." The major demand of the constructivists was that poetry should be rationalized according to technical principles, that it should be brought into a "system of the maximum exploitation of the theme." The slogan of "local" semantics in this connection means that every metaphor and every image was to be "motivated" obviously through the total theme, that the verse in all its aspects was to be related directly to the basic idea of the theme.

A co-author of the Declaration of Constructivism was the actual theoretician of the group, Kornelii Zelinski (born 1896), who, in 1929, published his subtle treatise *Poetry as Sense* (*Poeziya kak smysl*). Zelinski's definition of poetry—"a poem is a machine of sense"—is, however, in the language of the constructivists, likewise only a "local" metaphor, which arises from the idea of technical construction.

The theoretical demands of the constructivists could not be translated literally into practice. Whatever was achieved by the constructivists in this direction had already been tried out by the futurists.

## Ilya Selvinski

The most important representatives of this movement with its technical, local color were Ilya Selvinski, Vera Inber (born 1890) and Eduard Begritzki. In 1925 Ilya Selvinski (born 1899), the most convinced adherent of constructivism, published, in the Almanac of the Center of Constructivism (*Gosplan Literatury*— Official Literary Plan), a first section of the verse epic *The Ulyalayev Adventure* (*Ulyalayevshchina*, published as a book in 1927), which became his best known work. In this work, Selvinski especially fulfilled the constructivist demand for suitable local color. He generously adorned his novel-like story of the fights of the roving bands in the southeastern steppes of Russia with an exotic vocabulary, with numerous dialectic expressions, and with playful mockeries.

In addition to other poetic narratives, such as *Fur Trade* (*Pushtorg*, 1929), Selvinski wrote a number of dramas in verse that show an avant-garde attitude. To these belong *Commander of the Second Army* (*Komandarm 2*, 1929) and *Pao-Pao* (1933), the grotesque story of a man-ape who discovers his proletarian heart and accepts Marxism.

Selvinski's linguistic art, which is essentially more indebted to Khlebnikov and Pasternak than to the theories of the constructivists, ends the last phase of daring experiment born during the poetic revolution, whose point of departure in Russia was futurism.

## Eduard Bagritzki

The greatest purely lyrical poet among the constructivists was doubtless Eduard Bagritzki (pseudonym of E. Dzyubin, 1895–1934).

Bagritzki came from a poor Jewish family of Odessa. In 1925 he left Odessa and settled in Moscow, where in 1926 he joined the constructivists. During the Civil War, he participated as an agitator at the front in the partisan conflicts in Southern Russia (1929–30).

Bagritzki had begun in 1915 to write poems in the style of the later Blok and of the acmeists, but his first volume of poems, *Southwest* (*Yugo-zapada*), did not appear until 1928. In this volume, the best works of the years 1922–27 were collected, which made Bagritzki justifiably a highly esteemed poet. With his special predilection for the short, dramatically moving line, Bagritzki found his way as well to the ballad as to the dialogue poem and the dramatic narrative in verse.

In his poems, Bagritzki has obviously been influenced by Anglo-Saxon models: Burns and Scott, whom he translated, as well as Poe and Kipling. His romanticism is oriented in its spirit entirely toward the West. In 1922 Bagritzki wrote *A Legend of the Sea, The Sailors and the Flying Dutchman* (*Skazaniye o more, matrosach i Letuchem Gollandtze*). Several poetic monologues of the years 1921–22 hover around the figure of the Flemish Till Eulenspiegel, with whom the poet liked to compare himself in his vagabond pose.

Bagritzki's most successful ballads, among others, are the story of a wreck in the Black Sea, *The Watermelon* (*Arbuz*, 1924) and the nocturnal fantasy *The Cigarette Box* (*Papirosny korobok*, 1927), which resurrects the spirit of the poet of the Decembrists, Ryleyev, who was hanged a hundred years before. Ballad themes are also found in *The Smugglers* (*Kontrabandisty*, 1927) and in *Conversation with the Komsomol N. Dementyev* (*Razgovot s komsomoltzem N. Dementyevym*, 1927). In the latter, Bagritzki defends his romantic views. With a few convincing strokes, he presents a poetic vision of the Civil War and of the time when the knapsack of the fighter not only contained "matches and tobacco" but also "Tikhonov, Selvinski, and Pasternak," that is, the poems of young romanticists. But this time lies far in the past, and in his melancholy reflections, the poet brings in the crowing of the raven, from Poe's poem, and the fateful quotation "Nevermore."

The feeling of disappointment over the new reality and the idea of being excluded from life appear very clearly in many poems of the years 1925–27, such as *The Night* (*Noch*) and *The Verses of the Nightingale and the Poet* (*Stikhi o solovye i poete*). Nevertheless, in his later publications, *The Victors* (*Pobediteli,* 1932) and *The Last Night* (*Poslednaya noch,* 1932), Bagritzki definitely affirmed his Communism, regardless of his romantic feelings.

Bagritzki's chief work is the narrative in verse *The Tale of Opanas* (*Duma pro Opanasa,* 1926), which describes the tragic fate of a traitor who joined the forces of the bandit leader Makhno during the Civil War. This lyrically dramatic story, set in the Ukraine, is, in its form, influenced by constructivism (in the "local semantics") but it also contains folkloristic traditions. The historical Ukrainian *Duma* is really a form between folk ballad and epic, and, with this in mind, Bagritzki stylized his poem. Shortly before his death (1933), Bagritzki revised this work as a libretto for an opera.

## SOME ASPECTS OF PREWAR SOVIET THEATER

The golden age of the Moscow Art Theater (Stanislavski and Nemirovich-Danchenko) and the important experiments on the different "stages of style" (Meyerhold, Yevreinov, and others), had already indicated before 1914 what modern scenic effects the Russian theater was able to produce. In the 1920s it was especially the two artists Aleksandr Tairov and Meyerhold, both theater enthusiasts, who established the reputation of the Soviet stage.

Aleksandr Tairov (1885–1950) established his "chamber theater" (*Kamernyi Teatr*) in Moscow in 1914. Here a new stylistic epoch was realized: Russian futurism and Russian constructivism, with all their peripheral phenomena. Tairov, with his "unchained" theater, opposed the naturalistic theater as well as the "stylized stage" of the time of symbolism. His new style was a protest against the "literary" theater. Tairov envisioned a theater of pure dramatic art in which, above all, the actor was required to have complete control of all the physical means of expression (pantomime).

The repertory of this theater, before and after the Revolution, was very European (Scribe, Claudel, Wilde, Chesterton, Shaw,

O'Neill). Tairov was not even deterred from the operetta (*Giroflé-Giroflà* by Charles Lecocq, 1922). Only rarely did Tairov produce Russian plays—Annenski's *Thamyras Tzitharoedus*, 1916, and Ostrovski's *Storm*, 1924. In 1923, 1925, and 1930, the theater also played abroad, where it was enthusiastically received everywhere.

The other great experimental stage was Meyerhold's State Theater in Moscow (1920–38), in which the second and mature phase of the stage director began. Here, too, the style was geared toward action (the so-called "biomechanics"), and the actor almost always turned into an athlete and an acrobat. Meyerhold's entire method of staging was based on "motor symbolism," which filled out the entire stage space in its height, breadth, and depth. The imaginative decorations developed out of a pure stage constructivism, which the sculptor Vladimir Tatlin had largely inspired.

Meyerhold's most controversial productions were the liberal and arbitrary revisions of the Russian classics, among which were *Tarelkin's Death* by A. Sukhovo-Kobylin, *Forest* by Ostorovski, and *Auditor* by Gogol. In addition to this, however, he contributed substantially to modern Russian drama with plays such as *The Teacher Bubus* (*Uchitel Bubus*, 1925) by Aleksei Fayko (born 1893), or *The Mandate* (*Mandat*, 1925) by Nikolai Erdman (born 1902).

One of his most interesting productions was *Trust D.E.* (*Trest D.E.*); this was a montage based on the novel of the same name by Ilya Ehrenburg. He also adapted works by Upton Sinclair and *The Tunnel* by Bernhard Kellermann for the stage.

Memorable, above all, are the two productions of Mayakovski's late comedies *The Bedbug* (*Klop*, 1929) and *The Bath* (*Banya*, 1930). In 1918 Meyerhold had produced the *Mysterium buffo* in Saint Petersburg; in doing so, he had adapted his earlier style to the heroic-grotesque satire of Mayakovski. This grotesque buffo-style formed the characteristic element of the Meyerhold stage from the beginning, and the producer was therefore practically predestined to stage Mayakovski's later satirical prose comedies.

*The Bedbug* (1928) is a fantastic, grotesque piece, in which the philistine inclinations of Comrade Prisypkin, the average little Bolshevist, are pilloried. The bedbug, which, with Prisypkin, remains frozen in a block of ice for fifty years, is a burlesque reminiscence of the stage effects of symbolism. *The Bath* is a virulent satire directed toward the upper Soviet bureaucracy and especially against the jargon of the Soviet functionary. The comedy is likewise partly fanciful, because Mayakovski introduces a "time machine" from which the Communist bureaucrats are hurled on their journey into the future.

Among the leading lights of the Soviet theater of the 1920s were Nikolai Yevreinov (1879–1953), the expert in the "theater of the masses," who later went into exile, and the gifted, early deceased stage director Yevgenii Vakhtangov (1883–1922). There should be included, too, the poet V. Volkenshetyn (born 1883), who was prominent for many years as a theoretician of the drama and whose tragedy *Spartacus* (*Spartak*) created a deep impression in the "Theater of the Revolution" in 1923.

Other important events in the history of the Soviet drama include the stage versions of several successful contemporary novels. Mikhail Bulgakov's drama *The Days of the Brother and Sister Turbin* (*Dni Turbinykh*, a dramatic version of his novel *Belaya gvardiya*) was produced in 1926 for the first time in the Moscow Art Theater. This was followed by *The Armored Train 14-69* (*Bronepoyezd 14-69*) by Vsevolod Ivanov (Moscow Art Theater, 1927) and *The Badgers* (*Barsuki*) by Leonid Leonov (Vakhtangov-Theater, 1927).

Revisions were much in vogue at that time, and during the 1920s the First Studio of the Moscow Art Theater produced stage versions of Andrei Belyi's *Petersburg*, as well as the comedy *The Flea* (*Blokha*, 1925) by Yevgenii Zamyatin, and the *Lefthanded One* (*Levsha*), a revision of the story by Nikolai Leskov.

Mikhail Bulgakov, whose satiric comedy (*Zoyka's Dwelling* (*Zoykina kvartira*, 1926) was soon dropped from the program of the Vayhtangov Theater, later, as literary consultant of the Moscow Art Theater, revised Gogol's *Dead Souls* for the stage (produced by Stanislavski in 1923). In 1936 Bulgakov's historical drama *Molière* (*Molyer*) was also performed in the Art Theater, as one of the last productions of Stanislavski.

The Moscow Art Theater, revived after the Civil War, furthered the efforts of a number of talented Soviet authors. Among these may be included Konstantin Trenev (1876–1945), whose *Pictures of a Folk Tragedy* was produced under the title of *The Rebellion of Pugachev* (*Pugachevshchina*, 1924). Trenev's other successful piece, *Lyubov Yarovayga* (the title is the name of the hero, 1926), was later taken over by the Art Theater.

Among other playwrights who were produced more than occasionally Aleksandr Afinogenov (1904–41), Vsevolod Vishnevski (1900–51), and Nikolai Pogodin (1900–62) should be mentioned.

Afinogenov's best-known play is *Fear* (*Stradkh*, 1931), in which the favorite theme of the reeducation of the prewar intelligentsia is broached. To clarify the position of Professor Borodin, in whose opinion fear is the most important psychological stimulus of eighty percent of all Soviet citizens, was in those years a problem of great immediacy. Even if the change in attitude of the old professor is indicated at the close of the play, the problem of the relationship of scientific research and Communist politics still remains in all its sharpness.

Vishnevski is especially known through his plays *The First Mounted Army* (*Pervaya konnaya*, 1929) and *Optimistic Tragedy* (*Optimisticheskaya tragediya*, 1933), in which the struggles of the Red Army and the Red Navy are glorified.

Nikolai Pogodin was the author of several popular plays of the Five Year Plan, such as *Tempo* (*Temp*, 1929) and *The Poem of the Ax* (*Poema o topore*, 1931). In his historical drama *The Man with the Gun* (*Chelovek s ruzhyem*, 1937), he finally glorifies the role of Stalin during the October Revolution.

# PART III

# Contemporary Soviet Trends

# World War II: New Orientations

In the development of Soviet literature a line of demarcation, a caesura as it were, was drawn by World War II, but not only externally. The mobilization of the entire country and the revival of ideals of defense of the fatherland and of a people's war (in the special sense of Lev Tolstoi) aroused powerful patriotic forces, through which the notion of the "Russian" cause and the "general Russian disaster" (Vera Panova) steadily gained ground.

The spirit of sacrifice and the will to resist are not confined to the public sphere; they are called upon everywhere, in every situation, at every place of work, in the family, in the most private areas. War demands absolute solidarity, but it also gives the assurance that the common cause is the good cause. For literature this means that every possible life situation can express the common cause. In "total" war the whole man, even the threatened and suffering human being, is justly chosen as a literary subject. Not only the "political" man but also the "naked" man and finally even the dying man is the hero of this reality that enters into poetry, the story, and the novel, even while the war is still going on.

The war literature of the 1940s, inspired by recent and immediate experiences, was in many ways decidedly less critical than the later wave of war books of the 1950s and 1960s. The "conflict" did not broach the question of adequate or inadequate military preparation, or the rationale of individual strategic decisions. The "critical" war literature as such was made possible only by the post-1956 revision of Stalin's image. The war years actually produced a situation that enhanced Stalin's reputation, which was strengthened immeasurably by the heroic aura of Stalingrad. The subsequent renaming of this city, now called Volgograd, evoked a critical attitude in one of Viktor Nekrasov's recent stories.

During and immediately after the war, an entirely new generation of authors emerged. It consisted of Communist youths who had hardly participated actively in the revolutionary struggle, although they had grown up during the years of the turbulent reconstruction. Most of the members of this group were born about 1910. A number had published their first works in the 1930s or even earlier. In general, however, they became known only through World War II, with its entirely new and vital subject matter, which for many years dominated writing in Russia. To this younger group belong Vera Panova (born 1905), Olga Berggoltz (born 1910), Aleksandr Tvardovski (born 1910), Viktor Nekrasov (born 1911), Emmanuil Kazakevich (born 1913), Konstantin Simonov (born 1915), and many others.

The war literature of this generation attempted, first of all, to describe life and personal experiences at the front and in the rear areas, whereas the older generation of writers—Ilya Ehrenburg and others—considered the fight against "fascism" the real task of the time. In the typical works of the above-mentioned authors the Germans, who were, after all, the "fascists," assume a very subordinate role in comparison with their prominence in the literature of the 1950s and 1960s.

The almost complete lack of interest in the theme of "fascism" is reflected for example in the calm irony of a descriptive passage in Nekrasov's novel *In the Trenches of Stalingrad* (*V okopach Stalingrada*), showing the comfortable appearance of a captured German bunker:

> Above the gaming table with its green cloth and curved feet a fan of picture postcards; a fir twig with a dripping wax taper, a goggle-eyed pugdog, with a knocked-over inkwell, a dwarf with a red stocking cap, and an angel, hovering in the air. A little higher —the Führer, exalted with firmly pressed lips, in a shiny coat.

The political aspects of the war were so very obvious that writers felt no need to describe them. The literature of the last war years and the first postwar years therefore reflects distress, conflict, privation, fear, hope, and always the waiting for the return home. Most of the thoughts hover around home and family; writers show an ever increasing interest in the world of ordinary objects, in detail, in common things that lend themselves to clear and unequivocal description. This is also true of the war and postwar poetry.

During these war years the wave of patriotism gave poetry a special character, as in a poem by Yaroslav Smelyakov, reprinted in the magazine *Znamya* in 1945. A mystical exaltation of love for the Russian land, it makes the fallen young Red Army soldier a judge over the people of the world:

> And when indeed the time shall come,
> That human beings with all their sins
> From all countries shall be called
> Three times by the trumpet,
> Then rises at the throne of judgment
> Not God with a flowing beard,
> But the modest youth of the Red Army,
> Before the trampled mass,
> And he holds in his right hand,
> Which was crushed by Germans in battle,
> Not the symbols of heavenly glory,
> But a handful of Russian soil.

This new feeling of patriotism that flourished after the victory over Germany was directed into political channels by the party leaders. With Zhdanov's declaration in 1946 the absolute claim of the party to leadership in literary life was newly established and rigorously carried out. Under this new and fatal limitation of literary expression the members of the older generation who had been attacked, such as Mikhail Zoshchenko and Anna Akhmatova, suffered especially. Younger authors, however, were also hindered in their development. Because of the dogmatic and unintelligent interpretation of "socialist realism," as well as because of the disputatious and intolerant literary criticism, which scarcely deserved the designation any longer, literary production between 1947 and 1953 became increasingly sterile and barren in variety of viewpoints. The turn of the tide came in 1953, the year that Stalin died. In December of that year the magazine *Novyi mir* published *About Sincerity in Literature* (*Ob iskrennosti v literature*), the highly influential thesis of the novelist and journalist Vladimir Pomerantzev (born 1907). Setting up directness and sincerity against the dominant insincerity and mendacity, Pomerantzev deplored the escapist tendency of current literature, as well as its "comfortable opportunism," "cowardice," and "blind practicality." The writer's concern should not be "preaching" (*propoved*) but "confession" (*ispoved*). Descriptions of human beings and their environment were far more meaningful than mere annals of events.

Precisely with his reference to the almost complete lack of "confession" on the part of the writer, Pomerantzev revealed the basic weakness of the so-called "socialist realism." The tendency that Pomerantzev called the "scholastic" treatment of practical literary problems had led to the almost complete disappearance from literature of the portrayal of awareness and with that the tendency to experiment with individual stylistic schemes.

The errors indicated by Pomerantzev, including the cult of the "super-hero" (*sverchgeroi*) that had entered literature, were discussed heatedly at the Second Congress of Soviet Writers in 1954. Nothing very radical resulted, but the ground was prepared for the so-called "thaw" that Ilya Ehrenburg acclaimed in a short novel of the same title in 1954. After the Second Congress of Soviet Writers the "rehabilitation" of those authors who had been banned under Stalin was carried out. This tendency continued to increase markedly after the twentieth general convention of the Communist Party of the Soviet Union in February 1956.

Neither the party convention nor the lively discussion that arose in the same year over Vladimir Dudintsev's new novel *Not by Bread Alone* (*Ne khlebom yedinym*) marks a real turning point in the political control of literature. No such turning point has yet appeared, although the change of attitude toward Stalin and toward the "personality cult" indicated that certain elements of the party line were no longer tenable. A great many of the rehabilitations could only be carried out posthumously, but in 1956 and 1957 a remarkable increase occurred in subject matter of contemporary interest and in the quality of writing. Several community enterprises, such as *Literaturnaya Moskva*, were started and new literary journals like *Neva* (since 1957) and *Moskva* (since 1958) were founded. Literary discussion became livelier everywhere, the level of literary criticism rose in general, and writers again met, here and there, for common enterprises and joint expressions of opinion. This solidarity of separate groups is shown not only by the publication of new almanacs (up to *Tarusskiye stranitzy*, 1961), but also by the large number of poems of dedication in which various individual writers would join. The tentative high spot of this relaxation in the relations between literature and state policy is to be seen in the years 1961–62, although the development until then had not been in a straight line. The limits of tolerance as far as the party was concerned had already been shown very clearly by the Pasternak "affair."

After 1961–62 the younger generation—called here the generation of the "heirs" in reference to their birth after the October Revolution—found their own language and style. Perhaps at some later time these years, like the beginning of the 1960s, will be looked on as the start of a new epoch. For the present, such an interpretation must remain inconclusive. Because the roots of every new beginning lie deep in the past, such phenomena as "upheavals" in literature are only apparent and superficial. Certainly since at least 1958 several quite different and definitely new literary movements have been competing, and a personal and critical "consciousness" has dominated literature since that time.

Contemporary literature offers a fascinating variety of currents and viewpoints. No effort can be made here to go into each case of the favorable acceptance or the criticism of the works and authors to be discussed. The spontaneous reaction to works of Soviet literature, moreover, whether in the East or in the West, does not present a coherent picture of current literary development. A more profitable approach is to examine this literature by analyzing its intentions which, generally speaking, are reflected in literary allusions, style, and other generally accepted literary devices.

## SOCIALIST REALISM IN FICTION

The concept of socialist realism no longer carries with it any generally accepted ideas. In its narrower sense the term seems restricted in time to the literature of the Stalin era, from the first Congress of Soviet Writers (1934) to the "thaw" (1954–56). In a wider sense socialist realism is considered the only sensible method of literary creation in the era of socialism, as the obligatory expression of a "new" consciousness. The history of the last ten or twelve years has shown, however, that the concept is so burdened by its "official" connotation that it can no longer be considered the concept of an epoch (that of socialism) but only the name of an effort that has foundered in the meantime. That this view is also prevalent in the Soviet Union is shown by a very polemical study by Andrei Sinyavski (pseudonym of Abram Tertz), condemned in the so-called "authors' trial"; this study appeared only in the West, in French and English translation.

In the essay *What Is Socialist Realism? (Chto takoye socialistichesky realizm?)* Sinyavski asks whether realism could be "socialistic, capitalistic, Christian, or Mohammedan," indicating that an attempt has been made to link literature with a purely ideological concept. Sinyavski asks further whether socialist realism is not merely "fiction, myth, or propaganda."

The theoreticians of the historical development and especially of the genre poetry of realism connect socialist realism predominantly with Maksim Gorki, although his work actually represents a very arbitrary reaction to the crisis in the narrative genres that occurred shortly before the turn of the century. According to these critics, socialist realism was developed by the "proletarian" writers grouped around Gorki during the last ten or twelve years before the October Revolution.

The most important characteristic of the movement is considered to be its awakening social consciousness primarily in its "romantic" aspect. Thus, for example, K. D. Muratova writes in her book *The Genesis of Socialist Realism in Russian Literature (Vozniknoveniye socialisticheskovo realizma v russkoi literature,* 1966): "Revolutionary (social) romanticism, which was linked with the greatly strengthened active behavior of man toward life and man's aim in it, was the first to reveal the essence of emotional basis to the understanding of the world by socialist realism."

In any case, the name "socialist realism" was adopted by Stalin himself (October 26, 1932) at the same time that the expressions "monumental," "romantic," "tendentious," and "dynamic" came up for discussion. The commitment to socialist realism was included in the statutes of the Writers' Association after Zhdanov's speech at the First Central Congress of Soviet Writers in Moscow (1934). It read as follows:

> Socialist realism is the fundamental method of Soviet belles-lettres and criticism. It demands of the artist a truthful, historically factual description of reality in its revolutionary development. The truthfulness and the historical accuracy of the artistic representation of reality must be in accord with the task of an idealistic reconstruction and a reeducation of the workers in the spirit of socialism.

This early definition of socialist realism was amended by incorporating Lenin's requirement (1905) of loyalty to the party and through the designation of the writer as one of the "engineers of the human soul" (Stalin). From this point of view two important principles of literary presentation arise: the search for the "new man" and the readiness for an "optimistic" solution of all conflicts.

If the concept of socialist realism is reduced to the ideological and "party" qualifications in their narrower sense—those that Stalin himself set up for literature and that definitely include social "romanticism"—then clearly the age group designated as the "post-revolutionary" generation furnished most of the representatives of this movement. Further, although no one could have ignored the official position as a matter of principle during the two decades from 1934 to 1953, in practice a number of important deviations did occur.

Although socialist realism was never clearly defined as a "method," certain procedures and devices became axiomatic. The leading role of the "hero" demanded a clear separation of "positive" and "negative" actors in the action, and in the patterns of behavior different conventional simplifications and standardizations developed. These simplifications, as a matter of comparison, correspond to the creation of types in modern "Westerns," or from a different point of view, the stock characters in the "pseudo" classic tragedy of the 18th century. An exact description would require an exhaustive study. Basically, however, the fighter, organizer, hero of work, and party functionary, on one side, are clearly distinguished from the coward, pusher, saboteur, and traitor on the other side.

For the separation of the positive and negative phases numerous conventional "signals" help the reader to solve the plot and predict events. On the periphery a number of "naive" characters appear, among them young people as well as the reasoning "grandfather" with the flowing beard. The hero may occasionally take a false step, but it must always be a minor one.

The narrative style is primarily a mixture of conventional "literary language," official abbreviations, "folk language" in moderate doses, and various technical terms that belong to the "milieu" under consideration. The dialogue plays the principal role in the action. "Reality" on the other hand is presented in somewhat long-winded descriptions and explanations of industrial processes, as well as in "realistic" genre scenes, preferably "romantic" descriptions of nature and characterization of lesser figures through dialect.

The description of consciousness is either eliminated entirely or confined to subordinate and incidental circumstances. The description of consciousness is used to develop the action rather than to individualize and delineate individual characters. "Nature" is especially singled out as aesthetically relevant, as are the physical descriptions of persons and settings. Human consciousness is almost never portrayed; it appears predetermined by political, social, and other compelling circumstances. For this reason it is often difficult to find a structure that can be interpreted from the literary viewpoint. During the era of socialist realism literary criticism was therefore understood primarily as ideological criticism. Critics studied various "conflicts," in which political logic was the most important factor.

The area of realistic "cheap literature" will be completely avoided here. Only the most prestigious representatives of socialist realism will be mentioned.

## Six Exemplary Novelists

Today the fame of Semion Babayevski (born 1909) is almost forgotten. His *Knight of the Golden Star* (*Kaveler zolotoi zvezdy,* 1948) can be considered a typical expression of the personality cult. Boris Gorbatov (1908–54) must also be included as a representative of the "semi-official" literature. His "construction novel" *Donetz-Basin* (*Donbass,* 1951) shows all the weaknesses of this once popular emotional genre.

A more lasting influence was exerted by the gifted Vasilii Grossman (pseudonym of Yosif Solomonovich, 1905–64). Known for his reporting and for such war stories as *The Defense of Stalingrad* (*Oborona Stalingrada,* 1944) and the poignant *The People Are Immortal* (*Narod bessmerten,* 1942), Grossman was unable to finish his great novel of World War II, *For the Just Cause,* I (*Za pravoye delo,* I, 1952). In this monumental work he presented a vast panorama, linking the development of the global warfare with all kinds of possible single destinies. Overambitious in its attempt, Grossman's novel ends in Part I with the battle around Stalingrad.

The prolific Vera Ketlinskaya (born 1906 in Sebastopol) had already published two novels before the war. After her war novel *During the Siege* (*V osade,* 1947), she turned to the theme of reconstruction in *Days of Our Life* (*Dni nashei zhizni,* 1952). Her latest novel, *It Doesn't Pay to Live Otherwise* (*Inache zhit ne stoit,* 1961) is part of a "dilogy," in which she attempts to illuminate critically the period from 1936 to 1956. The daughter of a czarist admiral who went over to the Reds and was later murdered by the Whites, Ketlinskaya belongs to the intelligentsia by birth. Attempting to break away from socialist realism in her most recent work, she begins her novel with a war scene that is projected chronologically far ahead; she then weaves in the story.

The best known of this group of writers is probably Boris Polevoi (pseudonym of Boris Kampov, born 1908 in Moscow), a member of the Soviet Peace Committee and of the World Council for Peace. As a journalist—he was on the staff of *Pravda*—Polevoi has traveled all over the world; he has even visited America and China. During World War II, he was a well-known war correspondent. After the war his novel *Story of the True Man* (*Povest o nastoyashchem cheloveke*, 1946), which extolled the courage and energy of the Soviet fighters, established his reputation as a model political author. Polevoi has been writing since the 1920s; for his novel *The Hot Coalpit* (*Goryachy tzekh*, 1939), a study of Soviet industry, he visited such great industrial centers as the Volga-Don Canal and the Bratsk cofferdam at the Angara. One of Polevoi's last works, *At the Wild Shore* (*Na dikom brege*, 1962), is a "construction novel" in the exact sense of the expression, describing the construction of the great hydroelectric plant in the Taiga (Bratsk). This novel also portrays a careerist of the Stalinist type, who is as much a stock figure in the novels of industry and production written since 1956 as in those on scientific themes, such as the novels of Kaverin or Leonov.

During the 1950s and 1960s Polevoi returned to a war theme, widening his outlook to cover the conditions in the occupied areas and describing the resistance, both overt and underground, as in *Deep Back Country* (*Gluboky tyl*, 1958). Although Polevoi describes many gripping incidents with the skill of an experienced journalist, his reportorial descriptions and the many frequently trivial dialogues are often far removed from true art, leading critics to question Polevoi's reputation as a narrative writer.

Among authors favored by certain party circles are Vsevolod Kochetov (born 1912 in Novgorod), who publishes the semiofficial literary journal *October* (*Oktyabr*). Kochetov is a trained agronomist, but was already active before the war as a journalist. During the war he wrote the novel *Edge of the City* (*Predmestye*, 1944), which describes the incidents of the war from an unusual viewpoint. After producing the novel *Comrade Agronom* (*Tovarishch agronom*) in 1950 he published a novel about the dock workers, *The Zhurbins* (*Zhurbiny*, 1952), and an extensive family novel, *The Brothers Yershov* (*Bratya Yershovy*, 1958).

The last of the writers in this category is the once celebrated Vasilii Azhayev (born 1915), whose novel *Far from Moscow* (*Daleko ot Moskvy*, 1948) deals with the wartime construction of an oil pipeline in Siberia. Azhayev is now editor in chief of the journal *Soviet Literature*, published in German, English, Polish, and Spanish.

THE  WAR  POETS

The war years from 1941 to 1945 brought with them a remarkable expansion of lyric poetry. This phenomenon resulted from the use of new themes as well as from the new responsibilities given to creative writers. These artists were assigned the task of strengthening the will to resist on the "psychological" front and with providing suitable literary "ammunition" for the war efforts. Poetry transmitted by word of mouth, as many witnesses attest, rendered an invaluable service to the Russian cause during these years, superseding the superficial slogans of ideological propaganda. The era of the "show trials" was not entirely forgotten, but after the surprise attack by Hitler everyone felt called upon to defend "Russian earth" and the party leaders were clever enough to strengthen this patriotic will through many minor concessions.

The poetry of the war years was maintained in particular by the members of two generations, the "post-revolutionary" generation born shortly before 1914 or during World War I, and the generation born around 1900 and established in the 1930s.

The representatives of the latter group belonged only partly to the older "avant-garde"; in most cases they had served an unfruitful literary movement with faith and devotion. For many of them the war years meant a relaxation in their style and a liberation of their talent, making their war poetry otherwise rather colorless, worthy of mention for this reason alone.

Aleksei Surkov (born 1899 in the district of Yaroslavl), subsequently well known as a literary functionary, journalist, translator, and critic, belongs to the circle of writers who were quite definitely "war poets." His trench poetry, although traditional in language and structure, is notable for its simplicity and marked consciousness of national tradition.

This poetry is sometimes "poetry of experience" in the strictest sense of the word—unpretentious, perhaps, from the literary point of view, but also free of any false pretensions. Historic allusions are common, as in references to the Tatar invasions and to the year 1812. Both the "Russian heart" and Russian melancholy (*toska*) are prominent in this war poetry, as in Surkov's poem *When It Rains for a Long Time* (*Kogda dolgo idiot dozhd*, 1942):

The swampy dull night has white eyebrows.
On the damp, rotting wood lies mould.
Melancholy, like an old, bald rat,
Crawled under my cloak again in the dark.

Both Stepan Shchipachev (born 1899 in the district of Perm) and Aleksandr Prokofyev (born 1900 at Lake Ladoga) also became known as war poets. Although Shchipachev followed acmeist and imagist movements during the 1930s, his verse was never very bold, and his contacts with avant-garde tendencies remained external. During the war his book of poems *Lines of Love* (*Stroki lyubvi,* 1944) made an impression and for a time after the war Shchipachev retained great popularity among his readers. At the beginning of the 1950s he was one of the few poets who published regularly.

Aleksandr Prokofyev belongs to the poets who prefer a stylization based on folk language and who also imitate the forms of folk poetry. His war poetry stresses national characteristics, as in the narrative *Russia* (*Rossiya*). Prokofyev, too, has remained a tireless writer; in 1961 he was awarded the Lenin Prize.

The above-mentioned Yaroslav Smelyakov (born in 1913 in Luck, Volhynia) has not quite fulfilled the promise of his war poetry, producing rather conventional declamatory and journalistic poems.

The once popular poems of Yevgenii Dolmatovski (born 1915 in Moscow) also lack lasting significance. On the other hand, Aleksandr Yashin (born 1913 in the Government of Vologda), a poet profoundly influenced by Russian folklore, produced such impressive war songs as *The Cloak* (*Shinel,* 1941) and *Drunkenness* (*Khmel,* 1944). Since the 1950s Yashin has also published prose works.

NARRATIVES OF WAR

*Vera Panova*

Completely unknown until 1945, Vera Panova (born 1905 in Rostov on the Don) has since become famous, and not only in

Russia. She began work about 1923 as a journalist on a local paper in Rostov, and her important experiences on the southern periphery of the Soviet Union are reflected with great vivacity in her later book *Sentimental Novel* (*Sentimentalnyi roman,* 1958).

During the war Vera Panova journeyed to Perm; her experiences as a correspondent on a hospital train furnished the material for her first and remarkably successful novel *The Traveling Companions* (*Sputniki,* 1946). This chronicle, almost laconic but written with great warmth, can be considered one of the best Russian books about the war years, both for its human candor and for its convincing and suitable form of composition.

*The Traveling Companions* is constructed in a ring-shaped, symmetrical pattern that allowed the author to cover on barely 300 pages virtually everything from the outbreak of the war to its end in the hospital train. The leading characters remain together from the first day to the last; the chapters of the first and third parts are named for the main persons, in mirror symmetry. Even though the train grows continually in importance as the "milieu" (*byt*), several digressions reveal the life stories of the people involved, so that war and peace meet in the consciousness of the persons. The dynamic motif of the action is the war with all its horrors but also with all its scurrilous episodes. The hospital train captures the war like a revolving mirror.

Panova's novel is patriotic in the sense given that word in the years from 1941 to 1946. The word "Russian" is also enriched, and the author speaks very definitely of the "general Russian misfortune." The lovable and lifelike figures of Dr. Belov, nurse Lena, and the surgical nurse Yuliya Dmitriyevna radiate such virtues as patience and perseverance, and display unselfish and trustful love even when threatened by cruel disappointment. In accord with contemporary standards the real hero is the polit-commissar Danilov, but he, too, is given human qualities, probably because of the author's feminine perspective. *The Traveling Companions* is notable as well for its use of recollection and reflection. The later novels also feature retrospective and introspective digressions in the form of memories and excerpts from diaries.

Several of Panova's works were not quite successful; these include *Looking Ahead* (*Kruzhilikha,* 1947)—the Russian title is taken from the name of an industrial plant in the Urals—and *Bright Shore* (*Yasnyi bereg*, 1949), a novel about life on a large government-owned estate. Immediately after Stalin's death Panova published her novel *Seasons of the Year* (*Vremena goda*, 1953), a chronicle of two families noted for its social criticism, especially in the discussions of the theory of "lack of conflict" (*teoriya beskonfliktnosti*), which was already under attack by literary critics in 1952.

The new novel, set in 1950, is constructed in sections that describe winter, spring, summer, and fall, just as the threefold division of *The Traveling Companions* depicted "Night," "Morning," and "Day." In *Seasons of the Year* the action is framed by the preparations for the new year's celebrations that begin and end the year covered by the novel. In this story, too, set in a middle-sized Soviet city, the preliminary events are brought in through digressions that occupy entire chapters.

The conflicts occur both on the level of the family and on the social level. Gennadii Kupriyanov (Genya, "the lost son"), the spoiled son of an honorable communist, becomes criminally involved and is in the end fatally wounded with a dagger by bandits, while in the family Bortashevich the weak Seriozha dominates as a character of integrity, although his parents have fallen into the heresy of "making money" and dream of social prestige.

The new society has its old "conflicts," too, and one is reminded of the great family portraits of Gorki. Panova, with her implication that good parents are not necessarily blessed with good children, questioned some taboos. The "milieu theory" as the basis of a narrative is developed to the last extreme in this novel. The author's interest in the psychology of young people is quite manifest. In her portrayal of Serezha and his friends and the group around Yuliya, Gennadii Kupriyanov's sister, Panova places the new generation directly in the center. Serezha's diary (Chapter 9) gives an additional insight into Panova's technique, which inclined increasingly toward a reduction of description and an expansion of the confessional character of her writing.

A simplification and refinement of expression, somewhat in the style of Lev Tolstoi, appears especially in the stories about children that she wrote in her later years, such as *Valya and Volodya* (1960) or *Sasha* (1965). Simplicity and directness are the most important principles of Panova's style. In *Sentimental Novel* Panova relives her own youth and revives the colorful milieu of her native city Rostov on the Don. She also developed new stylistic techniques in this work. Thus, although much autobiographical material has been worked into the novel, Panova makes the budding young journalist Sevastyanov her hero and tells the entire story through his reminiscences. The frame of the novel is Sevastyanov's railroad trip to his home, after about thirty years, and the novel ends with the arrival of the hero in his city.

As the continuous reminescence goes on, the novel is transformed into a stream of sentences heard and thought. By means of questions, parentheses, ellipses, marks and additional comments the present is indicated. In this way there is a double perspective: events as they were experienced in the past and as they are reexperienced in the present. The book bears the motto "O my light-footed youth!" (*O yunost legkaya moya!*) from Pushkin's *Yevgenii Onegin*. The meaning of the novel is evoked through this motto, expressing a sentimental farewell to a time which, although gone forever, has been transfigured poetically into an eternal present.

Such a book could have been written only after the condemnation of Stalin, because the "golden" 1920s appear here for the first time freed of all ideological interpretation. They have been lightened by a sense of distance, in which affectionate melancholy and profound irony turn the events of the time into mere names, slogans, almost grotesque customs, and "revolutionary" discussions. The novel is a homage to the time of illusions, and hardly, as the Soviet critic L. Plotkin indicates, a novel of "lost illusions." The work is a "critique of good fortune"—a description of the way in which the "great" good fortune, symbolized by the figure of the big Zoya, is transformed into the "little" good fortune, little Zoya.

In this book, too, the human traits are impressive:

> The bells were still ringing. Then Sevastyanov and little Zoya looked quickly into the youth club and listened to a dispute: "May a Komsomol member eat Easter bread?" They agreed that he couldn't, but the next day Sevastyanov ate Easter bread at home with Aunt Manya and also at the home of Vanka Yakovenko, and

also at the home of little Zoya. For in all homes Easter was being celebrated; if not by the parents, then by the grandmothers and grandfathers. . . . Sevastyanov was not two-faced, it was simply that he was always hungry and good eating was a rarity in his life.

Panova settled in Leningrad soon after the war. She was successful with several plays and with material for film scripts. Films have been made of her *The Traveling Companions*, the stories *Yevdokiya* (1958), *Volodya* (1960), *Early in the Morning* (*Rano utrom*, 1964), and the film narrative (*kinopovest*) *Workers' Settlement* (*Rabochy posiolok*, 1964).

More recently Panova has been working on a collection of legendary stories from older Russian history under the title *Faces of the Dawn* (*Liki na zare*). In 1966 the magazine *Zvezda* published two excerpts, *The Legend of Olga* (*Skazaniye ob Olga*) and *Feodoretz, Belyi Klobuchok* (a story of the twelfth century).

### Aleksandr Tvardovski

Aleksandr Tvardovski (born 1910 in the region of Smolensk), the author of *Vasilii Terkin*, and the publisher of the distinguished journal *Novyi mir* since the 1950s, is one of the most prominent personalities of the Russian literary world. In 1961 he was awarded the Lenin Prize. Because of his fundamentally liberal editorial policy, he was exposed for years to hostile attacks, but he continued to follow consistently his policy of moderation. He began his journalistic activities in the 1930s but became widely known only with the publication of the verse epic *Vasilii Terkin* (1945). He wrote this popular poem from 1941 to 1945; parts of it were published from 1942 on.

Tvardovski's *Book about the Soldier* (*Kniga pro boika*) presents in thirty chapters a portrait of the unknown popular hero of World War II—the Soviet fighter at the front whose endurance and resourcefulness always save him from disaster. *Vasilii Terkin* is a book "without beginning or end" that describes the war in popular trochees, as it must have appeared from the point of view of the soldier at the front, simple and limited in judgment. The heroic-comic character Vasilii (Vasya) Terkin, around whom all the incidents of the book are centered, became a symbol of the art of surmounting and surviving danger. The character was invented during the war in Finland (1939–40) by an authors' collective that included Tvardovski. See *How Vasilii Terkin Was Written* (*Kak byl napisan Vasilii Terkin*, 1951, expanded 1962).

Parallels cannot be drawn with Hasek's *The Good Soldier Schweik*, however, because direct satire is completely missing in *Vasilii Terkin* and because it is not intended as an antithesis to war or as representing an individual point of view. Related features appear only in the ingenuous adaptation of the "naive" hero to the frequently grotesque circumstances of the war. Terkin does not think of praise and reward; he acts directly as circumstances require. Terkin does not fight "for fame but for life on this earth."

*Vasilii Terkin* is also a didactic epic with many instructive sayings, proverbs, and popular maxims. Facetious digressions about the very "ordinary" and not especially imposing person of the hero establish an atmosphere that challenges the reader to identify with him. Vasilii Terkin is the Russian Everyman; his inward gaiety, his love of the harmonica, his penchant for free and sometimes biting humor, his unselfishness, and his willing devotion explain the popularity of this completely unpolitical figure whose chief motivating force is naive and unquestioning patriotism.

As a poet Tvardovski is not particularly prominent, although he published several volumes of poems. Despite a gift for the "gnomic" (a style marked by pithy proverbial sayings), Tvardovski easily slips into rhymed colloquial speech or conventional discourse. Nikolai Nekrasov seems to be a closely imitated model; the drifting into popular and folkloristic style may easily appear to be a copied mannerism. Tvardovski,, however, attempts to avoid all false pathos and would rather understate than hyperbolize. Tvardovski's popular style often creates comic contrasts through prosaic interpolations.

Of his newer works special mention must be made of the narrative in verse *Distance after Distance* (*Za dalyu dal*, 1960), written in the form of a fictional travel diary describing a trip on the Trans-Siberian Express from Moscow to the Far East. Single parts of this work, which begin with the Korean War, were published in 1953. In all Tvardovski worked at it for ten years.

Adopting the style of the verse narratives of the nineteenth cen-

tury and using iambics, the author continually reflects on his intentions, his past life, and recent history. A double point of view thus
arises, one aspect following the movement of the train into the
distance and the other resembling a journey into the past: "Two
kinds of journeys exist: one, leaving a spot and moving into the
distance; the other, remaining seated at the spot and turning the
calendar backward."

By using the old and honorable device of a journey, Tvardovski
discusses the most recent history of Russia; the story culminates in
the penultimate chapter, *That's How It Was Then* (*Tak eto bylo*),
in an evaluation of Stalin's reign of terror. The moral problem is
discussed in a gingerly fashion, but the repulsive traits and the mania
of the dictator, "who not infrequently referred to himself in the third
person," and nominated himself as a divine being, are openly described:

> His greatness in eternity, which our whole chorus promised him,
> he himself wanted to see in his lifetime, together with the other
> works. He was in a hurry. And everything seemed still too little.
> Already the Volga joined the Don and Moscow shot up like some
> rare pavilion. . . . Only one canal was still missing, which one
> should have been able to see from Mars!

The central point in the book is marked by the author's dramatic
meeting, at a little railroad station in the Taiga, with a friend of his
youth whom he had presumed dead. The friend is traveling as a
released convict in the opposite direction, from the Far East to
Russia; the merely implied record of his suffering overshadows the
entire second half of the story. The ten days of the journey expand
to ten years of Russian history, which teaches the moral "that even
in the Kremlin no one is eternal."

From 1954 to 1963 Tvardovski wrote the verse travesty *Terkin
in the Underworld* (*Terkin na tom svete*, 1963) as a continuation
of the epic *Vasilii Terkin*. In this poem, clearly suggested by Dante's
*Divine Comedy*, Tvardovski ridicules his own work, exaggerating
the heroic-comic traits of Vasilii Terkin and transforming the whole
work into a satire of the police state of the Stalin era. From *Vasilii
Terkin* Tvardovski takes over the comic four-foot trochees and the
ironic discussion with the reader about the merits and the character

of his hero. The digressions here, as in *Distance after Distance*, acquire an important function as a means of composition. The work is expressly based on a grotesque fiction; in this form it can unfold its satire without restraint.

The underworld with its wholly absurd ceremonial, its investigations and hearings, its police terror and penal sections, is only the reflection of an all too familiar reality, which is here skillfully shown in a new form. Poor Vasya Terkin, whose guide in the various regions of the underworld is a former war comrade, never stops being amazed, especially when he learns that this is only the "normal" underworld, and that another "bourgeois" underworld exists nearby, in which the "discipline" is much weaker and which is exposed to lingering decomposition.

Hardly an area of life is spared the sarcasm of Tvardovski's pen. Indeed, this work can be considered one of the most amusing social-political satires of the last years. The preliminary sketches for *Terkin in the Underworld* are obviously far more extensive than the final version that Tvardovski used. A version deviating from the original in various details and episodes also appeared in ( 1963 ) in the almanac *Mosti*, published in Munich by emigré Russians.

The end of the journey through the underworld is Terkin's happy return to daylight and the characterization of the experiences as a "fairytale." Terkin has thus been saved for further adventures.

## *Viktor Nekrasov*

Viktor Nekrasov (born 191 1 in Kiev) spent his earliest childhood in France and Switzerland; his education was quite extensive, comprising architecture, dramatics, and playwriting. His most profound experiences, to which his stories often refer, occurred during his years as an officer at the front from 1941 until he was wounded in 1944, and especially the battle of Stalingrad.

Under the still fresh impressions of the war Nekrasov began a novel about Stalingrad; it was entitled *In the Trenches of Stalingrad* (*V okopach Stalingrada*, 1946).

With this book Nekrasov entered the ranks of the foremost and most successful authors of war books. The figure of the narrator,

Lieutenant Kerzhenzev, bears unmistakable autobiographical features, and the various experiences, confrontations, and complications, although fictional, in this way acquire the weight of authentic evidence.

In strictly chronological succession Nekrasov describes the retreat in the summer of 1942, and then depicts the various phases of the defense of the unfortunate city from the point of view of an officer of an engineer battalion in the front lines.

This novel, written without embellishments, carefully explores the experiences of soldiers, as humans and as members of the armed services, in the trenches. Avoiding glorification, Nekrasov portrays the "typical" Russian soldier of World War II, a man of unsentimental reality.

Life is not strictly divided into "war" and "no war," into soldiers and civilians, into "front" and "back country." To Nekrasov the scene in Stalingrad represents a normal continuation of life, even if under extremely difficult circumstances; only death remains ever foreign. Everything goes along very humanly in this book and Nekrasov has no desire to rouse "lofty" feelings. War is laborious, dirty, and boring; it demands exertions, annoyances, and physical pain.

Like Tolstoi in his stories of Sevastopol, Nekrasov eliminates all heroic expectations by pointing out the blindness of the one who is fettered to a fixed point in the action:

> In war, one never knows the least thing, possibly only that which happens directly under one's nose. If only the German isn't shooting at you, you think that it is quiet and peaceful on the whole earth, and when the bombs fall, you are already convinced that the entire front from the Baltic to the Black Sea is active.

The concepts "front" and "battle" as concrete images are often questioned by Nekrasov; as far as he is concerned, the scene is merely a matter of nearness, of details. These symbolic details, according to Nekrasov's own words, constitute the vivacity and authenticity of the book.

The little "realistic" details at one point reach a disturbing peak in the description of a soldier who has just fallen:

He lay on his back, his arms outstretched; a stump was glued
at his lips. A little, still smoldering cigarette stump. And that was
more horrible than everything that I saw before or since the war.

Although the party and socialism are almost never mentioned in
Nekrasov's novel, the book was extremely popular. It went through
numerous editions and secured official praise.

Nekrasov worked harder at his next works, but they did not come
up to his first book. These were his novel of the return home, in the
*Native City* (*V rodnom gorode*, 1954), and his collected war
novellas, which appeared in 1961 as *Vasya Konakov*.

The critics, however, considered the novella *Kira Georgiyevna*
(1961) a remarkable achievement, and Nekrasov became well
known for his travel reports, including, from Italy, *First Acquaintance* (*Pervoye znakomstvo*, 1958); from America, *On Both Sides
of the Ocean* (*Po obe storony okeana*, 1962); from France, *A
Month in France* (*Mesyatz vo Francii*, 1965); and from the
Kamchatka Peninsula, *12,000 Kilometers Wide* (*Za dvenadtzat
tysyach kilometrov*, 1965).

Whereas in the travel descriptions the personal experiences also
refer to the historic and geographical, the structure of the volumi-
nous novella *Kira Georgiyevna* is entirely based on actual and
"experienced" time, in which the characters apparently come together and soon drift apart again. The sculptress Kira Georgiyevna,
whose destiny has bound her in a second marriage to a man over
twenty years her senior, stands in the center of several "personal"
lapses of time, which correspond to all separate points of view and
which cannot be brought into harmony. Thus at the end the heroine
loses not only her former husband, released after serving twenty
years in a prison camp and condemned to invalidism after a heart
attack, but also her much younger friend, who had posed as a model
for some of her work.

The fateful two decades assume different shapes in the novella
and loom as an impassable barrier between Kira and her illusions
of a carefree life. In fact they represent advancing age, a distancing
from personal development, and the result of irreversible history.
Kira's journey to Kiev with Vadim, the companion of the happy

years of her youth, leads to alienation in its renewed meeting with the past. Kira's indecisiveness causes her to seem guilty toward all three men, in each of whom she seems to be reflected differently. Nekrasov introduces a hopeful element only in a suggestion that the aging Kira may renew her own youth through the joy of life of the likable, wholesome boy Yurochka.

For Kira, who has tried in vain to live past the hard fate of her generation and her people, the only honorable way at the end is resignation, which she can still share with her older companion, who has long since become inwardly isolated.

Because of the uncompromising attitude of the author and especially because of the interweaving of the narrative with many allusions and with contemporary history, *Kira Georgiyevna* was not very favorably received by official critics.

Questions of art are often suggested in the novella, with unmistakable criticism of the false "pomp" and "splendor" of "commercial realism." In this acquired superficiality Nekrasov finds the roots of the heroine's artistic failure.

The criticism of false standards of art is also a theme in his travelogues, especially in the account of his trip to France, where Nekrasov discusses in detail various problems of the film, the theater, the opera, the fine arts, and architecture. Nekrasov here proves that he is a keen observer and a liberal Soviet critic of culture. French culture comes off much better than with most Russian cultural critics of the nineteenth century; for Paris Nekrasov has only panegyrics. In this connection the description of his meeting with Le Corbusier is of special interest, as is his unconditional advocacy of the latter's architecture.

The story *The Experience at the Mamai Hill* (*Sluchai na Mamayevom kurgane*, 1965) is complicated in form. Introduced as the autobiographical account of a journey, the narrative develops into a fantastic confrontation with the past. The author's return to the scene of the battle of Stalingrad—unforgettable for the veteran—ends in a guardroom, which apparently sets the author back to October 1942, but also confronts him with figures from his Stalingrad novel, *In the Trenches of Stalingrad*, and his Stalingrad film, *Soldiers* (*Soldaty*, 1957).

In the story the problem of the contradiction between his own memories and tradition play an important role. The battle of Stalingrad rises expressly in all its "living" reality beside history and tradition. The figures that Nekrasov "invented and did not invent—living and dead friends of perhaps the most significant years" of his life— seem to be marked by a greater verisimilitude than the political decisions of the twenty-three years that have elapsed in the meantime and from which the historic truth seems to have vanished.

"How is one to explain all that to them?" asks the author with reference to the exposure of the personality cult and the renaming of the city of Stalingrad to Volgograd, as well as with reference to the gorgeous monuments for those who fell and the subsequent explanations of the guardians of the museums. "Words, words, words . . ." answers a character (Farber) of the novel, echoing Hamlet, "none of that hits the nail on the head."

Nekrasov's unexpressed thought is that the motives that the present ascribes to history cannot be found at all in the actual past and that the tendency has been to simplify the past. As a symbol for the gap between the present reality Nekrasov uses the flamboyant memorial postage stamps of the twentieth anniversary of the victory (1965), which the dreaming tourist shows his dream figures and which anticipate the monument that is to be erected in honor of the fighters who are still living. The fighters, however, are unable to recognize themselves in this symbol.

## Olga Berggoltz and Margarita Aliger

The two women who became known to wide circles of readers primarily through their war poetry actually first became prominent in the prewar era. Whereas Margarita Aliger initially seemed to follow the acmeist tradition, Olga Berggoltz (born 1910 in Saint Petersburg) directly joined the popular representatives of Russian poetry in the late 1920s and early 1930s, for example Eduard Bagritzki and Nikolai Tikhonov. In her manly, almost stoic pathos Berggoltz is unquestionably a poet of marked individuality, but her compressed language, filled with allusions, can hardly be imagined without her model Pasternak, whose verses occasionally serve her as a motto.

The theme of the war poems *February Diary* (*Fevralskyi dnevnik*, 1942), and *Leningrad Poem* (*Leningradskaya poema*, 1942) is the defense of Leningrad, which the poet lived through from beginning to end. Although Berggoltz describes the nomadic life in the starving, continually bombarded city in truly heartrending tones, she guards against false pathos. She speaks of the "primitive adornment of the hoar frost," of "rustic heaps of snow" under which the streetcar tracks have disappeared, and of the screeching runners of the sleds transporting firewood and corpses. The Leningraders live "in a closed-in ring, in darkness, in hunger, in pain," but they have not stopped reciting poems to one another occasionally in "dwellings black as caves, next to loudspeakers that are silent." Berggoltz herself worked on the Leningrad radio committee; her spoken comments appeared in 1946 in *Here Speaks Leningrad* (*Govorit Leningrad*).

Berggoltz was first married to the poet Boris Kornilov, who was shot during the time of the purges (about 1937). During the war she also lost her second husband. To the memory of these most difficult years (1937–45) she devotes especially her last volume of poems, *The Knot* (*Uzel*, 1965). Berggoltz called this thin volume "New Book of Poetry," but she included in it a great number of earlier poems, which speak of old losses and old despairs. The cycle *Affliction* (*Ispytaniye*) presents in unadorned, laconic form some of the poet's experiences; only in her love for her homeland did she find the strength that enabled her to endure. On the day of the outbreak of the war in June 1941 she makes the notation:

> On this day, too, I do not forget
> The bitter years of persecution and of evil,
> But in the blinding lightning I understood:
> That happened not to me, but happened to you,
> That was your waiting and your maturing.
> No, I have forgotten nothing!
> But even if I were dead or condemned,
> At your call I would rise out of the grave,
> We would all arise, not I alone.

With these verses addressed to Russia, Berggoltz expresses an attitude that was actually recorded in history. The poems *The Knot* form both an intimate confession and a public justification, and Berggoltz wants the confessional aspect of poetry to be understood in precisely this manner. In her prose volume *Stars by Day* (*Dnevniye zvezdy*, 1959) she terms her personal life the "most important book" that she could write, because in it "confession" and "announcement" (*ispoved, propoved*) necessarily coincide. In fact, this quite unchronologically planned book is the nucleus of an autobiography, in which the memories of childhood, travels, and reminiscences of the siege of Leningrad intermingle. The first part, *Trip to a Town of Childhood* (*Poyezdka v gorod detstva*), contains a very poetic description of the old Russian city of Uglich on the Volga. Corresponding to this in *The Knot* is the beautiful poem *Divnaya Church in Uglich* (*Cerkov Divnaya v Ugliche*, 1953). Memories of many years are part of the story *Excursion Beyond the Neva City Boundary* (*Pokhod za Nevskuyu zastavu*), which is dedicated to her home city, Saint Petersburg.

Margarita Aliger (born 1915 in Odessa) also lost her husband in the war; her war poetry in the volume *To the Memory of the Brave* (*Pamyati khrabrykh*, 1942) can be compared with Berggoltz's work in many ways. Aliger, too, uses a softened pathos, and many of her war poems picture the incidents only indirectly but nonetheless clearly, as in *From the Kazan Notebook* (*Iz Kazanskoi tetradi*, 1941) and *Music* (*Muzyka*, 1942). As the poet expresses it, the war seized her soul but "forgot it somewhere on the way":

> And at night thunder above it,
> Hurling stones from the railroad bed,
> Transports with crying children
> Who during the journey have lost their mothers,
> The wheels of crazed freight cars. . . .

The lament over her fallen husband becomes most impressive in the poem *Music*, which actually deals only with the piano that the dead man once played. Aliger always orients herself by visible objects in her immediate surroundings, by the physical "things" of the world, even when she begins to meditate philosophically. In her definitely worldly attitude and in the importance that she assigns to the sensory stimulation provided by her surroundings—tone, color, sound, and smell—the poet is completely loyal to the former demands of acmeism.

Poems of the postwar period that deserve special mention are *Poems from the Crimea* (*Krymskiye stikhi,* 1952), in which Aliger's "objective" poetry reaches its high point. Here she shows her delight not only in new and identifying adjectives but also in exotic names and sounds, as in *Vineyard* (*Vinograd*).

Her poems written from 1935 to 1956 are combined in the volume *Poems* (*Stichotvoreniya,* 1958); the continuation is the collection *Some Steps* (*Neskolko shagov,* 1962; expanded new edition, 1964). In this new book the "narrative" tendency is stronger than formerly, although this development was to be expected, because the poet had always cultivated epic narrative verse. The story in verse of the partisan girl Zoya Kosmodemyanskaya (*Zoya*) had appeared in 1942. Basically the cycle *Lenin Hills* (*Leninskiye gory,* 1953), which deals with the new buildings of Moscow University, is pure verse narrative.

Aliger also wrote numerous poetic reports, especially about her trips abroad at the end of the 1950s and the beginning of the 1960s. She visited Japan, Latin America, and both parts of Germany. The poems of Germany constitute an entire cycle, *Two Meetings: 1958, 1960* (*Dve vstrechi: 1958, 1960*), and the reports of Berlin, Weimar, Dresden, Nuremberg, and Munich, although they deal primarily with the fissure that goes through Germany, also demand an admission of guilt. The poet's impressions of the German landscape are very much like the harmless prettiness of picture postcards; from the distance she still recalls the "enduring little houses" and the "little dwarfs of earthenware":

> Have not their busy little hands
> Saved the fatherland from fire?
> But all the more tantalizingly, Germany,
> You withdraw from me.
>
> *From the Distance (Isdali)*

## Emmanuil Kazakevich and Konstantin Simonov

These two writers, whose themes in many instances overlap and who are about the same age, resemble one another, too, in that both are highly individualistic. Although in Simonov the later phase seems to be the more productive, at least quantitatively, Kazakevich, because of his early death, never completed his projected long novel, which was to cover the history of the last few decades. The few novellas that Kazakevich completed from 1961 to 1962 reveal a narrative and stylistic precision notably lacking in Simonov's novels. Kazakevich himself has a note in his diary (1961): "I have the feeling that only now my real life in literature is beginning."

Emmanuil Kazakevich (1913–62) was born in Kremenchug (Ukraine); both of his parents were teachers. After attending a technical institute in Kharkov, he went in 1931 with a group of Komsomols to the Far East, where he engaged in a great variety of occupations, among others, theater director in the autonomous Jewish state of Birobidzhan. In 1938 he settled in Moscow, to devote himself exclusively to literature. Kazakevich wrote stories, a novel in verse, poetry and a comedy, partly composed during the 1930s, in Yiddish. Not until after the war, in which he participated as a volunteer, did he write in Russian.

The work that suddenly made Kazakevich famous as a Russian writer was the war novel *Star* (*Zvezda*, 1947), notable for its compact form and clear style. "Star" is the password of a reconnaissance group behind the S.S. Division Viking, who are chased and finally destroyed by the Germans. The radio station with which the soldiers are in contact is the "earth." From this play with camouflage the story acquires its symbolic import. Kazakevich, who was given several decorations for bravery, was himself a member of such a reconnaissance detachment at the front, his descriptions in this respect are absolutely authentic. Kazakevich's language is unusually precise and laconic, although the dryness of his expressions frequently rises to sarcasm. Apotheosizing and glorifying the war are entirely foreign to Kazakevich, and pathetic tones are certainly intentionally avoided.

For *Two in the Steppe* (*Dvoye v stepi*, 1948), another novella
of the war, Kazakevich again chooses a very crucial situation, although a number of factors are introduced that limit the credibility
of the story. An officer is condemned to death by a court martial. In
the steppe the officer and his guard are overtaken by the war, and
after many adventurous complications and the death of the guard,
the officer gives himself up to the military authorities and is then
pardoned. The story is perhaps intelligible only under the peculiar
circumstances of Stalinism. In 1948 it meant a courageous review
of the "unjust" death sentences of the courts martial.

Kazakevich next published two novels that depicted the relationship between Germany and Russia, to which the author gave serious
attention. *Spring on the Oder* (*Vesna na Odere*, 1949) and *The
House on the Square* (*Dom na ploshchadi*, 1955) describe the
problems of the confrontation of Russian occupation troops and
the Germans. Apparently the immensity of the problem demanded
too much of the author, even apart from the politically almost in-
soluble question of maintaining an "objective" attitude, at least at
the time.

Kazakevich introduced a new phase in the historic narrative about
Lenin, which appeared in 1961 under the title *Sinyaya tetrad* and
which is set in the summer of 1917, when Lenin had to conceal
himself near Saint Petersburg from Kerenski's agents. Although
Lenin is quite possibly idealized here, no evidence of a special cult
of Lenin is apparent, because this would be counterbalanced by
Kazakevich's observation from close proximity and his fine irony.
Lenin is portrayed as the very opposite of a man of pathos. Kazakevich also planned to write a sequel about Stalin, in order to emphasize the contrast between the two figures.

Psychological analysis of character, together with sparing and
by no means devastating irony, are outstanding characteristics of
Kazakevich's last novella. *By Daylight* (*Pri svete dnya*, 1961) is a
complicated narrative in which the portrait of a captain fallen in the
war is drawn from a double close-up: in the naive and affectionate
account of a suddenly returned war comrade, and in the equally
naive but somewhat attenuated memories of the war widow who re-
married after two years. One point of view seems to contradict the
other, and the story ultimately questions the reality of this man.

The war has already become a legend here, and its truth, which is beginning to disturb people, can be divined, again in a rather naive manner, only by the twelve-year-old son of the fallen man, who lives with his mother and stepfather.

*The Father Visits His Son* (*Priyezd ottza v gosti k synu*, 1962) is also a narrative of the misjudging and misunderstanding of reality. The aged father, with the slyness of a peasant, attempts to swindle his son who, by Soviet standards, is living in very comfortable circumstances. Father and son are no longer able to understand one another or to look into each other's hearts. The modern theme of "alienation" introduced here actually goes through all of Kazakevich's novellas, right from the start, as in *Star*. The "official" public care of the community is in no case a guarantee of the security of Kazakevich's hero. The novella of the father's visit contains very disrespectful talk about the "radio voice striving to be sunny," as in the ironic comment: "The loudspeaker is jubilant in its childish transmission tone."

Konstantin Simonov (born 1915 in Petrograd), began in 1931 in Moscow as a common workman (lathe hand) and made his way through the Moscow Institute of Literature, from which he graduated in 1938. In 1939 he was sent as a reporter to Mongolia, where fierce border disputes with the Japanese took place at the Manchurian-Mongolian frontier. From 1940 to 1941 Simonov was trained by the Red Army as a war correspondent, and shortly before the outbreak of the war he was given a military rank. In the war, as a reporter for *Red Star*, Simonov often took part in operations in the very front lines and received several war decorations. The war also made Simonov known as a poet, and his verses were painted in huge letters on the house walls in beleaguered Leningrad.

Poems written during or about the war constitute the greater part of Simonov's poetic production, which he published in *Three Notebooks: Verses and Verse Narratives* (*Tri tetradi: Stikhi, poemi*). The middle volume (over 200 pages) is devoted to the war and contains, of course, the well-known lines, written in 1941:

> Wait for me, then I will come back.
> Only you must wait very much,
> Wait, when you become sad,

In yellow rain showers,
Wait, when the snow sweeps down,
Wait in the heat,
Wait, when one does not wait for others any more,
No longer thinking of yesterday.

Not all of Simonov's poems are as impressive as this, but many of his verses speak with his whole heart and soul of suffering humanity. Simonov's real domain is the ballad and the epic verse narrative, but · after the war he turned only intermittently to poetry. Between 1940 and 1952 Simonov also wrote nine dramas. The major part of his work, however, is from his last years, in the novel.

His first and immediately successful novel, which was awarded a Stalin Prize in 1946, appeared during the war as *Days and Nights* (*Dni i nochi*, 1944). This work describes the first phase of the defense of Stalingrad from the late summer of 1942 to the November offensive, which initiated the encirclement of Stalingrad and the German Sixth Army. In the middle of the action is the battalion led by Captain Saburov; it is thrown into the struggles in the city and goes through the "hell" of this battle. The environment described is that of the battalion commander himself, who, on the whole, is idealized much more than the officers in Nekrasov's Stalingrad novel.

Artistically, however, Simonov is quite the equal of the earlier Nekrasov, and in his almost naive attachment to truth and in the directness of his interpretations and evaluations, Simonov did not excel himself later. Through the battle in the city the front and the rear are brought together, and the little details clearly show the importance of defending home and hearth.

Later, Simonov returns persistently to the theme of the war. In the "new wave" of critical literature on World War II Simonov is one of the leading exponents of the exposure of the personality cult around Stalin. In the novel *One Is Not Born a Soldier* (*Soldatami ne rozhdayutsya*, 1964) he even has Stalin appear personally, and draws a rather accurate picture of the dictator in conversation with a commander at the front.

This novel is the third in a cycle of incomplete historic novels about World War II that began with *Comrades in Arms* (*Tovarishchi po oruzhiyu*, 1952). This first novel, revised in 1961, is set in the

Far East at the Mongolian frontier, and Simonov included a number of persons, such as the functionary and war correspondent Sincov, in the second part of the cycle.

The really "new" phase begins only with the novel *The Living and the Dead* (*Zhiviye i mertviye*, 1959), in which the fateful beginning of the war is described as far as the turn in events at the battle before Moscow. In this work, however, Simonov devotes more attention to historical justice than to literary problems, and the new novels, even though they use some of Tolstoi's artistic devices, do not present such convincing poetic truth as *Days and Nights*. Perhaps such a presentation is relatively difficult after twenty years; the aims of the "historical" novel may be entirely different. The extent to which Simonov exerted himself is indicated in the author's comments on his excerpts from the war diary *Every Day is Long* (*Kazhdy den—dlinnyi*, 1965). The immediate impressions, despite the fragmentary and incidental character of the notes, are far more vivid and convincing than the critical and brooding thoughts of the protagonists of the last cycle of novels, which is to be concluded with a fourth part.

## Boris Slutzki

Only in the middle of the 1950s, after the Twentieth Party Congress had led to a loosening of controls, was any attention given to the poet Boris Slutzki (born 1919 in Slavyansk), whose nonconformist poetry hardly reflected public taste before Stalin's death. In fact, Slutzki did not publish his first volume of collected poems, *Remembrance* (*Pamyat*), until 1957, although it contained poems from the 1940s and even a ballad of the war.

The ballad, which, according to the oral account of a Yugoslav teacher whom he met in the Balkans Slutzki had already composed, is entitled *The Cologne Pit* (*Kelnskaya yama*) and describes the destruction of thousands of prisoners of war in a cave near Cologne. Another balladlike poem from the postwar period, *Horses in the Ocean* (*Loshadi v okeane*), tells of a tragic incident in the war. The transport vessel *Gloria*, struck by a mine, goes down, and although the men are able to rescue themselves in the lifeboats, a hundred horses swimming in the water are doomed to drown:

> Horses can swim.
> But not well. Not far.

The peculiar style of this poem and of the majority of Slutzki's poems is formed by an intonation that is almost entirely "dry" and by a language that is prosaic, in fact, almost jejune; in spite of this an unusual, very "virile" poem is developed, with a strong rhythm that becomes apparent only when the verses are read aloud. Slutzki secures strong accents through his clear syntactical structure, in which he, incidentally, often follows Khlebnikov. Thus his language is not emotional but quite pithy, almost "primitive." Slutzki's simplicity is, like that of Khlebnikov, almost polemic; it expresses itself especially in the repetition of the same clauses, the same word families, or the same word-stems (*polyptoton*).

Slutzki never uses hackneyed words, and he is not afraid to introduce definitely "unpoetic" words and expressions. Typical, perhaps, is the poem *Bath* (*Banya*, 1947), in which in the very second line the unpoetic, modern word for "provincial" (*"periferiny,"* lying on the periphery) occurs. The district bathing establishment is probably not a very poetic subject, with its naked and partly war-crippled bathers, but that is the very thing that concerns Slutzki; he wants to preserve memories of the war, to present the theme man and war close up without fanfare and marble plaques. In the last stanza, Slutzki closes with a play on words: the word *ray* ("paradise" and an abbreviation for *"rayon,"* which means "district-" as a combining form) is used with a double meaning:

> You know the district bathhouse ["paradise bath," *raibanya*],
>       don't you?
> For every admission you pay two rubles.

Although Slutzki took part in all of World War II as a volunteer and was wounded three times, he wrote hardly anything during the war. The conflict was a favorite theme in his works, however. The title of his first book, *Remembrance*, may be understood in this sense, because it gives much space to the war. It was followed by the volumes *Time* (*Vremya*, 1958), *Today and Yesterday* (*Segodnya i vchera*, 1961), and *Work* (*Rabota*, 1964). Slutzki also frequently published poems in the annual *Day of Poetry* (*Den poezii*) and was a very active translator, of Berthold Brecht, for example. In smaller format, too, Slutzki, produced some very interesting experimental pieces. Today he belongs among the most modern poets of Russia.

His admonition (in a small poem in *Day of Poetry*, 1966) is "Don't pass off half-wits for wits, or half white for white."

# The Older Literary Avant-Garde

### CODA

The last vestiges of the avant-garde in Russian literature disappeared in the early 1930s. The term "avant-garde" in the general sense in which it is used with reference to a dominant movement of the time is, of course, not to be taken quite literally. Not every writer of the period in which avant-gardism prevailed can be classified as a representative of the avant-garde. Many belonged to it only intermittently and with only a few works.

Meanwhile, with the turn to a conservative, even reactionary cultural policy, a once tempestuous development was artificially suppressed or terminated. Many literary styles, of course, had probably reached their peak by 1930 in any case. On the other hand, the 1920s, as well as the first four or five years before World War I and certainly the years of the revolutionary discussions before and after October 1917, left inextinguishable traces in the minds of those involved. The final wave of memoirs and literary reminiscences entered the market, generally attempting to settle a feeling of an unredeemed guilt toward these years on the part of the older generation.

The names, facts, and experiments of the time of the young and innovation-loving avant-garde have in the meantime been "rehabilitated." It is of importance for the cultural process that the memories of competent witnesses of the epoch should no longer be suppressed. Unfortunately the ranks of the former avant-garde were frightfully thinned out through the "purges" of the 1930s and many witnesses, documents, and manuscripts no longer exist. Although these gloomy aspects of the epoch are no longer hidden, they are usually mentioned more or less laconically and not infrequently circumscribed. Thus L. Polyak's preface to a new edition (1966) of the stories of Isaac Babel (1894–1941) states: "On May 15, 1939, Babel was subjected to an illegal repression and lost his life." In the preface to another edition of Babel, which also appeared in 1966, Ilya Ehrenburg writes a comment that begs, as it were, for absolution: "Babel was arrested in the spring of 1939. I learned of it only later—I was in France. Mobilized troops marched through the streets, ladies strolled about with gas masks, the windows were pasted up with strips of paper."

### Some Poets, Novelists, and Memoirists

Among the oldest representatives of the avant-garde the interesting translator and author of children's books Samuil Marshak (1887–1964), the friend of many avant-garde poets, did not become known for his own poetry ("for adults") until after the war; his merits in children's literature and theater were also appreciated only in later years. A close friend of Maksim Gorki, he studied in London before World War II. He then published his universally praised translation of Shakespeare's sonnets—an effort that is both "classically" strict and eminently poetic. Also notable are Marshak's translations of works of Robert Burns, Byron, Shelley, Keats, Heine, and Petöfi.

Marshak's own best poems are simple and artless in their expression. They became shorter and pithier in form as his work matured. His other writings include *Poetic Epigrams* (*Liricheskiye epigrammy*, 1965), which manifest the wisdom of old age in simple and striking form:

> Time is dear at its time.
> One has much and little time.
> Long time is no time
> When it has run out.

Another poet of the older generation, Pavel Antokolski (born 1896 in Saint Petersburg), the son of an attorney and later an actor and director of the Vakhtangov Theater in Moscow, also became known in his later years to the general public. His verse narrative about the fallen soldier, *My Son* (*Syn*, 1943), belongs to the most impressive poetic works of the war. His language and images have a very traditional, even old-fashioned flavor, which is also characteristic of his partly autobiographical verse narrative about Moscow, *In the Alley Back of the Arbat* (*V pereulke za Arbatom*, 1954).

The memoirs of Mikhail Slonimski (born 1897 in Pavlovsk), published as *Book of Memories* (*Kniga vospominani*, 1966) and originating in the group known as the Serapion Brothers, especially enriches contemporary knowledge of the legendary House of the Arts (*Dom iskusstv*, Saint Petersburg, 1921–22). The author gives much space to Gorki and also to the recently rehabilitated Aleksandr Grin, Olga Forsh, Boris Pilnyak, Nikolai Nikitin, Mikhail Zoshchenko, and the playwright Yevgenii Shvartz.

Slonimski's later novels, *Engineers* (*Inzhenery*, 1950) and *True Friends* (*Verniye druzya*, 1951), unfortunately indicate that he was primarily a "fellow-traveler," who was inspired in his first and only successes by the atmosphere of a lively community.

Nikolai Tikhonov (born 1896 in Saint Petersburg), also formerly a member of the Serapion Brothers, devoted himself during and after the war almost entirely to publicity, reporting, and journalistic activities. His stories and verses are confined generally to political themes or exotic scenes, as in *Stories about Pakistan* (*Rasskazy o Pakistane*, 1950), the volume of poems *Two Streams, Verses about Pakistan and Afghanistan* (*Dva potoka, Stikhi o Pakistane i Afganistane*, 1951), and *Stories of the Hill Country* (*Rasskazy gornoi strany*, 1951), also set in Afghanistan.

During the war Tikhonov wrote articles and feuilletons in besieged Leningrad: *Tales of Leningrad* (*Leningradskiye rasskazy*) and *Leningrad Accepts the Challenge* (*Leningrad prinimayet boi*, 1942–44). Besides this, Tikhonov is a reconized translator, especially of middle-Asiatic poetry—Georgian, Armenian, Tadzhik, and Uzbek. Through a trip to China he was inspired to write *Verses about China* (*Stikhi o Kitaye*, 1959). The collected works of the poet appeared in 1958–59 in six volumes.

The collected works of Nikolai Aseyev (1898–1963) were published in five volumes, 1963–64. Aseyev's poems, however, indicate the difficulties encountered by the former "avant-gardists" in attempting to depart from their earlier attitudes. Whereas Aseyev's war verses contain solely rhetorical elements, his books that appeared after 1955 manifest an increasing effort to present a "new" Aseyev, appearing in the simpler, unadorned, and dispassionate style of old age. The volume *Harmony* (*Lad*, 1961) contains poems that sometimes resemble foreign works and in which the real Aseyev is missing. Unlike Pasternak, Aseyev did not experience a "rebirth," despite the flawless form of some of the very "small" poems, such as *Golden Balls* (*Zolotiye shari*, 1956). Such rhetorical poems as *Beginning* (*Nachalo*, 1960) or *Lenin's Time* (*Vremya Lenina*, 1960) may be ignored here, because they contain no new formal elements. A similar criticism applies to the volume *My Very Own Poems* (*Samiye moi stikhi*, 1962), in which, however, a confessional poem about the rehabilitated Velimir Khlebnikov (1885–1922) is striking.

Aseyev's poem *Dream* (*Son*) describes a vision of the return of Khlebnikov to the association of the poets (*soyuz poetov*). The "prophet," who has only to announce the "naked truth," stands among the moneychangers in the temple; he seems "helpless and honest in a dignified manner." The dreamer, however, seems paralyzed and cannot run to his aid.

> I have not sworn off, and no cock has crowed at midnight,
> But the dream broke off, and it was time to get up. . . .
> If one can't blow a grain of dust away with a thought,
> How could one possibly move a mountain with it?

Of the group of the former "constructivists" Vera Inber (born 1890 in Odessa) and Ilya Selvinski (born 1899 in Simferopol) are active in literature. Inber became known particularly through her long narrative in verse in besieged Leningrad, which was published in 1943 as *The Meridian Pulkovo* (*Pulkovski Meridian*). Somewhat later she published *Almost Three Years: Leningrad Diary* (*Pochti tri goda. Leningradski dnevnik*, 1946), which like so many other documents of these years described the time of terror in the besieged city.

Selvinski's works have been reprinted frequently during the last few years. His pedagogic work *Verse Studio* (*Studiya stikha*) appeared in 1962. Selvinski has preserved certain elements of constructivist poetry, and even the war poems contain elements of avant-gardism, as in *Ballads and Songs* (*Balladi i pesni*, 1943). His language is never hackneyed; rhythmic swing and wit are among his major characteristics. His newer poems include much occasional, satirical and children's verses. He wrote the following lines in 1956 to celebrate the Twentieth Party Congress:

> To you I talk, the platter-lickers,
> Who would like to wipe out all traces,
> Who are ready to exchange
> Socialism for a pig's trough.
> Don't thresh any empty straw
> About friendship, freedom and happiness!
> The people need the truth:
> The more bitter it is, the sweeter.

His most recent publications are *Lyrics* (*Lirika*, 1959), *About Time, About Destinies, About Love* (*O vremeni, o sudbach, o lubvi*, 1962), and *Lyrics* (*Lirika*, 1964).

Kornelii Zelinski (born 1896), the former theoretician of the "Literary Center of the Constructivists," published his memoirs as *At the Border of Two Epochs: Literary Confrontations from 1917 to 1920* (*Na rubezhe dvuch epoch. Literaturniye vstrechi 1917–1920 godov*, 1959).

Memoirs were also written by Viktor Shklovski (born 1893 in Saint Petersburg), whose production of technical works on literature, the film, and individual artists during the last few years is impressive. Of unusual importance in connection with the avantgarde is the volume of memoirs *Once Upon a Time* (*Zhili-byli*, 1964), which contains personal memories, memories of Mayakovski in *About Mayakovski* (*O Mayakovskrom*), and *Meetings* (*Vstrechi*), which discusses the avant-grade film as well as Isaac Babel, Yurii Tynyanov, and other contemporaries. The book *During Forty Years* (*Za sorok let*, 1965) is devoted to the development of the Soviet film; it is a major source for historians and film enthusiasts.

*Anna Akhmatova*

The death of Anna Akhmatova (1889–1966) extinguished the last great "star" of the Russian firmament of poets, whose light had risen before the Revolution. The personally very modest poet enjoyed widespread recognition at home and abroad only in her last years—a recognition that she had always deserved. In 1964 she was given the Etna-Taormina Prize in Italy, and in 1965 she was awarded an honorary doctor's degree at Oxford.

Today Akhmatova is admired not only for her poems, but also for her unswerving fidelity to her homeland during the most difficult times. Her verses manifest strong, direct, free, and natural feelings but at the same time old cultural traditions, to which she adhered despite all hostility.

A considerable part of her poetry written since 1940 was made available to the reader only after 1958, because Zhdanov had condemned her as the representative of the "hostile and reactionary ideals of the literary miasma."

Since 1958 a selection of volumes of her collected poems has again reappeared in the Soviet Union; most comprehensive is *The Flight of Time* (*Beg vremeni*, 1965). In 1965 a comprehensive edition of her works *Works I* (*Sochineniya I*) was also begun by Russian emigrants.

Akhmatova's principal work from her later period of activity is the verse epic *Poem Without Heroes* (*Poema bez geroya*), at which the poet worked from 1940. Several preliminary versions of this work exist; the most comprehensive appeared abroad, as in the almanac *Vozdushniye Puti*, 1960–61.

The principal story line, concerning the suicide of a twenty-year-old dragoon cornet in front of the house of a famous and faithless actress, is overshadowed by visions of an epochal confrontation that decides the destiny of Russia, which Akhmatova investigates paradigmatically in the legendary aura surrounding Saint Petersburg. The narrative is both a judgment on the past and a catharsis, because it is dominated by conscience. Externally this part of the epic is a carnival in which only masks appear; the personal and literary allusions are extraordinarily rich. The masks, however, are figures in a *roman à clef*; A. Pavlovski has explained them in his book *Anna Akhmatova* (Leningrad, 1966).

Akhmatova returns to the language of the Silver Age, that is, to the "code" of symbolism and its great figures, but the grotesque elements of this midnight "Hoffmanniade" point to Pushkin and Gogol as inspiration for the Saint Petersburg legend.

*Intermezzo*, the considerably shorter second part of the epic, is a discussion of the meaning of the story and a digression into personal matters. The theme of the poem is compared with a chrysanthemum crushed on the floor "after the coffin has been carried out."

The real hero of *Poem Without Heroes*, however, is the history or special legend of Saint Petersburg, which the author sought to express all her life. Thus the scene of action of the third part is Leningrad, the suffering Leningrad of the years of the war and blockade:

> And my city stands sewed-in,
> Heavily rest the grave stones
> On your sleepless eyes. . . .

At the time of these events the author had been evacuated to Tashkent (1942–44), but she sees herself chained to the fate of her beloved city:

> My shadow is on your walls,
> My reflection in the canals,
> The sound of my steps in the halls of the Hermitage. . . .

The epic deals with the downfall of the old world (1913) and the trials of the new years. This theme runs consistently through the literary productivity of the last decades, beginning with *Requiem* (*Rekviyem*) on which she worked from 1934 to 1940, expressing the suffering after the arrest of her son Lev Gumilev. It was published in Russian in Munich in 1963.

The Saint Petersburg that Akhmatova continually experienced in her literary tradition is present in *Northern Elegies* (*Severniye elegii*, 1943, including *Leningrad Elegies*). It appears in most of the poems of the war years, and also in *Summer Garden* (*Letni sad*, 1959), in *Second Anniversary* (*Vtoraya godovshchina*, 1946, describing the anniversary of the author's return to Leningrad), in *Three Poems* (*Tri stikhotvoreniya,* 1944–60, about Aleksandr Blok), and in numerous other poems.

Pushkin occupies a special place in her writings, as in *Pushkin* (*Pushkin,* 1943) and *City of Pushkin* (*Gorodu Pushkina,* 1957), and quite a few of her poems were dedicated to him. The town of Tzarskoye Selo (now Pushkin) remains an "ideal landscape," and in her *Ode on Tzarskoye Selo* (*Tzarskoselskaya oda,* 1961) she seeks to describe the city "like his Vitebsk-Chagall." The erotic theme appears in the postwar poetry in the cycle *Cinque* (1945/46), although deliberate rejection and renunciation become increasingly dominant, as in *Out of a Burned Up Notebook* (*Iz sozhzhennoi tetradi,* 1946).

A preponderance of the anthological and the epigrammatic appears in Akhmatova's later poetry; these styles are especially suited to her taut and pithy diction. She dedicated the cycle *Secrets of the Trade* (*Taini remesla,* 1936–60) to her own poetry. One of the poems from 1940 contains these lines:

> I find that in verse everything must be à propos (*nekstati*),
> No so, as in the case of human beings.
> If you knew out of what heaps of rubbish
> Verses grow, without knowing shame,
> Like yellow dandelions at the fence,
> Like burdocks and weeds.

Here Akhmatova shows why her poems cannot be termed "beautiful" and "harmonious" in the sense of classical poetry. Her secret consists of concealed dissonances and discords of images, rhymes and rhythms, deliberately avoiding smooth and graceful euphony.

During the extraordinarily fruitful Tashkent period, her poetry was enriched with oriental images. Tashkent and Leningrad overlap here and lead to an attractive neighborliness.

*The Seventh Book* (*Sedmaya kniga*) in *The Flight of Time* (1965) was to be Akhmatova's last book; she rests in the earth that she describes in *Native Soil* (*Rodnaya zemlya,* 1961):

> Yes, for us it is the dirt on the galoshes;
> Yes, for us it is the gnashing of one's teeth.
> And we grind, we knead and crumble

This dust involved in nothing.
But we are laid in it and become like it,
Therefore we call it so freely—ours.

*Boris Pasternak*

Shortly before World War II, after several critical pauses in his poetic activity, Boris Pasternak (1890–1960) found the style that characterizes his last period. His collection *On the Early Trains* (*Na rannikh poezdakh*, 1943) consists principally of the two cycles *Peredelkino* (January 1941), named after the writer's colony that was his last place of residence, and the *War Poems* (*Stikhi o voine*). In these cycles Pasternak's poetic meditation concerns itself mainly with the present, but it also touches on the living past and the timeless Russian destiny, as in *The Old Park* (*Stari park*, 1941) and *Winter Approaches* (*Zima priblizhayetsya*, 1943), and devotes itself to faith in the future, as in the title poem *On the Early Trains* (1941) and *Spring* (*Vesna*, 1944).

The poems are strongly accented and are bound by forceful rhymes and clearly marked syntactic grouping. Metaphors are used more sparingly than formerly, but they maintain their whole weight and their poetic power of suggestion, as in the images of stars in *The Cold Cavern of January*. The last volume of poems, *When It Clears Up* (*Kogda razgulyayetsya*), was published in Russian in the almost complete edition of *Poems and Narrative Verse* (*Stikhotvoreniya i poemy*, 1965). *When It Clears Up* contains the poems of 1956 to 1959 and is full of joy, spiritual gaiety, and confidence. Especially to be mentioned are the four poems about Aleksandr Blok, *Wind* (*Veter*), the beautiful poem *Music* (*Muzika*), which concludes with a suggestion of Tchaikovski's *Francesca da Rimini*, and the cycle *The Bacchanal* (*Vakchanaliya*), which was inspired by a factual occurrence, the premiere of *Maria Stuart* (in Pasternak's translation). Drama—the stage as the reflection of reality—always meant much to Pasternak, and therefore the metaphor of the play, which Pasternak describes as "insane daring," is of central importance.

In 1958 Pasternak was awarded the Nobel Prize for Literature, primarily for his poetry; for political reasons, however, he declined the award. Although a collection of the poems planned in 1956 never appeared, the preface (two versions, 1956, 1957) was published outside of Russia in 1959 under the title *Autobiography* (*Avtobiograficheski ocherk*); the English edition was entitled *I Remember*. The version of 1957, authorized by Pasternak's son, was published in 1967 in *Novyi mir* under the title *People and Situations* (*Lyudi i polozheniya*).

In his autobiography (1956) Pasternak refers to his novel *Doctor Zhivago*, which he had just completed, as "my decisive and important work, the only one of which I am not ashamed and for which I will courageously vouch." Pasternak regarded his previous poetic work as only the "first stage of the novel."

In form, the architectonic structure of the novel may appear both confusing and disappointing to the superficial reader. The many fateful "incidents" in the lives of the leading figures have often been criticized as weak points in the work, although certain critics have not fully recognized either the historical-chronological plan (covering the years between 1903 and 1943) or the symbolic scheme of the novel. As in the traditional novel the various stages in the story of Zhivago's life are set in the foreground of the narrative. Considered purely as a story, however, the book is actually a continued confession of the author and an optimistic vision, grounded in the depths of his consciousness, of the victory of light and of the inalienable freedom of the human soul.

Like Dostoyevski's late novels, *Doctor Zhivago* contains a definite, personal message, which Pasternak himself regarded as the essence of his life experiences and of his artistic objectives. The presentation of such a message is also the motivation for including in the novel a complete cycle of poems in Part XVII, *The Poems of Yurii Zhivago* (*Stikhotvoreniya Yuriya Zhivago*). The poems, which essentially present a variety of religious motifs, are woven into the action of the novel as part of the hero's consciousness.

The twenty-five poems, the first of which is entitled *Hamlet* and the last *The Garden of Gethsemane*, are, of course at the same time the work of the poet Pasternak and show his personal stamp. They are stylized only in the depiction of the epic figure, or rather Zhivago is a stylized portrait of Pasternak, although not an exact autobiographical representation. In a certain sense, of course, all the principal figures of the novel are "autogenous" (L. Rzhevski), but the author is no more a prototype for Zhivago than the figure of Hamlet (in Pasternak's interpretation) or even the figure of Christ (Viktor Frank).

The characters of the novel—especially Zhivago, Lara, Antipov-Strelnikov—are from the start firmly fixed as in a constellation. The characters, their encounters, and the intermingling of their destinies has to be understood symbolically: the house in the Urals (Varykino), the room in Moscow, the quarter around the Brest railroad station, and Petrovka, the landscape of Pasternak's own childhood. In this regard *Doctor Zhivago* is remarkably close to Andrei Belyi's symbolic novels *The Silver Dove* and *Saint Petersburg*.

Critics have repeatedly stressed the mystique of light in Pasternak —the gleaming candle in the "eye" of the window in Moscow—and indeed the shining light is the leitmotif and central symbol of the novel, as in the poem *Winter Night* (*Zimnayaya noch*).

Pasternak fits the historic revolutions and the difficult destinies of mankind in dark times into a symbolic scheme (the "Kingdom of God" in the world), and he expressly rejects man as the "proud" (Gorki) measure of history. In the highly compressed final portion (Part XV) Lara, at Zhivago's corpse, gives final and frankly polemic expression to the common faith:

> Just that, exactly that was the principal thing that made them similar and bound them together. Never, never, not even in the moments of the most heavenly, unconscious happiness did what was highest and breathtaking desert them: the joy in the whole pattern of the world, the involvement of themselves in the entire painting, the sensation of their belonging to the beauty of the whole spectacle, to the entire universe. Only in this communality had they breathed. Thus the elevation of man above the rest of nature, the fashionable coddling and worship of him, had not attracted them. The principles of a hollow sociability that had been transformed into politics looked to them like amateurish work and remained unintelligible to them.

The novel is told in a free "auctorial" manner and refers artistically and morally to the figure of the author, leading to the use of an elevated "literary" narrative language, free from all local color. The latter, in the form of familiar, vulgar, or dialectic speech, is introduced only at the periphery in subordinate figures or in dialogue typical of a given time. Pasternak's poetry abounds in sharply drawn landscape descriptions filled with suggestive comparisons, and the novel gains from the poetic intensity of such passages. In spare, masterly descriptions it evokes the Russian landscape as well as the "holy city" of Moscow of the years before the war, during the war, and in the revolution. The lyrical passages and the *Poems of Yurii Zhivago* correspond to the descriptions of consciousness and the thoughts of the chief characters, which approach a wholly "abstract" (L. Rzhevski) form of expression.

The first edition of *Doctor Zhivago* appeared in Italian (Milan, 1957). The novel has been printed in Russian only outside the Soviet Union. The complete edition (four volumes) of Boris Pasternak's works was published by the University of Michigan Press in 1961.

## Ilya Ehrenburg

Ilya Ehrenburg (1891–1967) vigorously opposed fascism during the war, which, he noted, actually began in the summer of 1936 with the Spanish Civil War. He attempted to record the incidents of these years, in more or less one-sided interpretations, on three different levels—as a journalist, as a novelist, and as the author of his personal memoirs.

The historic trilogy of the war novels is introduced by *The Fall of Paris* (*Padeniye Parizha*, 1942), describing an event that Ehrenburg witnessed as the Paris correspondent of *Izvestiya*.

Ehrenburg uses numerous figures from the different levels of French society to interpret the causes of the French collapse, materially and historically, and to refer it to an epochal conflict. The period of the narration extends from the middle of the 1930s across the people's front and the Spanish War to July 14, 1940, in occupied Paris. Ehrenburg's war novel *The Storm* (*Burya*, 1947) gains in moral intensity by presenting the world of the Gestapo and the concentration camps. The action of the novel ranges from France and

England throughout Europe to the Soviet-German front. In *The Storm* and *The Fall of Paris* Ehrenburg follows the historical situations precisely, and his imagination plays with all the possibilities that arise in the minds of the participants and observers affected simultaneously by the numerous incidents.

In contrast to his situation in World War I, which was shown in Ehrenburg's novel *Julio Jurenito* (*Yulio Yurenito*), the narrator is irrevocably committed to his own cause; the course of events is unified by the thought of the final victory. Self-irony has been displaced by bitter anger and the conviction of the unassailability of his own position, of the position of Communism and the cause of the Jewish people.

The subordination of the psychological elements to the pattern of friend-foe thinking during the war and in the postwar years also determines the action of the novel *The Ninth Wave* (*Devyati val,* 1952), which Ehrenburg, however, did not include in the last nine-volume edition of his works (1962).

The return to the psychological story and to the tradition of Chekhov in Ehrenburg's *The Thaw* (*Ottepel,* 1954) is a surprise for the reader and the critic. In this work, set among the small and intimate circles of the intelligentsia of an unimportant city on the Volga, the author's primary concern is with the feelings and views of people who think of no goal, who do not think at all.

Questions not yet solved, allusions, and chiaroscuro make a much stronger impression in this story than in Ehrenburg's earlier declarations. The title *The Thaw*, a happy and deliberate choice, became the slogan for the entire period of transition from the false monumentality of Stalinism to the present. In fact, Ehrenburg here applied his candid and unmistakable criticism to the cold and routine pseudo-art, the art "made to order"; he definitely shows his preference for the genuine "feeling" for a subject. True art must be rediscovered gradually and carefully: "Today Raphael would be denied admission to an artists' association."

The factory director and manager of the old school, who belongs to the "over-insurers" and those who would raise production to the level of "116%," is exposed with notable irony. In the end he loses his position through a sudden change of the weather in the literal sense of the word.

A very interesting feature of *The Thaw* is Ehrenburg's frequent use of reports of thoughts and of "interior monologues." This story follows a definite pattern in its indication that the intimate sphere of consciousness, comprising love, longing, and doubt, again count for something.

Among Ehrenburg's best works are the six books of memoirs *People, Years, Life* (*Lyudi, godi, zhizn*; first printing in *Novyi mir*, 1961–65). These gripping remembrances of his life extend from his childhood to 1954 and record an important phase of European political and intellectual development.

His range of acquaintances is particularly notable, comprising virtually every leftist active between 1911 and 1954. He expresses himself quite frankly about a whole chapter of Russian literature, from the symbolists and Voloshin, Mandelstamm, Yesenin, Mayakovski, Tzvetayeva, and Pasternak until almost the immediate present. As a witness and contemporary, Ehrenburg presents much detailed information and an extremely comprehensive view of his time.

Revelations about the Stalinist system and about Ehrenburg's personal relations with Stalin, which might have been expected at the appearance of the sixth book (1965), are given only sparingly and incidentally. Apparently this phase of public and private life cannot yet be treated in memoirs, as Ehrenburg indicated: "More than once I broached this chapter, made some outlines, tore up what I had written and realized finally, that I could not keep my promise. . . ."

## Konstantin Fedin

Konstantin Fedin, a very successful novelist even at the beginning of his career in the 1920s, began his principal work, a novel-trilogy not yet completed, in his maturity. In his *Author, Art, Time* (*Pisatel, iskusstvo, vremya*, 1957), Fedin himself explained the origin of the plan, which anticipated a number of essential questions arising from the author's recollections of historical events. He indicates that the great work had hovered in his imagination since the

1930s as a novel about the world of the theater; the war then impelled a transfer of emphasis to historical and historical-philosophical questions.

During the war Fedin composed the first part of his trilogy, *Early Joys* (*Perviye radosti,* 1945), set in the peaceful year of 1910 in Saratov on the Volga. The historical and social situation is of course determined by the revolution fermenting underground, but only later do the "positive" heroes—the student Kiril Izvekov and the illegally working railroad locksmith Petr Ragozin—participate in it directly.

The actual problematical character in the center of the story is the young writer and dramatic poet Aleksandr Pastukhov, who with his intelligent irony is primarily an observer and only reluctantly a participant. If Pastukhov is indeed the principal figure of the trilogy, then his development from the spoiled and superior worldling to the passionate proponent of the common cause and thus the executor of the historic necessity is the nucleus of the work. Pastukhov, grown obese through good living, is undoubtedly a descendant of Pierre Bezukhov in Tolstoi's *War and Peace.*

Fedin's trilogy is actually linked with Tolstoi in many ways. In the essay *The Art of Lev Tolstoi* (*Iskusstvo Lva Tolstovo,* 1954) and in the sketch *In the Summertime in Yasnaya Polyana* (*Letom v Yasnoi Polyane,* 1959) Fedin reveals the importance of Tolstoi's influence on his work. The trilogy is not an imitation of *War and Peace,* but it could not have been conceived without that great novel as a model.

Although Fedin's trilogy spans more years than Tolstoi's epic, it brings into play a peculiar and compelling continuity, especially in the historic phases that centered around the years 1910, 1919, and 1941. The large cast of characters remains recognizable throughout the interweaving of the narrative elements and thus makes the parts into an essentially homogeneous whole. The theme of art and stage develops its own dynamic power, carried along by Pastukhov's profession as writer and poet and by Anna Ulina (Anochka) who becomes an actress. Her story runs through all parts of the trilogy and tells how she joined her life to that of the organizer Kiril Izvekov, who is active in war and peace (and also in the party). A typical and not unimportant minor part is given the character actor Tzvetukhin, who acts as a kind of catalytic agent.

In the second part of the trilogy, *No Ordinary Summer* (*Neobyknovennoye leto*, 1947–48), the historic point of reference is the decisive crisis of the civil war in the summer of 1919, and the scene of action for long stretches is again the provincial city of Saratov. This middle section is most definitely determined by the rules of socialist realism and even by the personality cult, in that at the end Stalin personally appears in the Red Army camp and favors Kiril Izvekov with an encouraging greeting. Pastukhov, who at the end of the first part experiences the great shock of the news of the flight and death of Tolstoi, is pushed by the heroes of action somewhat into the background of the middle section. His final development is only outlined in the so far existing chapters of the third and most essential novel of the trilogy.

Fedin has been occupied with this work for many years; it reflects a synthesis of his entire literary activity. The symbolical title of this work, *The Funeral Pyre* (*Koster*), refers to the flame of the war as well as the flame of the united national resistance to Hitler. As a motto Fedin placed at the head of his novel: "The wind blows out the candle, but it blows up the flames of the pyre." The first book of this novel, in which the scenes of action are continually changing, is entitled *The Invasion of the Enemy* (*Vtorzheniye*, 1961) and has been completed. In it Fedin departs from the purely auctorial principle of the middle part, in order to illuminate the time of the outbreak of the war (June 1941) in a psychoanalytic manner.

The consistency with which the story in *No Ordinary Summer* is interrupted by digressions into military science and historiography has its counterpart in *The Funeral Pyre* in the consistency with which the personal experiences and memories are analyzed in various segments. The first book of the novel comprises only the two days of June 21 and 22, 1941, as well as the few days following the outbreak of the war. Because the point of view is shifted several times through other persons, the war breaks out three or four times, until finally a grouping of the different lines of action is possible.

Technically Fedin makes a connection with his first novels by means of these shifts in time, on which long memories of the past are imposed. Fedin's historical comments in the middle portion of the trilogy recall Tolstoi, as do the psychological analysis and the special use that Fedin makes in the third part of the inner monologue, of the "experienced speech" and the self-analysis of the hero. B. Brainina, in her study of Tolstoi and Fedin, and M. Borisova, in her investigation of the style of the first two parts of the trilogy, have already shown the connections.

Chapters 13 and 14 of the second book of the third part, *The Hour Is Here* (*Chas nastal*), were without doubt intended as the culminating point of the novel *The Funeral Pyre*. In these chapters the writer Pastukhov visits the Tolstoi memorial in Yasnaya Polyana in the face of the approaching German troops (*Novyi mir*, February 1967). For the time being Fedin describes the war and the actions in the war through the eyes of civilians; in this passage Tolstoi may have inspired him again. Especially typical is the episode in Brest, where Anna Ulina, just arrived as the guest of the theater, experiences the inferno of the night of June 22. The hours in Brest and the later flight show the war from a new and unusual point of view.

*The Hour Is Here* has not yet been completed, and the three published sections (*Novyi mir*, 1965–67) do not permit the expression of a final judgment. Here, too, the growing generation— the children of Pastukhov, Izvekov, and Ragozin—is assigned a major role.

Through a flashback in the first book (*Vtorzheniye*) Fedin attempts to present a characterization of Stalinism and of the excessive mistrust that prevailed in 1937, the year of the purge. Izvekov is involved in an affair and barely escapes his fate. The description of a visit to the Party Control Commission in the building of the ZK in Moscow clearly indicates the author's firsthand knowledge.

Fedin has occupied an influential position in public life for decades. He has been awarded many prizes in literature and belongs to the group of directors of the Soviet Authors' Association. His publishing activity is also extensive; a catalogue of his publications that appeared in 1966 listed over six hundred items. The last edition of his collected works appeared in 1959–62 in nine volumes.

*Konstantin Paustovski*

Konstantin Paustovski (1892–1968) has been one of the most reliable and stable of Russian literary figures. His extensive memoirs *Story of a Life* (*Povest o zhizni*, 1947–63) are generally regarded, and not only in Russia, as one of the most poetic of autobiographies. In accordance with the capacities of human memory the first of the five books are devoted to the most distant memories; they are the most colorful and the liveliest. On the other hand the last book, *Book of Wanderings* (*Kniga stikani*, 1963), covering the years 1923 to 1933, contains predominantly literary reminiscences.

In the first five books, *Childhood and School Days* (*Dalekiye godi*, 1947), *Slow Approach of Thunder* (*Bespokoinaya yunost*, 1955), *In That Dawn* (*Nachalo nevedomovo veka*, 1956), *Years of Hope* (*Vremya bolshikh ozhidani*, 1958), and *Excursion to the South* (*Brosok na yug*, 1960), Paustovski's real home, the south of Russia, provides the romantic, legendary background for his own life and for the entire epoch. The "historic" Ukraine, Kiev, Odessa, the southern Black Sea ports and the Caucasus reflect the life and at the same time the romantic bend of young Paustovski, who may have inherited a special feeling for the "oriental" atmosphere of these regions through his paternal grandmother, who came from Turkey.

In all instances Paustovski is a graphic narrator; closely bound to nature, he seems to miss no important detail. Paustovski clearly indicated, in his novel about the trade of the storyteller, *The Golden Rose* (*Zolotaya roza*, 1955), the importance that he attached to the right "seeing" and the right "memory." This focus can be seen in his memoirs.

Especially striking is the skill with which Paustovski makes tangible things and objects into the "heroes" of his story, vividly expressing the epoch through their attributes. Not only nature but also the objects of daily life or of special use radiate an atmosphere that seems to surround the reader completely.

Such achievements are not accidental, because Paustovski himself continually makes objects the keys to his poetic transformations, as indicated in *In That Dawn*.

> Things are made by our hands, as Pinocchio with the long nose
> is made out of a block of wood by the old joiner Carlo. . . . If
> things could come to life what confusion they would bring in our
> relationships and how much history might be enriched thereby!
> They would indeed know something to tell.

Nothing short of symbolic, from this point of view, is the impression made by the description of his early childhood with memories of the Ukraine—such as the *Bazaar* (*Basar*), drawn with a few strokes. A special fascination is also exerted by the colorful ports from Odessa to Batum as Paustovski depicts them in his story. The fourth book describes only Odessa in the stirring years of 1920 to 1921; it clearly indicates the role that this city played in the 1920s in the literary life of the Soviet Union.

Paustovski's many novellas and short stories are less impressive in their inventiveness than in the vividness of the images and the tangible symbols that are so important in his work. In his restrained depiction of human circumstances and in his gentle, unobtrusive, and indirect psychological sketching Paustovski sometimes follows Chekhov, although the actual atmosphere more closely resembles that of Bunin or even of Kuprin.

The last stories often reflect primarily anecdotal material—writers' biographies, travel experiences—and avoid every display of personal intervention. Typical of this attitude, which approaches the "pure" story of Pushkin, is *The Fairytale Teller* (*Skazochnik*, 1955), a story about the Danish writer Hans Christian Andersen. Paustovski's travel experiences in Naples are described in *The Crowd at the Wharf* (*Tolpa na naberezhnoi*, 1958), and those at the Bulgarian Black Sea coast form the subject of *The Amphora* (*Amfora*, 1961).

Paustovski's experiences in World War II have been recorded in the novels *The Smoke of the Fatherland* (*Dym otechestva*, 1964) and *Story of the Woods* (*Povest o lesach*, 1948). In the latter, Paustovski, following his frequent practice, combines memories and anecdotal and documentary material in a loose narrative sequence; in the beginning even the composer Tchaikovski appears.

For several years Paustovski was the director of a seminar for prose at the Gorki Literature Institute in Moscow; as a friend and promoter of many young talents he aided the development of Russian literature after the war.

His *The Golden Rose* discusses his pedagogical activity. A book about art and the artist, it offers many personal insights and experiences. Paustovski makes an end of all "ceremonious" pretensions in art and complains about the saccharine Tchaikovski monument in Moscow, which reflects the official concept: "No! Inspiration is a strict working condition of man. The elevation of the spirit is not expressed in theatrical pose and loftiness."

In Russian and world literature Paustovski especially discusses Andersen, Balzac, Chekhov, Flaubert, Gorki, Aleksandr Grin, Victor Hugo, and Prishvin. He particularly commends Aksakov, Bunin, Leskov, and A. N. Tolstoi.

Paustovski also gives some valuable information about the origin of a number of his own stories, including the collection and sifting of the material. The material, Paustovski remarks, cannot be "ordered" from without; the artist must live inwardly in the material itself. Various digressions into memory, imagination, "the study of maps," imaginary dictionaries, and "nature and language" illuminate Paustovski's manner of working quite graphically. Paustovski's collected works appeared in 1957 and 1958 in six volumes and, beginning in 1967, in eight volumes.

## Leonid Leonov

Leonid Leonov is generally regarded as the classicist of Soviet literature. The years 1938 to 1947 are marked in his works by a transfer of creative emphasis to drama and journalism.

Leonov's journalistic work is, of course, especially related to World War II and its aftermath. Leonov worked as a war correspondent at various sectors at the front and was later sent as a reporter to the Nuremberg Trials. In 1947 he issued a widely observed admonition to conserve the forest reserves of Russia in *In Defense of a Friend* (*V zashchitu druga*), which is also the ideological point of reference of Leonov's imposing novel *The Russian Forest* (*Russki les*, 1953).

During the war he published the highly stylized epic narrative *The Capture of Velikoshumsk* (*Vzyatiye Velikoshumska*, 1944), in which he attempted a poetically elevated description of the great tank battle west of Kiev in December 1943. Leonov is concerned here primarily with the dominant role of the people, the fusion of Russian and Ukrainian heroic traditions, and a romantic transfiguration of reality. Linguistic echoes of the folk epic and poetic descriptions in the manner of Gogol are a part of this choice style, which also includes numerous metaphors and allegories.

*The Russian Forest*, Leonov's true Russian epic, comprises many more periods of time and themes than the summer of 1941 and the following winter of war of 1941–42, which stand in the foreground. This work provides a combination of all of Leonov's former tendencies and artistic devices; it must be considered his most personal prose work.

The action is always equally divided between historical action and present action and the story, as in the novels *The Thief* (*Vor*, 1927) and *The Way to the Ocean* (*Doroga na Okean*, 1934), proceeds on several tracks, forming a double novel. The form of composition leads on the two chronological levels to a progressive "reciprocal elucidation" of the nature and the destinies of the chief characters, who belong to two different generations and are rooted in different social traditions.

The young student Apollinariya (Polya) Vikhrova, who occupies the center of attention on one side, gradually explores the story of her separated parents, especially of her father, a professor of forestry exposed to vicious aspersions. The problem of the overcoming of class barriers and of the complicated social consciousness already appears here, in that Polya's mother grew up as the daughter of a once rich owner of an estate, Polya is the connecting link between the two narrative tracks; her gradual discoveries become striking revelation: on the one hand the outbreak of the war in June 1941, the autumn and winter of 1941–42 in Moscow, and the conditions at the Moscow front until the partisans appear; on the other, the historical, political, and social development of Russia since the 1890s.

The actual plot is determined less by the involved family story than by the lifelong scientific and moral "duel" of the two protagonists, Professor Vikhrov and his questionable adversary Professor Gratzianski, with whose unmasking and shameful defeat the novel ends. The moral question concerns the absolute purity of the means to an end. Leonov's novel is therefore the first clear signal of the "thaw," which became fully apparent only in 1956 after the Twentieth Party Congress.

The ideological questions deal with the preservation for the whole people and for the coming generations of the economic potential of the Russian forest, so passionately protected by Vikhrov. In fulfilling his "social obligation" Leonov goes through the entire discussion of the forest by the two professorial opponents and even cites a two-hour lecture by Vikhrov, which takes up forty pages and is a brilliant achievement of stylized rhetoric.

The impressive high point of the novel occurs midway, in the wait for the memorable parade in Red Square on November 7, 1941, which Polya attends:

> Polya vainly spurred on the hands of the clock, and for the first time she realized the insensibility of history, which lets nothing happen until all preliminaries have passed. The latecomers had not yet arrived, the chain of guards in front of the grandstands had not yet been formed, the motion picture photographers had not yet set up their cameras in all directions, so that generations a century later could also see how everything took place.

In his epic calm and fine irony of description Leonov almost reaches the dimensions of *War and Peace*.

Leonov's story is interspersed with philosophical reflections and general maxims, as in *The Thief*. Youth is now seen by Leonov rather from the affectionate, ironic angle of old age. The wisdom and originality of the people are again the foundation. The theme of the forest with its natural life cycle is expanded to a comprehensive history in which fable and legend have their place as well as the mighty and the humble and the partisans, who share their expectation of death and their last hopes with one another.

The forest is the leitmotif, expressed or unexpressed, and the beauty of the forest is probably nowhere in Russian literature so impressive as in Leonov—as a summer and winter landscape, as a symbol for the spaciousness of life, as a striking expression of survival. Leonov's novel is a very national Russian epic, a chronicle of Russian history, evidence of the power of resistance in the war, a record of typical "Russian" discussions and brooding. Leonov's undogmatic though pronounced world view is above all borne by a believer in life, and "an invitation to life" appears at the very beginning of the novel in the stirring "epoch" (a favorite word of Leonov) witnessed by the author.

In 1963 Leonov published a very peculiar novella with a circumscribed Latin title, *Evgenia Ivanovna*. In this story, begun as early as 1938, Leonov describes the destiny of an emigrant and the ruinous reaction of Russian homesickness. At the beginning of the 1920s Evgenia Ivanovna visits Georgia with her husband, an English archeologist, and meets again the man who deserted her so shamelessly as an emigrant. Evgenia Ivanovna makes a fool of this man, who acts as a guide for foreign visitors, but despite the affectionate devotion of Pickering, her present husband, she survives the trip to her Russian fatherland by only a few months.

The novella is once again stylized in the manner of the ironic sentimental stories of the eighteenth century, of which Mikhail Kuzmin was such a master. This novella once more shows Leonov's skill in stylization, which already manifested itself in the 1920s and on which Leonov's lasting successes are based.

Leonov's collected works appeared in a nine-volume Russian edition in 1960 to 1962. The third volume contains the novel *The Thief* in a version revised by the author in 1959.

### Veniamin Kaverin

One of the first Soviet authors with whom the German reading public became reacquainted after 1945 was Veniamin Kaverin. His two-part novel *Two Captains* (*Dva kapitana*, 1940, 1944) is a weaving together of travels and explorations in the northern polar regions—the search for Captain Tatarinov, missing since 1914. Finally World War II and the mission of the Russian air force in the extreme north are drawn into the plot.

Because of its adventurous subject this novel became a favorite work for juveniles, and the Soviet military administration distributed it in German translation immediately after the war. Actually Kaverin had already taken up the novel of the explorer and discoverer with the previously mentioned *Fulfillment of Wishes*. By connecting his episodes to a series of scientific problems Kaverin found a new technique of epic composition.

The novel trilogy *The Open Book* (*Otktrytaya kniga*, 1949–56) is also the story of the life of a research scientist, in this case that of the bacteriologist and microbiologist Tatyana Vlasenkova; the story is told in the first person. Soviet critics of Stalin's time rejected the first part of the trilogy, later published as *Time of Youth* (*Yunost*, 1949), as a flight into the "exotic" and a "formalistic" deviation from the norm, but especially because of the almost entirely unpolitical story of childhood set in the fictitious provincial city of Lopakhin (probably Pskov). Kaverin's feelings for adventurous complications, his delight in curiosities and intellectual calisthenics is really less pronounced here than in the earlier stories of the epoch of the Serapion Brothers; seen as a whole the trilogy is not particularly exciting. Kaverin even quite obviously has difficulty in covering so great an area with the first-person form, because the rigid point of view must finally lead to monotony.

The second part, *Doctor Vlasenkova* (1952), later issued as *On the Search* (*Poiski*), is devoted to the life of the explorer, the turmoils of love and marriage, motherhood, expeditions for combating epidemics, and the varied activities in the Moscow laboratory.

The restriction caused by the commands and prohibitions of socialist realism are greatly in evidence in the middle of the trilogy, especially because the 1930s are described. The actual conflicts of the trilogy—the confrontations and arguments with Professor Kramov, the head of the institute, and the arrest and deportation of Andrei Lvov, the husband of Tatyana Vlasenkova—become apparent only in the third part, which appeared in 1956 as *Searching and Hoping* (*Poiski i nadezhdi*—final title *Nadezhdi, Hoping*).

In the argument about Stalinism in science, through which the marriage of the scientists is violently torn apart, the dynamic motif of the book is expressed. The conciliatory fade-out of the trilogy— Tatyana's husband returns in June 1953 from camp—cannot conceal the pervasive gloom of the third volume. Tatyana's adversary Kramov appears as the incarnation of corrupted scientific honor, and his two-faced mendacity reminds Tatyana of a mysterious picture by Goya.

For the edition of his collected works (six volumes, 1963–66), Kaverin once more revised the entire trilogy and gave the different parts their present titles.

After a long, serious illness Kaverin began to write his memoirs at the end of the 1950s; the first part, extending until his student years in Saint Petersburg, was published in 1960 under the title of *Unknown Friend* (*Neizvestnii drug*). The very witty and vivaciously written memories of his youth in Pskov and his first literary friendships and meetings belong to the best that Kaverin has written. There the author has given his sparkling self-irony free rein.

The 1960s quite unexpectedly brought new literary successes by Kaverin, including a number of stories and a novel. Especially remarkable in its subject is the story *Seven Pairs of Devils* (*Sem par nechistikh*, 1962), which returns to the outbreak of World War II. On the old freight steamer *Onega*, which ironically once belonged to the Solovetzki Monastery and had been christened with the name *Lyubov* (Love), convicts, including victims of political court action, are being transported across the Barents Sea. A mutiny on the vessel is prevented at the last moment only because of the turbulent incidents of the first days of the war. Here Kaverin is again in his real element; the action combines the purely adventurous—including German air attacks on the ship—with an open accusation against Stalinism.

The generation gap and the problem of the solitary mature wife and mother, severely oppressed by life, form the axis about which the novel *Slanting Rain* (*Kosoi dozhd*, 1962) moves like a motion picture. The action is partly set in Italy, where a group of Russian tourists is continually exposed to new and exciting impressions. The plot in Russia (concerning the teen-agers at home) and the story in Italy (on the part of the grown-ups) culminate at exactly the same time in a symbolic, meaningful cloudburst, which fails heavily in "slanting strokes" from the sky, in Florence as well as in Murmansk. The filmlike "cuttings," which constituted a favorite principle of composition even in Kaverin's earliest stories are emphasized here through a discussion of Fellini's motion picture *La dolce vita,* which thrills the tourists to Italy.

The novel *Double Portrait* (*Dvoinoi portret,* 1966) can be compared in many respects with the earlier novel *Unknown Master* (*Khudozhnik neizvesten,* 1931). The plot is determined by the procedure of technical investigation, in this case the investigation of the moral crime of a scientist of the Stalin era. The work recalls Leonov's *The Russian Forest,* especially in the struggle of the two rival ichthyologists and oceanographers, although Kaverin poses the problem far more radically and on the basis of principle by using the device of the investigation by detectives. The action takes place in 1954, when Professor Ostrogradski, deported to a camp through the complicity of his adversary, returns to Moscow, severely ill, without being formally rehabilitated. A journalist and the narrator in the first person further this rehabilitation, but before it is attained, Ostrogradski dies of heart disease.

The psychologically interesting figure of his opponent, Professor Snegirev, through his apparently friendly advances and suppression of the truth, attempts to minimize events, but is unable to recognize his own guilt. The question of guilt, however, is asked with much insistence; the narrator compares his work with the restoration of a palimpsest.

This novel is one of the most important about the time of Stalin, and the atmosphere of the years after 1937 is described here without mercy. In the new epilogue composed for the last edition of the novel the narrator closes with the confessional statement:

> I, too, was deceived, guilty without guilt, and punished with degradation and fear. I, too, believed and did not believe, worked diligently and stumbled at every step, got involved in contradictions, in order to prove to myself that a lie was true. And I grieved in the effort to forget the dismal dreams, in which one had to come to terms with the nonsense, in dissimulation and hypocrisy. But that's an entirely different book that I must write some time.

The novel actually consists of the assembling of the details that have been ascertained; the action runs off either scenically, as in an explanatory film, or as a report of the narrator in the first person about his researches and interviews. *Double Portrait* is also a novel about the development of a story, except that this story is not told in connection with the whole. One of the high points of the novel is the image, conjured up out of the memories of the narrator, of the burning of all sources for the authentic history of the Russian people, such as private diaries, letters, and photographs. Documents pass through Leningrad in 1937 as a thin smoke from the backyards —"splinters of time" that will forever be missing in the total picture: "They were evidently long forgotten, expunged in memory, these days, an empty courtyard, the smell of something burning, the pigeons flying up and off, light ashes in the beams of the autumn sun!"

## Nikolai Zabolotzki

Nikolai Zabolotzki, forgotten for almost twenty years, was re-discovered by readers and critics only at the beginning of the "de-Stalinization" (since 1956). Now that Zabolotzki's total production is available in a Soviet edition and in an edition of the Russian emigrants (both 1965), he can be seen to belong to the really great poets of Russia.

His arrest, incarceration, and deportation (1938–46) did not leave Zabolotzki unharmed, but twelve creative years remained in which he could give new evidence of his marked personal gifts. His translations are characteristic of his second productive period; they include an adaptation of *The Song of Igor's Campaign* (1946); translations from the Georgian (1947–58); translations of classical and modern poems from the German, Serbian, Hungarian, Italian, Uzbek, and Tadzhik. Equally significant are his new poems of 1946 to 1958, inspired by reflections on man and the cosmos.

The fruit of these years appeared in magazines and almanacs as well as in various comparatively limited single editions: *Poems* (*Stikhotvoreniya*, 1947, 1948, 1959) and *Selected Works* (*Izbran-noye*, 1960). Several important poems were published posthumously in the Soviet edition of 1965.

As early as the 1930s Zabolotzki had given up the paradoxical play of fancy reminiscent of surrealism, and the grotesque, plastic style of his early poems. His work of the 1940s and 1950s has its roots in symbolism and the Russian classics, even though Zabolotzki was fundamentally concerned with securing a modern effect by means of a surprising compression of a theme and series of metaphors. In his nature poems and his philosophical verse Zabolotzki copies neither Derzhavin, Baratinski, Tyutchev, nor Bryusov, although he owes much to the Russian tradition represented by these writers.

In Zabolotzki's poems nature is not actually thought of as a "subject" but as a contrast to the questionable and unstable existence of man, as a firm counterbalance to doubt, despair, unfulfillable longing. Zabolotzki's poems are built on the principle that human life and extra-human elements become firmly mortised into one another. Corresponding to the poetry of classicism Zabolotzki also works with personifications, allegorical metaphors, and mythological associations—gods, heroes, and muses:

> With his eyebrows raised at a late hour
> There gazes at us attentively
> Bloody Mars out of the blue depths.
> *Opposition of Mars*
> (*Protivostoyaniye Marsa*, 1956)

In his predilection for musical instruments and musical comparisons Zabolotzki repeatedly brings into play the "music of the worlds"; nature once becomes a concert hall for him:

> Begin with the serenade, starling!
> For the drums and tambourines of history
> You are our first singer of spring
> Out of the conservatory of birches.
> *Beethoven* (1946)

In nature man finds his world once more; thus the birches turn into schoolgirls, for whom the school bell tolls, and they hear how the waterfall "conjugates verbs." Pools look like transparent saucers, in *Thaw* (*Ottepel*, 1948), and the soul of the crying roosters is compared with the face of old clocks, in *The Roosters Crow* (*Petukhi poyut*, 1958). Wars let their wings rotate like "crazed windmills," which sweep together houses in a white whirl, and the "bloody-headed thistles," the "stars with sharp corners," have been "scratched directly into the heart" of the poet in *Thistle* (*Chertopolokh*, 1956).

Mythology is as familiar to the poet as the classical themes of Russian poetry—birch glade, winter landscape, rain, night, storm, sea, and microcosm and macrocosm—as in *The Peak of the Caucasus* (*Kazbek*, 1957), *Portrait* (*Portret*, 1953), *Poet* (*Poet*, 1953), *Remembrance* (*Vospominaniye*, 1952), *Legacy* (*Zaveshchaniye*, 1947), and *Through Leeuwenhoek's Marvelous Apparatus* (*Skvoz volshebni pribor Levenguka*).

Zabolotzki also continued the series of classical poems about Venice, which he visited in 1957 (*Venetziya*, 1957). Of especially impressive vividness are such poems as *The Laundry* (*Stirka bleya*, 1957), *The Woods of Gombori* (*Gomborski les*, 1957), and *Evening at the Oka* (*Vecher na Oke*). In *The Woods of Gombori* the poet dreams of penetrating the painting and dissolving in nature:

> I became the neural system of vegetation,
> I became the thought of the stone crags,
> And the experience of my autumnal observations
> I wish to give again as a gift to mankind.

The poems with musical motifs include, in addition to *Beethoven* the poem about Ravel, *Bolero* (1957), the *Poem of Spring* (*Poema vesny*, 1956), *Across the Sea* (*Nad morem*, 1956), and *Late Spring* (*Pozdnyaya vesna*, 1948).

Zabolotzki's poems of the 1950s deal almost exclusively with "great" poetic themes, through which human comprehension repeatedly approaches the limits of its capacity.

The problem of the erotic is broached in the impressive cycle *Last Love* (*Poslednyaya lyubov*, 1956–57). Drawing on his own experience the poet depicts human paths of suffering in such verses as *Somewhere in the Open Air at Magadan* (*Gde-to v pole vozle Magadana*, 1956), *Flight to Egypt* (*Begstvo v Egipet*, 1955), or *At the Railroad Station* (*Na vokzale*, 1958).

The verse narrative *Rubruck in Mongolia* (*Rubruk v Mongolii*, 1958) is really a heroic-comic epic; it describes the journey of a

Flemish Franciscan monk Wilhelm von Rubruck (Rubruquis) to the descendants of Genghis Khan in Karakorum (1254). The story is ironic in its deliberate anachronisms as well as in its allusions to Stalin's rule. The Khan is introduced as the "Generalissimo of the Steppes," the Mongolian warriors are termed "active," and the Mongolian wagon-train performs the "sixth symphony of the devil." The four-foot iambus is in the unbroken Russian tradition, and here and there the style of the classical narrative in verse is deliberately parodied.

## Mikhail Svetlov and Semen Kirsanov

Through the development of Soviet literature during World War II, and especially during the very last years, new names have appeared, which stood in the shadow of greater contemporaries in the epoch after the revolution.

Mikhail Svetlov (1903–1964), born in a petty bourgeois Jewish family became known in the 1920s as a poet of the Komsomol, although at that time only a few of his poems, such as the ballad *Grenada* (1926), had really become popular everywhere. During World War II Svetlov turned from purely lyrical poetry to narrative verse in cycles about the heroes of the war: *Twenty-eight* (*Dvadtzat vosem*, 1942) and *Liza Chaykina* (1942). The first cycle mourns the death of twenty-eight soldiers of the guard, and the other the sacrifice of a young partisan girl.

Combative pathos, combined with a youthful, communistic, romantic mood, remained Svetlov's characteristic style until the beginning of the 1950s, although the poet had almost become silent during these years. An entirely new Svetlov appeared in the collection *Horizon* (*Gorizont*, 1959) and especially in the last volume, *The Hunting Lodge* (*Okhotnichii domik*, 1964).

Svetlov's new poems, including *Loneliness* (*Odinochestvo*, 1957), discuss the theme of aging and express pensive reflections over the loss of the romantic dreams of youth:

> At night love goes through the world.
> But why didn't you come to the poet?

Fear of declining health and grief over the irretrievable presence of past time are the tragic basic motifs of Svetlov's later poetry. The poet turns to Pushkin, Tyutchev, and Blok in *To Pushkin* (*Pushkinu*) and *Rain* (*Dozhd*). He who has waited for the fulfillment of his dream must confess:

> How I have dreamed about the black brows
> That wait at the bridge,
> But not as a maiden, as a widowed woman
> You come to me, my dream!

In his old age, too, Svetlov remained faithful to his predominantly lyrical style, but in his choice of words and in expression he approaches the best classical and modern models. Self-irony, also appears in the poems of his old age, and in one of the last poems, *In the Hospital* (*V bolnice*, 1964):

> It seems to me, that one already surrounds me
> With honors like a herring with onions.

Svetlov was also very popular as a teacher at the Gorki Institute of Literature; Gennadii Aygi, for example, was his pupil. Three years after his death Svetlov was finally granted the Lenin Prize (1967). The collected poems appeared in 1966 in an edition of the *Biblioteka poeta*, which was virtually equivalent to reaching the status of a "classic."

Semen Kirsanov was born even later than Svetlov (1906 in Odessa), but his debut also occurred in the 1920s. At that time Kirsanov organized a branch of the Left Front of the Arts (LEF) in Odessa and was a friend of Mayakovski. Strikingly, however, in *Book of Poems* (*Kniga liriki*, 1965), the volume issued on his fortieth anniversary as a poet, he included comparatively few poems of earlier origin. Kirsanov had always stood in the shadow of Maykovski, and the 1930s were, moreover, no longer a very fruitful time for Russian poetry. Kirsanov did include the verse narrative *Your Poem* (*Tvoya poema*, 1937), which contains some interesting passages and ends with a passionate espousal of the cause of the Spanish republicans in the civil war.

Kirsanov's war poems can be distinguished very sharply from the average of the poetry of the front of that time. The peculiar poem *Waltz of the Front (Frontovoi vals)* deserves special mention. Here Kirsanov conspicuously shows his predilection for stylization, as suggested in the verse narrative *Poem of the Poets (Poema poetov)*, not completed until long after the war (1956). Kirsanov presents a fictionalized gathering of five (later six) "unknown" poets, each of whom writes poems in his own style. One of the sections is entirely in the style of the popular *Rayeshniki* (peepshow verse, rhymes of fools and wags). A supplement appeared as Kirsanov's epic *Legend of the Emperor Maximilian (Skazaniye pro carya Maksa-Yeme-lyana,* 1964); it shows a similar stylization and is arranged in thirteen pieces, or *skaz*, possibly in the sense of the Arabic *makame*.

The ironic grotesque verse narrative *Seven Days of the Week (Sem dne nedeli,* 1956) is a kind of travesty of the story of creation in which the poet dreams—at first in vain—of the renewal of the "false hearts" dating from the Stalin era:

> Everywhere the stores offered
> Hearts of tin or even of rubber,
> Also for blowing up, with a squeaking head,
> Or stuffing, with the inscription "Good luck."
> Flasks like hearts with sweet perfume,
> Heart albums with insinuating verses,
> Hearts like money boxes, so that very little is spent,
> Macaroni hearts for the soup,
> And little frames for the lovely ladies,
> For personal and family festive days.

Kirsanov's poetry of the last ten years is often very surprising in its stylization: profound and facetious, playful or sensitive, seldom dignified, always mature and unembarrassed.

The theme of Saint Petersburg is treated in a rather peculiar manner in the cycle *Leningrad Notebook (Leningradskaya tetrad,* 1960). Here Kirsanov comes closest to tradition, but his points of view are quite personal and unconventional. The *Bridges (Mosti),* the *Lions and Sphinxes (Lvi i sfinksi),* and the *Caryatids (Kariatidi)* are dismembered as anecdotes and taken up for momentary reflection.

Among the editions of the last years the collection *Selected Works* (*Izbranniye proizvedeniya*, two volumes, 1961) offers the most comprehensive cross section of the work, also collected in *Book of Poems* (1965). The latest collection with new poems appeared in 1964: *The One Time, Tomorrow, Verses and Poems* (*Odnazhdi zavtra, stikhi, poemi*).

## Leonid Martynov

During the last ten years Leonid Martynov (born 1905 in Omsk) has secured long overdue recognition as one of the typical representatives of the still fruitful tradition of the 1920s.

Martynov, whose home Siberia plays a special role in his poetry, borrows especially from the language of Yesenin, Khlebnikov, and Pasternak. At times his work even recalls Villon and Rimbaud, whom he admired.

The poems of the 1920s and the early 1930s are of relatively little importance in connection with his later work. The first volume of poems, *Verse and Verse Narratives* (*Stikhi i poemi*), appeared in 1939. Already at this time the tendency toward witty or polemical wordplay and burlesque narration is evident. Among the verse epics completed by that time are portraits of the Siberian past, as in *The Chronicler of Tobolsk* (*Tobolski letopisetz*, 1937). The burlesque epic *The Homespun Venus* (*Domotkanaya Venera*, 1939) is also set in Tobolsk. Another parody epic, directed at the symbolist Konstantin Balmont, is *Poetry as Sorcery* (*Poeziya kak volshebstvo*, 1939).

After the war Martynov produced several new volumes in which the tone is partly facetious and partly ironic-pathetic, as in *The Gulf* (*Lukomorye*, 1945). The motifs are taken in part from Russian folklore; in the foreground are the Russian landscape, the Russian climate, the natural resources, the rhythm of the seasons, and Russian history. Martynov's poetry is characterized by a combination of mythical-utopian ideas and entirely prosaic reality. Human standards are determined by the world of the workers' fists as well as by the world of legend and myth. Both strands are woven into the vocabulary, in which fragments of ancient myths are placed next to prosaic or even idiomatic expressions, as in the poems *Nordic Fairytale*

(*Severnaya skazka*, 1946) and *The Crossing* (*Pereprava*, 1946). This technique is also the determining factor in such later poems as *Ovidiopolis* (*Ovidiopol*, 1961) or *Aphrodite* (*Afrodita*, 1961). Only with the publication of his later volumes of poems, *Verses* (*Stikhi*, 1955), *Poetry* (*Lirika*, 1958), and *Poems* (*Stikhotvoreniya*, 1961), did Martynov become known as more than a "regional" talent. The poet memorialized the 1920s in the poem *The Twenties* (*Dvadtzatiye godi*, 1954). Several poems of 1954 and 1955 are also devoted to the theme of the "thaw," as in *Voices* (*Golosa*) and *One Degree of Heat* (*Gradus tepla*). The themes "Healing of the Lepers" and the "Resurrection of the Innocently Executed" recur in several poems, which deal more concretely than ever before with questions of human life.

Although Martynov seems to subscribe completely to Communist optimism about progress and ridicules the Russian past with its "byzantine, ghostlike faces, its pine shavings and candles, and its sobbing harmonicas," his newest poems are increasingly dominated by melancholy memories, as *Memoirs* (*Memuari*, 1964):

> O, my atomic age,
> Antiquarians surround you
> Like janissaries
> Around the pasha!
> I did not intend to write memoirs,
> But, it's a fact,
> I am writing them.

Martynov has collected the production of his last years in the volumes *New Book* (*Novaya kniga*, 1962) and *Primogeniture* (*Pervorodstvo*, 1965). A selection of the poems also appeared in 1965 in *Poems and Verse Narratives* (*Stikhotvoreniya i poemi*, two volumes). Martynov's verse is always written according to the rules; he continues the tradition of symbolism as well as the attainments of its successors. The tonal qualities predominate; the repetitions of tones sometimes degenerate into a consciously dalliant manner, which can be compared with the former habits of the Rayeshniki. Surprising tonal associations and wordplay are integrating components of Martynov's poetry, which seldom yields to usual conventions and definitely ignores the classical standards.

## Mikhail Sholokhov

With the completion of the four-volume novel *The Silent Don* (*Tikhii Don*, 1928–40), Mikhail Sholokhov (born 1905 in the region of the Don cossacks) became known as the epic master of elementary contradictions and as the prophet of the psyche of the south Russian cossack.

Through the war Sholokhov was taken from his work. Like a number of other writers he actively participated in world events as a war correspondent. Many of his open letters and reports of World War II are now important historic documents, such as the *Letter to American Friends* (*Pismo amerikanskim druzhyam*, 1943).

During this time Sholokhov published only one story, *The Science of Hatred* (*Nauka nenavisti*, 1942), an account of the gruesome experiences of an officer in a German prison camp and his eventual escape. The same theme appears in the novella *The Fate of a Man* (*Sudba cheloveka*, 1957), which presents horrifying details of the treatment of Soviet prisoners in the enemy's camps. The problem of the prisoner of war was generally avoided in literature until 1956, and these stories not only bring accusations against the Germans but also call for the moral rehabilitation of the soldiers who were taken prisoner.

Here Sholokhov, in other instances so concerned with authenticity, cannot report from personal observation and experience, and the literary importance of the novella is therefore not to be found in this excerpt from the memories of the narrator, but rather in the concept of blind destiny and in the popularly stylized narrative form.

The frame for the story is the classic "accidental" meeting with the narrator, in this case at the ferry on a tributary of the Don. Into the frame is also brought the little boy, entirely alone in the world, who is the secret hero of the story, inasmuch as he believes that he has found his father in Andrei Sokolov. The two orphaned survivors—Sokolov had lost his wife, children, and house through violence—meet immediately after the war and form a new, unexpected relationship, the intimacy of which can be explained only by the loss of all other human contacts and through extreme, despairing loneliness.

The deep involvement with which Sholokhov portrays the despair and then this new father-son relationship lifts the story above the merely anecdotal and makes it a parable for the constant testing of man, possibly in the sense of the story of Job. A Soviet critic, A. Britikov, compared the novella with Hemingway's *The Old Man and the Sea*, which became known in a Russian translation a year and a half before Sholokhov's work.

In 1960 Sholokhov published the long-awaited second part of his novel of the collective, *Seeds of Tomorrow* (*Podniataya celina*, Part I, 1932). The cossack milieu and the melancholy landscape at the lower Don carry the structure of the plot as in the first part, the ideological implications of which have been discussed in detail by Soviet critics. The almost completed manuscript of this continuation was apparently destroyed during the war, and Sholokhov had to resume work on it later.

With his direct portrayals and his indirect delineation of character the author was again very successful in creating living figures, but the language is less stylized and in the new form much less "naive" than in the first part. The change in style of the epoch must be considered; admirers of the early Sholokhov may be somewhat disappointed by the polished and refined language of the later works. Much more psychology is introduced into the descriptions, and on occasion Sholokhov's scurrilous humor becomes dominant, as in the episode of the cock crowing at the wrong time in the fourth chapter.

For this second book of his novel Sholokhov was awarded the Lenin Prize in 1960; in 1965 he received the Nobel Prize for Literature.

The long war novel that Sholokhov began in 1942, with advance copies appearing in 1943 and in the 1950s, has not yet been completed. Tentatively entitled *They Fought for Their Country* (*Oni srazhalis za rodinu*), it is apparently set in the landscape of the Don and deals with the withdrawal of the Red Army in the summer of 1942. World War II is portrayed as a popular war, and the heroes, representing various strata of society—peasants, workers, and intellectuals—achieve a new solidarity through the war.

# The Revolution's Critical Heirs

## THE REDEMPTION FROM
## SOCIALIST REALISM

The voice of the younger Soviet writers, most of whom were born many years after the revolution, was given greater attention after the party congress of 1956. The literature of the heirs of the revolutionary upheaval of the 1920s and of the stagnation that followed, was "critical" from its beginning. Criticism was directed at socialist realism itself, as well as at moral and social standards, which were subsequently uncontested and considered valid beyond Stalin's death into the middle of the 1950s.

The first breaches in the front of "dogmatism" had already been made by the older generation—Ilya Ehrenburg and Leonid Leonov —but the direct and polemical concern with the moral and aesthetic problems could begin only after the public condemnation of Stalin and the personality cult. Among the writers who protested most vocally was Aleksandr Solzhenitzyn (born 1918), who was condemned to silence at that time. The general discussion began with Vladimir Dudintzev (born 1918) and his novel *Not by Bread Alone* (*Ne khlebom yedinim*, 1956); the movement was soon joined by such authors as Daniil Granin (born 1919), Yurii Nagibin (born 1920), and Aleksandr Yashin (born 1913).

## Dudintzev and Others

Dudintzev's novel, which appeared in the late summer of 1956, actually still entirely reflects the program of socialist realism, with a great industrial combine at the center of the plot and with little apparent modification of the basic form. Most striking perhaps is the title itself, which is an allusion to the scriptural passage "Man does not live by bread alone." In any case the literary value of the novel is far less than its political and social importance, and the critics reacted with special sensitivity to the latter. The novel provoked unrest and consternation; after the first favorable comments it was severely attacked in November 1956.

The positive hero of the novel, the engineer and "inventor" Lopatkin was decried as an individualistic "ascetic" and "kinetic" type, and the whole novel—and rightfully so—as an "attack on society." In fact, Dudintzev's novel offers the first criticism of the industrial petty bourgeoisie, although it is less a social than a moral critique. The factory manager Drozdov is the corrupt, authoritarian bureaucrat, behind whom, however, as is indicated, other "archangels and prophets" stand.

Lopatkin, on the other hand, is no longer the former "hero of socialism," nor the man of iron will power whom one was accustomed to see; he listens to Chopin and Rachmaninov and really preaches something like asceticism: "Man has not been born to suffer degradation in the name of good eating and living, to lie and to practice deceit." Dudintzev would like to see this "joy of the worms that are warmed by the sun" replaced by man's "becoming inflamed" for his cause (his symbol is the comet). Ironically critics pointed out to Dudintzev that the scorn of material goods was abnormal and that asceticism was of value only in the battle for the material progress of mankind. This was exactly the belief that Dudintzev denied.

In the same year (1956) several shorter stories appeared, presenting an equally skeptical picture of Soviet society. The poet Aleksandr Yashin published the short story *The Levers* (*Richagi*), which expresses an almost parodistic criticism of the style of the party meetings. In a *kolkhoz* a number of functionaries decide, because the regional committee has ordered two meetings a month, to constitute themselves as a party gathering. The radio is turned off and all suddenly transform themselves into masks, or, as the title indicates, into *levers* of the party. Just before the transformation they still made such cynical remarks as: "With us here in the region truth is placed only in the honorary chairmanship, so that it is not insulted and keeps its mouth shut." All at once the five members follow the same ritual, until the desired end of the session has come. The various utterances of the participants are also intended as parodies, thus irritating the critics all the more.

Daniil Granin (born 1919) had already published his novel about scientists, *Those Who Seek* (*Iskateli*) in 1954; he also fought against careerism and bureaucracy, against the degradation of man to a mere cog in the wheel. Granin's story *A Personal Opinion* (*Sobstvennoye mneniye*, 1956) was published at the same time as Dudintzev's novel. Here too the conflict smolders between the courageous engineer Olkhovski and Minyev, the director of the institute, who dodges every risk and remains devoted to the personality cult.

Granin, who had studied electromechanics, maintained his interest in technology. In 1962 he published his novel *I Fly Toward the Storm* (*Idu na grozu*), which dealt with weather reconnaissance pilots. *One Month Upside Down* (*Mesyatz v verch nogami*), Granin's amusing and detailed report on his trip to Australia, appeared in 1966.

Yurii Nagibin (born 1920 in Moscow) also belongs to this group of critical realists, although he worked principally as a screen writer. His numerous stories are highly regarded, as are his travelogues, especially those of Scandinavia.

Nagibin's best-known short story, *A Light in the Window* (*Svet v okne*), appeared in the second volume of *Literaturnaya Moskva* (1956). A brief psychological study, it portrays the director of a convalescent home, in which a complete three-room apartment with television and billiard table has long been unoccupied in anticipation of the arrival of a mysterious important guest. Despite the over-crowding of the home and although the director would have liked to give the rooms to other guests, they remain empty. They are more carefully tended by the maid Nastya than are her own rooms. The personality cult is symbolized in the touching eagerness with which the windows are cleaned every day:

> Here her ordinary work became creative activity. One can just clean a window, but one can also perform a miracle, that is, make it so transparent, so glistening and sunny, that it virtually draws into the room the blue of the sky, the white of the snow, and the green of the pine needles. The walls disappear and the room be-comes a part of the wide world.

The director is finally compelled to take action when one night he sees light in the windows and the reflection of the television set in operation. Nastya, tired of the long and futile waiting, has finally unlocked the rooms for the staff of the home. The director shouts, threatens and stamps his feet, but also feels that the others are right, and he becomes aware of the peculiar feeling that "presses forward into the very tips of his fingers . . . the feeling of an unbearable loathing of himself."

Nagibin's story *The Chazaric Ornament* (*Khazarski ornament*), also published in 1956, was well received, because it expressed the backwardness of the Russian village and the entire agricultural system as mercilessly as in Solzhenitzyn's story *Matriona's Yard* (*Matrionin dvor*, 1963).

Offshoots of socialist realism are represented by the works of the two younger writers Anatolii Kuznetzov and Georgii Vladimov. In 1957 Kuznetzov (born 1929 in Kiev) published his novel of devel-opment *Continuation of a Legend* (*Prodolzheniye legendi*), which is notable for the deromanticizing of the modern world of work and the destruction of the clichés of the "hero of work." The college graduate Tolya, who travels to Siberia on his own in order to gather his first life experiences at the building of a cofferdam, is confronted by the necessity of organizing his personal life, which does not seem possible without resistance to his environment, and to indifference and routine. A similar theme is found in the story *Masha* (1959); recently however, Kuznetzov has gone over to the exotic. The story *Storm on the Journey to Stockholm* (*Shtorm na puti v Stokgolm*, 1965) questions the goodness of a world in which a Russian girl and a Swedish youth, who fall in love on a boat trip to Stockholm, have no real possibility of ever meeting again.

Georgii Vladimov (born 1931 in Kharkov) has published relatively few works. His story *The Big Ore* (*Bolshaya ruda*, 1961) presents a completely unadorned description of the real life of the worker. Exactly this sobriety and lack of illusion had been lacking in the socialist realism of the Stalin era.

During the past ten years socialist realism has gradually been transformed into a new realism, represented not only by such authors as Solzhenitzyn but also by Bondarev, Aksenov, or Gladilin, who all belong to the generation that is currently setting the literary fashion. Other writers of the same generation, who will be discussed later, attempt to carry on the traditions of the nineteenth century or of the realists of the early twentieth century (Chekhov, Bunin). The designation "traditionalists" is meant only in this general and perhaps somewhat vague sense.

### THE NEW REALISTS

#### *Aleksandr Solzhenitzyn*

Aleksandr Solzhenitzyn (born 1918 in Kislovodsk) is considered one of the most interesting Russian writers of fiction. Clearly, however, this author's total production has not yet appeared in print. His two great novels, a Stalin novel with the title *The First Circle* (*V kruge pervom*) and the novel *The Cancer Ward* (*Rakovy korpus*), have been denied publication in the Soviet Union up to this time.

Solzhenitzyn, who grew up in South Russia, in Rostov on the Don, studied mathematics, history, philosophy, and literature in Moscow before the war. He had to give up the idea of becoming an actor because of a chronic throat condition. After World War II and internment in a camp (1945–53) he finally made his living as a mathematics teacher. Until 1956 he lived in exile; only later on was he rehabilitated and finally settled in the central Russian city of Ryazan.

Solzhenitzyn's first work, published by permission of the highest authorities, was the novel *One Day in the Life of Ivan Denisovich* (*Odin den Ivana Denisovicha*, 1962), in which the camp life of the forced laborers at the time of the terror is described in an exemplary and authentic manner. Contrary to the assumption generally accepted at the time, this novel is not the chance product of a beginner, but the mature work of a professional writer, who had been condemned to silence until then. By Solzhenitzyn's own admission, the novel, in its form, recalls a favorite thought of Lev Tolstoi, that is, to make the events of a single day the subject of a novel, as in Tolstoi's first work, *Story of Yesterday* (*Istoriya vcherashnevo dnya*, 1851).

Solzhenitzyn, certainly for good reasons, waives every intent of justifying his estimate of the convict Ivan Denisovich Shukhov before the conscience of a personal narrator and of assuming an attitude from a distance. Everything is observed through the consciousness of the carpenter Shukhov, who works under very sharply defined conditions. The overt expression of these observations is often made in impersonal, generalized statements that use the indefinite pronoun "one," which in Russian has many circumscribed variations, or the indefinite "you," (second person singular). The personal narrative form "he" alternates constantly with the supraindividual "we," producing a continuous, deindividualized stream of consciousness that coincides with a collective experience.

The hero Ivan Denisovich is indeed the point of departure for the narrator's point of view, but this figure is intended as a representative for all the others. His individuality is nothing more definite than his number as a convict. Corresponding to this is the concept of time, which reaches only a relatively fixed point. The story ends with the sarcastic sentence: "The day was past, not clouded by anything, almost happy. Such were the days during his confinement from reveille to taps: 3653. Three days additional, because of the leap years."

The day behind the barbed wire, the fiction of a January day of the year 1951, is not marked by the values and the vocabulary of the normal, free human being. Solzhenitzyn grasps the values and the language that actually arise from the immediacy and the general misery of the camp—the blunt speech of the long-term prisoner, the jargon that reflects this degraded reality. The medium of the story, Ivan Denisovich Shukhov, nevertheless reveals meaningful moral traits. The proverbs and sayings of the Russian people that are interwoven in the lively narration vouch for the survival of a centuries-old truth, which asserts itself against spiritual and physical pressure even behind barbed wire. Shukhov is a shrewd child of this world, practically a rogue, whom we owe our silent sympathy rather than our pity. The lack of suspense in the plot is balanced by the interest that the existence of this one day arouses—a complicated problem that incessantly demands not only physical stamina but the foresight of deduction.

Solzhenitzyn's accurate and laconic, and apparently "disinterested" report represents in language and form a seamless work of art, which has already assumed a special place in Russian literature.

Mention should also be made again of Solzhenitzyn's story *Matriona's Yard*, which can be taken as a salute to poverty and frugality, to helpfulness and cheerfulness. The heroine of the story, which is still set in the 1950s, the old peasant Matriona, is less a real person than the symbolic center of an imaginary world, the world of the old, disappearing Russia. Matriona's way is the way of the righteous, as she is expressly described with the biblical expression, but a righteous one in the midst of the world, a righteous one in the midst of the Russian people.

The narrator, whose fate is only indirectly outlined (he, too, returns home from exile) observes and fathoms Matriona in her environment; after her tragic death he finally becomes the "hagiographer" who writes down the legend of Matriona. The story could almost be termed edifying, but Solzhenitzyn avoids any didactic attitude or any sort of triviality with his ironic humor.

Solzhenitzyn flirts in his language and literary props with the religious legends of the Russian people. The real meaning of the story, however, is not the glorification of the pious life of Matriona but the sarcastic exposure of the average interests of men and the average concerns of this world. The narrator finds more righteousness and honesty in Matriona's kitchen scraps than in most men, and he mentions the scraps respectfully: "I had become accustomed to them, for in their rustling there was no evil, no lie. They lived to rustle."

In the story *An Incident at the Krechetovka Station* (*Sluchai na stantzii Krechetovka*), also published in 1963, Solzhenitzyn conjures up the tragedy of October 1941, the first month of the war, through a portrayal of the so-called *okruzhentzi*, the soldiers who escaped from the great battles of encirclement and barely saved their lives. These former fighters are sent away in collective transports, and, subject to the secret police, are considered almost outlaws.

The young Lieutenant Vasya Tzotov, on duty as the railroad commandant, talks with one of these unfortunates, a graying actor of the Moscow Dramatic Theater, but his spontaneous, human feelings are quickly suppressed. An honest but only average representative of middle Soviet intelligence, Tzotov begins to suspect, through a misunderstanding, that he is dealing with an *agent provocateur*; he finally turns the actor over to the secret police.

Solzhenitzyn leaves no doubt that the inwardly free man must accept the role of a victim and that Tzotov, who sits at a lesser point of control of power, was raised in a manner that left him uninformed and unfree in his judgments. A sharply sarcastic remark indicates that Tzotov has never heard of Lieutenant Colonel Vershinin (in Chekhov's *Three Sisters*) and that his greatest reading experience—after the outbreak of the war—was the first volume of *Das Kapital* by Karl Marx.

Equally significant is the following passage:

> Tzotov: "Best of all I like the pieces by Gorki. Yes, Gorki! Our wisest, our most humane, our greatest author. Don't you think so, too?" Tveritinov furrowed his eyebrows to find an answer, but he found none and remained silent.

The manner of speaking in the dialogue is everywhere carefully graded and contains (as in the dialogue of Chekhov himself) the most varied intermediate tones, and also those that indicate reticence.

Another story of 1963, *For the Good of the Cause* (*Dlya polzy dela*), deals with everyday Soviet life after Stalin's death. Students of a technical school in a self-help program have completed a new school building. At the last moment this building is taken from them by the administration because a superior institute of research claims it. Solzhenitzyn treats the affair dramatically, almost exclusively through dialogue, as a struggle between justice and injustice, in which for the time being injustice triumphs. The methods of Stalin (whose name is conspicuously absent) continue to exist on the lower level. Of course, the "fear of truth" has been overcome in the meantime; the conflict is carried on openly to the end. The fact remains that the self-sacrificing pupils are cheated out of the fruit of their enthusiasm. Solzhenitzyn's obvious conclusion (expressed by the secretary of the municipal committee) is that communism can be built more easily in stone than in the hearts of men.

## Grigorii Baklanov

Of the younger authors specializing in war books Grigorii Baklanov (born 1923 in Voronezh) especially deserves mention. Baklanov belongs to those young Russian officers who went to the front voluntarily and only after the war learned the literary craft in the Moscow Gorki Institute of Literature. He has written three novellas and a novel about the war. Baklanov's battle descriptions are especially typical of the revised version of the battles of the last war, which was promulgated after the twentieth party congress (1956).

In the foreground are the sanguinary facts of the unimaginably great attrition of living human beings and the problem of the moral responsibility of the leaders to their own soldiers and their own people.

In the center of the story *South of the Main Attack* (*Yuzhneye glavnovo udara*, 1958), which originally appeared as *Nine Days* (*Devyat dnei*), are the battles of the Russian artillery at Lake Balaton (in Hungary) in the last winter of the war, the defense against the heavy German counterattacks in view of the early victory, and the eagerly desired end of the war.

The expansive story *A Short Stretch of Ground* (*Pyad zemli*, 1959) describes the bloody holding of a bridgehead at the Dniester in the summer of 1944. Baklanov's choice of the first person for narration (through the eyes of the artillery lieutenant Motovilov) lends the story the necessary verisimilitude, even though the description is crude and consciously limited to one point of view. In any case it gives an idea of the situation of the Soviet soldiers in the iron clamp between the German tank attacks and the constant threat of court-martial, the stockades, and execution because of cowardice before the enemy.

Baklanov obviously chooses extreme situations, such as the fight for almost lost positions, in order to give his stories sharp outlines, and to give a clear view of the superhuman efforts and sacrifices of the Soviet side in World War II.

The title of the story *No Shame Falls on the Dead* (*Mertviye sramu ne imut*, 1961) alludes to the historic Nestor Chronicle (for the year 971) and recalls the phrase that Prince Svyatoslav used to the Russian warriors in their battle against the Byzantines. In the winter, during the recapture of the Ukraine an artillery division encounters a severe attack in ambush and is almost totally destroyed by tanks.

This story, related from an "Olympian" viewpoint and overlooking all human and tactical contingencies, deals primarily with science in personal engagement and resistance to panic. The surviving chief of staff of the division, Captain Ishchenko, has escaped disaster only through surrender of himself and his duty, and his own conscience delivers him to shame, although the story does not indicate whether he will be court-martialed.

Not surprisingly the image of the Germans, who play roles in part as prisoners, as murderers of Russian prisoners, or as merciless occupation troops, is repulsive in the highest degree, with one notable exception (in *No Shame Falls on the Dead*).

In his novel *July 1941* (*Iyul 41 goda*, 1965) Baklanov attempted to bring the destinies of selected characters into harmony with the extensive historical background of the military catastrophe of the summer of 1941 and to provide an exact description of strategic decisions on the level of an army corps. Because Baklanov intended to expose the mistakes and errors of omission of Stalin and the highest military and political leadership of the Red Army, and at the same time to demonstrate the moral superiority of the Soviet soldiers over their adversaries, the plot cannot develop freely; occasionally it seems artificially constructed. The Soviet publications on military science adequately support the thesis of the "omniscient historian." This approach, however, removes the actual characters of the novel from their leading position, and everything finally proceeds like a judicial hearing.

Unlike *War and Peace*, this novel contains no true personal motivation, although Baklanov partially adopts Tolstoi's manner of having the author comment. Baklanov's history of philosophy, moreover, is basically materialistic and provides no room for unexpected judgments.

The disease of the period of paralyzing threat against free thought ("How is one to treat a disease if its name may not even be mentioned?") is, however, exposed mercilessly by Baklanov, placing this novel, too, among the revealing books of the time of the revision of Stalin's image.


### Yurii Bondarev

Yurii Bondarev (born 1924 in Orsk) also belongs to the authors of the younger front-fighter generation that entered the public arena after the twentieth party congress. He studied in the Gorki Institute of Literature, and his first stories, written under the influence of Konstantin Paustovski, were collected in 1953 as *At the Big Stream* (*Na bolshoi reke*). His novel *The Battalion Asks for Artillery Support* (*Batalyoni prosyat ognya*) is undoubtedly just as typical of the new wave of war literature as Baklanov's novels and stories.

In his novel Bondarev deals primarily with the sacrifice of soldiers left to their fate in the interest of strategic decisions made far behind the lines. From the point of view of a front officer in the artillery, who experiences the complete annihilation of the infantrymen entrusted to him, Bondarev depicts the complete hopelessness and the despairing insanity of the war as it rages in the front lines. Bondarev combines the continuous development of a given strategic situation (the futile formation of a bridgehead on the Dnieper in October 1943) with objective physical and psychological reality as the individual experiences it within and through himself. Even though patriotism finally triumphs over all adversities, the Soviet fighter bears an unusually heavy burden with the enemy before him and the unmerciful court-martial behind him. Bondarev presents the entire picture truthfully.

A discussion of the responsibility of the commander for the life and death of the soldiers under him is also the theme of Bondarev's war novel *The Last Salvos* (*Posledniye zalpi*, 1959). The action occurs on the frontier between Poland and Czechoslovakia in the Carpathian Mountains, and the military situation is again the bloody repulse of a German tank breakthrough (in the fall of 1944). Even more clearly than in the earlier novel, the major concern is with the individual's readiness to sacrifice his life, his personal behavior, and his fear of death. The events are focused on a single artillery battery and the nurse assigned to it. The time involved is only one day and two nights.

Bondarev refrains almost completely from detailed descriptions and auctorial generalizations. His strength is in the isolation of personal perception, and in the exact description of atmospheric details and physical stimuli. Side by side with the terse colloquial language of the dialogue is the obvious reality of human life, with signals and impulses that manifest themselves particularly in an abundance of meaningful verbs.

Bondarev's next novel, *Silence* (*Tishina*, 1962), received considerable attention in the West. In this work the author attempted to express the feelings of the members of his own generation, who after their happy return home from World War II consciously experienced the silence of naked injustice and cold terror for the first time. The ominous quiet that suddenly confronts the returning soldiers, aged before their time through their experiences at the front, only seems to be filled by a nervous greed for life, as expressed by study, love, and indifferent cynicism.

The former schoolfriends Sergei Vokhmintzev and Konstantin Korabelnikov, who meet again in Moscow in 1945, feel as though they are surrounded by ugly masks; they are sickened by the faint-hearted caution, shabby ambition, and suppression of true opinions that they see on all sides. Bondarev invents a rather melodramatic plot to make the confused actions plausible, thus inadvertently indicating that his plan has not entirely matured. This fault is overcome in the continuation of the novel, *The Two* (*Dvoye*, 1964), where Konstantin and his young wife Asya, Sergei's sister, stand alone in the midst of the action. In *Silence* the psychological point of departure of the story is Sergei, who is the same age as the author. The victim of unjust accusations, Sergei is expelled from the Mining Institute after the arrest of his father. At the end Sergei faces a void and must seek his fortune as a miner in central Asia.

In *The Two* Bondarev is occupied with the last days before Stalin's death, from the end of February to the beginning of March 1953. Konstantin, a cabdriver in Moscow, becomes involved in an inconsequential discussion in front of a hotel in the center of the city. At one point he displays one of his war souvenirs, a Walther pistol that he had previously concealed. Through several thoughtless remarks he becomes entangled in the invisible tentacles of a system that seems to encircle him with a persistence that is silent and therefore all the more frightening. The extreme situation of the hero partially resembles Raskolnikov's feverish dreams, and several episodes also recall Dostoyevski in character and style. The news of Stalin's death removes all inhibitions, and the action apparently enters a new phase. The persistent sense of spiritual confinement, however, is expressed symbolically in the frightening congestion of the human masses that have surged together to see the dead dictator once more. During the turmoil Konstantin and his wife Asya are almost crushed to death.

The time span, confined to a few days, has its spatial counterpart in the penetrating description of certain parts of the center of Moscow through which the hero drives several times; their distinguishing characteristics become the visible symbols of the ever tightening net, in which the "circles become narrower and narrower."

Bondarev undoubtedly owes much to Dostoyevski in his accounts of ambiguous meetings, and in his description of interiors, with their symbolic references to congestion, walls, inner courtyards, and stairs.

States of physical overstimulation, excessive perspiration, disgust, and hectic monologues also recall Dostoyevski.

Despite such similarities Bondarev remains a typical contemporary writer; his characters act carelessly and callously in their technological environment. Flirting, sex, alcohol, and excessive smoking belong to this life style, as does constant riding around in automobiles, subways, and buses.

## Nikolai Arzhak and Abram Tertz

The two writers Arzhak and Tertz, whose works until now have been published only outside the Sovet Union, were arrested in September 1965 after their pseudonyms had been revealed. After a double trial in February 1966 they were condemned to five and seven years, respectively, at hard labor.

Arzhak and Tertz both attempt to overcome pure critical realism and to recover the realm of the fantastic, the absurd, and the utopian for modern Soviet literature. As in the 1920s, this free element of the unreal and weird is used as satire aimed at reality and thus committed to criticism. The charge of an "anti-Soviet" tendency raised during the trial can hardly be accepted in the sense of the court, because the incriminating works, although published abroad, were not planned with reference to the countries in which they appeared. Most of the allusions are not to world problems but to discussions and tensions within the Soviet Union.

Nikolai Arzhak (born about 1925, with the family name of Yulii Daniel, known as a paraphraser and translator of Ukrainian, Armenian, and Caucasian) is the author of four satiric-grotesque novellas, each provocatively based on a somewhat absurd assumption.

In *Moscow Speaking* (*Govorit Moskva*, 1962) Arzhak toys with the idea that the government might announce a new festive day, the "day of open murder." This malicious provocation, however, leads nowhere, because only a few people avail themselves of the opportunity to kill their fellow citizens, "transportation workers and military personnel excepted." The reaction is an overall fear, an eagerness for reconciliation, and unconcealed antiheroism.

In *The Hands* (*Ruki*, 1963) a former member of the secret police tells how blank cartridges were mysteriously placed in his gun just before the scheduled execution of a priest. When the unharmed victim came toward him, the executioner suffered a nervous collapse; now he can no longer use his hands.

Arzhak resembles Yevgenii Zamyatin in his use of imaginary, experimental situations, which are to be tried out on people. The stories are so composed that the reader foresees a high point; they end in a kind of anticlimax (Margaret Dalton) with the actual formulation or posing of the problem.

The somewhat overrated *The Man from Minap* (*Chelovek iz Minapa*, 1963) is really a not quite serious burlesque. In *The Atonement* (*Izkupleniye*, 1964) Arzhak tackled a theme that is generally taboo in Soviet literature: the problem of the informers of the years up to 1953, now living unpunished among those given amnesty. Arzhak reverses the problem: The hero of the story, Viktor Volski, is not an informer at all; only suspected of being one, he is harassed so long that he is driven into complete isolation and shame, and has to be taken to a mental institution.

This explicit shifting of the question of guilt places conscience before a far weightier problem: Are not all really guilty, victims and executioners—guilty of the passive tolerance of injustice, guilty because they have done or do nothing, "nothing good and nothing bad"? This question is probably derived from Kafka's *The Trial*, with which Abram Tertz also seems to take issue (in *The Court Appears*).

Abram Tertz (born about 1925 with the family name of Andrei Sinyavski, a noted literary historian and critic) had his *Fantastic Stories* (*Fantasticheskiye rasskazy*) printed in Paris in 1961.

Whereas Arzhak is primarily concerned with moral-ethical questions, Tertz is a sharp critic of the cliché, the "unreal" language of daily reality, and of the type of mind that entrenches itself behind all sorts of fictions. Typical of this is the satire *The Graphomanes* (*Grafomani*, 1960), in which the literary production of Moscow is dissected and impaled mercilessly. Tertz does not even spare noted authorities, because they, as the narrator remarks, have "transformed literature into an impregnable fortress."

The little story *The Subtenants* (*Kvartiranti*, 1959) is an entirely contemporary monologue, the monologue of a ghost voice, in which the actual colloquial language is parodied. The ghost, capable of a number of material changes, speaks directly with a person, Sergei Sergeyevich, whose replies, however, cannot be heard. In the long stories *The Court Appears* (*Sud idiot*, 1960) and *Slippery Ice* (*Golodleditza*, 1961) Tertz gives his imagination free rein and disturbs the normal balance of everyday life through absurd and grotesque shifts.

The situation of the accused in the authors' trial (1966) is really anticipated in the prologue and in the epilogue. The author, however, is constantly concerned with matters that occur outside of reality, and this play permits and requires exaggerations, which can only be judged on the basis of artistic expression. The prologue of *The Court Appears*, for example, describes the grotesque transformation of Moscow at the appearance of the gigantic hand of the "lord in the house" (*Chotzyain*) in the morning sky:

> The buildings of the cathedrals and the ministries rose like banks of coral. On the slender points of the skyscrapers grew decorations and medals, emblems and lacework. Moulded, cast, and carved adornments, all of pure gold, covered the massive blocks of stone. That was granite covered with lace, iron cement painted over with bouquets and monograms, stainless steel coated with cream to beautify it.

The utopian novel *Lyubimov* (the name of an imaginary city in the novel), written in the years from 1962 to 1963, also deals with the social utopia. Tertz again subjects language and modes of expression to a parodistic critique. The manner of the spokesmen is extremely funny and full of crazy inspirations, which sometimes rise to the grotesque, as in the correspondent of the bourgeois newspaper *Perdit intrigan vrot okh Amerika*. The novel contains many quotations, paradoxes, and plays on words.

Tertz thus continues a tradition founded in the 1920s by Ehrenburg, Ilf and Petrov, and Zoshchenko. His work cannot be properly evaluated in translation.

*Vasilii Aksenov and Anatolii Gladilin*

Several authors loosen up the strict schematic narrative form of socialist realism by introducing short monologues (diary notes) by the supporting characters, or through a special technique of segmentation (several narrators in the first person take turns in making a report).

The individual points of view can, for example, supersede one another as in Boris Pilnyak's *The Naked Year* (*Golyi god*, 1922), so that the same incidents are seen from different sides and judged by different standards. Not only are human values renewed through such techniques, but morality is individualized and psychologically analyzed—a practice that contradicts the totalitarian and "party" principle of socialist realism. These techniques can be studied especially well in the works of Vasilii Aksenov and Anatolii Gladilin.

Vasilii Aksenov (born 1932 in Kazan) spent several years of his life (a part of his school years) in the Far East; he also studied medicine. His first stories appeared in 1959 in the then especially lively youthful magazine *Yunost*. With his novel *The Starred Ticket* (*Zvezdni bilet*, 1961) Aksenov furnished a typical example of the demolition of the traditional narrative frame and the technique of reporting from changing points of view. He uses the star-shaped hole punched into the railroad ticket for validation as metaphor for the sky glimpsed above a Moscow backyard.

Two brothers relieve one another in telling the story; the first and third parts are told by the older brother Viktor, a young scientist, who dies in an airplane accident. In the fourth part the narrator is Viktor's brother Dimka, born eleven years after he was. Now only seventeen years old, Dimka joins a small group of dropouts and attempts to live his own life in the west (Estonia). The young runaways also appear in the second part, where the story is told in the third person.

The destiny of each brother is reflected in that of the other. After the death of the older brother, Dimka enters a new phase of awareness and recognizes Viktor's "starred ticket" (the segment of the night sky in the narrow square of a Moscow backyard).

Aksenov did not find an entirely convincing solution for the problem presented by the several lines of action. The novel is notable, however, for the vivacity of the narration and for its use of Soviet teen-age slang. Different sections of dialogue are introduced, as in the script of a play, merely by giving the speaker's name.

Throughout the novel Aksenov allows his heroes to act according to their own moral principles, even though the method casts doubt on the "official" interpretation of life. Aksenov considers the feelings of the rising generation as a general protest against adults, "bourgeois" saturation, and clichés. His work thus resembles much western writing, as an American critic has suggested, citing the possible influence of J. D. Salinger, whose novel *The Catcher in the Rye* (1951) appeared in Russia in 1960.

In 1964 Aksenov published his stories in *Catapult* (*Katapulta*), which also contains the short novel *Oranges from Morocco* (*Apelsini iz Marokko*) first published in 1963 in *Yunost*. Aksenov's youthful romanticism is aroused by technology and sports, including skindiving, football, skiing, and jet flights; by such fetishes of "Western" civilization as records, dance, films from Italy and Poland, and teen-age fashions; and by the extent of Soviet territory and the technical development of distant areas. Aksenov's heroes include doctors, engineers, architects, artists, athletes, workmen, pilots, and sailors—all with little experience in life—whom the author places in the arena of first decisions and responsibility.

In Aksenov the tangible conflicts, if they can be specified at all, are rather banal; attitudes of suspense are almost entirely absent. On the other hand Aksenov has not been afraid to try to introduce into literary use another language—the careless colloquial language of the 1960s. Aksenov has been severely criticized for this, and in the second edition of *Oranges from Morocco* (1964) the author deliberately smoothed out much of the slang.

*Oranges from Morocco* consists largely of youthful dialogue; the eighteen sections of the story deal primarily with the individual reports of the various characters. All of these reports describe a single winter's evening at a fictitious scene on the Pacific coast.

The plot revolves around the sale of recently arrived Morocco oranges in a tiny harbor, where all the participants meet at a late hour. The events are seen from different viewpoints, and several sections recall the style of continuous narration known as *skaz*. In the wintry landscape of the Russian Far East the young actors seem isolated from civilization. They choose the "oranges from Morocco" as a fetish-like goal of their romantic wishes, and at the end everything centers around them.

In Aksenov's story *Half a Trip to the Moon* (*Na polputi k lune*, 1962), the very successful truckdriver and former convict Valerii starts a vacation trip from the Far East to Moscow. Valerii has hoarded a pile of money, and he shows that he can spend it with inimitable nonchalance. After an unsuccessful brief love affair in Khabarovsk, he falls in love with a stewardess on the flight to Moscow. In the vague hope of meeting her again, he continues to travel between Moscow and Khabarovsk until his money, his hopes, and his days of leave dwindle away.

More recently Aksenov has written the hypercritical short story, as in *The Victory* (*Pobeda*, 1965), and the ironic-humorous analysis of society, as in *Too Bad You Were Not There* (*Zhal chto was ne bylo s nami*, 1965). In the latter Aksenov portrays the milieu of the artists and people of the film, who lead a glittering superficial life. As in other stories Aksenov here skirts the limits of elevated feuilletonism, which strives primarily for gags and amusing effects.

Like Aksenov, Anatolii Gladilin (born 1935 in Moscow), author of the journal *Yunost*, was especially devoted to the psychology of young people, and he attempts to describe their development. In the story *Smoke in the Eyes* (*Dym v glaza*, 1959) the plot is determined by the brilliant career of Igor Serov, a young football star, who because of an injury must return to "normal" life. His adjustment to reality fails, and in his despair he also fails in business. He finds his way back to society very tortuously. The last stage is his disappointment in the romantic expectations nourished by Rudyard Kipling, which lead him to the dangerous life of a sailor on a fishing steamer.

The impossibility of leading a heroic existence is indicated in the title of the story and by the subtitle *A Story of Ambition* (*Povest o chestolyubii*). In this respect, too, the story contributes to the compromising of false heroic pathos in the eyes of the younger generation. Igor's fame as a football star is like a hypnosis; after the trance ends nothing remarkable remains.

Gladilin also experimented with the changing points of view of different narrators in the first person. Some narrative segments appear in the form of personal confessions—inner monologues, diary notes, letters, and reports of dreams.

Gladilin's story *New Year's Day (Pervii den Novovo goda*, 1963) consists of alternating reports of a young artist and his father, who is seriously ill in a Moscow hospital. The contrast between the two generations—the father's generation of the Civil War and the son's, which grew up and gained independence only after World War II—is described with great psychological precision in the narrative form chosen. The reports, and an interpolated letter from the son's sweetheart, combine the characteristics both of monologue and of diary entries; the story is told from the particular narrator's point of view.

Whereas the father with his memories and dreams lives primarily in a heroic or hero-worshipping past, the son quarrels with an unsatisfactory present: "I am a human being who has been drained by everything: family, trade, and television; I am a disciplined tenant." Here again the youthful hero expresses more or less open cynicism: "Dust, stirred up by thousands of feet, is in my opinion more harmful than radioactive fallout."

## THE TRADITIONALISTS

### Vladimir Tendryakov

Vladimir Tendryakov (born 1923 in the region of Voronezh) has been an important figure in literary and ideological discussions since the beginning of the 1960s.

His first volume of narrative prose, *In the Woods (Sredi lesov)*, appeared in 1954. Tendryakov's first novel, *In the Quickstep of the Days (Za begushchim dnem*, 1959) deals with a Russian provincial school teacher. The controversy about more child-centered methods of instruction is, however, overshadowed by the problem of unhappy marriages. The story, told in the first person, repeatedly returns to this intimate dilemma and attempts, analyzing rather too abstractly, to find an honorable solution, which is finally attained in the reasonable separation of two incompatible marriages and the union of true lovers. In this novel, Tendryakov assails conventions and conformity, behind which he recognizes self-deception and cowardice.

The motivating force in Tendryakov's last stories and novels is his fanatical love of truth, the rejection of every convenient readiness to compromise, the insight that no pure goal can be reached by evil means. In Tendryakov, however, the pathos of frankness and love of truth is not as radical and above all not as provocative as in Lev Tolstoi, although his work sometimes recalls Tolstoi, as in the novella *The Court* (*Sud*, 1961), which alludes to Nekhlyudov in Tolstoi's *Resurrection*.

This story clearly shows Tendryakov's principal concern: the testing of conscience in profoundly human conflicts. A young bystander is shot in a tragic hunting accident. One of the three hunters, who did not fire at the decisive moment, finds a bullet that identifies the guilty marksman, who was not the little army surgeon, as had been assumed, but the highly esteemed official in an important and influential position. The old bear hunter Semen Teterin, the hero of the novella, angrily throws away the piece of evidence that no one wants to see.

The end of the trial is very simple: no one is condemned. The one who is really innocent, however, is considered morally guilty despite the lack of proof, and Semen Teterin, who knows better, is truly punished after the trial. He who violated truth feels the deepest guilt. The story therefore ends with the sentence: "There is no severer judgment than the judgment of conscience."

Tendryakov treats the problem of justice further in his later story *The Find* (*Nakhodka*, 1966), which is concerned with a case of child exposure. The supervisor of fisheries, Trofim, strict and hardened in his feelings, is led to the insight that life is far more complicated than his police conscience would have it, and that a relentless persecution of violations against law and custom is not always the best way. Tendryakov's moral in this story is that the hangman can no longer feel at home in human society and that behavior influenced by no human feelings of pity leads to lonely bitterness. A similar viewpoint appears in other stories. He indicates that "new human beings" exist in socialist society, and that the moral problems and temptations of man remain constant: every man must live his own life.

A theme typical of Tendryakov is treated in the story *A Case Out of Line* (*Khrezvychainoye*, 1962). The daughter of a party functionary of a provincial high school, a girl in the upper class, and her mathematics teacher, are discovered to be believing Christians. The director of the school must take suitable steps; the party also becomes involved. The story describes the failure of the efforts of the director to retain the teacher at the school and to induce the student, through a relaxation of the strict methods of instruction, to reconsider her not too firmly grounded convictions.

The director finally suffers a heart attack and hears of the end of the affair on his sickbed. His plea for humanity and tolerance, for overcoming narrow-mindedness, and for open discussion fades away unheard. At the most important point in the story, however, the student precipitously marries an above-average young man and renounces her faith, not because she has been convinced otherwise, but because her husband "also does not believe." With her early marriage she descends to a lower spiritual level.

The novel *Meeting Again with Nefertiti* (*Svidaniye s Nefertiti*), which appeared in 1964 in the journal *Moskva*, describes the development of Fiodor Materin, the son of a peasant, who goes directly from the war to the academy for painting in Moscow. Much space is devoted to the discussions of permitted and "forbidden" experiments in painting, and of the preservation and dissolution of moral integrity among young art students during the Stalin epoch. Tendryakov also pleads for tolerance and for the absolute validity of ethical and aesthetic criteria, and for the individual's freedom of decision.

The end of the novel is formed by an invocation of the death watch before Stalin's corpse: "But in Moscow, in the hall of the columns funeral music drifts between the wreaths and over those watching the somber wax face. The people look searchingly into the future."

In this novel and in his subsequent stories, Tendryakov experimented with a special stylistic technique, producing a directly "experienced" narrative in the name of the hero or of another person who seems to identify himself with the hero. This story is a further development of "experienced speech," which excludes the first person singular. The third person singular, however, is transformed in this "unreal" speech, alternating in the various impersonal expressions, as in Solzhenitzyn's *One Day in the Life of Ivan Denisovich.* An illustration of this technique occurs in a scene from the war episodes, although many characteristics of the style are lost in translation. At the height of the winter battle around Stalingrad, Materin listens to a violin played by a Rumanian prisoner of war:

> And the violin sings. . . . Grief? . . . Perhaps. Lament? . . .
> Possibly. . . . The violin sings. . . . But in front of you you have
> the battle. And surely, directly from the movement, after a whole
> day's march, when you are already collapsing, without waiting for
> the chow truck, then you will still load the heavy cable reels on
> your back and crawl through the frozen steppe, crawl and tear the
> skin from your bleeding hands, pressing your face to the cold
> ground under fire. And perhaps they will shoot you dead. . . . Dead?
> Good Lord! At that moment one would not care a rap for anything,
> nothing means anything any more—battle, hunger, fatigue, death—
> thumb your nose at it! There is this voice, the pure voice—sobbing
> and passion, lament and happiness . . . in the middle of the war, for
> a moment holding up the stormy forward march, a violin sings.
> And all around heavy breathing was to be heard.

This narrative style, which had already appeared in Belyi's *Silver Dove,* also pervades Tendryakov's remarkable kolkhoz story *Short-lived is the Mayfly (Podenka-vek korotki,* 1965), one of the few peasant tragedies. In *The Find* the story is extensively blended with Trofim Rusanov's consciousness, and the partly ornamental style (with its rhetorical figures and stereotyped repetitions) also recalls Belyi. Continuous symbolic comparisons and plastic expressions lead to peculiar complications in the world described, which makes them mysterious and pregnant with meaning for the reader.

*Vladimir Soloukhin*

Since the beginning of the 1960s Vladimir Soloukhin (born 1924 in the Central Russian region of Vladimir) has come before the public as a surprisingly vital exponent of a national Russian current in Soviet literature.

The author grew up in the country; after the war he attended the Gorki Institute of Literature in Moscow. His early poems and articles, beginning in 1951, were not widely read. Soloukhin is the representative of a genuine new romanticism, which rests on the traditions of folklore but goes far beyond the narrowness and prejudice of pure "regional fiction."

His first volumes of poetry bore such conventional titles as *Rain in the Steppe* (*Dozhd v stepi*, 1953) and *Back of the Blue Seas* (*Za Sin -moryami*, 1956). Later collections, including *How One Drinks Up the Sun* (*Kak vypit solntze*, 1961), *He Who Carries Flowers in His Hands* (*Imeyushchi v rukach tzveti*, 1962), and *Living on Earth* (*Zhit na zemle*, 1965), are pretentious in their message and in the form of language.

Soloukhin is rather unique in his use of free verse, in which he was surely not inspired solely by folk poetry. In his volume of essays *From Poetic Positions* (*S liricheskich pozitzii*, 1965) Soloukhin, speaking for the whole new poetry, points out a tendency toward the "freeing of verse" (*raskreposhchniye stikha*). From this tendency Soloukhin has deduced several important and radical consequences.

For him, rhyme is only accidental, and the line of verse is characterized neither by typical stress nor by a uniform number of syllables. The articulation of the poems in verses is attained solely through emphatic intonation or through rhythmic tendencies within the word groups, whereby the boundaries between verse and rhythmic prose often disappear entirely. His "modern" stylistic devices include frequent repetition of words, phrases, or units of intonation, as in the works of such poets as Voznesenski, Rozhdestvenski, and Yevtushenko:

> I took the words and tried them out
> As to their weight,
> As to their taste,
> As to their odor,
> As to their color,
> As to their firmness,
> As to the nuances of their taste, color and odor. . . .
> Forty times tinkling fall of drops,
> Forty snowstorms in winter,
> Forty black nights in the fall,
> Forty times summer rainbows,
> Forty years.
> Forty times I tasted the spring in advance.
> Forty years.
> Forty times nature sank into sleep.
> Forty years.
> Am I sorry that it is already forty and not twenty?
> No.

Soloukhin's poetry is syntactical in that the semantic relationships are controlled through simple syntactical means. Deliberately and as a matter of principle he declines to use metaphors. In this respect his poems are pure *texts*, which cannot always be judged as poems in the conventional sense. The themes of the poems are man, the Russian landscape, and technology. Nature is often played off against technology, as in *Man Goes Over the Earth on Foot* (*Chelovek peshkom idet po zemle*).

Soloukhin shows his true romantic vein in his prose works, which include his "lyric" articles and memoirs, such as *A Walk in Rural Russia* (*Vladimirskiye proselki*, 1957), *A Drop of Dew* (*Kaplya rosi*, 1960), several stories, and more recently the novel *Mother-Stepmother* (*Mat-machekha*, 1966).

The hero of this undoubtedly partly autobiographical novel is a Russian peasant's son who is demobilized after the war and admitted to the Moscow Institute of Literature. His name is Mitya Tolushkin (*Tolushka* is the Russian word for Cinderella). During the 1940s he personally experiences the temptations and conflicts of the late Stalin era. For him, Russia is at the same time a mother and a bad stepmother; the symbolism of the title is indicated in the novel in numerous ways.

The scene of action is not exclusively Moscow; Mitya's native village, which remains a fixed place of reference for the hero, is drawn into the plot. The events are related strictly from the author's point of view, as by a biographer at a distance. The author's language nevertheless depends on the environment described; sometimes it approaches the *skaz*, that is, a highly stylized form of speech. In this way Soloukhin introduces fairytale motifs as well as folkloristic, ornamental turns of speech.

After the hero's attempt at suicide, this novel of development concludes with an almost pagan hymn to nature. The work also suggests a deeper piety, in the Christian sense of the word, behind the author's free and confident attitude toward life.

Soloukhin's narrative style has been considerably influenced by Russian tradition, especially by such writers as Leonov, Prishvin, and Paustovski, and through them by Russian literature of the nineteenth century.

In his essays Soloukhin is a passionate champion of the Russian past. He defends folk art and icon painting, and the sacred and secular architecture of past centuries, from careless disdain in the era of such technological achievements as spacecraft, atomic reactors, and daring functional structures. In his campaign for the preservation of Russian tradition he goes far beyond the official "protection of monuments" and the mere maintenance of tourist attractions.

Surprisingly enough Soloukhin announced the spiritual values of the past, and his writings are full of concealed polemics against the present. He rejects the entire "avant-gardist" Western European art of the twentieth century, which he discusses very disparagingly in his book *From Poetic Positions*, where he speaks of "splitting the soul," "denationalization," and the complete leveling of the national traditions of all the arts. Soloukhin thus virtually represents a new Slavophile tendency, as indicated by his dedication of the essay *Aksakov's Magic Wand* (*Volshebnaya palochka Aksakova*) to Sergei Aksakov.

Among Russian artists Soloukhin shows a special preference for such definitely nationalistic painters and composers as Shishkin, Surikov, Levitan, Vasnetzov, Kustodiyev, Nesterov; Mussorgski,

Tchaikovski, and Rachmaninov. Among the poets he prefers Tyutchev, Fet, Blok, and, surprisingly, Gumilev.

The destiny, presentation, and cultivation of Russian national art are discussed in Soloukhin's poetic essay *Letters from the Russian Museum (Pishma iz Russkovo muzeya*, published in the journal *Molodaya gvardiya* in 1966. For the form of his report Soloukhin refers to Karamzin's *Letters of a Russian Traveler*, and the findings of the traveler in contemporary Russia are as startling as Karamzin's observations in Europe at the end of the eighteenth century. Soloukhin lists over four hundred valuable monuments destroyed by Stalin in Moscow alone. He complains of the preponderance of contemporary art in the national museums in contrast with the barely represented folk art and the modest number of icons. Soloukhin's survey of the storage rooms of the museums is especially striking; in two museums alone (Leningrad and Moscow) altogether 10,000 old icons have been stored. In this courageous, factual account, written in lively style, Soloukhin proves himself a connoisseur, and *Letters from the Russian Museum* suggests a significant change in attitude toward national traditions.

### Yurii Kazakov

The internationally successful Yurii Kazakov (born 1927 in Moscow) is notable for the psychological character of his mood painting. Often regarded as a successor to Chekhov, he is particularly esteemed as a writer of subtle, poetically sentimental short stories. He has also been influenced by such American writers as Mark Twain, Jack London, and Ernest Hemingway, and his manly heroes, the exoticism of the "white sea," and his brief, vividly drawn episodes differ from Chekhov's subtle depictions of social relationships. The story *Damned North (Proklyati sever*, 1965), however, definitely recalls Chekhov in its dissatisfaction with the world, its inner restlessness, its melancholy, and its poetic impressions.

Educated as a musician, Kazakov shows a remarkable facility in his early stories, written in the 1950s. His reputation was established by two longer animal stories, *Teddy (Teddi*, 1956) and *Arktur, the*

*Hunting Dog* (*Arktur—gonchi pos*, 1957). The former tells of a bear's escape from a circus; the animal's longing for the "other" life is unappeased even in the freedom of the wilderness. In this story, possibly influenced by London's *The Call of the Wild*, Kazakov handles his narrative technique and language with assurance.

In the stories of the 1950s Kazakov is always concerned with the striking portrait and realistic detail. He also attempts to bring nature close to the reader through simple and precise descriptions, in which he follows Mikhail Prishvin and Konstantin Paustovki, to both of whom he dedictated several of his stories.

The Russian natural scene (fishing, hunting, lonely coasts and woods, bright nights and frost-crackling winters) plays an important role with Kazakov. Longer stays in northern Russia (the area of Archangelsk) have left definite traces in his works. Especially in the beginning many of his short stories and narratives are concerned with people living along the northern coasts of Russia, as in *Nikishka's Secrets* (*Nikishkiny taini*, 1957), *The Old Woman of the Sea* (*Pomorka*, 1957), and *Manka* (*Manka*, 1958).

Kazakov's special technique of description was developed especially from 1959 to 1961. In the story *Nonsense* (*Trali-vali*, 1959), originally *The Apostate* (*Otshchepenetz*), he brings reality close to the senses through the new description of such entirely everyday domestic activities as eating and drinking, smoking, working, and singing. Kazakov concentrates on the shapes and colors of objects as well as on noises, odors, inner bodily reactions, and thoughts.

As in most of Kazakov's stories the theme of *Nonsense* is the erotic relationship between man and woman, which Kazakov was one of the first of his generation to describe frankly. Yegor, in charge of river buoys and widowed through an accident, is visited regularly by young Alenka. This relationship is developed by Kazakov as a matter of course and with complete naturalness. Yegor is, to be sure, a rather lazy drunkard, but he is also the original, free, triumphant, and desirable man, to whom self-discipline and moral demands are totally foreign. Yegor's human core expresses itself in song, the heartrending song that seems to express his never appeased longing and his inner, gnawing pain. Yegor is born to sing; singing is his secret beauty.

The human condition is Kazakov's most important theme, but, as with Chekhov, life is always led beyond itself and directed toward an abstract vanishing point. Thus even the most precise descriptions often end in an abstraction:

> The air is already getting cold. The swallows sweep across the water and screech penetratingly. Near the shore fish splash about, and at every splash Yegor makes a face as if he were well acquainted with just this fish. From the shore a fragrance of strawberries, hay, and dew-covered shrubs is wafted, and the boat smells of fish, petroleum, and swamp grass. From the water, however, a hardly perceptible mist is rising; it smells of depth and seclusion.

Another example appears in Kazakov's later story *Night's Lodging* (*Nochleg*, 1964):

> She did not take leave, she did not go, nor did she become livelier, no, she seemed to be made of stone: blue-eyed, somewhat buxom, strong, fragrant; and her fragrance was sincere, it was that of powder, of a woman, of milk, of the village. And she was still taciturn, distant.

Kazakov's language is direct and saturated like the language of Bunin; it is accentuated by syntactic series, accumulation, and modulated rhythms. The plasticity of his language is grounded less in comparisons than in the accumulation of striking definitions (*epitheta*).

In Kazakov's stories great importance is assigned to the erotic tension in transitory or unsuccessful or paradigmatic meetings between the sexes. Kazakov describes these tensions with considerable persistence and in suggestive nuances then new in Soviet literature. Even when failures or the absence of expected fulfillment are unavoidable, Kazakov finds a way to solve the suspense poetically or to introduce in any case a contrasting, deflecting motif.

Tragedy is foreign to Kazakov; often the ending is kept inconclusive rather than have it come to an irrevocable catastrophe. This trait characterizes such novellas and short stories as *There Goes a Dog!* (*Von bezhit sobaka!*, 1961), *Two in December* (*Dvoye v dekabre*, 1962), *On the Island* (*Na ostrove*, 1963), and *The Ugly One* (*Nekrasivaya*, 1964).

In *On the Island* the already married accountant Zabavin has a short and sudden love affair during a business trip to a little island in the White Sea; it promises him all the unknown happiness that he has sought in vain in everyday life. A prosaic telegram calls him back to Archangelsk, and a sudden parting interrupts his affair with the young director of the meteorological station, who remains behind in the misty solitude with her unfulfilled dreams, far from Archangelsk or even Leningrad.

The story ends in disappointment, but the apparently unhappy experience fades out, at least for Zabavin, in the somnolent lurching and pitching of the little local steamer, in the calming splashing of the water behind the cabin wall. Zabavin is the seducer at the very first opportunity, but he also seduces his own power of imagination. This attitude is typical of Kazakov's view of the relations between man and woman: extenuating circumstances always exist.

Strikingly objective, too, is the picture presented in *The Ugly One*. The homely young teacher with the beautiful name of Sonya approaches a certain disappointment with open eyes, when she becomes involved with Nikolai, the idol of the girls. For the moment wish and longing are intense, but through her humiliation Sonya gains sufficient strength for self-preservation, so that no tragedy results:

> Suddenly she noticed the penetrating beauty of the world, and how the stars falling down wrote their course in the sky. She noticed the night, the distant camp fires, which she probably just imagined, and the good people who sat around these fires, and she felt the already tired, peaceful power of the earth. . . .

With all his realistic description of the everyday, Kazakov disposes of so much wistfully wise irony that he predicts consolation for real pain as in *The Fragrance of Bread* (*Zapakh khleba*, 1961), which appeared in the famous almanac *Tarusskiye stranitz*. The relation of the heroine to the death of her mother, who has died in a distant village, is already peculiarly affected by the receipt of the telegram on new year's morning. Only much later when the daughter visits the grave of her mother does the stored-up anguish break forth in an abrupt, vehement funereal wail based on a centuries-old traditional Russian ritual, which, however, Kazakov scarcely indicates.

After the completely exhausted Dusya has been carried home from the cemetery, she falls asleep, and the narrative continues:

The next day after she had already got ready to return to Moscow, she still had a cup of tea with her sister. She was gay and told what a wonderful apartment they had in Moscow and how much comfort. So she left gay and serene, giving Misha ten rubles. Two weeks later new people came, they opened the house of the old mother again, scrubbed the floors, brought their things and began to live in the house.

In some stories, contrasting memories are superimposed on the main theme, as in *Autumn in the Oak Forests* (*Osen v dubovikh lesakh*, 1961), but in every story many unexpressed expectations can be recognized in the distance. Often too, Kazakov uses music to ease unbearable suspense, as in the episode of recollection in *Autumn in the Oak Forests*.

Aside from publication in magazines, Kazakov has already issued several volumes of collections of stories in larger editions. The most important are *On the Way Station* (*Na polustanke,* 1959), *On the Way* (*Po doroge,* 1961), *Blue and Green* (*Goluboye i zelenoye,* 1963), and *Two in December.* Kazakov's most popular stories have thus been reprinted frequently.

## *Viktor Konetzki*

The pronounced romantic tendency among such recent writers as Kazakov, is also apparent in the work of Viktor Konetzki (born in 1929 in Leningrad), who had served in the navy.

Konetzki cherishes the ports of the northern coast of Russia, the White Sea, the wastes of ice of the "northern sea route, the testing of character beyond the boundaries of civilization." For this reason Konetzki has been compared with Jack London and Hemingway, and these names, in fact, indicate his general tendency. In any case, however, the regions lying on the periphery of Russia—the Arctic, the Far East, Kamchatka, the shores of the Black Sea—have again become fashionable in literature since the 1950s, as in the works of Kaverin, Paustovski, Aksenov, and Nebrasov, where an extensive homesickness seems to be expressed.

In Konetzki's *The Worries of Tomorrow* (*Zavtrashniye zaboty*, 1961) the crossing of the northern sea route around Siberia to the Far East is only the apparent theme. The hero of the story, Captain Gleb Volnov, is also on a journey into his own past; with the aid of bits of memories of a hopeless love affair during a "white" night in Archangelsk he attempts to draw his own self, piece by piece, from the obscurity of instinctive experience to the light of consciousness. Like Kazakov and Paustovski, Konetzki favors animal stories and sentimental descriptions of nature. The story *Bandit's Last Night* (*Poslednaya noch bandita*, 1963) describes from a thoroughly human point of view the observations and thoughts of an old and finally moribund circus dog. In other instances, too, Konetzki shows his deep interest in the life and behavior of animals. His attempt to describe consciousness, which manifests itself particularly in these animal stories, gives these narratives and stories (*povesti*) their real vigor.

Konetzki makes reflection an actual event, and the process of remembering becomes a theme in itself or is inserted as a digression in the course of the story. The *Story of the Radio Operator Kamushkin* (*Povest o radiste Kamushkine*, 1962) is especially rich in such digressions. In this case memory is given an added motivation by the hero's head injury:

> Life appeared sharply and clearly before his eyes, episode after episode. And this clearness of the memories was disturbing. Fiodor Ivanovich realized that behind the host of smallest and exact details, behind the speed and relentlessness of remembrance, illness remained.

Konetzki's stories involve confrontations of the heroes with themselves, with their own guilt and inadequacy, as shown especially in *Over the White Road Cross* (*Nad belym perekrestkom*, 1960), which is the title story of a volume of the same name (1966) and which includes the best-known stories. It concerns guilty war memories that relentlessly pursue an air force officer.

Leningrad, Konetzki's native city, plays a special role in his stories as a landscape of the soul, as *The Story of the Radio Operator Kamushkin*. In his descriptions Konetzki succeeds in abstracting new and unusual charms from this city. The following paragraph is taken from Konetzki's *He Who Looks at the Clouds* (*Kto smotrit na oblaka*, published in *Znamya*, 1967):

> He showed her the Prayazhka with the crumbling, somber building of the hospital "To the Wonderworking Nicholas," where the gray robes of the patients could be seen behind the window gratings. Above the hospital, in the distance, the cranes of the wharves were moving, and in the space between the houses the Neva glistened, very broad here, but thronged with tugboats, motor launches, old vessels that were waiting for repairs and new, giant ones bright with red lead. The rotting planks quivered under their steps. The oily water of the canals, gleaming like a rainbow from the petroleum, flowed along slowly. Fences and the walls of houses were steeped in moisture and looked unsightly, and not all people were able to notice the beauty under this unsightliness.

In this work, too, the point of view is the determining factor; it corresponds to the three parts into which the book is divided. The stories are unified by the plot, in which a group of persons acts in a loose spatial and temporal connection, but where at every stage another figure and another year (1943, 1950, 1960) occupy the center.

The story ends without a definite fulfillment for any of the persons involved and resembles a question rather than an answer. Recent history is drawn into the plot through Captain Basargin's difficulties with the authorities and through his banishment to the far north until his amnesty in 1956.

In Konetzki's stories the conflicts play the role primarily of the trigger for reflection, in which the real human nuances emerge. The conflicts often remain unresolved, but Konetzki knows how to arouse the sympathy of the reader and to fascinate him through personal and subjectively arranged perspectives.

# New Tendencies in Soviet Poetry

## LYRIC AND ''CHAMBER''
## MUSIC IN POETRY

The variety of tendencies in contemporary Russian poetry permits a differentiation according to the most varied criteria. The arrangement attempted here is based on the dominant factor in the poetic text and not on the idea of the demarcation of certain procedures from one poet to another. Tradition as a whole is open to every poet for his personal use, and every poet would like to appear "new" and unchangeable. Nevertheless, a regularity exists in the approach to the individual poem, emerging in the realization of one's own best capacity. The singable character of the word and the line of verse can fascinate the poet as much as the new "text" in its entirety, which results from free associations and stylistic innovation.

The poet concerned with the lyrical development of his theme will give most attention to the melody and musicality of the verses, without minimizing the importance of the structural elements, because his "dominant factor" can prove its strength only in resisting the other components. Pure melody in language is as unthinkable as pure sound.

In contemporary Russian literature singable verse still plays a decisive role; it maintains itself as "song" in the strictest sense as well as in the rhymed poem of strophes. The genres of the eighteenth and nineteenth centuries, long ago discarded, are occasionally revived in ironic reminiscence and quotations. The minstrel and ballad forms are much in evidence, compared with their relative neglect under Stalin.

### Bulat Okudzhava

During the last decade Bulat Okudzhava (born 1924 in Moscow) has become known as a protagonist of this *scenic* lyric poetry (song, minstrel song, ballad, "little song"). Although he usually accompanies himself on the guitar, he is neither a cabaret performer nor a "protest" singer. His poems, often profoundly cryptic and filled with a poignant clairvoyance, have their place in "real" literature.

The son of a victim of Stalinist persecution and not really of Russian but of South Caucasian descent, Okudzhava participated as a young volunteer in the battles for the defense of Transcaucasia. These war experiences led to a remarkable piece of prose, *Hello, Scholar!* (*Bud zdorov, shkolyar!*, 1961). His war experiences, reported without illusions, have a decidedly antimilitaristic undertone, and his poetic repertory includes songs against war:

> Don't believe in war, my lad; don't believe, it is sad. It is sad, my lad, like high boots, so narrow. Your wild horses, they accomplish nothing there, for you are always as on an outstretched hand, and all bullets seek only one.

Many of Okudzhava's songs have been recorded, and they are very popular with Soviet youth. Records made abroad show his skill in recitation.

Okudzhava's literary models are to be sought not only in folk poetry and folk songs, but also in the romances of the nineteenth century (Gypsy romance), in the romantic song, in the ballad of the nineteenth and twentieth centuries, and in the tragic note of the poetry of Aleksandr Blok. Several pieces, including the ballad *Korol, the King* (*Lenka Koroliov*, 1962), the *Midnight Trolleybus* (*Polnochyi trolleibus*, 1962), and *Little Song of Arbat* (*Pesenka ob Arbate*), belong to the contemporary poems most popular among the intellectuals.

Okudzhava's poetry appeared in Russia in the little volumes

*Islands* (*Ostrova*, 1959) and *The Jolly Drummer* (*Veselyi baraban-shchik*, 1964). These volumes were also printed abroad, with expanded contents.

## Rimma Kazakova

The lyrical forms, influenced by tradition, which are suitable for anecdotal incidents as well as for the expression of purely lyrical moods, now also have a place in the work of several younger women poets, notably Rimma Kazakova (born 1932 in Sevastopol). Her earliest volume of poems, *We Will Meet in the East* (*Vstremtimsya na Vostoke*), appeared in 1958 in Khabarovsk. It was followed by *There, Where You Are* (*Tam, gde ty*, 1960), *Verses* (*Stikhi*, 1962), and *Free Days* (*Pyatnitzi*, 1965).

Kazakova spent several years in the Far East, and her poetry has been linked with all the landscapes of Russia. The most personal poems, however, are connected with her native city Sevastopol, as in *Thoughts at the Grave of My Grandfather in Sevastopol* (*Razmyshleniye na mogile moyevo deda v Sevastopol*) and the poem to war, *The Ballad of the Return of the Fallen Father*. Motifs and forms of ballad singers and minstrels are found very frequently in Kazakova's works. Tragic humor and self-irony are characteristic of the poet. Seeking extreme simplification of expression, popular but by no means vulgar language, and unemotional statements, she shows a close relationship to Okudzhava in *Little Song of the Sail* (*Pesenka o paruse*), *Trains* (*Poyezda*), and *There Are Fools in this World* (*Zhivut na svete duraki*).

The tradition from Lermontov to Bagritzki is evident in her poems, and the frequently complicated plays of rhyme and sound also recall Tsvetayeva, Pasternak, and their contemporaries. Such poems as *Drizzle* (*Gribnoi dozhd*) and *Malakhov Hill* (*Malakhov kurgan*, an old fortress in Sevastopol) are stylized in folk language. Frequently, however, the poet mingles the folk language with modern foreign words, abstract concepts, and surprisingly up-to-date expressions. Kazakova looks on her "craft" quite unceremoniously and unpretentiously as work suitable for a servant, as in *Handicraft* (*Remeslo*):

I am your ugly duckling, Cinderella,
Tomorrow—Eve, today still a rib. . . .
With bare hands I wash gold,
Out of the parent rock I scratch silver.

## Yunna Moritz and Bella Akhmadulina

The poetry of Yunna Moritz (born 1937 in Kiev) is somewhat different in style. Her singable, musical poems deal with dreams and the imagination, using abstract and flexible metaphors, as in *Autumnal Borderland* (*Osennyaya okraina*, 1966). Moritz is really a romantic poet, and her volume *Cape of Longing* (*Mys zhelaniya*, 1961), set at the extreme end of the Arctic island of Novaya Zemlya, is a continuous dream that transforms birds, fish, sea, and icebergs into important signs and symbols.

The poetic spirit of the poet remains "naive," however, combining folk and fairytale features as in Marc Chagall's paintings. The impressions of Moritz's trip to the Arctic and the north Siberian gold mines are depicted in *Cape of Longing* in sparkling, almost exotic colors.

Moritz is by no means one-sided. Belligerent and satirical tones occur in such poems as *On Juliet's Death* (*Na smert Dzhulyetti*, 1966) and *French Ballad* (*Frantzuzskaya ballada*, 1965). She has published two volumes of poetry in addition to *Cape of Longing*: *Discussion about Happiness* (*Razgovor o shchastye*, 1957) and *Birth of the Wing* (*Rozhdeniye kryla, 1965*).

The "spoken" rather than sung type of poetic language (in the sense of the differentiations of B. Eichenbaum) is represented by the poet Bella Akhmadulina (born 1937 in Moscow). The title of the collection *Strings* (*Struna*, 1961) indicates that the individual poems, despite their strict strophic form, have a distinct lyrical quality. The intonation, vocabulary, and syntactic arrangement, however, are not derived from "melodic" poetry.

Akhmadulina's poems are based primarily on the acmeist tradition; in addition, she frequently alludes to Pushkin. Sober, prosaic images and a calm, well-poised diction are as typical of her as the structural compactness and transparency of every line of her verse. The themes are clearly limited; often they are domestic and everyday, as in *Entrance into the Cold* (*Vstupleniye v prostudu*, 1962). A single object can inspire a poem, as in *The Candle* (*Svecha*) or *Traffic Lights* (*Svetofori*). The world of technology means a great deal to the poet, evoking astonishment and a surprising play of thoughts, as in *Tape Recorder* (*Magnetofon*, 1962). Akhmadulina is by no means a "harmless" poet, and despite the worldliness of her themes, her associatively active imagination often leads her beyond reality to the expression of a decidedly "avant-garde" element.

The term "chamber poetry" can be applied to Akhmadulina's work, in which intimate human concerns take precedence over romantic extravagance as well as over metaphysical brooding. Even where occasional rhetorical pathos appears, as in *My Family Tree* (*Moya rodoslovnaya*, 1964; the title recalls a poem of the same name by Pushkin), the poet quickly returns to the periphery of the personal world.

## NONCONFORMIST POETS

Truly "modern" and avant-garde poetry, in the contemporary sense, runs counter to official Soviet policy. The younger representatives of this movement in Russia are therefore well known only to the initiated, and their poems are circulated only in manuscript form. Several poets have become well known through publication and translation abroad, but this poetry cannot yet be definitely classified and evaluated in an overall historical context. Although much of this poetry was written in the 1960s, it actually belongs to a new and still incomplete period of Russian literature.

Contemporary avant-garde poetry is no longer directed to a large audience; it is difficult to understand, and in most cases not suitable for political purposes. This poetry is also differentiated from other modern Russian poetry, such as that of Yevtushenko or Voznesenski, in that it fails to present a precisely defined message.

The poets of the new avant-garde use metaphors arising from complex emotions or from language itself; they are seldom based on the principle of pure substitution. The plasticity tends toward complete transformation and demands a good deal of effort from the reader. Whole areas of tradition can nevertheless flow through the images into the poem, and the resolution of the suspense is then left to the poet.

## Gennadii Aygi

Undoubtedly the most important representative of this movement in the Soviet Union is Gennadii Aygi (born 1934). A member of the nation of the Chuvash, he wrote his first volumes of poems (1958, 1962) in his mother tongue, writing in Russian only since 1960, on the advice of Nazim Hikmet and Boris Pasternak. Although he has translated his earlier poems into Russian, few have been published in the Soviet Union. His popularity in Czechoslovakia led to a translation by Olga Mašková, from the original Russian manuscript, of the volume *Here (Tady)*, published in Prague in 1967 and covering the entire period from 1954 to 1966.

His poems of the 1960s, which can hardly be compared with any others in Russian literature, present many "abstract" metaphors and surprising associations. Aygi frequently uses free verse, which clashes somewhat with his general approach to poetry. He has also translated works by Villon, García Lorca, and Aragon, among others. As Mašková has noted, Aygi "really comes from modern world poetry," and "for him there is not a single section in the Soviet literary file."

Even the titles of the various poems are informative and speak a new language: *Baudelaire, Kafka's Childhood on the Moldau, Kazimir Malevich, Early Winter Requiem* (for Pasternak). The title *Requiem* is repeated several times, expressing a concept now very popular in the Soviet Union as the designation of a genre. The "litany" also occurs in Aygi, and as a rare genre, the madrigal.

## Viktor Sosnora

One of the less radical but still remarkable "moderns" is Viktor Sosnora (born 1936 in Alupka, Crimea). Sosnora fundamentally imitates Velimir Khlebnikov, but he knows how to make this tradition fruitful. As a young man Sosnora traveled much in Russia, and during his school years in Lvov he became enthusiastic over the language of the old Russian chronicles and *The Song of Igor's Campaign*, as shown in his volume of *January Rain* (*Yanvarskyi liven*, 1962), which has an introduction by Nikolai Aseyev. Sosnora draws his associations largely from the language itself; his images are often adjusted to the sonic undertones, as in the untranslatable poem *First Snow* (*Pervyi sneg*, 1962), which begins with the words

> Pervyi sneg
> Peresmekh
> Pervertishei snezhinok.

In *Cleansing* (*Ochishchenye*, 1965) Sosnora uses the associations that result from the similarly sounding words *chisto* ("clean") and *chislo* ("number"). This word play is not, however, intended to produce a grotesque effect as is so often the case with Voznesenski; it is the free play of a tranquil imagination. Sometimes Sosnora elaborates certain images in order to enjoy the burgeoning metaphors to the full. The poem *Slippery Ice* (*Gololeditza*, 1965) transforms the smooth trail into "glass carps" for the fishermen, steel for the locksmith, and lollipops for the children:

> And the king, the deceiver,
> Promises golden hills.
> But then suddenly a boy will cry
> That the king lacks clothes!

Sosnora's poems are certainly more playful and less adjusted to a metaphysical plan than the poems of Aygi, showing a conscious avoidance of clichés. Even folkloric motifs, as in *Stinging Nettle* (*Krapiva*, 1962), are transformed in a wholly unique manner.

## Iosif Brodski

The works of Iosif Brodski (born 1940) have hardly been printed in the Soviet Union. A member of a circle of younger Leningrad poets, Brodski was already active and known as a translator from English, Spanish, and Polish when, in 1964, he was tried and condemned as a "work dodger." He was apparently released from the work camp in 1966.

Brodski's poetry can be found in various émigré magazines, and in 1965 a volume of his poems was compiled and printed abroad as *Poems and Narratives in Verse (Stikhotvoreniya i poemy)*. Brodski's metaphors and images often symbolize certain of the poet's experiences. These images recall the Bible as well as the Jewish tradition with which Brodski is thoroughly acquainted.

The peculiar litany *Fish in Winter (Ryby zimoi)* names the fish that live under the ice in winter but that seek the light. The fish is here a symbol of renewal and rebirth, as in Christian symbolism and in many paintings by Chagall.

*Fish in Winter* and other poems show a slight change in wording from line to line, the result of experiments in "grammatical meditations." Syntactical parallelisms also occur quite frequently, as in much Russian "underground" poetry; one journal of this movement is called *Syntax (Sintaksis)*.

Brodski's chief works are *Great Elegy (Bolshaya elegiya)*, a long song of lament over the English poet John Donne, and the verse narrative *Solemn Procession (Shestviye)*. He has also composed a number of romances, sonnets, and "strophes."

Brodski's evocative metaphor appears prominently in *Verbs (Glagoli)*, in which the active words ("hungry verbs, naked verbs, principal verbs, deaf verbs") have turned into human beings that live in cellars and come into the world as verbs separated from substantives. Every morning they go to work, mix mortar and drag stones, construct the city—"the monument of their own loneliness" —and finally go the way to Golgotha. As at a locked door someone knocks and hammers in nails, "into the preterit, into the present, into the future":

No one comes and no one takes them down.
The hammer beats,
It becomes eternal rhythm.
The hyperbola of the earth lies under them,
Like the heaven of metaphors floating over them!

The poem is thus an expanded *concetto* in which verbs are people and people verbs.

Brodski's works contain no central dogma. For him life is a solemn procession as in the poem of that name; a pilgrimage, as in *The Pilgrims* (*Piligrimi*), and a blind groping, as in *Verses About the Blind Musicians* (*Stikhi o slepikh muzikantakh*). The journey is a recurrent theme in Brodski's work, but he does not believe in changing the world:

> The world remains in the lie.
> The world remains forever.
> Perhaps comprehensible,
> But still infinite.

The theme of death is thoroughly familiar to this young poet, and the elegy and the song of lament occur frequently in his works, as in *Solemn Procession*. Melancholy thoughts are expressed in the poem about the Leningrad Jewish cemetery, where the former "lawyers, merchants, musicians, and revolutionaries" now lie under the earth:

> Remembering nothing
> Forgetting nothing.
> Behind the crooked fence of rotting plywood,
> Four kilometers distant from the streetcar.

### THE POETRY OF PATHOS AND SENTIMENT

#### Robert Rozhdestvenski

One of the most recent of Mayakovski's successors among the younger poets is Robert Rozhdestvenski (born 1932 in the Altai region), who recalls his model both by his declamatory pathos and by his romantic irony. Not a mere follower, however, he is notably individualistic in his selection of themes, and his interesting poems are those most remote from their model. They include the poem *The Bazaar in that Year* (*Bazar tovo goda*), dedicated to Yurii Kazakov, the poems about his various journeys, and his meditations on the present. His purely journalistic poems, including the exaggeratedly pathetic verse narrative *Letter to the 30th Century* (*Pishmo v tridtzati vek*, 1963), are relatively unimportant.

Like so many others, Rozhdestvenski, a well-known athlete in his youth, learned his poetic craft in the Gorki Institute of Literature in Moscow. His first important work, *Uninhabited Islands* (*Neobitayemiye Ostrova*, 1962), contains the well-known *Requiem* (*Rekviyem*), written for the soldiers who fell in World War II. Here, Rozhdestvenski shows his pathos not only in the panegyrics on the dead but in his impressive use of such ritualistic elements as outcries and expressions of pain. The obstinate repetitions determine the syntactic structure of the separate sections, transforming the poem into a great and solemn litany.

Rozhdestvenski's pathos is national and communistic. In this poem his language is determined primarily by tradition (including folk tradition). In his next volumes, *Radius of Action* (*Radius deistvivya*, 1965) and *Son of Faith* (*Syn very*, 1966) modern and traditional elements, political and emotional rhetoric, reflection and irony are colorfully mingled. He joined the general criticism of Stalinism in *Winter 1938* (*Zima tridtzat vosmovo*). Not especially optimistic about the present, he expresses as much pathos as anger in the poem of "the killed-off time":

> One kills it at noon.
> One kills it in the night.
> One kills time brazenly and ardently.
> One kills time shamefully and desperately.
> One kills it directly before the windows of the militia!
> (How so "before the windows"? Behind the windows too. . . .)

The murderers of time wash their hands, and "the dead minutes are silent, they do not feel offended."

In *Son of Faith* the poet engages in a similar deliberation about the confusion of music from many radios ("all transistor antennae are bared like swords") or about the pedestrians on the street, who give themselves a certain air, behind which "nothing" is concealed ("an addition to the mustache and a modest pedestal for the cigar . . ."):

> And there, uttering words with a strain,
> Swinging about their pale hands,
> Stride young foundations.
> Without walls (not to speak of roofs!)

Rozhdestvenski's irony appears particularly in the poems about such foreign cities as Rome, Paris, New York, San Francisco, and Los Angeles. Rozhdestvenski complains most about the annoying individuals who shadowed him in New York ("taciturn fellows of a pedestrian type"): "We have already shown you the city twice. . . ."

Although many of these verses are only rhymed journalism, they still convey a definite style. A romantic element frequently appears as in *Venice* (*Venetziya*), and the language is by no means banal. The romantic poems also include *In Memory of Mikhail Svetlov* (*Pamyati Mikhaila Svetlova*) and especially most of the pieces in *For Grownups* (*Vzroslym*) in the third section of *Son of Faith*.

## Yevgenii Vinokurov and Novella Matveyeva

The transformation in Russian poetry during the last decade is further indicated in the treatment of the "current" poetic themes. Childhood and growing up, journey and stopping, distance, sea and sky, the rhythm of human life and nature, holiday and workday—all have been liberated from the stereotyped forms of the past and can be newly discovered by the poets of the present. The naive approach has, of course, gone out of fashion, and the simple themes are developed through internal reflection.

Two poets who definitely pursue different paths in this area and yet have much in common in their attitude are Yevgenii Vinokurov and Novella Matveyeva. Both seek to reflect the whole of life, the general as well as the particular, and both meditate on their own egos and on their stations as poets.

Yevgenii Vinokurov (born 1925 in Briansk) grew up in Moscow and took part in World War II as a volunteer. Later he was graduated from the Gorki Institute of Literature and in 1951 issued his first volume of poetry, *Verses about Duty* (*Stikhi o dolge*). These early poems deal mostly with the war and maintain a wholly unpretentious, unemotional tone. Vinokurov has always cultivated an absolute neatness of style; on this modest level he at first worked for many years toward self-improvement.

In 1960 Vinokurov adopted a new approach, gaining general respect and even fame. After the volumes *The Word* (*Slovo*) and *Poetry* (*Lirika*), both published in 1962, Vinokurov issued the collection *Music* (*Musyka*, 1964), and in 1965 he published "new poems" in *Characters* (*Kharakteri*).

Vinokurov should be termed a sentimental or at least a sensitive poet; he is not concerned with the world as immediate subject matter but rather as experience expressed in reflection and sensation. Vinokurov's view of the world is suggested in *The Period Lost by Cutting Class* (*Pobeg s uroka*, 1965), where he combines the joy of discovery of the world with the sweet feeling of guilt of a period cut at school. The world is dipped in a special light, and in everyday life and in the language of the everyday surprising things are found, as in *Everyday* (*Budni*).

He advises poets always to "finger" the world in order to learn its truth:

> Only the poet who goes barefoot has sense:
> From between the toes the mud must press forth.

Vinokurov's philosophy is "to live," "to walk," "to be among people" ("Socrates is in the market the whole day"), "to miss the right train and rather see the stars in the sky," as in *Come Too Late* (*Opozdal*).

One of Vinokurov's most important poems, *Seizing Possession* (*Ovladevanye*), concerns mastery of the world and one's own destiny. The "seizure of possession" ends with the universe taking possession of the poet and "things" slip out of the outstretched hands. In another poem *I* (*Ya*) Vinokurov worries about identity with his "I" and concludes with the daring formula of the I:

It is in me. It has been hammered in with a
Single blow up to the "head," like a nail.

Not merely a philosophizing poet, Vinokurov is also a poet of the
everyday and of the "purely" human; his metaphors are therefore
primarily worldly and materialistic. The soul has the shape of a
metal jug, and the disintegration and origin of worlds is compared
with repairing a dwelling. Vinokurov is not without self-irony; he
is entirely averse to the tragic pose.

The language of his last poems is less simple than it seems at first,
but the different layers, which reach into the scholarly, even sacred,
sphere, are smoothly merged. The apparently colloquial language
suddenly becomes complicated through wholly abstract, rare and
"difficult" expressions, so that Vinokurov's language always appears
surprising and novel.

Novella Matveyeva (born 1934 in Pushkino, near Moscow) also
shows a marked affinity for questions of the relationship of man to
his world. She is gifted with a romantic feeling that appears not only
in such poems as *Land of Childhood* (*Strana detstva*) but also in
*Robert Burns* (*Robert Biorns*, 1959) and *Kipling's Songs* (*Pesni
Kiplinga*, 1961).

Matveyeva's poetry first appeared only in scattered editions; the
first little volume, *Poetry* (*Lirika*), dates from 1961. It was followed
by *The Little Ship* (*Korablik*, 1963) and *The Soul of Things* (*Dusha
veshchei*, 1966). Although she does not follow an actual model in
her diction, she seems close to the symbolist tradition. Many of her
verses have a facetious, epigrammatic tinge and some decidedly
grotesque inspirations ("The cook marries the compote . . ."). Often
seeking to astound the readers she asserts in *Stencil* (*Shtamp*) that
she fears the devil less than the stereotype.

Her metaphors are often constructed on the principle of contrasting series, as in *Wooden Bodies* (*Drevesina*), where the annual rings
of a tree are related to the rings on the surface of the water into
which someone has dived. Entire metaphorical complexes belong
to such frequently recurring concepts as *echo, traces, resonances,*
and *reflection.* The images that form certain equivalents clearly
reveal their montage character. In the "unrelated connection" the

poet attempts to relate "Mars, Athena, and an old shoe" or makes
the following arrangement of images:

> Last Judgment and dirt on the roads,
> Wind, mirror, brush, a cart,
> And on the old wallpaper the moist stripe.
>
> *Resonance (Otgolosok)*

Matveyeva reflects on her craft in many poems, including *County
Road* (*Doroga*), *Waterfall* (*Vodopad*), *Moonlight Night* (*Lunnaya
noch*), and *Steppe* (*Step*). Although the titles often appear innoc-
uous and traditional, the themes are completely renewed through
startling associations and audacious language, completely surpassing
old-fashioned descriptions of nature. In *The Soul of Things* she
remarks:

> I like houses, where things are not property,
> Where things are lighter than boots at the rope. . . .

For Matveyeva, too, the world is not subject matter but the echo
of her reflections and a magic realm behind the visible objects.


TWO CONTROVERSIAL POETS


*Yevgenii Yevtushenko*


The internationally famous Yevgenii Yevtushenko (born 1933 in
the settlement Zima-Stantziya at Irkutsk) is a poet of great versatility. Settling in Moscow and—during World War II—in Siberia,
he began to write when he was only sixteen.

His work should not be judged solely on the basis of his well-
known emotional verses which he recited on his trips abroad; more
sensitive tones occur in his collection *The Apple* (*Yabloko*, 1960).
This sensitivity is frequently relieved by irony, and his work occasionally recalls the Russian symbolist poetry of Balmont and Blok,
although his rhyme technique and word play are of course more
modern than that of the symbolists. He also shows his familiarity
with the acmeists, with Mayakovski, and especially with Pasternak.

His poems of 1957 to 1960 especially show Blok's influence and also that of Yesenin. In *When I Think of Blok* (*Kogda ya dumayu o Bloke*, 1957), the poet appeals to Blok and his Saint Petersburg:

> And as in an enigmatic prologue
> Whose essence is not transparent and deep,
> The rattling of the cabs passes in the fog,
> Paving stone, Blok and the clouds. . . .

In 1961 and 1962 Yevtushenko published his internationally celebrated political poems: *Babi Yar* (1961), a confrontation with anti-Semitism in all of Europe; *Stalin's Heirs* (*Nasledniki Stalina*, 1962); and *Fear* (*Strakh*, 1962). In the collection *Delicacy* (*Nezhnost*, 1962) he published the first great ballads as well as poems about France, the United States, and Cuba.

The "real" Yevtushenko also appears before the public in 1962, with the publication of *Verses about Foreign Countries* (*Stikhi o zagranitze*) in the collection of *Swinging of the Hand* (*Vzmakh ruku*, 1962).

Agitatory pathos appears in poems aiming at purely objective description, as in *Hail in Kharkov* (*Grad v Kharkove*), as well as in the political odes from Cuba, such as *The Aggressors* (*Agressori*). The illustrative element often predominates, especially in the poems that Yevtushenko wrote during his trips abroad.

Among the many themes treated by Yevtushenko are the market of Paris, in *Onion Soup* (*Lukovi sup*); Fidel Castro, in *Verses about Fidel* (*Stikhi o Fidel*); the bar of the airport in Barcelona, in *Don Quixote* (*Don Kikhot*), the beatniks of New York, in *Beatnik Monologue* (*Monolog bitnikov*); the rubber plantations of Liberia, in *Rubber Trees* (*Kauchukoviye derevya*); and the panopticon in Hamburg (first published in the magazine *Moskva*, 1965, as a result of the trip to Germany in 1963), in *Panopticon in Hamburg* (*Panoptikum v Gamburge*).

Yevtushenko is overwhelmingly extroverted when he deals with himself as a poet and leader. In his emotional poem from Paris, *The Exclamation Point* (*Vosklikatelni znak*), he sees himself incarnated as the "hand of Moscow," which writes the exclamation point after a slogan against the Algerian war on the wall of a house in Paris:

What is it doing, my exclamation point?
It makes me as proud as a poem.

Yevtushenko's formal accomplishments appear not so much in plastic expression or rhythm as in rhyme, word play, and the phonetic structure of the verse line. His language is dominated by the assonances and alliteration (in sentimental as well as humorous texts) so popular in Russia, "sound-painting," and skillful melodious variations. The latter can, of course, become a mannerism, and the poet has not always avoided this fault.

Seeking new formal expressions, as in *Connecting Boat* (*Kater svyazi*, 1966), Yevtushenko approaches various new genres. This collection maintains the tension between poetry and feuilletonism (as Yevtushenko himself has described some of his poetry) and includes meditative or programmatic poems, such as *Uncertainty* (*Neuverennost*), *The Third Memory* (*Tretya pamyat*), *Perfection* (*Sovershenstvo*), as well as rhymed reports, legends and anecdotes.

The poems from Italy, in the cycle *Italian Italy* (*Italyanskaya Italiya*), contain the most arbitrary language in this volume. The poem *Rhythms of Rome* (*Ritmi Rima*), fifteen pages long, is full of startling expressions in its burlesque stylization.

The ballad, still a popular genre in Soviet poetry, has a special character in Yevtushenko's poems. Many of his ballads appeared as occasional poems, as in the ballad on the 150th anniversary of Lermontov's death, *Ballad of the Chief of the Gendarmes and the Poem on the Death of the Poet* (*Ballada o shefe zhandarmov i o stikhotvorenii na smert poeta*), and *The Ballad of the Fish Killing* (*Ballada o brakonyerstve*, 1965, published in *Novyi mir*).

In the spring of 1965 the magazine *Yunost* printed Yevtushenko's ambitious verse narrative *The Bratsk Cofferdam* (*Bratskaya GES*), which unfolds a panorama of Russian history and the historical experiences of mankind. The work, consisting of more than thirty chapters, opens with the introductory *Prayer Before the Poem*, wherein Yevtushenko invokes Pushkin, Lermontov, Nekrasov, Blok, Pasternak, Yesenin, and Mayakovski. The first chapter begins with a skeptical *Monologue of the Egyptian Pyramid*, which continues as an argument between the pyramid and the Bratsk Dam about unbelief and belief and the justification of revolutions. Soviet construction dominates the second part, which depicts certain figures and focal points as representatives of all others.

In the first part Yevtushenko seems overly ambitious; his philosophy of history remains superficial. Clever montages "confirm" the revolution, but Yevtushenko's cultural interpretation, as with Dostoyevski (*Petrashevtzi*), is amateurish.

The poet plays with the different "cultural goods"; he singles out Pushkin, Tolstoi, and Lenin as "the three noblest names of Russia," and pays special homage to Mayakovski. As a whole, however, the work seems amorphous and "eclectic" (A. Sinyavski).

The work is nonetheless important for a study of Yevtushenko's style, because the various chapters are thematically motivated and brought into line with tradition through several covert or overt quotations.

## Andrei Voznesenski

Andrei Voznesenski (born 1933) can be considered the poet of the cities (Moscow, New York, Paris, and Rome), as well as of the technological age of automation, artificial fabrics, and nuclear fission. He has moved toward the liberation of modern existence, but always with pain and protest, never with cheap acclaim.

Although Voznesenski is not actually a metaphysical poet, his work is so extensively developed from studied and paradoxical metaphors that he sometimes, perhaps unintentionally, appears to continue the tradition of the late Renaissance and the Baroque. The present and history coexist in his work without mediation—in the metaphor, the *concetto*, and in the subjective elimination or even reversal of chronology.

The title of one of Voznesenski's volumes of poems (1964) is taken from his earlier poem *Antiworlds* (*Antimiry*, 1961), which appeared in the cycle *The Three-Cornered Pear, 40 Digressions from a Lyric Poem* (*Treugolnaya grusha, 40 liricheskich otstupleni iz poemi*, 1962). The *Antiworlds* are always afterthoughts, added to daily life; they break into reality in a surprising manner. Both the thematic and the formal development of his theme is determined by the reversal of historical events and causality, by anagrams, reflections and metamorphoses, inverted metaphors and comparisons, and the idea of the "absurd world."

With his "local" semantics and "local" color, taken over by his own admission from García Lorca, Voznesenski is also an heir of the constructivists of the 1920s, who expected the "maximum exploitation of the theme" from a poem. Typical of this style of composition is *Night Airport in New York* (*Nochnoi aeroport v Nyu Yorke*), which deals with the construction of the modern airport building, expressing the concept of the "antimatter" structure.

The verse narrative *Master* (*Mastera*, 1959) is similarly constructed on the basis of local semantics, forming a kind of "Antipoem" (an antihistorical poem), in which the building of the sixteenth-century Vasilii–Blazhenni Cathedral in Moscow is treated as a metaphor or parable for artistic creativity in general.

Significantly, Voznesenski studied painting and architecture, and he has indicated that he feels himself closely drawn to Joan Miró and to the buildings of Le Corbusier. Buildings play a great role in Voznesenski's work, and his sense of the "material" of language and objects in the world is extraordinarily well developed. On the "local" level of structure the sound material plays the principal role.

Voznesenski goes far beyond any other living Russian poet in illustrating his thoughts and associations through sound. From intensive alliteration to word play and the thematic anagram, as in *Crowns and Roots* (*Krony i korni*, 1960) Voznesenski uses sound structure for his local semantics and metaphors. He also favors the futurist "inner flection" or "pseudo-flection" (varying or pseudo-paradigmatic changes of a recurring series of sounds in a nucleus). He uses this technique most successfully and most convincingly in the famous *Goya* (*Goyya*, 1959).

In regard to the materials for his metaphors Voznesenski speaks with gentle self-irony in the homage to Lorca, *I Love Lorca* (*Lyu blyu Lorku*):

> The metaphor is the motor of form. The twentieth century is the century of transformations, of metamorphoses. What is the pine tree of today? Perlon? Plexiglass of the rocket? My furry pullover of silon dreams at night about silver firs. It dreams of the rustling of the needles of his ancestors.

Voznesenski looks for his metaphors with great circumspection, weaving entire chains, genealogies, and hierarchies. Nature and "art" (technology) are generally the two phases, which are borne in the "local" associations and bind the different worlds to one another, often in tense and even grotesque proximity. The comparisons from the world of technology (cliff-climbing motorcycles, electric trains, aircraft carriers, rockets, atomic piles) always refer to the human world and are directly integrated in it. In "Discovery of America" the preface to *The Three-Cornered Pear*, Voznesenski compares that historical event with the descent into the object, "as in the subway": the three-cornered lights of a New York subway station are the point of departure for the metaphor "three-cornered pears" (another play of thoughts).

The same poem also deals with the discoverer Columbus ("You look for India—you find America") and the comparison of the globe to a watermelon from which the peel has been removed. This comparison ("net of the lines of latitude and longitude"—"net shopping bag" with the "watermelon") appeared earlier in *Trade in Watermelons* (*Torguyut arbuzami*, 1956).

In this way Voznesenski approaches his own "emblems," which may be partly linked to the baroque tradition (fire, torch, the phoenix). The allusions to Lomonsov's odes also point in this direction, as in *Ballad of Work* (*Ballada raboty*, 1959): "The oaks of the hatchets bent themselves to bows, and the shavings bored themselves into Istanbul and Paris!"

The *Ballad of Work* is really a double *concetto*, because all statements refer simultaneously to Peter the Great and to the Flemish painter Peter Rubens.

Voznesenski's ballads are related in part to García Lorca's ballads, but they also show grotesque and paradoxical strains as in *Ballad of the Place of Execution* (*Lobnaya ballada*, 1961) and *Ballad— Dissertation* (*Ballada—dissertatziya*, 1963). This last poem with its "nose" themes refers to the tradition of the eighteenth century and Gogol. Elegiac tones occur in *The Sick Ballad* (*Bolnaya ballada*, 1964), in which life is compared to the trip on a swaying vessel; strictly speaking, it deals with seasickness.

The ironic-grotesque features predominate increasingly in Voznesenski's recent poems, *Lament over Two Unborn Poems* (*Plach po dvum nerozhdennym poemam,* 1965), *The Unknown—Requiem in Two Steps, with an Epilogue* (*Neizvestni—rekviyem v dvukh shagakh, s epilogom,* 1964), and *Sketch of a Poem* (*Eskiz poemy,* 1965). The latter is a pure grotesque.

Inversion and conversion ("absurd world") can be followed best in the verse narrative *Oza* (1964); the title can be interpreted as an anagram. The scene of action is principally the institute for atomic research in Dubna. Several prose sections expand the vision of a nuclear explosion or of a devilish experiment for the "absurd world":

> The nose was in its place, but only inserted from behind, like a hollow dagger sheath. The tip of the nose, not finding more room, grew out of the nape of the neck. The trees lay on their backs like ramified lakes, but their shadows stood upright, as though cut out by shears. They rustled softly in the wind, like tissue paper. The depth of the well rose like a black bundle of light out of the search-light. In it lay the pail that had fallen and particles of mud floated in it.

Voznesenski uses the same technique of inversion with an entirely different purpose, sometimes for satirical effect. In *The Torches of Florence* (*Florentiskiye fakeli,* 1962) he exposes the anachronism of socialist realism and the artistic ideals of the Stalin era. Florentine architecture is here ironically passed off as the "tracing" of the exercise assignments of Moscow architecture students:

> The baptistery is sleeping like the further development
> Of my plans for an institution for sobering up.
> Sinful child of socialist realism,
> Thus I enter the squares full of torches.
> You are a "tracing" of my youth, Florence!
> I saunter through the past!

Similarly, in the verse narrative *Longjumeau* (1962), Lenin in the emigration is seen as "the heart of Russia" ("One lies, that Lenin was in the emigration"), whereas Saint Petersburg society and the Czar are the real (secret) emigrants.

Voznesenski has repeatedly rearranged his poems in various editions and integrated them into new cycles. A basic stock of poems is thus represented in all his books: *Parable* (*Parabola*, 1960), *Mosaic* (*Mozaika*, 1960), *The Three-Cornered Pear, Antiworlds* and *The Heart of Achilles* (*Akhillesovo serdtze*), 1966).

# SUPPLEMENT

*This Supplement is based in part on Dr. Markstein's article "The Difficulty of Writing about Soviet Literature" in* Mosaic: A Quarterly Journal for the Comparative Study of Literature and Ideas *(Winter, 1970), published by the University of Manitoba Press and used with their kind permission. The article was revised and expanded by the author for this volume.*

# Censorship, Samizdat, and New Trends

## ELISABETH MARKSTEIN

There is a Russian proverb that says, "Seven nurses turn a child into a cripple." Soviet literature has no lack of nurses, guardians, administrators, and advisers. Everyone seems to claim the right to tell it where to go, beginning with Stalin, whose example was followed first by Khrushchev, then by Brezhnev, not to speak of others, some army generals and youth leaders, all of them anxious of course to protect the "ordinary" Soviet reader and therefore deeming it wise, for safety's sake, to place a very fine filter between the writer and the reader in the shape of a censorship. That is the main difficulty: we do not really know Soviet literature, and we cannot know it. In the interests of accuracy we ought to put this proviso at the top of any essay on modern Soviet literature, or indeed any other form of Soviet Russian artistic activity. One day perhaps it may be possible to examine the true influence of the censorship on the development of Soviet literature, but not yet.[1]

Toward the end of 1966 the literary periodical *Novyi mir* listed, in accordance with its usual practice, its attractions for the coming year. Readers were promised fourteen substantial works by well-known authors, which were either "already in print or in the process of being set." Of these fourteen, nine did not appear—neither in 1967 nor after. A further list published in 1968 included these

[1] I am confining myself in this essay to Soviet *Russian* literature, though the censorship naturally affects non-Russian Soviet writers also.

missing works as well as new ones by other authors: in all, twelve titles, plus thirty-one contributions unspecified by title. All of them prose works. In the ten numbers of *Novyi mir* published up to December 1969 only ten of these forty-three advertised contributions had appeared.

It is no accident that we have chosen the year 1969 to illustrate our point; it was the last year in which *Novyi mir* was authentically itself. Early in 1970 its entire editorial staff was replaced. Only a short while before this happened, Aleksandr Tvardovski was using the full weight of his authority to fight his final battle against censorship: he had given his anti-Stalinist poem *The Right Not to Forget* (*Po pravu pamyati*) to the printers. The censors eliminated it even after type had been set. A few weeks later, Tvardovski was dismissed from the magazine. Among the authors still held up in the censorship machine are V. Voynovich, I. Grekova, Kuznetzov (who has since emigrated to the west), V. Syomin, A. Bek, A. Rybakov, Baklanov, Kaverin. This is also true of the posthumous work of Paustovski as well as the work of lesser-known writers.

But that is the snag: why "lesser-known"? Aleksandr Solzhenitzyn was once a *Novyi mir* author. As we know, his first book, *One Day in the Life of Ivan Denisovich*, was allowed to appear only after Khrushchev had personally intervened. We also know that Solzhenitzyn's *Cancer Ward* did not appear in *Novyi mir*, though a contract was signed for it. Officially Solzhenitzyn's literary career ended in 1965, the year in which his story *Zakhar-Kalita* appeared in *Novyi mir*. Since then he has existed in the press simply as a punchball for salaried officials of literature to exercise their muscles on. Critics may mention him only as a warning example. Finally, with his expulsion from the Soviet Writers' Union in November 1969 Aleksandr Solzhenitzyn—a "not ungifted writer," in the words of S. Mikhalkov—was officially pronounced null and void.

Well, one has heard of Solzhenitzyn. His *Cancer Ward* and his *The First Circle* were issued in duplicated form by *samizdat*, and distributed among an admittedly very small group of Russian readers, most of them intellectuals. *Samizdat* is the Soviet Union's underground press, a system by which manuscripts, which have been reproduced in the home, by a mimeograph machine for example, are illicitly handed around. In the west Solzhenitzyn's books have become bestsellers and have made a lot of money for their publishers. In June of 1971, Solzhenitzyn's most recent novel, *August 1914 (Avgust chetyrnadtzatogo)*, was published in Paris, this time with Solzhenitzyn's full approval. But supposing Solzhenitzyn had been a much younger man and his *Ivan Denisovich* had not slipped past the censor because it happened to strike a sympathetic chord in Khrushchev in his hatred against Stalin? It would not alter the fact that Solzhenitzyn is an important Russian writer, but who knows if we should ever have heard of him?

To take another and very different case: the lyric poet Iosif Brodski became known through the scandalous trial in which he was involved in Leningrad in 1964. He is not a member of any official association, and since the trial he is not allowed to publish his poems. So what would we know of him if it had not been for the trial? In that same year the literary periodical *Yunost* published a short story by Friedrich Gorenstein, who is probably (to judge by his name) of German extraction.[2] The story showed every sign of a remarkable new talent. Not a single line from his pen has appeared since. An older man, Varlam Shalamov—whose face reminds one somewhat of Dostoyevski—published a few little poems in the annual *Poetry Days*. Is he a true poet? In this case we know the answer: he is a poet and also a notable writer of prose; his somber tales of prison camp life have appeared in the west and have been circulated privately in Russia.

Every judgment must be regarded as conditional—even in connection with apparently established writers. (As we recently discovered, even Sholokhov, the celebrated Nobel Prize winner, has not got past the censor completely unscathed.) Konstantin Simonov is sufficiently established to have his collected works published in his lifetime. Six volumes were promised, and five of them appeared punctually. The sixth volume is still awaited. It is to contain his wartime diary of 1941, *One Hundred Days of War (Sto sutok voiny)*, and all who have read it swear that it is his best work. At the funeral of the writer Aleksei Kosterin a young man made a

---

[2] Friedrich Gorenstein, *The House with the Turret (Dom s bashenkoi)*, in *Yunost*, No. 6, 1964.

speech. He said: "On the bus I heard people talking about the
funeral of an author whose name meant nothing to me. But, since
he was an author, and in this country you cannot judge the talent or
significance of an author by establishing whether he was famous or
unknown, I decided to attend the funeral."[3]

Any attempt to make analyses on the strength only of the printed,
as opposed to the written, word must consequently lead to mere
hypotheses. Contemporary Soviet literature is, for example, constantly being reproached for being formally conservative. This may
well be true so far as "official" literature is concerned. But the blame
is being put on the wrong people. It is not the creators of literature
who are guilty. It is the administrators of literature, those imposing
censorship that is the tool of an official ideology that can by now
be maintained only by administrative means, who are to be charged
with this sin.

If, for instance, anyone were to attempt a survey of the influence
in Russia of the modern theater or, more specifically, the influence
of the theater of the absurd or antitheater, how could he even begin?
There are simply too many unknown factors. Vasilii Aksenov's play
*Always for Sale* (*Vsegda v prodazhe*), which is clearly influenced
by Ionesco, can be taken as a prototype for other and perhaps more
important plays: it has never been published, and its few performances have taken place on only rare occasions in the experimentally
minded Sovremennik in Moscow. Most of the productions at the
Theater on the Taganka by the stage director Lyubimov (a montage
of Mayakovski poems under the title *Poslushaite!*, Voznesenski's
*Antiworlds*, Molière's *Tartuffe*, Gorki's *Mother*) have been attacked
as "modernistic."[4] What exactly is meant by "modernism" is not
clear from the criticisms themselves. Might it be that Lyubimov has
turned away from the canonized Stanislavski style? However, whatever it is, the result remains the same: "modernistic" productions
are either taken off entirely or the number of performances dras-

[3] Quoted from *Samizdat* I, Paris 1969, pp. 478 ff.
[4] The modernizing, that is to say revitalization, of older well-known works,
such as was practiced by Tovstonogov in Leningrad, and others, is usually a
thorn in the flesh of the guardians of "safe" classics. A modern adaptation of
Griboyedov's *Intelligence Brings Suffering* was promptly closed.

tically reduced. The periodical *Teatr*, which showed too kind an attitude toward such experiments and an apparent tendency to despise the classics, was subjected to an official investigation, as a result of which the editor, J. Rybakov, was removed from his post. How then can one report on new and genuinely modern developments in the Soviet theater? One would simply end up by tripping over the "repertory committee," which censors theatrical activity in the same way that Glavlit censors literary output.

The purity of art, as defined by the censor, is not simply a matter of politics. Morals also must be kept under strict control. This is a relatively easy task. The main thing is to look out for beds, and then forbid them. It is perhaps no more than ridiculous when in books and films love scenes are brought to an end by rows of dots or pan shots of the sea at the very point where our grandmothers would have felt constrained to blush. But it is no longer ridiculous when writers are forced to confine themselves to the emotional responses of a pair of lovers as depicted by approved writers of the nineteenth century (to whom, of course, Dostoyevski could not in this regard be considered to belong). And it becomes alarming when desecration goes so far as to cut out of the Russian translation of Heinrich Böll's *Ansichten eines Clowns* the scene in which Marie on her wedding night washes the sheets in the cold kitchen. Antonioni's *Zabriskie Point*—despite its anticapitalist and anti-American Way of Life tendencies, tendencies that Soviet propagandists would ordinarily welcome—was performed only in private showings for people in the know: the sexual hallucinations that the protagonists experience in the desert could not be "inflicted upon" the general public. Pasolini's film *Teorema* could never have been shot in Russia, and obviously it cannot be shown. Sexuality, a permissible subject when regarded as a social need and psychiatric problem, is in the eyes of the art censors nothing but plain pornography.

If we dissect Solzhenitzyn's banned novel *Cancer Ward* in a deliberately schematic way—in order to make our point—we get the following picture: Stalinism and factors of dehumanization—this is the social aspect, depicted almost satirically in the figure of Pavel Rusanov. Life and death: inescapable death by cancer, love and sexuality, God and the meaning of life—these are the religious and philosophical aspects. In Solzhenitzyn's case it could not have been the form of his work that provoked the ban. Either of the two aspects was enough. Thus we can recognize the subjects that stand on the censor's blacklist. This list also carries an item, applicable in other cases, under "modernistic" form.

For the outside observer to ignore the existence of the censor would be to help the censor play his own game. True, it is not primarily the observer of literature who suffers from the censor, but literature itself. It is simply not true to say that nothing can hold up the march of progress. The censor can intervene, can forbid, distort and conceal. He can destroy live babies, but equally he can permit thalidomide babies to grow crippled in their mother's womb. He can draw up maps with blank spaces (each of which might be a new America). And—to make things even more difficult—he can set the signposts on the existing portion of the map pointing in the wrong direction, as happened in Czechoslovakia in 1968. Every artist who wishes to have his brainchild blessed by official censorship is bound to make concessions.[5]

Vasilii Aksenov is doubtless one of the most gifted members of that generation represented in the west by the name of Yevgenii Yevtushenko. For anybody seriously interested in contemporary Russian prose literature, he is to be regarded as a central figure. He is a storyteller who has undergone a very clearly defined development, from realism of a traditional cast, as in *Colleagues* (*Kollegi*, 1960), to a highly individual synthesis of realism and fantasy— *Wild* (*Dikoi*, 1964) and the play *Always for Sale*—that links him to Gogol's *The Nose* and above all to Mikhail Bulgakov. *A Wagon Load of Empty Barrels* (*Zatovarennaya bochkotara*), published in the March 1968 issue of *Yunost*, reveals that he was developing his talent for satire. But in 1971 he published his novel of the Revolution, *Love of Electricity* (*Lyubov k elektrichestvu*),[6] in which he

---

[5] In his review (*Novyi mir*, No. 2, 1969) of the book *Textology of the Works of Soviet Literature*, V. Lakshin pointed out that even celebrated writers such as Gladkov and Fadeyev made corrections in their books (which are incidentally considered to be standard works of socialist realism) years after they first appeared. These were made on "second thoughts that had nothing to do with literary considerations."

[6] In *Yunost*, Nos. 3, 4, 5, 1971.

returned, even in style, to his literary beginnings. But does recognition of this throwback give us the right to pronounce judgment on Aksenov? The presence of censorship again reduces us to an approach that is unscientific—the hypothetical approach. Was Aksenov allowed to publish everything he wrote? How large was the role played by the "inner censor," that played by the official censor, in the composition of this most recent work? Can we formulate an analysis of Aksenov when it must be based on censored writings? Respect for Aksenov's undeniable talent compels us to be cautious at the very least.

Conflict is unavoidable. The censor demands his pounds of flesh. Solzhenitzyn refused to "edit" his *Cancer Ward.* As a result his brainchildren were declared illegitimate, unworthy of support and above all forbidden to mix with others. The loss was the Russian reader's.

With Solzhenitzyn's expulsion from the Soviet Writers' Union the blank spaces on the map were, one might say, approved and legalized and the existence of two Russian literatures more or less recognized. On the one side the union, the publishing houses, large circulations, trips abroad, publicity; on the other, self-publishing, loss of income, persecution. But we must be careful with generalizations. There are in fact genuine writers on both sides.

It would of course be easier if we had literature on the one side and censorship on the other, that is to say, if censors and writers were constant factors. But convenient journalistic clichés, dividing people up into Stalinists, conservatives, liberals, intellectuals and so on, simply do not always fit the case. Solzhenitzyn, for instance, is both a writer and an anti-Stalinist, but he is not a liberal. Chalmayev, the former chief ideologist of the periodical *Molodaya gvardiya,* is no Marxist, though he is antimodernist. The artistic adviser of *Novyi mir,* the veteran critic M. Livshits, is certainly a Marxist, though he is both anti-Stalinist and antimodernist. And Sholokhov, the court poet, is no longer a writer; whether when writing his superb *The Silent Don* he was a socialist realist in the statutory sense is something that would have to be proved. Yevtushenko is certainly the best-known Russian poet in the west, but he is not the most significant. Arsenii Tarkovski—who is no longer young and who up to a few years ago was known only as a translator—is certainly more significant; he is one of the greatest of the lyric poets of whom we have heard.[7] If we are to be realistic, we must recognize that both the censorship (or the official ideology that power supports and that supports power) and literary production are throughout the scale variable and by no means homogeneous concepts.

It must be admitted, of course, that in recent years the conflicting attitudes have hardened. As late as 1969 it was still possible to speak of a certain modest pluralism among the various semiofficial literary journals published in Russia, which traditionally provide the most up-to-date reflection of current literary work. *Novyi mir*, though not perhaps entirely homogeneous, adhered to the Marxist line given it by Plekhanov, Lunacharski, and the Hungarian Georg Lukács.[8] It also voiced the demands of the progressive faction (which is the majority of the intellectuals in opposition) for the abolishment of censorship and the elimination of the administrative control of the arts and sciences, and for a genuine economic reform. *Novyi mir* was consistently anti-Stalinist, a stand that was to prove its undoing. But what finally brought *Novyi mir* to grief was its refusal to accept the official doctrine of socialist realism. The same position that the thesis of limited sovereignty holds in Brezhnev's doctrine came to be occupied in socialist realism by the thesis of qualified truth ("look to the future"; "serve the future"; "create models for the young"). The attacks on *Novyi mir* struck home here, and ultimately brought about its de facto liquidation. And indeed, by its attempts to seize upon actual, not just imaginary, reality; by its effort to accord the right to existence of the "little" truth of the here and now as well as the "large" truth of history; and still more, by its wish to promote "the truth of the fact"—by these means *Novyi mir* was weakening the foundations on which the dogmas of socialist realism rest.[9]

While *Novyi mir* was still fighting the battle that would end in its

[7] Arsenii Tarkovski, in *Vestnik*, Moscow 1969.

[8] This position is made clear in *Novyi mir*'s polemic against the Russist ideologists of *Molodaya gvardiya*. See A. Dement'ev's "Tradition and Folk Tradition," No. 4, 1969, and the editorial in No. 7, 1969.

[9] An example are the attacks on the novel by N. Voronov, *Youth in Zheleznodolska* (*Yunost v Zheleznodol'ske*), published in No. 11, 1968, and No. 12, 1968. See also the aggressive criticism in *Literaturnaya gazeta*, 5 March 1969.

death, the journal *Oktyabr*—the totally orthodox organ of the Writers' Union of the Russian Federation—published the neo-Stalinist novel *What Do You Want?* (*Chevo zhe ty khochesh?*),[10] written by its own editor-in-chief, Vsevolod Kochetov. The censors saw nothing objectionable in it. Nor did they object to the memoirs of General Shtemenko, with their glorification of Stalin, nor to Aleksandr Chakovski's novel about rehabilitation, *Blockade* (*Blokada*).[11] Some nonliterary details may be mentioned in passing. Shtemenko is the Chief of Staff of the Warsaw Pact nations. Chakovski is the editor-in-chief of the official *Literaturnaya gazeta*.

Perhaps the most saddening example of the damage done by censorship and administrative meddling is the journal *Yunost*, aimed at young readers. Before the removal of its former editor Valentin Katayev, it strove successfully to provide a forum for beginning writers and to allow experiments with literary forms. Founded in 1954, it had introduced a whole school of young writers, men who today are a part of the middle generation: Aksenov, Gladilin, Kuznetzov, Yevtushenko, Voznesenski, Akhmadulina, Gorenstein, and the poet Oleg Chukhontzev, who is to be regarded as a supreme discovery. With the arrival of the new chief editor Boris Polevoi, the journal lost all color, but even this was not enough. In May 1969 another purge swept the editorial office. Thus *Yunost* lost its individual, young, nonconformist complexion. This middle group reveals with particular vividness the psychological effects of pressure from above. Its members had received its initial impetus from the liberalization by the Twentieth Party Congress and developed with unequaled intensity. Hardly ten years later, they were subjected to the disappointment of the government's failure to democratize and humanize society as promised. As the days of the thaw receded, Aksenov wrote his *Love of Electricity*; Yevtushenko wrote his poem on Lenin, *Kazan University* (*Kazanski universitet*);[12] Voznesenski withdrew into painting and visual poetry; Kuznetzov left the Soviet

[10] *Oktyabr*, No. 9, 1969 and No. 10, 1969.

[11] S. M. Shtemenko, *General Staff during the War Years* (*Generalni stab v gody voiny*), Moscow: Voyenizdat, 1968. Chakovski's novel ran in *Znamya* in the following issues: No. 1, 1970; No. 2, 1970; No. 3, 1970; No. 6, 1971; No. 7, 1971, No. 8, 1971.

[12] *Novyi mir*, No. 4, 1970.

Union; Gorenstein and Chukhontzev are not publishing—which does not mean that they are not writing. In opposition to the so-called westernized liberals of *Novyi mir* and the self-indulgent sophisticates of *Yunost* arose a new intellectual creed: Russism. For three years, until 1970, it found its official platform in *Molodaya gvardiya*, the literary organ of the Young People's Union. Stated briefly, Russism means: nationalism; the messianism of Russia, both religious and political; anti-intellectualism; antimodernism. In literary practice, it means Russian birch trees, Russian stoves, Russian folk custom, linguistic purism (down with words of foreign derivation), puritanism in the love between the sexes (down with sexual liberties). This is not the place to offer an analysis of Russism, as represented by Chalmayev, Kozhinov, Palievski, its exponents. The time is probably not ripe for it, because the movement, which, after all, is subject to censorship like all literary movements, has not yet become sufficiently differentiated. An initial impetus toward such differentiation in the area of politics may have been provided by the occupation of Czechoslovakia. As nineteenth-century Russians were divided by their reactions to the Polish uprisings of 1830 and 1861, present-day Russians are divided according to their views of the events in Czechoslovakia in 1968. Since "patriotism" lies at the heart of Russism, the Russists feel compelled to condemn the intervention in Czechoslovakia, while the "patriotism" of others leads them to affirm Russian imperialism.

In today's literary confrontation, the exponents of Russism have already made their position sufficiently clear. While the core of the socialist-realist camp is faithfulness to the party, closeness to the people, and communist education, the major allegiance of the Russists is faithfulness to the Russian people. It is the Russian people whom they are invoking, rather than the party's conception of the future, when they condemn "denigratory," "naturalistic," or "modernistic" writers such as Syomin, Grekova, A. Makarov, or Katayev. These writers are attacked not because they are untrue to socialism, as Zhdanov would have accused them of being, but because, the Russists claim, they denigrate the Russian people as a whole. Indeed, the accusations hurled by *Molodaya gvardiya* writers at the "naturalists" bear a striking resemblance to the accusations made against

Visarion Belinski's "naturalist school" in the 1840s. All the trappings of Marxist literary criticism, both popular and scholarly, are thrown overboard. National characteristics are stressed as rising out of Russia's past. And, with a truly astonishing blindness, the Russists ignore realities such as the scientific and technological revolution, or the changes that have occurred in the economic and social structure.

Yet all the Stalinist features of Russism—Stalin the great strategist, Stalin the great "organizer," Stalin the embodiment of Russia's will to become a great power; all the sniping in support of the official repression of the long-haired, tight-trousered, and excessively thoughtful figures around *Yunost*; the existence of influential protectors in the Red Army—all these were powerless to shield the theoreticians of blood-and-soil literature from the all-leveling arm of Russia's managers of ideology. The propaganda apparatus, no matter how hollow and ossified its phraseology has become, of a multination state, such as the U. S. S. R., cannot tolerate in its midst so explosive an ideology as nationalism represents. In January 1971, Anatolii Nikonov, editor-in-chief of *Molodaya gvardiya,* was dismissed, as, soon after, were several members of the editorial staff.

But intellectual forces cannot always be restrained by administrative control. In the same month in which *Molodaya gvardiya* was "restored to the party line," a newcomer made its appearance in *samizdat*. This was *Veche*, a "Russian, patriotic" journal, whose editorial group, headed by Vladimir Osipov, defined its purposes as follows: "to turn our eyes upon our homeland . . . to preserve and revitalize our national culture, our moral and spiritual heritage . . . to continue the work of the Slavophiles and of Dostoyevski, which shall be our guide."[13]

Thus by the end of 1971 one sees on the one hand suppression of authorized journals and on the other hand, the growing strength of the *samizdat*. By means of this illicit circulation of the written word, all factions, from the neocommunists to the chauvinists, can

[13] Quoted from *Chronicle of Current Events* (*Khronika tekushchikh sobiti*) in *Samizdat*, March 1971. English translation by Amnesty International, London.

gain a hearing, and literary works of vastly different merit can find "publication." (An example from the American literary scene are Ernest Hemingway's *For Whom the Bell Tolls* and Margaret Mitchell's *Gone with the Wind*—two works that for various reasons were not allowed to appear in Russian translation.)

*Samizdat* is the direct result of censorship: the larger the number of literary themes and forms on the "forbidden" list, the larger the number of works that are forced to turn to the resources of *samizdat*.

The task of the scholar specializing in modern Soviet literature is thus becoming ever more difficult—but ever more interesting. *Samizdat* is a phenomenon without parallel today. What a paradoxical and unique situation: that in a country with an exceedingly rich literary tradition, in an age distinguished for the enormous power of the mass media and for its overproduction of printed matter, an "underground press," without access to modern technology and the country's media, is an outlet for such a rich crop of works of art.

The task of the Slavic scholar is further complicated by the fact that there is, obviously, no hard and fast dividing line between free and controlled literature. Topics that are freely discussed in the underground press cannot be totally suppressed in the authorized literature, despite the most relentless watchfulness of the censors. An example of this is the discussion about the Slavophile movement that was published in the journal *Voprosi literaturi* (devoted to literary theory) in 1969. The journal offered both the "Westernizers" and the Russists an opportunity to present their opposing viewpoints in an authorized framework.[14]

Another example is the recent fruitful development of lyrical "rural" prose. It is no accident that this new literary school grew out of Solzhenitzyn's *One Day in the Life of Ivan Denisovich* and *Matriona's Yard*, and that its ideology partly coincides with the Russist beliefs. It is true literature, though curiously enough it has not yet found recognition in the west. The writers are of various ages, and they include V. Belov (born 1933), V. Likhonosov (born 1935), V. Astafyev (born 1924), E. Nosov (born 1925), J. Galkin,

---

[14] *Voprosi literaturi*, No. 5, 1969; No. 7, 1969; No. 10, 1969; No. 12, 1969.

and M. Roshchin. Vasilii Shukshin, born in 1929, stands somewhat apart from this group, though he is linked to it by his choice of theme. They represent something new in both Russian and European literature. They are not regional authors, but writers who view country life from the inside and from the bottom. They are not plow-pushing Tolstois, but farm workers, bound to their villages by the ties of family and education—and consequently with no literary background. They are seeking a substitute for religion, fleeing from the wastes of the cities, not forward in the direction of socialist hope (now discredited), but back to the eternal moral values that are kept alive by "simple folk" alone. (We must not forget that God has been banished by the censor to the fields of antireligious propaganda.) For these contain the meaning of man's life: tilling the earth and sowing, bearing children and bringing them up, not consciously trying to do good, but trying to avoid evil.

It is the longing for security. But let us not be too quick to label it conservatism. In Russia there are still villages, and it is only in recent years that the number of people living in towns passed the fifty percent mark. It is not a case of an imagined reality created in order to satisfy romantic illusions. There are other rural writers whose sober evidence provides proof of the facts and problems of rural life. Soberness is of course no guarantee of quality, but neither does it imply indifference or libel, as "patriotic" critics like to suggest. Above all, Boris Mozhayev's outstanding picaresque novel *From the Life of Fjodor Kuzkin (Iz zhizni Fiodora Kuzkina)*[15] should be read. Not only Mozhayev, but A. Makarov, V. Syomin and V. Tendryakov as well, sometimes move perilously close to the censor's net with their clear social criticism.

This rural lyric prose is political in the sense that it adopts a negative attitude toward politics. It attempts to avoid a head-on collision with prevailing social and economic conditions (emigration to the towns, poverty in rural areas, troubles in communal farms) by presenting chief characters who, inwardly impervious to social change, seek release from worldly cares in eternal values. Here they come close to the *Molodaya gvardiya* recipe, to the efficacy of the

---

[15] Mozhayev's novel, published in *Novyi mir*, No. 7, 1966, was not permitted by the censors to be published as a book.

Russian national character, deeply rooted in the people's soul, as a panacea for all evils. It is an attitude that can become dangerous when the intuitively "good" man is contrasted with the introspective doubter, the intellectual. Then, by implication, it becomes a comparison between the profound, nonrational East and the superficial, rational West.[16]

To return now to our starting point—to the censorship. Here, in a "free" territory, we see developing in the space of only a few years a completely original and quite remarkable literary movement. It is a sign not only of the potential richness of this movement in itself, but also of the continued existence of classical Russian realism, which is by no means yet exhausted. This new movement, as is evident from the attitude of at least some of its members, has moved as far away from orthodox socialist realism and party loyalty as the forbidden Solzhenitsyn himself. In contrast to Solzhenitzyn, it does not storm the strongholds of power, for it is held in the grip of a dream and is not in search of culprits.

One can call this movement interesting and fruitful, but it would be unwise to go farther. One cannot say with certainty what place it occupies in present-day Russian literature as it really is. Doubtless in a free literary atmosphere, untrammeled by censorship, other intellectual and artistic movements would develop and become no less vigorous and rewarding. But of course we can bring no evidence to prove it. That is why it is so difficult to write about Soviet literature.

<hr>

[16] An example is Likhonosov's *I Love You Brightly* (*Lyubliyu tebya svetlo*) in *Nash sovremennik*, No. 9, 1969.

# *Bibliography*

Alexandrova, Vera. *A History of Soviet Literature 1917–1964. From Gorki to Solzhenitzyn.* New York, 1964.

Becka, Jiří; Drozda, Miroslav; and others. *Slovník spisovatelů národů SSSR.* Prague, 1966.

Bowra, C. M. *The Creative Experiment.* London, 1949.

————, ed. *A Second Book of Russian Verse.* London, 1948.

Brown, E. J. *The Proletarian Episode in Russian Literature 1928–1932.* New York, 1953.

Dox, Georg. *Die russische Sowjetliteratur: Namen, Daten, Werke.* Berlin, 1961.

Franěk, Jiří. *See* Mathesius, Bohumil.

Gibian, George. *Interval of Freedom: Soviet Literature during the Thaw 1954–1957.* Minneapolis, Minnesota, 1960.

van der Eng-Liedmeier, A. M. *Soviet Literary Characters: An Investigation into the Portrayal of Soviet Men in Russian Prose 1917–1953.* The Hague, 1959.

Guerney, Bernard, ed. *An Anthology of Russian Literature in the Soviet Period from Gorki to Pasternak.* New York, 1960.

Hayward, Max, and Crowley, Edward, eds. *Soviet Literature in the Sixties. An International Symposium.* New York-London, 1964.

Hayward, Max, and Labedz, Leopold, eds. *Literature and Revolution in Soviet Russia 1917–1962.* London, 1963.

*Istoriya russko sovetskoi literaturi,* Part III (1941–1957). Moscow, 1961. (A revision of this "History of Russian Soviet Literature," published by the Institute for World Literature of the Academy of Sciences of the USSR, was begun in 1967.)

Kaun, Alexander. *Soviet Poets and Poetry.* Freeport, New York, 1943.

Lewanski, Richard C., ed. *The Slavic Literatures* (Vol. II of *The*

*Literatures of the World in English Translation: A Bibliography).* New York, 1965.

Lo Gatto, Ettore. *Storia della letteratura russa contemporanea.* Milan, 1959.

Mathesius, Bohumil, and Franěk, Jiří. *Prehled sovetske literatury.* Prague, 1965. (A new, revised edition is being prepared by Jiří Franěk.)

Mirski, Dmitri S. *A History of Russian Literature.* New York, 1949.

Obolensky, Dmitri, ed. *The Penguin Book of Russian Verse.* Baltimore, 1962.

Poggioli, Renato. *The Poets of Russia 1890–1930.* Cambridge, Massachusetts, 1960.

Reavey, George. *Soviet Literature Today.* New York, 1946.

Rühle, Jürgen. *Literature and Revolution.* New York, 1969.

*Russkiye Sovetskiye pisateli. Prozaiki. Bibliograficheski ukazatel.* Leningrad, 1959 ff.

Slonim, Marc. *Soviet Russian Literature, Writers and Problems.* New York, 1964.

Steininger, Alexander. *Literatur und Politik in der Sowjetunion nach Stalins Tod.* Wiesbaden, 1965.

Stillman, E., ed. *The Bitter Harvest.* New York, 1959.

Struve, Gleb. *Soviet Russian Literature: 1917–1950,* third ed. Norman, Oklahoma, 1951.

Vickery, Walter. *The Cult of Optimism, Political and Ideological Problems of Recent Soviet Literature.* Bloomington, 1963.

Yarmolinsky, Avraham, ed. *A Treasury of Russian Verse.* New York, 1949.

———. *Literature under Communism.* New York, 1960.

Zavalishin, Vyacheslav. *Early Soviet Writers.* New York, 1958.

# Index

*About Literature, Revolution, Entropy and Other Things* (Zamyatin), 97
*About Mayakovski* (Shklovski), 188
*About Myself II* (Khodasevich), 74
*About Sincerity in Literature* (Pomerantzev), 154
*About Splendid Clarity* (Kuzmin), 65
*About Synthesism* (Zamyatin), 93
*About That* (Mayakovski), 82
*About Theurgy* (Belyi), 36
*About Time, About Destinies, About Love* (Selvinski), 188
*Abyss, The* (Andreyev), 48
Acmeism, 41, 62, 141, 144, 256, 266
  acmeism creed, 65–72
  acmeism reconsidered, 73–75
*Across the Sea* (Zabolotzki), 212
Adamovich, Georgii, 40
*Adolescence of Zhanya Luvers, The* (Pasternak), 84
*Adventures of Chichikov, The* (M. Bulgakov), 114
*Adventures of a Fakir, The* (Vsevolod Ivanov), 102
*Aelita* (A. N. Tolstoi), 108
*Affliction* (Berggoltz), 174

*Afghanistanian Ballad* (Tikhonov), 142
Afinogenov, Aleksandr, 148
*Aggressors, The* (Yevtushenko), 267
*Aimé Leboeuf's Adventure* (Kuzmin), 65
Akhmadulina, Bella, 256–57, 285
Akhmatova, Anna, 66, 68–70, 82, 85, 137, 153, 189–92
*Akhru-Saint Petersburg Report* (Remizov), 61
*Aksakov's Magic Wand* (Soloukhin), 245
Aksenov, Vasilii, 224, 236–38, 280, 282–83, 285
*Alexandrian Songs* (Kuzmin), 63
Aliger, Margarita, 173, 175–76
*All Motifs* (Bryusov), 15
*Alliance of the Five, The* (A. N. Tolstoi), 109
*Almost Three Years: Leningrad Diary* (Inber), 187
*Altar of Victory, The* (Bryusov), 27
*Always for Sale* (Aksenov), 280, 282
*Amphora, The* (Paustovski), 202
*Anathema* (Andreyev), 49
Anderson, Hans Christian, 128, 133, 202

Andreyev, Leonid, 11, 22, 48–49, 59, 118, 128
Andreyevski, Sergei, 5
*Anna Akhmatova* (Pavlovski), 190
Annenski, Innokentii, 41–43, 66
*Anno Domini MCMXXI* (Akhmatova), 70
*Anonymous Artist, The* (Kaverin), 100
*Ansichten eines Clowns* (Böll), 281
*Anti-Christ, Peter and Alexei* (Merezhkovski), 8
*Antiworlds* (Voznesenski), 269, 273, 280
Antokolski, Pavel, 186
*Antonov Apples* (Bunin), 56
*Antony* (Bryusov), 16
*Anxiety at the Railroad Station* (Annenski), 42–43
*Aphrodite* (Martynov), 217
*Apocalypse of Our Time, The* (Rozanov), 33, 34
*Apocalypse in Russian Poetry, The* (Belyi), 12
*Apollo and Dionysos* (Veresayev), 50
*Apollon* magazine, 41, 65, 66, 73
*Apollonius of Tyre* (Remizov), 61
*Apostate, The* (Kazakov), 247
*Apotheosis of Rootlessness, The* (Shestov), 10
*Apple, The* (Yevtushenko), 266
*Arktur, the Hunting Dog* (Kazakov), 246–47
*Armored Train* (Vsevolod Ivanov), 101, 147
*Art of Lev Tolstoi, The* (Fedin), 198
*Artamonov Business, The* (Gorki), 107
Arzhak, Nikolai, 233–34
Aseyev, Nikolai, 83, 137, 138–39, 187, 259

*Ashes* (Belyi), 38
Astafyev, V., 288
*At the Big Stream* (Bondarev), 230
*At the Border of Two Epochs: Literary Confrontations from 1917 to 1920* (Zelinski), 188
*At the Crossroads* (Kuprin), 52
*At the Railroad Station* (Zabolotzki), 212
*At the Walls of the Invisible City* (Prishvin), 53
*At the Wild Shore* (Polevoi), 160
*At the World's End* (Zamyatin), 94
*Atonement, The* (Arzhak), 234
*Auditor* (Gogol), 146
*Auditor, The* (Kaverin), 100
*August 1914* (Solzhenitzyn), 279
*Author, Art, Time* (Fedin), 197–200
*Autobiography* (Pasternak), 193
*Automobile* (Khodasevich), 75
*Autumn in the Oak Forests* (Kazakov), 250
*Autumnal Borderland* (Moritz), 256
Avant-garde in Russian literature, 71, 143, 184
the older literary avant-garde, 184–219
poetry of contemporary avant-garde, 257–58
*Awakening* (Babel), 123
*Away over the Barriers* (Pasternak), 83
Aygi, Gennadii, 214, 258
*Azef* (A. N. Tolstoi), 109
Azhayev, Vasilii, 160

Babayevski, Semion, 159
Babel, Isaac, 121–24, 185, 188
*Babi Yar* (Yevtushenko), 267
*Bacchanal, The* (Pasternak), 192

*Back of the Blue Seas* (Soloukhin), 243

*Badgers, The* (Leonov), 128–29, 147

Bagritzki, Eduard, 143–45, 173

Baklanov, Grigorii, 228–30, 278

*Bakunin in Dresden* (Fedin), 103

*Ballad* (Khodasevich), 74

*Ballad of the Blue Package* (Tikhonov), 141

*Ballad of the Chief of the Gendarmes and the Poem on the Death of the Poet* (Yevtushenko), 268

*Ballad—Dissertation* (Voznesenski), 271

*Ballad of the Fish Killing, The* (Yevtushenko), 268

*Ballad of the Nails* (Tikhonov), 142

*Ballad of the Place of Execution* (Voznesenski), 271

*Ballad of the Return of the Fallen Father, The* (Kazakova), 255

*Ballad of Work* (Voznesenski), 271

*Ballads and Songs* (Selvinski), 188

Balmont, Konstantin, 12–13, 216

Baltrušaitis, Jurgis, 18

*Bandit's Last Night* (Konetzki), 251

*Bare Year, The* (Pilnyak), 125–26

*Bath* (Slutzki), 182

*Bath, The* (Mayakovski), 146, 147

*Battalion Asks for Artillery Support, The* (Bondarev), 230–231

*Battle for Idealism, The* (Volynski), 6

*Bazaar* (Paustovski), 202

*Bazaar in That Year, The* (Rozhdestvenski), 262

*Beatnik Monologue* (Yevtushenko), 267

*Beautiful!* (Mayakovski), 138

*Beautiful Land* (Romanov), 112

*Beautiful Life, A* (Bunin), 57

*Bedbug, The* (Mayakovski), 146–147

*Beethoven* (Zabolotzki), 211, 212

*Beginning* (Aseyev), 187

*Behind the Scenes* (Zamyatin), 96

Bek, A., 278

Belinski, Visarion, 287

Belov, V., 288

Belyi, Andrei, 12, 15, 19, 29–33, 36–38, 50, 59, 62, 82, 94, 125, 137, 147, 194

Berdyayev, Nikolai, 10, 34

Berggoltz, Olga, 152, 173–75

Beyond symbolism, *see* Symbolism, transition from

*Big Gamble, The* (Kaverin), 99

*Big Ore, The* (Vladimov), 224

*Birth of a Man, The* (Gorki), 47

*Birth of the Wing* (Moritz), 256

*Black Arab, The* (Prishvin), 53

*Black Blood* (Blok), 20

*Black Prince, The* (Aseyev), 139

*Black Prince, The* (Zoshchenko), 106, 139

*Black Sea, The* (Paustovski), 111

*Blockade* (Chakovski), 285

Blok, Aleksandr, 15, 19–22, 22–24, 144, 191, 192, 254, 267, 268

*Blooming Staff, The* (Gorodetzki), 73

*Blue Book* (Zoshchenko), 106

*Blue Cities* (A. N. Tolstoi), 109

*Blue and Green* (Kazakov), 250

*Blue Sands* (Vsevolod Ivanov), 102

Bobrov, Sergei, 83

*Bolero* (Zabolotzki), 212

*Bomb, The* (Aseyev), 139

Bondarev, Yurii, 224, 230–33
Book about the Soldier (Tvardovski), 166
Book of Death (Andreyevski), 5
Book of Memories (Slonimski), 186
Book of Poems (Kirsanov), 214, 216
Book of Reflections (Annenski), 43
Book of Wanderings (Paustovski), 201
Borisova, M., 200
Boundaries of Art, The (Vyacheslav Ivanov), 40
Bracelet of Garnets, The (Kuprin), 52
Brainina, B., 200
Bratsk Cofferdam, The (Yevtushenko), 268
Brew, The (Tikhonov), 141
Brezhnev, Leonid, 277, 284
Bridges (Kirsanov), 215
Bright Shore (Panova), 164
Brik, Osip, 137
Britikov, A., 219
Brodski, Iosif, 260–61, 279
Brothers, The (Fedin), 102
Brothers Yershov, The (Kochetov), 160
Bryusov, Valerii, 14–17, 24, 26–29, 39, 137
Büchner, Georg, 109
Budennyi (Aseyev), 139
Budetliane futurists, 76
Bulgakov, Mikhail, 113–14, 147, 282
Bulgakov, Sergei, 10
Bunin, Ivan, 10, 11, 51, 55–59, 202, 224, 248
Burlyuk, David, 77, 79, 80, 139
Burning Buildings (Balmont), 13
Buryga (Leonov), 128
By Daylight (Kazakevich), 178

Call of the Wild, The (London), 247
Camp of the Swans, The (Tzvetayeva), 85
Cancer Ward, The (Solzhenitzyn), 224, 278, 281–82, 283
Candle, The (Akhmadulina), 257
Cape of Longing (Moritz), 256
Čapek, Karel, 109
Capture of Velikoshumsk, The (Leonov), 204
Card of Diamonds, A (Kaverin), 99
Carmen (Blok), 20
Carmina amoebaea (Vyacheslav Ivanov and Bryusov), 39
Caryatids (Kirsanov), 215
Case Out of Line, A (Tendryakov), 241
Catapult (Aksenov), 237
Catcher in the Rye, The (Salinger), 237
Cave, The (Zamyatin), 95
Cement (Gladkov), 118
Censorship, 277–90
  in the theater, 280–81
  of moral issues, 281–82
  samizdat as direct result of, 288
  writers forced to make concessions because of, 282–83
Chadzhi-Tarkhan (Khlebnikov), 79
Chakovski, Aleksandr, 285
Chalmayev, 283, 286
Chansons de Bilitis (Louÿs), 63
Chapayev (Furmanov), 116–17
Characters (Vinokurov), 264
Chazaric Ornament, The (Nagibin), 223
Chefs d'oeuvre (Bryusov), 15
Chekhov, Anton, 4, 5, 6–7, 10, 11, 22, 36, 43, 44, 51, 54, 112, 196, 202, 224, 246, 248

*Cherry Orchard, The* (Chekhov), 7, 11
*Cherry Stone, The* (Olesha), 132–133
*Childhood and School Days* (Paustovski), 201
*Christ and Antichrist* (Merezhkovski), 8, 31
*Christians* (Andreyev), 48
*Chronicler of Tobolsk, The* (Martynov), 216
Chukhontsev, Oleg, 285, 286
Chuzhak, Nikolai, 137
*Cigarette Box, The* (Bagritzki), 144
*Cinque* (Akhmatova), 191
*Circle of Flame, The* (Sologub), 18
*Circular Letter No. 37* (Luntz), 98
*Cities and Years* (Fedin), 102
*City, The* (Blok), 19, 20
*City of Justice, The* (Luntz), 98
*City of Okurov, The* (Gorki), 47
*City of Pushkin* (Akhmatova), 191
*City of the Winds* (Pilnyak), 127
Civil War, and the literary situation, 49, 54, 63, 67, 91, 107, 116, 119, 121, 137, 139, 144
*Clay Doves* (Kuzmin), 64
*Cleansing* (Sosnora), 259
*Cloak, The* (Yashin), 162
*Cloud in Trousers, A* (Mayakovski), 80–81
*Cold Cavern of January, The* (Pasternak), 192
*Colleagues* (Aksenov), 282
*Collected Poems* (Gippius), 14
*Cologne Pit, The* (Slutzki), 181–182
*Colored Winds* (Vsevolod Ivanov), 102

*Columns* (Zabolotzki), 140
*Come Too Late* (Vinokurov), 264
*Commander of the Second Army* (Selvinski), 143
*Comments on Present-Day Russian Literature* (Ehrenburg), 121
*Comrade* (Yesenin), 87
*Comrade Agronom* (Kochetov), 160
*Comrade Kislyakov* (Romanov), 112
*Comrades in Arms* (Simonov), 180–81
*Concerning the Causes of the Decline, and the New Currents in Contemporary Russian Literature* (Merezhkovski), 3–4
*Confession, The* (Gorki), 47
*Confession of a Hooligan, The* (Yesenin), 87
*Connecting Boat* (Yevtushenko), 268
*Consolation* (Sologub), 24
Constructivists, 80, 118, 131, 142–45, 146, 159, 160, 187, 188, 270
*Contemporaries* (Forsh), 109–10
Contemporary Soviet literary trends, 150–273
   new orientations, World War II, 151–83
   new tendencies in Soviet poetry, 253–73
   new trends since 1968, 286–87, 288–90
   older literary avant-garde, 184–219
   Revolution's critical heirs, 220–52
*Continuation of a Legend* (Kuznetzov), 223

*Conversation with the Komsomol N. Dementyev* (Bagritzki), 144

*Cor ardens* (Vyacheslav Ivanov), 39

*Correspondence between Two Corners of the Room* (V. Ivanov and Gershenzon), 41

*County Road* (Matveyeva), 266

*Court, The* (Tendryakov), 239

*Court Appears, The* (Tertz), 235

*Created Legend, The* (Sologub), 24–25

*Crème de violettes* (Severyanin), 76

Critical literary heirs of the Revolution, 220–52
  new realists, 224–39
  redemption from socialist realism, 220–24
  traditionalists, 224, 239–52

*Crossing, The* (Martynov), 217

*Crowd at the Wharf, The* (Paustovski), 202

*Crowns and Roots* (Voznesenski), 270

*Cry, The* (Bunin), 58

Cult of personality, and Stalin, 154, 180, 220

Cult of the "super-hero" in literature, 154

Curtius, E. R., 41

Czechoslovakia, 1968 uprising, 282, 286

*Damned North* (Kazakov), 246

*Dance of Death* (Blok), 20

*Dante Street* (Babel), 124

*Danton's Death* (A. N. Tolstoi), 109

*Dark Countenance, The* (Rozanov), 34

*Day of Peter the Great, The* (A. N. Tolstoi), 108

*Days of Brother and Sister Turbinych, The* (M. Bulgakov), 113, 147

*Days and Nights* (Simonov), 180

*Days of Our Life* (Ketlinskaya), 159

*De profundis amavi* (Vyacheslav Ivanov), 40

*Dead Souls, The* (Gogol), 114, 147

*Death After the Announcement* (Sologub), 24

*Death of the Gods, The* (Merezhkovski), 8

*Death of Wazir-Muchtar, The* (Tynyanov), 110

*Deeds of Alexander the Great* (Kuzmin), 65

*Deep Back Country* (Polevoi), 160

*Defeat, The* (Fadeyev), 117

*Defense of Stalingrad, The* (Grossman), 159

*Defrauders, The* (Katayev), 112–113

*Delicacy* (Yevtushenko), 267

*Demon* (Lermontov), 20

*Dethroned Jupiter, The* (Bryusov), 29

*Devil Haunting* (M. Bulgakov), 113

*Devil's Swing, The* (Sologub), 18

Diaghilev, Sergei, 9

*Diary of a Poet* (Aseyev), 139

"Discovery of America," in *The Three-Cornered Pear* (Voznesenski), 271

*Discussion about Happiness* (Moritz), 256

*Distance after Distance* (Tvardovski), 167, 169

*Distances* (Bryusov), 137

*Divnaya Church in Uglich* (Berggoltz), 175

*Doctor Vlasenkova* (Kaverin), 207
*Doctor Zhivago* (Pasternak), 83, 193–95
*Dog of the Gray King, The* (Sologub), 18
Dolmatovski, Yevgenii, 162
*Don Quixote* (Yevtushenko), 267
*Donetz-Basin* (Gorbatov), 159
Dostoyevski, Feodor, 4, 6, 20, 26, 40, 50, 54, 60, 128, 129, 281
*Double, The* (Dostoyevski), 20, 128
*Double Portrait* (Kaverin), 209–210
*Dragon, The* (Zamyatin), 95
*Dream* (Aseyev), 187
*Drizzle* (Kazakova), 255
*Drop of Dew, A* (Soloukhin), 244
*Drunkenness* (Yashin), 162
Dudintzev, Vladimir, 154, 220, 221
*Duel, The* (Kuprin), 52
*During Forty Years* (Shklovski), 188
*During the Siege* (Ketlinskaya), 159

*Early Joys* (Fedin), 197
*Early in the Morning* (Panova), 166
*Earth Axis* (Bryusov), 26
*East* (Bunin), 58
*Eccentric of Moscow, The* (Belyi), 33
*Edge of the City* (Kochetov), 160
Ehrenburg, Ilya, 118–21, 146, 152, 154, 185, 195–97, 220, 230
Eichenbaum, Boris, 92
*Elektriada* (Aseyev), 139
*Eleventh Axiom, The* (Kaverin), 99

*Embarkation for the Isle of Cytherea* (G. Ivanov), 67
*Emblematics of Sense, The* (Belyi), 36
Emigration of writers from Soviet Russia, 40, 49, 52, 54, 55, 59, 61, 63, 66, 68, 74, 77, 108, 128, 137, 147, 169, 278
*Enclosed in Stone* (Forsh), 109–110
*End of the Den of Thieves, The* (Kaverin), 99–100
*End of the Little Man, The* (Leonov), 128
*End of the Old Folks' Home, The* (Babel), 124
*Enemies, The* (Gorki), 46
*Engineers* (Slonimski), 186
Entelechism, 77
*Entrance into the Cold* (Akhmadulina), 257
*Envy* (Olesha), 131–32
Erdman, Nikolai, 146
*Eros* (Vyacheslav Ivanov), 39
Escapist writing, in interwar period, 110–12
*Eternal Truth of the Idols, The* (Bryusov), 16
*Evening* (Akhmatova), 68, 69
*Evening Album* (Tzvetayeva), 85
*Evening Glow* (Vyacheslav Ivanov), 40
*Evening at the Oka* (Zabolotzki), 212
*Evenings Not of This World* (Kuzmin), 64
*Every Day Is Long* (Simonov), 181
*Everyday* (Vinokurov), 264
*Eugenia Ivanovna* (Leonov), 206
*Exclamation Point, The* (Yevtushenko), 267–68
*Excursion Beyond the Neva City Boundary* (Berggoltz), 175

*Excursion to the South* (Paustovski), 201
*Experience at the Mamai Hill, The* (Nekrasov), 172–73
Expressionism, 75, 85, 102

*Faces of the Dawn* (Panova), 166
Fadeyev, Aleksandr, 116, 117, 282n
*Fairy Tales about Italy* (Gorki), 46, 47
*Fairytale Teller, The* (Paustovski), 202
*Fall of Paris, The* (Ehrenburg), 195–96
*Fallen Leaves* (Rozanov), 33
*Family Question, The* (Rozanov), 34
*Fantastic Stories* (Tertz), 234
*Far from Moscow* (Azhayev), 160
*Fatal Eggs, The* (M. Bulgakov), 113
*Fate of Charles Lonceville, The* (Paustovski), 111
*Fate of a Man, The* (Sholokhov), 218
*Father, A* (Babel), 123
*Father Visits His Son, The* (Kazakevich), 179
*Favorites of the Centuries* (Bryusov), 15–16
Fayko, Aleksei, 146
*Fear* (Afinogenov), 148
*Fear* (Yevtushenko), 267
*February Diary* (Berggoltz), 174
Fedin, Konstantin, 92, 102–3, 197–200
*Feodoretz, Belyi Klobuchok* (Panova), 166
Feuilletonism, 82, 119, 139, 238, 268
*Fiery Angel, The* (Bryusov), 26, 27–29

*Fifth Pestilence, The* (Remizov), 59
*Find, The* (Tendryakov), 240–41, 242
*Fire, The* (Aseyev), 139
*Fires of St. Dominic, The* (Zamyatin), 97–98
*First Acquaintance* (Nekrasov), 171
*First Circle, The* (Solzhenitzyn), 224, 278
First Congress of Soviet Writers (1934), 156, 157
*First Meeting, The* (Belyi), 33
*First Mounted Army, The* (Vishnevski), 148
*First Snow* (Sosnora), 259
*Fish in Winter* (Brodski), 260
Five Year Plan, 113, 136, 148
*Flea, The* (Zamyatin), 147
*Flight to Egypt* (Zabolotzki), 212
*Flight of Time, The* (Akhmatova), 189, 191
*Flood, The* (Zamyatin), 96
*Flower Path, The* (Katayev), 113
*Flute Made of a Spinal Column* (Mayakovski), 80–81
Fofanov, Konstantin, 4
*Foma Gordeyev* (Gorki), 46, 107, 135
*For the Good of the Cause* (Solzhenitzyn), 228
*For Grownups* (Rozhdestvenski), 263
*For the Just Cause* (Grossman), 159
*For Whom the Bell Tolls* (Hemingway), 288
*Forest* (Ostrovski), 146
Formalism, in prose and literary criticism, 92, 138
Forsh, Olga, 109–10, 186
*Fragrance of Bread, The* (Kazakov), 249–50

Frank, Semen, 10
Frank, Viktor, 194
*Free Days* (Kazakova), 255
*French Ballad* (Moritz), 256
*From the Kazan Notebook* (Aliger), 175
*From the Life of Fjodor Kuzkin* (Mozhayev), 289
*From Marxism to Idealism* (S. Bulgakov), 10
*From Poetic Positions* (Soloukhin), 243, 245
*Fujiyama in the Tea Cups* (Kuzmin), 64
*Fulfillment of Wishes, The* (Kaverin), 101, 207
*Funeral Pyre, The* (Fedin), 199, 200
*Funeral Service* (Yesenin), 86
*Fur Trade* (Selvinski), 143
Furmanov, Dmitri, 116–17
*Furrows and Frontiers* (Vyacheslav Ivanov), 40
Futurism, 62, 64, 75–83, 137–41, 145
cubo-futurists, 76
ego-futurists, 76

Galkin, J., 288
*Gapa Guzhva* (Babel), 124
*Gardens* (G. Ivanov), 68
Garin, Nikolai, 6
Garshin, Vsevolod, 4, 5
*General Staff during the War Years* (Shtemenko), 285n
*Genesis of Socialist Realism in Russian Literature, The* (Muratova), 156–57
*Gentleman from San Francisco, The* (Bunin), 58
Gershenzon, Mikhail, 41
Gippius, Zinaida, 12, 13–14, 19, 34

Gladilin, Anatolii, 224, 236, 238–239, 285
Gladkov, Fiodor, 118, 282n
Glavlit, censorship bureau, 281
*Goat, The* (Zoshchenko), 104
Gogol, Nikolai, 4, 32, 59, 100, 113, 114–15, 146, 190, 203, 271, 282
*Gogol and the Devil* (Merezhkovski), 4
*Gogol in Life* (Veresayev), 51
*Gogol's Mastership* (Belyi), 33
*Gold in Azure* (Belyi), 37
"Golden age" in Russian cultural development, 9
*Golden Ass, The,* by Apuleius (Kuzmin translation), 65
*Golden Balls* (Aseyev), 187
*Golden Calf, The* (Ilf and Petrov), 115
*Golden Fleece, The,* symbolist journal, 9
*Golden Rose, The* (Paustovski), 201, 203
*Gone with the Wind* (Mitchell), 288
*Good in the Teaching of Tolstoi and Nietzsche, The* (Shestov), 10
Gorbatov, Boris, 159
Gorenstein, Friedrich, 279, 285, 286
Gorki, Maksim, 10, 11, 22, 44–47, 50, 51, 59, 91, 93, 98, 103, 106–7, 117, 121, 128, 134, 156, 185, 186, 280
Gorki Institute of Literature in Moscow, 179, 203, 214, 228, 230, 243, 262, 264
Gorodetzki, Sergei, 18–19, 65, 73, 78
*Governor, The* (Andreyev), 48–49
*Goya* (Voznesenski), 270

Granin, Daniil, 220, 222
*Graphomanes, The* (Tertz), 234–235
*Gray-eyed King, The* (Akhmatova), 68
*Great Conflagrations* (novel by twenty-five Soviet writers), 111
*Great Elegy* (Brodski), 260
*Green Nightingale, The* (Kuzmin), 65
Grekova, I., 278, 286
*Grenada* (Svetlov), 213
Griboyedov, Aleksandr, 110, 280n
*Grieving Bride, The* (Sologub), 24
Grin, Aleksandr, 111, 186
Grossman, Vasilii, 159
*Guiding Stars* (Vyacheslav Ivanov), 39
Guild of Poets, 66, 67
*Gulf, The* (Martynov), 216
*Gulliver Plays Cards* (Tikhonov), 142
Gumilev, Nikolai, 66, 67, 68, 91, 141
Guro, Yelena, 77

*Hagia Sophia* (Mandelstamm), 72
*Hail in Kharkov* (Yevtushenko), 267
*Half a Trip to the Moon* (Aksenov), 238
*Handicraft* (Kazakova), 255–56
*Hands, The* (Arzhak), 234
*Hangman of Nuremburg, The* (Sologub), 18
*Happy Little House, The* (Khodasevich), 74
*Harmony* (Aseyev), 187
*Harps and Violins* (Blok), 20
*He Who Carries Flowers in His Hands* (Soloukhin), 243
*He Who Looks at the Clouds* (Konetzki), 252

*Heart of Achilles, The* (Voznesenski), 273
*Heather* (G. Ivanov), 68
*Heavy Lyre, The* (Khodasevich), 74
*Hello, Scholar!* (Okudzhava), 254
*Here* (Aygi), 258
*Here Speaks Leningrad* (Berggoltz), 174
*Heritage of Symbolism, The* (Vyacheslav Ivanov), 38–39
*Heritage of Symbolism and Acmeism, The* (Gumilev), 66
Historical novel in interwar period, 108–10
Hoffmann, E. T. A., 91, 93, 99
*Homeland* (Blok), 21
*Homespun Venus, The* (Martynov), 216
*Horde, The* (Tikhonov), 141
*Horizon* (Svetlov), 213
*Horrible World* (Blok), 20
*Horses in the Ocean* (Slutzki), 181–82
*Hot Coalpit, The* (Polevoi), 160
*Hour Is Here, The* (Fedin), 200
*House, The* (Khodasevich), 75
House of Art, 91, 92, 109, 186
House of the Scholars, 91
*House on the Square, The* (Kazakevich), 178
House of the Writers, 91
*House with the Turret, The* (Gorenstein), 279n
*How It Was Done in Odessa* (Babel), 123
*How One Drinks Up the Sun* (Soloukhin), 243
*Howling John* (Bunin), 58
*Huns of the Future, The* (Bryusov), 16
*Hunting Lodge, The* (Svetlov), 213

*I* (Mayakovski), 81
*I* (Vinokurov), 264–65
*I and E* (Khlebnikov), 79
*I Fly Toward the Storm* (Granin), 222
*I Love Lorca* (Voznesenski), 270
*I Love You Brightly* (Likhonosov), 290n
*I Remember* (Pasternak), 193
*Ideal, The* (Annenski), 42
Ilf, Ilya, 114–15, 235
Imagists, 76, 87
*In the Alley Back of the Arbat* (Antokolski), 186
*In America* (Gorki), 46
*In the Basement* (Babel), 123
*In the Crowd* (Sologub), 24, 25
*In Defense of a Friend* (Leonov), 203
*In the Fog* (Andreyev), 48
*In the Hospital* (Svetlov), 214
*In the Land of the Frightened Birds* (Prishvin), 53
*In Memory of Mikhail Svetlov* (Rozhdestvenski), 263
*In the Quickstep of the Days* (Tendryakov), 239–40
*In St. Valentine's Church* (Babel), 123
*In the Summertime in Yasnaya Polyana* (Fedin), 198
*In the Trenches of Stalingrad* (Nekrasov), 152, 169–71, 172
*In the Underground Dungeon* (Bryusov), 26
*In the Woods* (Tendryakov), 239
*In the World* (Gorki), 47
*In That Dawn* (Paustovski), 201
Inber, Vera, 143, 187
*Incident at the Krechetovka Station, An* (Solzhenitzyn), 227
*Infamous Stories* (Zamyatin), 98
*Inoniya* (Yesenin), 87

*Insane Ship, The* (Forsh), 109
*Intelligence Brings Suffering* (Griboyedov), 280n
*Intermezzo* (Akhmatova), 190
International Congress of Writers in Paris (1935), 142
*Interviews* (Gorki), 46
*Invasion of the Enemy, The* (Fedin), 199
*Islanders, The* (Zamyatin), 94, 95
*Islands* (Okudzhava), 255
*It Doesn't Pay to Live Otherwise* (Ketlinskaya), 159
*Italian Italy* (Yevtushenko), 268
*Ivan-Moskva* (Pilnyak), 126
Ivaniov, Ryurik, 87
Ivanov, Georgii, 66, 67–68, 78
Ivanov, Vsevolod, 92, 101–2, 137, 147
Ivanov, Vyacheslav, 18, 34, 38–41, 50, 62
Ivanov-Razumnik, R., 21, 53, 86, 88
Ivask, George, 36, 71
Ivnev, R., 76

Jakobson, Roman, 81
*January Rain* (Sosnora), 259
*Jolly Drummer, The* (Okudzhava), 255
*Jolly Experience, A* (Zoshchenko), 106
*Journey of Sir John Fairfax Through Turkey and Other Remarkable Countries, The* (Kuzmin), 65
*Julio Jurenito* (Ehrenburg), 119–120, 196
*Julius Caesar* (Bryusov), 16
*July 1941* (Baklanov), 229–30

*Ka* (Khlebnikov), 79
Kamenski, Vasilii, 77–78
Kandinski, Vasili, 75

*Karl-Yankel* (Babel), 124
*Kashchei's Chain* (Prishvin), 108
Katayev, Valentin, 112–13, 285, 286
Kaverin, Veniamin, 92, 93, 99–101, 111, 160, 206–10, 278
Kazakevich, Emmanuil, 152, 177–79
Kazakov, Yurii, 246–50, 251, 262
Kazakova, Rimma, 255–56
*Kazan University* (Yevtushenko), 285
*Kerenski* (Zoshchenko), 106
Ketlinskaya, Vera, 159
Khlebnikov, Velimir, 73, 76, 78–80, 137, 141, 143, 182, 187, 216, 259
Khodasevich, Vladislav, 74–75, 81, 137
Khrushchev, Nikita, 277, 278, 279
*King, The* (Babel), 123
*King on the Plaza, The* (Blok), 23
*King's Girl, The* (Tzvetayeva), 85
*Kipling's Songs* (Matveyeva), 265
*Kira Georgiyevna* (Nekrasov), 171–72
Kirsanov, Semen, 214–16
*Klim Samgin's Life* (Gorki), 107
Klyuyev, Nikolai, 88
*Knight of the Golden Star* (Babayevski), 159
*Knot, The* (Berggoltz), 174, 175
"Knowledge" (*Znaniye*) group, 11
Kochetov, Vsevolod, 160, 285
Kommissarzhevskaya, Vera, 23
Konetzki, Viktor, 250–52
Konevskoi, Ivan, 18
Kornilov, Boris, 174
*Korol, the King* (Okudzhava), 254
Korolenko, Vladimir, 5, 11
Kosterin, Aleksei, 279–80

*Kotik Letayev* (Belyi), 32
*Kovyakin's Notes* (Leonov), 128
Kozhinov, 286
*Krasnaya Nov* journal, 121, 128
*Kremlin in the Snowstorm at the End of 1918, The* (Pasternak), 84
Kruchenykh, Aleksei, 76–77, 79
Kuprin, Aleksandr, 10, 11, 51–52, 118, 128, 202
*Kurymushka* (Prishvin), 107
Kusikov, Aleksandr, 87
Kuzmin, Mikhail, 63–65, 137, 206
Kuznetzov, Anatolii, 223–24, 278, 285
Kyukhelbeker, V., 110
*Kyukhlya* (Tynyanov), 110

*Ladomir* (Khlebnikov), 80
*Laestrigonies, The* (Kuprin), 51
*Lakes in the Fall* (Kuzmin), 64
Lakshin, V., 282n
*Lament over Two Unborn Poems* (Voznesenski), 272
*Land of Childhood* (Matveyeva), 265
*Landscape by Gauguin* (Kuzmin), 64
*Last Judgment, The* (Prishvin), 53
*Last Love* (Zabolotzki), 212
*Last Martyrs, The* (Bryusov), 26, 27
*Last Night, The* (Bagritzki), 145
*Last Salvos, The* (Bondarev), 231
*Late Spring* (Zabolotzki), 212
*Laundry, The* (Zabolotzki), 212
*Lef* journal, 121, 138
*Lef* movement (Left Front of the Arts), 83, 137–38, 214
*Lefthanded One* (Leskov), 147
*Legacy* (Zabolotzki), 212

*Legend of the Emperor Maximilian* (Kirsanov), 215
*Legend of Olga, The* (Panova), 166
*Legend of the Sea, A* (Bagritzki), 144
*Legends of King Solomon* (Remizov), 60
*Leimonarium* (Remizov), 60
Lenin, Nikolai, 157, 178, 269, 272
*Lenin Hills* (Aliger), 176
Lenin Prize, 162, 166, 214, 219
*Leningrad Accepts the Challenge* (Tikhonov), 186
*Leningrad Elegies* (Akhmatova), 190
*Leningrad Notebook* (Kirsanov), 215
*Leningrad Poem* (Berggoltz), 174
*Lenin's Time* (Aseyev), 187
Leonov, Leonid, 111, 128–31, 147, 160, 203–6, 220, 245
Leontiyev, Konstantin, 3, 33
Lermontov, Mikhail, 20, 84, 268
Leskov, Nikolai, 6, 147
*Let Us Be like the Sun* (Balmont), 13
*Letopis* monthly, of Gorki, 121
*Letter to American Friends* (Sholokhov), 218
*Letter of Safe-Conduct* (Pasternak), 85
*Letter to the 30th Century* (Rozhdestvenski), 262
*Letters from the Russian Museum* (Soloukhin), 246
*Letters from Tula* (Pasternak), 84
*Lev Tolstoi* (Gorki), 47
*Levers, The* (Yashin), 221–22
*Lieutenant Schmidt* (Pasternak), 140
*Life of Man, The* (Andreyev), 49
*Life of Matvei Koshemyakin, The* (Gorki), 47

*Light in the Window, A* (Nagibin), 222–23
*Like a Spaniard* (Balmont), 13
Likhonosov, V., 288, 290n
*Lilac Is Blooming, The* (Zoshchenko), 106
*Lines of Love* (Shchipachev), 162
*Lions and Sphinxes* (Kirsanov), 215
*List of Good Deeds, The* (Olesha), 133
Literary life in Russia at turn of century, 3–11
  critical foundations, 3–4
  decline of the novel, 4–7
  importance of literary criticism, 4, 5–6
  journalism and the realists, 10–11
  Merezhkovski and his followers, 8–10
  reconsideration of values, 8–11
  religio-philosophical idealism, development of, 9–10
  symbolism, acceptance of, 8–9
Literary trends, contemporary, *see* Contemporary Soviet literary trends
*Literaturnaya gazeta* magazine, 285
*Literaturnaya Moskva* community enterprises, 155
*Literaturniye ocherki* (Andreyevski), 5
*Little Box of Cypress Wood, The* (Annenski), 42, 43
*Little Devil, The* (Gippius), 14
*Little Ship, The* (Matveyeva), 265
*Little Song of Arbat* (Okudzhava), 254
*Little Song of the Sail* (Kazakova), 255
*Liubka the Cossack* (Babel), 123

*Living and the Dead* (Simonov), 181
*Living on Earth* (Soloukhin), 243
*Living Life* (Veresayev), 50
Livshitz, Benedikt, 77–78
Livshitz, M., 283
*Liza Chaykina* (Svetlov), 213
*Loneliness* (Svetlov), 213
*Longjumeau* (Voznesenski), 272
*Looking Ahead* (Panova), 163–64
Lorca, García, 270, 271
*Love of Electricity* (Aksenov), 282–83, 285
*Lower Depths, The* (Gorki), 45, 46
Lozinski, Mikhail, 66, 73
Lukács, Georg, 284
Lunacharski, 284
Luntz, Lev, 92, 93, 98, 99
*Lyrical Digression* (Aseyev), 139
*Lyrics* (Selvinski), 188
Lyubimov, 280
*Lyubimov* (Tertz), 235
*Lyubov Yarovayga* (Trenev), 148

*Machines and Wolves* (Pilnyak), 126
*Magic Lantern* (Tzvetayeva), 85
*Magic of Words, The* (Belyi), 36, 62
*Mahogony* (Pilnyak), 127
Makarov, A., 286, 289
Makovski, Sergei, 41
*Malakhov Hill* (Kazakova), 255
*Malva* (Gorki), 45
*Mamai* (Zamyatin), 95
*Man* (Mayakovski), 81
*Man Goes Over the Earth on Foot* (Soloukhin), 244
*Man Hunter, The* (Zamyatin), 95
*Man Is Man's Devil* (Sologub), 25
*Man from Minap, The* (Arzhak), 234

*Man Old as the Hills, A* (Bunin), 57
*Man with the Gun, The* (Pogodin), 148
*Mandate, The* (Erdman), 146
Mandelstamm, Osip, 66, 71–72, 137, 197
*Manka* (Kazakov), 247
*Manner, Personality and Style* (Vyacheslav Ivanov), 40
*Manual Work* (Tzvetayeva), 85
*Mara* (Remizov), 61
*Mares' Boars, The* (Yesenin), 87
*Marfa, the Wife of Posadnik* (Yesenin), 86
*Maria* (Babel), 124
Mariengof, Anatolii, 87
*Marksman with One and a Half Eyes, The* (Livshitz), 78
Marshak, Samuil, 185
Martynov, Leonid, 216–17
Marxism, 10, 46, 47, 50, 283, 284
Marxist literary criticism, 287
*Masha* (Kuznetzov), 224
Mašková, Olga, 258
*Master* (Voznesenski), 270
*Master and Journeymen* (Kaverin), 99
*Matriona's Yard* (Solzhenitzyn), 223, 226–27, 288
Matveyeva, Novella, 263, 265–67
Mayakovski, Vladimir, 64, 76, 77, 79, 80–83, 137, 138, 146–47, 188, 197, 214, 266, 268, 269, 280
*Me eum esse* (Bryusov), 15
*Mea* (Bryusov), 137
*Meaning of Art, The* (Belyi), 36
*Measured Stakes* (Tzvetayeva), 85
*Meeting Again with Nefertiti* (Tendryakov), 241–42
*Memoirs* (Martynov), 217
Memoirs of Andrei Belyi, 33
*Memories* (Gorki), 47

*Memories* (Veresayev), 51
*Memory of a Demon* (Lermontov), 84
*Mephistopheles* (Pasternak), 84
Merezhkovski, Dmitri, 3–4, 6, 7, 8–10, 11, 13, 19, 28, 31, 34, 44, 50
*Meridian Pulkovo, The* (Inber), 187
*Mess-mend or a Yankee in Petrograd* (Shaginyan), 111
Meyerhold, Vsevolod, 22–23, 49, 82, 145, 146
*Michael Sinyagin* (Zoshchenko), 106
*Midnight Trolleybus* (Okudzhava), 254
Mikhalkov, S., 278
Minski, Nikolai, 4
*Miracle, The* (Zamyatin), 95
Mirski, D. S., 5, 7, 30, 35, 60, 109, 135
*Model Book of Verse, The* (Khlebnikov), 78
*Molière* (M. Bulgakov), 147
*Moloch, The* (Kuprin), 52, 118
*Molodaya gvardiya* magazine, 283, 286–87, 289–90
*Monologue of the Egyptian Pyramid* (Yevtushenko), 268–69
*Month in France, A* (Nekrasov), 171
*Moonlight Night* (Matveyeva), 266
Moritz, Yunna, 256
*Mosaic* (Voznesenski), 273
Moscow Art Theatre, 8, 22, 46, 49, 109, 145, 147
First Studio of, 147
*Moscow Speaking* (Arzhak), 233
*Moscow Under the Push* (Belyi), 33
*Moskva* literary journal, 155, 241, 267

*Mosti* almanac, 169
*Mother, The* (Gorki), 46, 280
*Mother-Stepmother* (Soloukhin), 244–45
*Mountain Spring, The* (Lozinski), 73
Mozhayev, Boris, 289
Muratova, K. D., 156
*Music* (Aliger), 175
*Music* (Pasternak), 192
*Music* (Vinokurov), 264
*My Childhood* (Gorki), 47
*My Family Tree* (Akhmadulina), 257
*My Heartache* (Annenski), 42
*My Sister, Life* (Pasternak), 83–84
*My Son* (Antokolski), 186
*My Universities* (Gorki), 47, 107
*My Very Own Poems* (Aseyev), 187
*Mysterium buffo* (Mayakovski), 81, 82, 146

Nagibin, Yurii, 220, 222–23
*Naked Year, The* (Pasternak), 236
Narrative style of 20th century in Russia, 59
Narratives of war, World War II, 162–83
*Native City* (Nekrasov), 171
*Native Soil* (Akhmatova), 191
*Nature's Calendar* (Prishvin), 108–10
Nekrasov, Viktor, 152, 169–73, 180
Nemirovich-Danchenko, Vladimir, 22, 145
Neo-realism, 92, 93, 94
NEP (New Economic Policy) period of Soviet life, 114, 129, 130, 139

*Nerves, a Phonograph Record* (Annenski), 43
*Nets* (Kuzmin), 64
*Neva* literary journal, 155
*Never Emptied Chalice, The* (Smeliov), 54
*New Book* (Martynov), 217
*New Russian Prose, The* (Zamyatin), 93, 115
*New Table of the Law, The* (Romanov), 112
*New Way, The,* magazine, 9
*New Year's Day* (Gladilin), 239
*Nicholas Parables* (Remizov), 61
Nietzsche, Friedrich Wilhelm, 3, 9, 36, 37, 38, 40, 45, 50
*Night, The* (Bagritzki), 145
*Night Airport in New York* (Voznesenski), 270
*Night in the Trenches, The* (Khlebnikov), 79
*Night's Lodging* (Kazakov), 248
*Nikishka's Secrets* (Kazakov), 247
*Nikita's Childhood* (A. N. Tolstoi), 108
Nikitin, Nikolai, 92, 186
Nikonov, Anatolii, 287
*Nine Days* (Baklanov), 228
*Nine-Tenths of Fate* (Kaverin), 100
*Ninth Wave, The* (Ehrenburg), 196
*No Ordinary Summer* (Fedin), 199
*No Shame Falls on the Dead* (Baklanov), 229
Nobel Prize for Literature, 55, 83, 193, 219, 279
*Noises of the City* (Remizov), 61
*Nomads of Beauty* (Vyacheslav Ivanov), 39
*Nonsense* (Kazakov), 247

*Nordic Fairytale* (Martynov), 216
*Nordic Symphony* (Belyi), 37
*North, The* (Zamyatin), 95
*Northern Elegies* (Akhmatova), 190
*Nose, The* (Gogol), 282
Nosov, E., 288
*Not by Bread Alone* (Dudintzev), 154, 220–21
*Notes of a Doctor* (Veresayev), 50
*Notes of an Eccentric* (Belyi), 32–33
*Notes of a Writer* (Teleshov), 11
*Notre Dame* (Mandelstamm), 72
*Novyi mir* magazine, 154, 166, 193, 196, 200, 277–78, 283, 284, 286
*Now, However, That I Am Awake* (Bryusov), 26
*Nymph and the Spirit of the Woods, The* (Khlebnikov), 79

*October* semiofficial literary journal, 160
*Ode on Tzarskoye Selo* (Akhmatova), 191
*Of Foreign Blood* (Smeliov), 54
*Ogonek* magazine, 111
*Oktober* (Mayakovski), 138
*Oktyabr* magazine, 285
Okudzhava, Bulat, 254–55
Okup, 82
*Old Isergil, The* (Gorki), 45
*Old Man and the Sea, The* (Hemingway), 219
*Old Park, The* (Pasternak), 192
*Old Woman of the Sea, The* (Kazakov), 247
Olesha, Yurii, 131–33
*On Both Sides of the Ocean* (Nekrasov), 171

*On the Early Trains* (Pasternak), 192
*On the Island* (Kazakov), 248, 249
*On Juliet's Death* (Moritz), 256
*On the Rack* (A. N. Tolstoi), 109
*On the Search* (Kaverin), 207
*On the Steamer* (Gorki), 47
*On the Street* (Belyi), 37
*On the Trail of the Magic Bread* (Prishvin), 53
*On the Way* (Kazakov), 250
*On the Way Station* (Kazakov), 250
*Once Upon a Time* (Shklovski), 188
*One Day in the Life of Ivan Denisovich* (Solzhenitzyn), 225–26, 242, 278, 279, 288
*One Degree of Heat* (Martynov), 217
*One Hundred Days of War* (Simonov), 279
*One Is Not Born a Soldier* (Simonov), 180
*One Month Upside Down* (Granin), 222
*One-Story America* (Ilf and Petrov), 115
*One Time, Tomorrow, Verses and Poems, The* (Kirsanov), 216
*150,000,000* (Mayakovski), 81, 82
*Onion Soup* (Yevtushenko), 267
*Open Book, The* (Kaverin), 207
*Opposition of Mars* (Zabolotzki), 211
*Optimistic Tragedy* (Vishnevski), 148
*Oranges from Morocco* (Aksenov), 237–38
*Orest Kiprenskii* (Paustovski), 111
Osipov, Vladimir, 287

*Otchar* (Yesenin), 86
*Out of a Burned Up Notebook* (Akhmatova), 191
*Over the White Road Cross* (Konetzki), 251
*Overcoat, The* (Gogol), 105
*Ovidiopolis* (Martynov), 217
*Oza* (Voznesenski), 272

Palievski, 286
*Panopticon in Hamburg* (Yevtushenko), 267
Panova, Vera, 151, 152, 162–66
*Pao-Pao* (Selvinski), 143
*Parable* (Voznesenski), 273
*Parkhomenko* (Vsevolod Ivanov), 102
Parnassians, 14, 41
Pasternak, Boris, 83–85, 121, 137, 138, 140, 143, 144, 174, 192–95, 197, 216, 266, 268
the Pasternak "affair," 155
*Pasture, The* (Gorodetzki), 73
Paustovski, Konstantin, 53, 111, 201–3, 230, 245, 247, 251, 278
Pavlovski, A., 190
*Peak of the Caucasus, The* (Zabolotzki), 212
*Pearls* (Gumilev), 67
*People Are Immortal, The* (Grossman), 159
*People and Situations* (Pasternak), 193
*People, Years, Life* (Ehrenburg), 197
*Peredelkino* (Pasternak), 192
*Perfection* (Yevtushenko), 268
*Period Lost by Cutting Class, The* (Vinokurov), 264
*Persian Motifs* (Yesenin), 88
*Personal Opinion, A* (Granin), 222

Personality cult, and Stalin, 154,
180, 220
*Perun* (Gorodetzki), 73
*Peter the Great* (A. N. Tolstoi),
109
*Peterburgski Almanakh* almanac,
64
Petrov, G., 141
Petrov, Yevgenii, 114–15, 235
*Petty Demon, The* (Sologub), 25–
26
*Petushok* (Remizov), 60
*Philosophy of Tragedy, Dostoyev-
ski and Nietzsche, The*
(Shestov), 10
*Pictures of a Folk Tragedy* (Tre-
nev), 148
*Pilgrims, The* (Brodski), 261
*Pillar of Fire, The* (Gumilev), 67
Pilnyak, Boris, 125–27, 186, 236
*Pineapple in Champagne* (Seve-
ryanin), 76
*Pit, The* (Kuprin), 52
Plekhanov, 284
*Plot of the Czarina, The* (A. N.
Tolstoi), 109
Plotkin, L., 165
*Poem of the Ax, The* (Pogodin),
148
*Poem of the Poets* (Kirsanov),
215
*Poem of Spring* (Zabolotzki), 212
*Poem Without Heroes* (Akhma-
tova), 70, 189, 190
*Poems* (Aliger), 176
*Poems* (Mandelstamm), 72
*Poems* (Martynov), 217
*Poems* (Zabolotzki), 210
*Poems from the Crimea* (Aliger),
176
*Poems and Narrative Verse* (Pas-
ternak), 192
*Poems and Narratives in Verse*
(Brodski), 260

*Poems and Verse Narratives*
(Martynov), 217
*Poems of Yurii Zhivago* (Paster-
nak), 193, 195
*Poet* (Zabolotzki), 212
*Poet, The* (Khlebnikov), 80
*Poetic Epigrams* (Marshak), 185
*Poetry* (Martynov), 217
*Poetry* (Matveyeva), 265
*Poetry* (Vinokurov), 264
Poetry, developments in, in inter-
war period, 137–48
constructivists, 142–45
futurists, 137–41
Serapion Brothers, 141–42
some aspects of prewar Soviet
theater, 145–48
Poetry, new tendencies in, *see*
Soviet poetry, new tendencies
in
*Poetry as Sense* (Zelinski), 142
*Poetry as Sorcery* (Martynov),
216
*Poetry Days* annual, 279
Poetry of propaganda, 73
Poggioli, Renato, 69, 71
Pogodin, Nikolai, 148
Polevoi, Boris, 159–60, 285
Polyak, L., 185
Pomerantzev, Vladimir, 154
*Pond, The* (Remizov), 60
*Poslushaite!* (Mayakovski), 280
*Praise of the Crowd* (Bryusov),
16
*Prayer Before the Poem* (Yev-
tushenko), 268
*Prayer of the Forty Days, The*
(Yesenin), 87
*Present, The* (Bryusov), 16
*Primogeniture* (Martynov), 217
*Princess Mymra* (Remizov), 60
Prishvin, Mikhail, 52–53, 107–8,
245, 247
Prokofyev, Aleksandr, 162

Proletarian writers, 115–18, 133, 156
*Prometei* (Vyacheslav Ivanov), 40
*Prosa* (Tzvetayeva), 86
Prose, development of, in interwar period, 91–136
escapist writing, 110–12
Gorki after the Revolution, 106–7
historical novel, 108–10
humor and everyday life, 112–115
proletarian writers, 115–18, 133, 156
Serapion Brothers, 91–106
six major figures, 118–36
*Psyche* (Tzvetayeva), 85
Publishing House of the Writers, 50–51
*Puppet Show, The* (Blok), 23
*Pushkin* (Akhmatova), 191
Pushkin, Aleksandr, 9, 69, 74, 84, 140, 190, 202, 256, 268, 269
*Pushkin in Life* (Veresayev), 51
*Pushkin's Poetic Economy* (Khodasevich), 74

*Quiet Lullaby* (Sologub), 18
*Quiet Songs* (Annenski), 41, 42
*Quiver, The* (Gumilev), 67

*Radishchev* (Forsh), 110
*Radius of Action* (Rozhdestvenski), 262
*Rain* (Svetlov), 214
*Rain in the Steppe* (Soloukhin), 243
*Rape of Europa, The* (Fedin), 103
Realism, 44–61, 128, 138, 144, 282
Gorki and Andreyev, as masters of, 44–49
in the realist tradition, 49–59
proletarian, 117

restructured realism, 59–61
*see also* Socialist realism
Realists, new type of, 224–39
*Realm of the Karamazovs, The* (Volynski), 6
*Rebellion of Pugachev, The* (Trenev), 148
*Recovered Youth* (Zoshchenko), 106
*Red Cavalry* (Babel), 122
*Red Howling* (Klyuyev), 88
*Red Laughter, The* (Andreyev), 49
"Rehabilitation" of previously banned authors, 124, 133, 154, 184, 186, 187
*Remarks from the Diary, Memories* (Gorki), 47
*Remembrance* (Slutzki), 181, 182
*Remembrance* (Zabolotzki), 212
Remizov, Aleksei, 34, 53, 59–61, 125, 126
*Renewal* (Aseyev), 139
*Republic of the Southern Cross, The* (Bryusov), 27
*Requiem* (Akhmatova), 190
*Requiem* (Rozhdestvenski), 262
*Retaliation* (Blok), 20
*Return, The* (Yesenin), 87
*Revolt of the Machines, The* (A. N. Tolstoi), 109
Revolution of 1905, 12, 16, 17, 24, 34, 37, 56
Revolution of 1917, 34, 51, 54, 63, 64, 78, 80, 83, 86, 88, 97, 102, 103, 107, 113, 118, 119, 121, 124, 125, 130, 138, 139, 140
followed by stagnation of intellectual life, 91, 107, 220
literature of critical heirs of, 220–52
*Rhythms of Rome* (Yevtushenko), 268

*Right Not to Forget, The* (Tvardovski), 278
*Road to Calvary, The* (A. N. Tolstoi), 108
*Road Grass* (Akhmatova), 70
*Robert Burns* (Matveyeva), 265
Rococo epoch, 63, 64
*Rogue, The* (Gorki), 45
*Roman Sonnets* (Vyacheslav Ivanov), 40
*Romance of Leonardo da Vinci, The* (Merezhkovski), 8
Romanov, Panteleimon, 112
*Roosters Crow, The* (Zabolotzki), 211
*Rose and the Cross, The* (Blok), 23–24
Roshchin, M., 289
Rozanov, Vasilii, 9, 33–36, 60
Rozhdestvenski, Robert, 243, 261–63
*Rubber Trees* (Yevtushenko), 267
*Rubruck in Mongolia* (Zabolotzki), 212–13
*R.U.R.* (Čapek), 109
"Rural" prose, 288–90
*Russia* (Prokofyev), 162
*Russia* (Romanov), 112
*Russian Forest, The* (Leonov), 204–6, 209
Russian Revolutions, *see* Revolution of 1905; Revolution of 1917
*Russian Symbolists* pamphlets, 14
Russian theatre, revival of, with founding of Moscow Art Theatre, 22
Russian version of Dante's *Divine Comedy* (Lozinski), 73
Russism, 286–87, 288
Russo-Japanese War, 12, 16, 49, 52
Rybakov, A., 278
Rybakov, J., 281
Rzhevski, L., 194, 195

*Sailors and the Flying Dutchman, The* (Bagritzki), 144
*Saint George* (Kuzmin), 64
*Saint Petersburg* (Belyi), 30–31, 95, 147, 194
Saint Petersburg Dramatic Theater, 23
Salinger, J. D., 237
*Sallow Horse, The* (Bryusov), 16–17
*Samizdat* underground press, 278, 287–88
*Sanatorium Arktur* (Fedin), 103
*Sasha* (Panova), 165
*Scar on the Sky* (Khlebnikov), 79
*Science of Hatred, The* (Sholokhov), 218
*Scythians, The* (Blok), 21, 22
"Scythians" movement, 53, 86, 87, 94, 125
*Seagull, The* (Chekhov), 7
*Search for a Hero, The* (Tikhonov), 142
*Search by Night* (Khlebnikov), 80
*Searching and Hoping* (Kaverin), 207
*Seasickness* (Kuprin), 52
*Seasons of the Year* (Panova), 164
*Second Anniversary* (Akhmatova), 190
*Second Birth* (Pasternak), 140
*Second Book* (Zabolotzki), 141
*Second Book, The* (Mandelstamm), 71
Second Congress of Soviet Writers (1954), 154
*Second of November, The* (Khodasevich), 75
*Secrets of the Trade* (Akhmatova), 191
*Seeds of Tomorrow* (Sholokhov), 134, 135–36, 219
*Seizing Possession* (Vinokurov), 264

*Selected Works* (Kirsanov), 216
*Selected Works* (Zabolotzki), 210
*Selections* (Aseyev), 139
Selvinski, Ilya, 143, 144, 187, 188
*Sentimental Novel* (Panova), 163, 165
*Sentimental Novellas* (Zoshchenko), 104
*Sentimental Pilgrimage, A* (Shklovski), 92
Serapion Brothers, society of, 91–106, 107, 141–42, 186, 207
*Seven Colors of the Rainbow* (Bryusov), 15
*Seven Days of the Week* (Kirsanov), 215
*Seven Days in Which the World Was Robbed* (A. N. Tolstoi), 109
*Seven Pairs of Devil* (Kaverin), 208
*Seven That Were Hanged, The* (Andreyev), 48
*Seventh Book, The* (Akhmatova), 191
*Severnyi Vestnik* magazine, 6
Severyanin, Igor, 76
*Shadow of the Friend, The* (Tikhonov), 142
*Shadow Mirror* (Bryusov), 15
*Shadows* (Sologub), 24
Shaginyan, Marietta, 111
*Shakespeare* (Pasternak), 84
Shalamov, Varlam, 279
*Shaman and Venus, The* (Khlebnikov), 79
Shchipachev, Stepan, 162
Shershenevich, Vadim, 76, 87
Shestov, Lev, 9–10
*Shipovnik* almanac, 128
*Shirt of the Patient, The* (Pasternak), 84
Shklovski, Viktor, 35, 92, 188
Sholokhov, Mikhail, 133–36, 218–19, 279, 283

*Short-lived Is the Mayfly* (Tendryakov), 242
*Short Stretch of Ground, A* (Baklanov), 229
Shtemenko, General S. M., 285
Shukshin, Vasilii, 289
Shvartz, Yevgenii, 186
*Sick Ballad* (Voznesenski), 271
*Silence* (Bondarev), 231–32
*Silent Don, The* (Sholokhov), 134, 135, 218, 283
*Silent Teams of Horses* (Zaitzev), 55
"Silver age" in Russian cultural development, 9, 190
*Silver Dove, The* (Belyi), 29–30, 194, 242
Simonov, Konstantin, 152, 177, 179–81, 279
*Simple Stories* (Pilnyak), 127
Sinclair, Upton, 146
*Singing Call, The* (Yesenin), 86
Sinyavski, Andrei (pseudonym: Abram Tertz), 156, 233, 234–35, 269
*Sinyaya tetrad* (Kazakevich), 178
*Sisters, The* (A. N. Tolstoi), 108
*Sisters of the Cross, The* (Remizov), 60
*Skaz* narrative style, 59, 104, 238, 245
*Sketches of the Sea* (Paustovski), 111
*Skutarevshi* (Leonov), 131
*Slanting Rain* (Kaverin), 208
*Slap in the Face of Public Taste, A* (Khlebnikov), 79
*Slippery Ice* (Sosnora), 259
*Slippery Ice* (Tertz), 235
Slonimski, Mikhail, 92, 186
*Slovo* almanac, 51
*Slow Approach of Thunder* (Paustovski), 201
Slutzki, Boris, 181–83
Smeliov, Ivan, 54

Smelyakov, Yaroslav, 153, 162
*Smoke in the Eyes* (Gladilin), 238
*Smoke of the Fatherland, The*
    (Paustovski), 202
*Smugglers, The* (Bagritzki), 144
*Snow Mask, The* (Blok), 20
Socialist realism, 97, 102, 110,
    117, 153, 154, 272, 282n,
    284, 286,
    concept of, 156–58
    in fiction, 156–60
    redemption from, 220–24, 236
    transformation of, into a new
        realism, 224
Society for the Study of Poetic
    Language, 92
*Soldiers* (Nekrasov), 172
*Solemn Procession* (Brodski),
    260, 261
*Solitaria* (Rozanov), 33, 35
Sologub, Fiodor, 17–18, 22, 23,
    24–26
Soloukhin, Vladimir, 243–46
Solovyev, Vladimir, 4, 16, 19, 36,
    38
Solzhenitzyn, Aleksandr, 220,
    223, 224–28, 278–79, 281–
    282, 283, 288, 290
*Some Currents in the Russian Po-
    etry of the Present* (Goro-
    detzki), 73
*Some Steps* (Aliger), 176
*Somewhere in the Open Air at
    Magadon* (Zabolotzki), 212
*Son of Faith* (Rozhdestvenski),
    262, 263
*Song of Bread, The* (Yesenin), 87
*Song of Igor's Campaign, The*
    (Zabolotzki's adaptation of),
    210
*Song of Praise* (Klyuyev), 88
*Sonnet to Form, The* (Bryusov),
    15
Sosnora, Viktor, 259
*Sot* (Leonov), 131

*Soul of Things, The* (Matveyeva),
    265, 266
*South of the Main Attack* (Bak-
    lanov), 228
*Southwest* (Bagritzki), 144
Soviet Authors' Association, 200
*Soviet Literature* journal, 160
Soviet poetry, new tendencies in,
    253–73
    lyric and "chamber" music in
        poetry, 253–57
    nonconformist poets, 257–61
    poetry of pathos and sentiment,
        261–66
    two controversial poets, 266–73
Soviet theater, prewar, some as-
    pects of, 145–48
Soviet Writers' Union, 278, 283
Sovremennik theater, 280
*Spartacus* (Volkenshetyn), 147
*Spektorski* (Pasternak), 140
*Spring* (Pasternak), 192
*Spring Night, A* (Bunin), 58
*Spring on the Oder* (Kazakevich),
    178
*Squaring of the Circle* (Katayev),
    113
Sreda group of realists, 11
*Staff Captain Rybnikov* (Kuprin),
    51
Stalin, Joseph V.
    death of, 154, 232
    personality cult around, 154,
        180, 220, 277, 279
    post-1956 revision of Stalin
        image, 151–52
    process of "de-Stalinization,"
        210, 220, 230
Stalin Prize, 180
Stalinism, 154, 168, 178, 196,
    197, 200, 207, 208, 209, 230,
    246, 262, 272, 281, 284, 285,
    287
Stalinist purges, 124, 127, 174,
    183, 200

*Stalin's Heirs* (Yevtushenko), 267
Stanislavski, Konstantin, 22, 46, 49, 145, 147, 280
*Star* (Kazakevich), 177
*Starred Ticket, The* (Aksenov), 236–37
*Stars by Day* (Berggoltz), 175
State Theater in Moscow, of Meyerhold, 146
*Steel Nightingale, The* (Aseyev), 139
Steiner, Rudolph, 31, 36
*Stencil* (Matveyeva), 265
*Stenka Razin* (Kamenski), 78
*Stephanos* (Bryusov), 15, 16
*Steppe* (Matveyeva), 266
Stepun, Fiodor, 128
*Sting of Death, The* (Sologub), 24, 25
*Stinging Nettle* (Sosnora), 259
*Stone, The* (Mandelstamm), 71
*Stories about Pakistan* (Tikhonov), 186
*Stories of the Hill Country* (Tikhonov), 186
*Storm* (Ostrovski), 146
*Storm, The* (Ehrenburg), 195–96
*Storm on the Journey to Stockholm* (Kuznetzov), 224
*Stormy Life of Lazik Roytshvanetz, The* (Ehrenburg), 120
*Story of Ambition, A* (Gladilin), 238–39
*Story of a Life* (Paustovski), 201
*Story of the Radio Operator Kamushkin* (Konetzki), 251
*Story of Troubled Times* (A. N. Tolstoi), 108
*Story of the True Man* (Polevoi), 160
*Story of What Is of Supreme Importance, The* (Zamyatin), 98
*Story of Yesterday* (L. Tolstoi), 225

*Story of the Woods* (Paustovski), 202
Strakhov, Nikolai, 3, 33
*Strange Sky* (Gumilev), 67
*Strasti-Mordasti* (Gorki), 47
Stravinski, Igor, 73
*Streetcar That Strayed, The* (Gumilev), 67
*Strings* (Akhmadulina), 256
Struve, Gleb, 106, 133, 141
Studio for Literature at the House of Art, 91
*Subtenants, The* (Tertz), 235
*Sukhodol* (Bunin), 57–58
Sukhovo-Kobylin, A., 146
*Summer Garden* (Akhmatova), 190
*Sunset* (Babel), 124
Surkov, Aleksei, 161
Surrealism, 79, 83, 94, 132
Svetlov, Mikhail, 213–14
*Swinging of the Hand* (Yevtushenko), 267
Symbolism, 12–43, 190, 197, 211
  beginning of, in Russia, 8–9, 12
  early symbolist poetry, 12–19
  high point of symbolism in Russia, 19–24
  journals of, at beginning of century, 9
  later symbolist poets, 36–43
  symbolist prose, 24–36
  symbolist theater, 22–24
  and theory of language, 62
*Symbolism* (Belyi), 36
Symbolism, transition from, 62–88
  acmeism creed, 65–72
  acmeism reconsidered, 73–75
  futurism, theory and practice of, 75–83
  major synthesizers, 83–88
  Mikhail Kuzmin, as transitional figure, 63–65

*Syntax* journal, 260
Syomin, V., 278, 286, 289

Tairov, Aleksandr, 43, 145–46
*Tale of Opanas, The* (Bagritzki), 145
*Tale of the Unextinguished Moon, The* (Pilnyak), 126–27
*Tales of the Don, The* (Sholokhov), 134
*Tales of Leningrad* (Tikhonov), 186
*Tales of Odessa* (Babel), 122, 123, 124
*Tape Recorder* (Akhmadulina), 257
*Taras Shevchenko* (Zoshchenko), 106
*Tarelkin's Death* (Sukhovo-Kobylin), 146
Tarkovski, Arsenii, 283–84
*Tartuffe* (Molière), 280
Tatlin, Vladimir, 80, 146
*Tchelkache* (Gorki), 45
*Teacher Bubus, The* (Fayko), 146
*Teatr* magazine, 281
*Teddy* (Kazakov), 246–47
Teleshov, Nikolai, 11
*Tempo* (Pogodin), 148
*Ten Days That Shook the World* (Reed), 109
*Tender Joseph* (Kuzmin), 64–65
Tendryakov, Vladimir, 239–43, 289
*Teorema* film (Pasolini), 281
*Terkin in the Underworld* (Tvardovski), 168–69
*Terrible Night, A* (Zoshchenko), 105
*Tertia vigilia* (Bryusov), 15, 16
Tertz, Abram (pseudonym of Andrei Sinyavski), 156, 233, 234–35, 269

*Textology of the Works of Soviet Literature,* 282n
*Thamyras citharoedus* (Annenski), 43, 146
*That's How It Was Then* (Tvardovski), 168
*Thaw, The* (Ehrenburg), 196–97
*Thaw* (Zabolotzki), 211
"Thaw" in relations between literature and state policy, 154, 156, 205, 217, 285
*Thaw in the Woods* (Prishvin), 108
Theater, modern trends in influence of, in Russia, 280–81
*Theater of Euripides, The* (Annenski), 41
"Theater of the Revolution," 147
Theater on the Taganka, 280
*Themes and Variations* (Pasternak), 84
*There Are Fools in This World* (Kazakova), 255
*There Goes a Dog!* (Kazakov), 248
*There, Where You Are* (Kazakova), 255
*Theseus to Ariadne* (Bryusov), 16
*They Fought for Their Country* (Sholokhov), 219
*Thief, The* (Leonov), 129–30, 204, 205, 206
*Third Memory, The* (Yevtushenko), 268
*Thirteen Pipes* (Ehrenburg), 120
*Thistle* (Zabolotzki), 212
*Those Traveling by Sea* (Kuzmin), 64–65
*Those Who Seek* (Granin), 222
*Thoughts about Chaplin* (Olesha), 133
*Thoughts about Symbolism* (Vyacheslav Ivanov), 41

*Thoughts at the Grave of My Grandfather in Sevastopol* (Kazakova), 255
*Three-Cornered Pear, The, 40 Digressions from a Lyric Poem* (Voznesenski), 269, 271, 273
*Three Fat Men, The* (Olesha), 133
*Three Notebooks: Verses and Verse Narratives* (Simonov), 179–80
*Three Poems* (Akhmatova), 191
*Three Sisters, The* (Chekhov), 7
*Through Leeuwenhoek's Marvelous Apparatus* (Zabolotzki), 212
*Through Russia* (Gorki), 47
*Thunder Against Marble* (Aseyev), 139
*Thunder-Foaming Cup, The* (Severyanin), 76
Tikhonov, Nikolai, 92, 141, 144, 173, 186
*Time* (Slutzki), 183
*Time Ahead* (Katayev), 113
*Time of Youth* (Kaverin), 207
*To the Memory of the Brave* (Aliger), 175
*To Pushkin* (Svetlov), 214
*To the Sea* (Pushkin), 84
*Today and Yesterday* (Slutzki), 183
Tolstoi, Aleksei N., 51, 108–9, 111
Tolstoi, Lev, 4, 44, 48, 50, 117, 134, 151, 164, 169, 198, 200, 225, 230, 240, 269
*Tolstoi and Dostoyevski* (Merezhkovski), 4
*Too Bad You Were Not There* (Aksenov), 238
*Torches of Florence, The* (Voznesenski), 272

Tovstonogov, 280n
*Toward Life* (Veresayev), 50
*Toward the Stars* (Vyacheslav Ivanov), 40
*Toward the West* (Luntz), 98
*Trade in Watermelons* (Voznesenski), 271
Traditionalists, 224, 239–52
*Traffic Lights* (Akhmadulina), 257
*Trains* (Kazakova), 255
*Transfiguration, The* (Yesenin), 87
*Transparency* (Vyacheslav Ivanov), 39
*Trava-Murava* (Remizov), 61
*Traveling Companions, The* (Panova), 163, 164, 166
Trenev, Konstantin, 148
Tretyakov, Sergei, 138, 139
*Trial, The* (Kafka), 234
*Trip to a Town of Childhood* (Berggoltz), 175
*Tristia* (Mandelstamm), 71, 72
*Triumph of Agriculture, The* (Zabolotzki), 141
*Triumph of Death, The* (Sologub), 23
*Troublemaker, The, or Evenings on the Island of Vasilyev* (Kaverin), 100
*True Friends* (Slonimski), 186
*Trust D. E.* (Ehrenburg), 146
*Tuatamur* (Leonov), 128
*Tunnel, The* (Kellermann), 146
Tvardovski, Aleksandr, 152, 166–169, 278
*Twelve, The* (Blok), 21–22
*Twelve Chairs* (Ilf and Petrov), 114, 115
*12,000 Kilometers Wide* (Nekrasov), 171
*Twenties, The* (Martynov), 217

Twentieth Party Congress (1956), 154, 181, 188, 205, 220, 230, 285
*Twenty-eight* (Svetlov), 213
*Twenty-six and One* (Gorki), 47
*Twin in the Clouds, The* (Pasternak), 83
*Two, The* (Bondarev), 232
*Two Captains* (Kaverin), 206–7
*Two in December* (Kazakov), 248, 250
*Two Meetings* (Aliger), 176
*Two in the Steppe* (Kazakevich), 178
*Two Streams, Verses about Pakistan and Afghanistan* (Tikhonov), 186
Tynyanov, Yurii, 92, 99, 110, 188
*Tzentrifuga* group, 83, 139
Tzvetayeva, Marina, 85–86, 137, 197

*Ugly One, The* (Kazakov), 248, 249
*Ulyalayev Adventure, The* (Selvinski), 143
*Uncertainty* (Yevtushenko), 268
*Uncle Vanya* (Chekhov), 7
*Under Northern Skies* (Balmont), 13
Underground press, *see Samizdat*
"Underground" Russian poetry, 260
*Unedited Khlebnikov, The,* 78
*Uninhabited Islands* (Rozhdestvenski), 262
*Unknown Friend* (Kaverin), 208
*Unknown Master* (Kaverin), 209
*Unknown, The—Requiem in Two Steps, with an Epilogue* (Voznesenski), 272
*Unknown Woman, The* (Blok), 19, 23
*Urbi et orbi* (Bryusov), 15, 16
*Urn, The* (Belyi), 38

Vakhtangov, Yevgenii, 147
Vakhtangov Theater in Moscow, 147, 186
*Valet Vanka and the Page Jean, The* (Sologub), 23
*Valley of the Unicorn, The* (Klyuyev), 88
*Valya and Volodya* (Panova), 164
*Valya's Doll* (Leonov), 128
*Vasilii Terkin* (Tvardovski), 166–167
*Vasya Konakov* (Nekrasov), 171
*Veche* magazine, 287
*Venice* (Akhmatova), 68–69
*Venice* (Pasternak), 83
*Venice* (Rozhdestvenski), 263
*Verbs* (Brodski), 260
Veresayev, Vikentii, 50–51
Verhaeren, Émile, 16
*Verse Studio* (Selvinski), 188
*Verse and Verse Narratives* (Martynov), 216
*Verses* (Kazakova), 255
*Verses* (Khlebnikov), 78
*Verses* (Martynov), 217
*Verses about the Blind Musicians* (Brodski), 261
*Verses about China* (Tikhonov), 186
*Verses about Duty* (Vinokurov), 264
*Verses about Fidel* (Yevtushenko), 267
*Verses about Foreign Countries* (Yevtushenko), 267
*Verses of the Beautiful Lady, The* (Blok), 19
*Verses of the Nightingale, The* (Bagritzki), 145
*Vesy* journal, 9, 26, 27, 29
*Victors, The* (Bagritzki), 145
*Victory, The* (Aksenov), 238
*Village, The* (Bunin), 56
Vinokurov, Yevgenii, 263–65

*Visa of the Time, The* (Ehren-
burg), 120
Vishnevski, Vsevolod, 148
*Vladimir Ilyich Lenin* (Mayakov-
ski), 138
*Vladimir Mayakovski* (Mayakov-
ski), 80
Vladimov, Georgii, 223, 224
*Voices* (Martynov), 217
*Voices of the Violins, The* (Blok),
21
*Volga Flows into the Caspian Sea,
The* (Pilnyak), 127
Volkenshetyn, V., 147
*Volodya* (Panova), 166
Voloshin, Maksimilian, 18, 197
Volynski, Akim, 6
*Voprosi literaturi* magazine, 288
Voronov, N., 284n
Voynovich, V., 278
Voznesenski, Andrei, 243, 257,
259, 269–73, 280, 285

*Wagon Load of Empty Barrels, A*
(Aksenov), 282
*Waiter Out of the Restaurant, The*
(Smeliov), 54
*Walk in Rural Russia, A* (Solou-
khin), 244
*Wall, The* (Andreyev), 48
*Waltz of the Front* (Kirsanov),
215
War books of the 1950s and
1960s, 151–52, 228
*War and Peace* (L. Tolstoi), 198,
205
*War Poems* (Pasternak), 192
War poets, World War II, 161–62
*Waterfall* (Matveyeva), 266
*Watermelon, The* (Bagritzki), 144
*Way to Damascus, The* (Solo-
gub), 24
*Way of an Enthusiast, The* (Ka-
menski), 78

*Way of the Grain, The* (Khoda-
sevich), 74, 75
*Way to the Ocean, The* (Leonov),
131, 204
*We* (Zamyatin), 96–97
*We Will Meet in the East* (Kaza-
kova), 255
Wells, H. G., 96, 108
*What Do You Want?* (Kochetov),
285
*What Is Socialist Realism?* (Si-
nyavski), 156
*What the Nightingale Sang* (Zosh-
chenko), 104, 105
*When I Think of Blok* (Yev-
tushenko), 267
*When It Clears Up* (Pasternak),
192
*When It Rains for a Long Time*
(Surkov), 161–62
*White Flock, The* (Akhmatova),
69
*White Guard, The* (M. Bulgakov),
113
*White Sail Gleams, The* (Kata-
yev), 113
*Why We Are Serapion Brothers*
(Luntz), 98
*Wild* (Aksenov), 282
*Willowtree, The* (Akhmatova), 70
*Wind* (Pasternak), 192
*Wings* (Kuzmin), 65
*Winter Approaches* (Pasternak),
192
*Winter Night* (Pasternak), 194
*Winter 1938* (Rozhdestvenski),
262
*Winter Sonnets* (Vyacheslav Iva-
nov), 40
*Wisdom* (Zoshchenko), 104
*Woman, The* (Gorki), 47
*Wonderful Life of Joseph Bal-
samo, Count Cagliostro*
(Kuzmin), 65
*Wooden Bodies* (Matveyeva), 265

*Wooden Queen, The* (Leonov),
128
*Woods of Gombori, The* (Zabo-
lotzki), 212
*Word, The* (Vinokurov), 264
*Word as Such, The* (Kruchenykh
and Khlebnikov), 76–77
*Work* (Slutzki), 183
*Workers' Settlement* (Panova),
166
*Works I* (Akhmatova), 189
*World of Art* magazine, 9
World War II: new orientations,
151–83
general atmosphere, 151–55
narratives of war, 162–83
socialist realism in fiction, 156–
160
the war poets, 161–62
*Worries of Tomorrow, The*
(Konetzki), 251
*Wreath of Roses, The* (Akhma-
tova), 68, 69
Writers' Union of the Russian
Federation, 285

*Yar* (Gorodetzki), 73
Yashin, Aleksandr, 162, 220,
221–22
*Year 1905, The* (Pasternak), 140
*Years of Hope* (Paustovski), 201
*Yegorushka's Downfall* (Leonov),
128
*Yerlas* (Gorki), 47
Yesenin, Sergei, 73, 86–88, 137,
197, 216, 267, 268
*Yevdokiya* (Panova), 166
*Yevgenii Onegin* (Pushkin), 140,
165

Yevreinov, Nikolai, 145, 147
Yevtushenko, Yevgenii, 243, 257,
266–69, 282, 283, 285
Young People's Union, 286
*Your Poem* (Kirsanov), 214
*Youth* (Khodasevich), 74
*Youth in Zheleznodolska* (Voro-
nov), 284n
*Yunost* magazine, 236, 237, 238,
268, 279, 282, 285–86, 287

Zabolotzki, Nikolai, 140–41, 210–
213
*Zabriskie Point* film (Antonioni),
281
*Zachar Vorobiov* (Bunin), 57
Zaitzev, Boris, 51, 54–55, 59
*Zakhar-Kalita* (Solzhenitzyn),
278
Zamyatin, Yevgenii, 59, 91, 92,
93–98, 99, 104, 107, 115–16,
120, 121, 147, 234
*Zangesi* (Khlebnikov), 80
Zavalishin, V., 106, 111
Zelinski, Kornelii, 142, 188
Zhdanov, Andrei, and political
control of literature, 70, 106,
153, 154, 157, 189, 286
*Zhuravl* (Khlebnikov), 79
*Zhurbins, The* (Kochetov), 160
*Znamya* magazine, 153
Znaniye group, 51, 54, 55
*Zoo, The, or Letters Not About
Love* (Shklovski), 92
Zoshchenko, Mikhail, 92, 103–6,
112, 153, 186, 235
*Zoyka's Dwelling* (M. Bulgakov),
147
*Zvezda* magazine, 166